# Methods in Behavioral Research

## EIGHTH EDITION

## PAUL C. COZBY

California State University, Fullerton

Northcentral University

Boston   Burr Ridge, IL   Dubuque, IA   Madison, WI   New York   San Francisco   St. Louis
Bangkok   Bogotá   Caracas   Kuala Lumpur   Lisbon   London   Madrid   Mexico City
Milan   Montreal   New Delhi   Santiago   Seoul   Singapore   Sydney   Taipei   Toronto

**METHODS IN BEHAVIORAL RESEARCH, EIGHTH EDITION**

Published by McGraw-Hill, a business unit of The McGraw-Hill Companies, Inc., 1221 Avenue of the Americas, New York, NY 10020. Copyright © 2004 by The McGraw-Hill Companies, Inc. All rights reserved. Previous editions © 2001, 1997, 1993, 1989, 1985, 1981 by Mayfield Publishing Company, © 1977 by Paul C. Cozby. No part of this publication may be reproduced or distributed in any form or by any means, or stored in a database or retrieval system, without the prior written consent of The McGraw-Hill Companies, Inc., including, but not limited to, any network or other electronic storage or transmission, or broadcast for distance learning.

Some ancillaries, including electronic and print components, may not be available to customers outside the United States.

1 2 3 4 5 6 7 8 9 0 DOC/DOC 0 9 8 7 6 5 4 3

Vice president and editor-in-chief: *Thalia Dorwick*
Publisher: *Ken King*
Marketing manager: *Melissa Caughlin*
Production services manager: *Jennifer Mills*
Production service: *Penmarin Books*
Manuscript editor: *Adrienne Armstrong*
Art director: *Jeanne M. Schreiber*
Design manager and cover designer: *Cassandra Chu*
Interior designer: *Claire Seng-Niemoeller*
Art manager: *Robin Mouat*
Illustrators: *Larry Daste and Lotus Art*
Production supervisor: *Tandra Jorgensen*

The text was set in 10.5/12 Legacy Serif Book by Carlisle Communication, Inc., and printed on acid-free, 45# New Era Matte by R. R. Donnelly, Crawfordsville.

Cover image: *People Look at House Puzzle* © Paul Schulenburg/SIS

The credits for this book are on page 387, a continuation of the copyright page.

**Library of Congress Cataloging-in-Publication Data**

Cozby, Paul C.
    Methods in behavioral research / Paul C. Cozby. — 8th ed.
        p. cm.
Includes bibliographical references and index.
    ISBN 0-07-252342-5
    1. Psychology—Research—Methodology.    2. Social Sciences—Research—Methodology.    I. Title.
    BF76.5.C67 2003
    150′.7′2—dc21

2003051308

www.mhhe.com

# Contents

## 4    STUDYING BEHAVIOR     61

## 5    MEASUREMENT CONCEPTS     84

## 6    OBSERVING BEHAVIOR     99

## 10 COMPLEX EXPERIMENTAL DESIGNS        177

## 11 QUASI-EXPERIMENTAL AND SINGLE CASE EXPERIMENTAL DESIGNS        194

## 12 UNDERSTANDING RESEARCH RESULTS: DESCRIPTION AND CORRELATION        212

## 13  UNDERSTANDING RESEARCH RESULTS: STATISTICAL INFERENCE    233

## 14  GENERALIZING RESULTS    257

# Preface

Teaching and learning about research methods is both challenging and a great deal of fun. This new edition of *Methods in Behavioral Research* maintains the features of previous editions that have been appreciated by both the instructors and the students. Clear communication of concepts is my highest priority. I have tried to present material clearly and use interesting examples. I have also tried to enhance learning by describing many important concepts in several contexts throughout the book; research shows that redundancy aids understanding. I have also emphasized the need to study behavior using a variety of research approaches. An outline precedes each chapter; study terms and review and activity questions appear at the end of each chapter. Important terms are boldfaced in the text and defined in the glossary.

## RESOURCES

A Web site devoted to learning about research methods is maintained at http://methods.fullerton.edu. This site provides an easy way to obtain more information about the topics presented in the text through resources available on the World Wide Web.

An Online Learning Center is available for both students and instructors at www.mhhe.com/cozby8. For students, this online resource provides numerous study aids to enhance the learning experience. Students will find practice quizzes and Internet exercises and links that complement the text. For instructors, this online resource contains the *Instructor's Manual*, an image bank, and Web links to help prepare course material. The *Instructor's Manual* contains many student activities and assignments as well as exam questions.

## ORGANIZATION

The organization generally follows the sequence of planning and conducting a research investigation. However, the chapters are relatively independent to provide instructors maximum flexibility in assigning the order of chapters. For example, chapters on research ethics and survey research methods are presented early in the book, but instructors who wish to present this material later in a course can easily do so. Chapter 1 gives an overview of the scientific approach to knowledge and distinguishes between basic and applied research. Chapter 2 discusses sources of ideas for research and the importance of library research. Chapter 3 focuses on research ethics; ethical issues are covered in depth here and emphasized throughout the book. Chapter 4 examines psychological variables and the distinction between experimental and nonexperimental approaches to studying relationships among variables. Chapter 5 focuses on measurement issues, including reliability and validity. Nonexperimental research approaches, including naturalistic observation, case studies, and content analysis, are described in Chapter 6. Chapter 7 covers sampling as well as the design of questionnaires and interviews. Chapters 8 and 9 present the basics of designing and conducting experiments. Factorial designs are emphasized in Chapter 10. Chapter 11 discusses the advantages and disadvantages of quasi-experimental and single-case experimental designs. Chapters 12 and 13 focus on the use of statistics to understand research results. Finally, Chapter 14 discusses generalization issues, meta-analyses, and the importance of replications. Appendixes on writing research reports, conducting statistical analyses, and constructing Latin squares are included as well.

## NEW TO THIS EDITION

This edition has incorporated many changes suggested by users of previous editions. The ethics chapter has been reorganized to reflect the themes of the *Belmont Report,* and the new APA Ethics Code is referenced. The fifth edition of the APA *Publication Manual* has been incorporated into Appendix A. Also, there is a new example article. Statistical information has been expanded to include material on effect size and confidence intervals. New graphing material has been included in the chapter on complex experimental designs. All quasi-experimental designs now appear together in a single chapter as well.

## ACKNOWLEDGMENTS

Many individuals helped to produce this and previous editions of this book. Franklin Graham, who guided this book through previous editions at Mayfield Publishing Company, has retired and is very much missed. Fortunately, Ken King at McGraw-Hill has done a wonderful job as the editor for this edition. Thanks go to Adrienne Armstrong for editing the manuscript and Hal Lockwood of Penmarin Books for production management. Mitch Okada did a wonderful job updating the *Instructor's Manual,* and Diana Kyle did a superb job in creating the Online Learning Center. I am extremely grateful for the input I have received from numerous students and instructors, and I particularly thank the following individuals who provided detailed reviews for this edition:

Paul Atchley, University of Kansas
Lindsey L. Cohen, West Virginia University

Margaret M. Gittis, Youngstown State University

Merrill Hiscock, University of Houston

Diana Kyle, Fullerton College

Harold Sigall, University of Maryland, College Park

Ed de St. Aubin, Marquette University

Theodore E. Steiner, San Francisco State University

On a personal note, I would like to thank the people in my life who have helped in numerous ways in producing the book: Jeanne King, Josh Cozby, Brisco Cozby, Don Hecht, Gil Linne, David Perkins, Tom Klammer, Greg Robinson, Claire Palmerino, Dan Kee, Kathy Brown, Frank Bagrash, William Smith, Stan Woll, Dennis Berg, Bill Marelich, Kim Shattuck, and Lisa Marr.

I am always interested in receiving comments and suggestions from students and instructors. Please send e-mail to cozby@fullerton.edu or ccozby@ncu.edu.

# Scientific Understanding of Behavior

What are the causes of aggression and violence? How do we remember things, what causes us to forget, and how can memory be improved? What are the effects of stressful environments on health and social interaction? How do early childhood experiences affect later development? What are the best ways to treat depression? How can we reduce prejudice and intergroup conflict? Curiosity about questions such as these is probably the most important reason that many students decide to take courses in the behavioral sciences. Scientific research provides us with a means of addressing such questions and providing answers. In this book, we will examine the methods of scientific research in the behavioral sciences. In this introductory chapter, we will focus on ways in which knowledge of research methods can be useful in understanding the world around us. Further, we will review the characteristics of a scientific approach to the study of behavior and the general types of research questions that concern behavioral scientists.

## USES OF RESEARCH METHODS

Informed citizens in our society increasingly need knowledge of research methods. Daily newspapers, general-interest magazines, and other media are continually reporting research results: "Eating Disorders May Be More Common in Warm Places," "Ginkgo Biloba Enhances Memory," or "Smoking Linked to Poor Grades." Articles and books make claims about the beneficial or harmful effects of particular diets or vitamins on one's sex life, personality, or health. Survey results are frequently reported that draw conclusions about our beliefs concerning a variety of topics. How do you evaluate such reports? Do you simply accept the findings because they are supposed to be scientific? A background in research methods will help you to read these reports critically, evaluate the methods employed, and decide whether the conclusions are reasonable.

Many occupations require the use of research findings. For example, mental health professionals must make decisions about treatment methods, assignment of clients to different types of facilities, medications, and testing procedures. Such decisions are made on the basis of research; to make good decisions, mental health professionals must be able to read the research literature in the field and apply it in their professional lives. Similarly, people who work in business environments frequently rely on research to make decisions about marketing strategies, ways of improving employee productivity and morale, and methods of selecting and training new employees. Educators must keep up with research on topics such as the effectiveness of different teaching strategies or programs to deal with special student problems. Knowledge of research methods and the ability to evaluate research reports are useful in many fields.

It is also important to recognize that scientific research has become increasingly important in public policy decisions. Legislators and political leaders at all levels of government frequently take political positions and propose legislation based on research findings. Research may also influence judicial decisions: A prime example of this is the *Social Science Brief* that was prepared by psychologists and accepted as evidence in the landmark 1954 case of *Brown v. Board of Education* in which the U.S. Supreme Court banned school segregation in the United States. One of the studies cited in the brief was conducted by Clark and Clark (1947). The study found that when allowed to choose between light-skinned and dark-skinned dolls, both Black and White children preferred to play with the light-skinned dolls (see Stephan, 1983, for a further discussion of the implications of this study). Legislation and public opinion regarding the availability of pornographic materials have been informed by behavioral research investigations of this topic (see, for example, Koop, 1987; Linz, Donnerstein, & Penrod, 1987), and psychological research on sex stereotyping greatly influenced the outcome of a Supreme Court decision on sex discrimination by employers (Fiske, Bersoff, Borgida, Deaux, & Heilman, 1991). In addition, psychologists studying ways to improve the accuracy of eyewitness identification (e.g., Wells et al., 1998; Wells, 2001) greatly influenced recommended procedures for law enforcement agencies to follow in criminal investigations (U.S. Department of Justice, 1999).

Research is also important when developing and assessing the effectiveness of programs designed to achieve certain goals; for example, to increase retention of students in school, influence people to engage in behaviors that reduce their risk of contracting HIV, or enable employees in a company to learn how to reduce the effects of stress. We need to be able to determine whether these programs are successfully meeting their goals.

## THE SCIENTIFIC APPROACH

We opened this chapter with several questions about human behavior and suggested that scientific research is a valuable means of answering them. How does the scientific approach differ from other ways of learning about behavior? People have always observed the world around them and sought explanations for what they see and experience. However, instead of using a scientific approach, many people rely on intuition and authority as ways of knowing.

### The Limitations of Intuition and Authority

Most of us either know or have heard about a married couple that, after years of trying to conceive, adopts a child. Then, within a very short period of time, the couple finds that the woman is pregnant. This observation leads to a common belief that adoption increases the likelihood of pregnancy among couples who are having difficulties conceiving a child. Such a conclusion seems intuitively reasonable and people usually have an explanation for this effect; for example, the adoption reduces a major source of marital stress, and the stress reduction in turn increases the chances of conception (see Gilovich, 1991).

This example illustrates the use of intuition and anecdotal evidence to draw general conclusions about the world around us. When you rely on intuition, you accept unquestioningly what your own personal judgment or a single story about one person's experience tells you about the world. The intuitive approach takes many forms. Often, it involves finding an explanation for our own behaviors or the behaviors of others. For example, you might develop an explanation for why you keep having conflicts with a co-worker, such as "that other person wants my job" or "having to share a telephone puts us in a conflict situation." Other times, intuition is used to explain intriguing events that you observe, as in the case of concluding that adoption increases the chances of conception among couples having difficulty conceiving a child.

A problem with intuition is that numerous cognitive and motivational biases affect our perceptions, and so we may draw erroneous conclusions about cause and effect (cf. Fiske & Taylor, 1984; Nisbett & Ross, 1980; Nisbett & Wilson, 1977; Gilovich, 1991). Gilovich points out that there is in fact no relationship between adoption and subsequent pregnancy according to scientific research investigations. So why do we hold this belief? Most likely it is because of a cognitive bias called *illusory correlation* that occurs when we focus on two events that stand out and occur together. When an adoption is closely followed by a pregnancy, our attention is drawn to the situation, and we are biased to conclude that there must be a causal connection. Such illusory correlations are also likely to occur when we are highly motivated to believe in the causal relationship. Although this is a natural thing for us to do, it is not scientific. A scientific approach requires much more evidence before conclusions can be drawn.

## Authority

The philosopher Aristotle was concerned with the factors associated with persuasion or attitude change. In his *Rhetoric,* Aristotle describes the relationship between persuasion and credibility: "Persuasion is achieved by the speaker's personal character when the speech is so spoken as to make us think him credible. We believe good men more fully and readily than others." Thus, Aristotle would argue that we are more likely to be persuaded by a speaker who seems prestigious, trustworthy, and respectable than by one who lacks such qualities.

Many of us might accept Aristotle's arguments simply because he is considered a prestigious "authority" and his writings remain important. Similarly, many people are all too ready to accept anything they learn from the news media, books, government officials, or religious figures. They believe that the statements of such authorities must be true. The problem, of course, is that the statements may not be true. The scientific approach rejects the notion that one can accept *on faith* the statements of any authority; again, more evidence is needed before we can draw scientific conclusions.

## Skepticism, Science, and the Empirical Approach

The scientific approach to knowledge recognizes that both intuition and authority are sources of ideas about behavior. However, scientists do not unquestioningly accept anyone's intuitions—including their own. Scientists recognize

```
Observations accurately reported to others

+

Search for discovery and verification of ideas

+

Open exchange and competition among ideas

+

Peer review of research
```

**FIGURE 1.1**
Elements of Goodstein's evolved theory of science

that their ideas are just as likely to be wrong as anyone else's. Also, scientists do not accept on faith the pronouncements of anyone, regardless of that person's prestige or authority. Thus, scientists are very skeptical about what they see and hear. Scientific skepticism means that ideas must be evaluated on the basis of careful logic and results from scientific investigations.

If scientists reject intuition and blind acceptance of authority as ways of knowing about the world, how do they go about gaining knowledge? The fundamental characteristic of the scientific method is **empiricism**—knowledge is based on observations. Data are collected that form the basis of conclusions about the nature of the world. The scientific method embodies a number of rules for collecting and evaluating data; these rules will be explored throughout the book.

The power of the scientific approach can be seen all around us. Whether you look at biology, chemistry, medicine, physics, anthropology, or psychology, you see amazing advances over the past 25, 50, or 100 years. We have a greater understanding of the world around us, and the applications of that understanding have kept pace. Goodstein (2000) describes an "evolved theory of science" that defines the characteristics of scientific inquiry. These are summarized in Figure 1.1.

The first is that scientists make observations that are accurately reported to other scientists and the public; others can replicate the methods used and obtain the same results. In addition, fabricating data is inherently unethical and dealt with by strong sanctions. Second, scientists enthusiastically search for observations that will verify their ideas about the world. They develop theories, argue that existing data support their theories, and conduct research that can increase our confidence that the theories are correct. Third, science flourishes when there is an open system for the exchange of ideas. Research can be conducted to test any idea that is advanced; supporters of the idea and those who disagree with the idea can report their research findings and these can be evaluated by others. Some ideas, even some very good ideas, may prove to be false; research fails to provide support for them. When this occurs, science is also advanced because it will spur the development of new and better ideas. Finally, peer review of research is very important in making sure that only the best research is published. Before a study is published in a scientific publication, it must be reviewed by peers. This ensures that research with major flaws will not become part of the scientific literature. In essence, science exists in a free market of ideas in which the best ideas are supported by research and scientists can build upon the research of others to make further advances.

### Integrating Intuition, Skepticism, and Authority

The advantage of the scientific approach over other ways of knowing about the world is that it provides an objective set of rules for gathering, evaluating, and reporting information. It is an open system that allows ideas to be refuted or supported by others. This does not mean that intuition and authority are not important, however. As noted previously, scientists often rely on intuition and assertions of authorities for ideas for research. Moreover, there is nothing wrong with accepting the assertions of authority as long as we do not accept them as scientific evidence. Often, scientific evidence is not obtainable as, for example, when religions ask us to accept certain beliefs on faith. Some beliefs cannot be tested and thus are beyond the realm of science. In science, however, ideas must be evaluated on the basis of available evidence that can be used to support or refute the ideas.

There is also nothing wrong with having opinions or beliefs as long as they are presented simply as opinions or beliefs. However, we should always ask whether the opinion can be tested scientifically or whether scientific evidence exists that relates to the opinion. For example, opinions on whether exposure to television violence increases aggression are only opinions until scientific evidence on the issue is gathered.

As you learn more about scientific methods, you will become increasingly skeptical of the research results reported in the media and the assertions of scientists as well. You should be aware that scientists often become authorities when they express their ideas. When someone claims to be a scientist, should we be more willing to accept what he or she has to say? First, ask about the credentials of the individual. I am much more likely to pay attention to someone with an established reputation in the field; I would also be influenced by the reputation of the institution represented by the person. It is also worthwhile to examine the researcher's funding source; you might be a bit suspicious when research funded by a drug company supports the effectiveness of a drug manufactured by that company, for example. Similarly, when an organization with a particular social-political agenda funds the research that supports that agenda, I tend to be skeptical of the findings and closely examine the methods of the study. Also, there are many "pseudoscientists" using scientific terms to substantiate their claims—these may range from astrologers to marketers asking you to purchase products to enhance your memory or sex drive. And finally, we are all increasingly susceptible to false reports of scientific findings circulated via the Internet. Many of these claim to be associated with a reputable scientist or scientific organization and then they take on a life of their own. A recent one that received wide coverage was a report, supposedly from the World Health Organization, that claimed that the gene for blond hair was being selected out of the human gene pool. Blond hair would be a disappearing trait! A general rule is to be highly skeptical when scientific assertions are made that are supported by only vague or improbable evidence.

## GOALS OF SCIENCE

Scientific research has four general goals: (1) to describe behavior, (2) to predict behavior, (3) to determine the causes of behavior, and (4) to understand or explain behavior.

### Description of Behavior

The scientist begins with careful observation because the first goal of science is to describe events. Cunningham and his colleagues examined judgments of physical attractiveness over time (Cunningham, Druen, & Barbee, 1997). Male college students in 1976 rated the attractiveness of a large number of females shown in photographs. The same photographs were rated in 1993 by another group of students. The judgments of attractiveness of the females were virtually identical; standards of attractiveness apparently changed very little over this time period. In another study, Cunningham compared the facial characteristics of females who were movie stars in the 1930s and 1940s with those of female stars of the 1990s. Such measures included eye height, eye width, nose length, cheekbone prominence, and smile width, among others. These facial characteristics were highly similar across the two time periods, again indicating that standards of attractiveness remain constant over time.

Researchers are often interested in describing the ways in which events are systematically related to one another. Do jurors judge attractive defendants more leniently than unattractive defendants? Are people more likely to be persuaded by a speaker who has high credibility? In what ways do cognitive abilities change as people grow older? Do students who study with a television set on score lower on exams than students who study in a quiet environment?

### Prediction of Behavior

Another goal of science is to predict behavior. Once it has been observed with some regularity that two events are systematically related to one another (e.g., greater credibility is associated with greater attitude change), it becomes possible to make predictions. One implication of this is that we can anticipate events. If we know that one candidate in an election is considered more credible than the other, we may be able to predict the outcome of the election. Further, the ability to predict often helps us make better decisions. For example, many college students take a measure of occupational interests such as the Strong-Campbell Interest Inventory at the college counseling center because awareness of their scores can help them make better decisions about possible career goals and choice of a major.

## Determining the Causes of Behavior

A third goal of science is to determine the causes of behavior. Although we might accurately predict the occurrence of a behavior, we might not have correctly identified its cause. For example, aptitude test scores do not cause college grades. The aptitude test is an indicator of other factors that are the actual causes; research may be undertaken to study these factors. Similarly, research shows that a child's aggressive behavior may be predicted by knowing how much violence the child views on television. Unfortunately, unless we know that exposure to television violence is a *cause* of behavior, we cannot assert that aggressive behavior can be reduced by limiting scenes of violence on television. Thus, to know how to *change* behavior, we need to know the *causes* of behavior.

Identification of a cause of a behavior requires three types of evidence. It is not enough to know that two events occur together, as in the case of knowing that watching television violence is a predictor of actual aggression. To conclude causation, three things must occur:

1. There is a temporal order of events in which the cause precedes the effect. This is called **temporal precedence.** Thus, we need to know that television viewing occurred first and aggression then followed.

2. When the cause is present, the effect occurs; when the cause is not present, the effect does not occur. This is called **covariation of the cause and effect.** We need to know that children who watch television violence behave aggressively and that children who do not watch television violence do not behave aggressively.

3. Nothing other than a causal variable could be responsible for the observed effect. This is called elimination of **alternative explanations.** There should be no other plausible alternative explanation for the relationship. This third point about alternative explanations is very important; suppose that the children who watch a lot of television violence are left alone more than are children who don't view television violence. In this case, the increased aggression could have an alternative explanation—lack of parental supervision. Causation will be discussed again in later chapters.

## Explanation of Behavior

A final goal of science is to explain the events that have been described. The scientist seeks to understand *why* the behavior occurs. Consider the relationship between television violence and aggression; even if we know that TV violence is a cause of aggressiveness, we need to explain this relationship. Is it due to imitation or "modeling" of the violence seen on TV? Is it the result of psychological desensitization to violence and its effects? Or does watching TV violence lead to a belief that aggression is a normal response to frustration and conflict? Further research is necessary to shed light on possible explanations of what has been observed. Usually, additional research like this is carried out by testing theories that are developed to explain particular behaviors.

Description, prediction, determination of cause, and explanation are all closely intertwined. Determining cause and explaining behavior are particularly closely related because it is difficult ever to know the true cause or all the causes of any behavior. An explanation that appears satisfactory may turn out to be inadequate when other causes are identified in subsequent research. For example, when early research showed that speaker credibility is related to attitude change, the researchers explained the finding by stating that people are more willing to believe what is said by a person with high credibility than by one with low credibility. However, this explanation has given way to a more complex theory of attitude change that takes into account many other factors that are related to persuasion (Petty & Cacioppo, 1986). In short, there is a certain amount of ambiguity in the enterprise of scientific inquiry. New research findings almost always pose new questions that must be addressed by further research; explanations of behavior often must be discarded or revised as new evidence is gathered. Such ambiguity is part of the excitement and fun of science.

## BASIC AND APPLIED RESEARCH

### Basic Research

Basic research tries to answer fundamental questions about the nature of behavior. Studies are often designed to address theoretical issues concerning phenomena such as cognition, emotion, motivation, learning, psychobiology, personality development, and social behavior. Here are citations of a few journal articles that pertain to some basic research questions:

Marian, V., & Neisser, U. (2000). Language dependent recall of autobiographical memories. *Journal of Experimental Psychology: General, 129,* 361–368.

Bilingual Russian-English speakers recalled more information about the period in their lives when they spoke Russian when interviewed in that language. The same people recalled more about the English-speaking times of their lives when interviewed in English.

Watkins, M. J., LeCompte, D. C., & Kyungmi, K. (2000). Role of study strategy in recall of mixed lists of common and rare words. *Journal of Experimental Psychology: Learning, Memory, and Cognition, 26,* 239–245.

When research participants were asked to recall common and rare words presented in separate lists, they recalled more of the common words. However, if the same words were presented in mixed lists, the participants remembered more rare words; when both are together, the study strategy is apparently to focus on the rare words.

Raine, A., Reynolds, C., Venables, P. H., & Mednick, S. A. (2002). Stimulation seeking and intelligence: A prospective longitudinal study. *Journal of Personality and Social Psychology, 82,* 663–674.

High-stimulation-seeking 3-year-olds had higher intelligence test scores at age 11 than did low-stimulation-seeking 3-year-olds. Children with high-stimulation-seeking dispositions may seek and create more cognitively stimulating environments; this in turn would enhance cognitive abilities.

## Applied Research

The research articles listed previously were concerned with basic processes of behavior and cognition rather than any immediate practical implications. In contrast, applied research is conducted to address issues in which there are practical problems and potential solutions. To illustrate, here are a few journal article titles:

Wells, M., & Perrine, R. (2001). Critters in the cube farm: Perceived psychological and organizational effects of pets in the workplace. *Journal of Occupational Health Psychology, 6,* 81–87.

People working in companies that allow employees to bring pets to work were asked about their experiences. Overall, the respondents believed that the presence of pets reduced work stress and benefited the organization; this effect was stronger among the employees participating by bringing pets to work than among others who either did not bring pets to work or did not have pets in their household.

Bushman, B. J., & Bonacci, A. M. (2002). Violence and sex impair memory for television ads. *Journal of Applied Psychology, 87,* 557–564.

Participants viewed a television program that contained violence, contained sex, or was neutral with neither violence nor sex. The programs included the same advertisements. Participants were telephoned the next day to measure their recall of the ads. Participants in the neutral content condition recalled more ads than did those viewing the sexual or violent content programs.

Straughan, R. D., & Lynn, M. (2002). The effects of salesperson compensation on perceptions of salesperson honesty. *Journal of Applied Social Psychology, 32,* 719–731.

Participants rated the honesty of male and female salespersons working on salary or commissions. Male salespersons working on commissions were judged as less honest than those on salary. However, compensation did not affect the honesty ratings of female salespersons.

A major area of applied research is called **program evaluation.** Program evaluation research evaluates the social reforms and innovations that occur in government, education, the criminal justice system, industry, health care, and mental health institutions. In an influential paper on "reforms as experiments," Campbell (1969) noted that social programs are really experiments designed to achieve certain outcomes. He argued persuasively that social scientists should evaluate each program to determine whether it is having its intended effect. If it is not, alternative programs should be tried. This is an important point that people in all organizations too often fail to remember when new ideas are implemented; the scientific approach dictates that new programs should be evaluated. Here are two sample journal articles:

> Grossman, J. B., & Tierney, J. P. (1998). Does mentoring work? An impact study of the Big Brothers Big Sisters program. *Evaluation Review, 22,* 403–426.
>
> An experiment was conducted to evaluate the impact of participation in the Big Brothers Big Sisters program. The 10–16-year-old youths participating in the program were less likely to skip school, begin using drugs or alcohol, or get into fights than the youths in the control group.
>
> Celio, A. A., Winzelberg, A. J., Dev, P., & Taylor, C. B. (2002). Improving compliance in on-line, structured self-help programs: Evaluation of an eating disorder prevention program. *Journal of Psychiatric Practice, 8,* 14–20.
>
> College women used one of four different computer-based self-help programs designed to reduce eating disorders. A program using a structured approach with e-mail reminders was associated with reading more of the program screens and greater behavioral improvement.

Much applied research is conducted in settings such as large business firms, marketing research companies, government agencies, and public polling organizations and is not published but rather is used within the company or by clients of the company. Whether or not such results are published, however, they are used to help people make better decisions concerning problems that require immediate action.

### Comparing Basic and Applied Research

Both basic and applied research are important, and neither can be considered superior to the other. In fact, progress in science is dependent on a synergy between basic and applied research. Much applied research is guided by the theories and findings of basic research investigations. For example, applied research on expert testimony in jury trials is guided by basic research in perception and cognition. In turn, the findings obtained in applied settings often require modification of existing theories and spur more basic research. Thus, the study of actual eyewitness testimony leads to richer and more accurate knowledge of basic perceptual and cognitive processes.

In recent years, many in our society, including legislators who control the budgets of research-granting agencies of the government, have demanded that research be directly relevant to specific social issues. The problem with this attitude toward research is that we can never predict the ultimate applications of basic research. Psychologist B. F. Skinner, for example, conducted basic research in the 1930s on operant conditioning, which carefully described the effects of reinforcement on such behaviors as bar pressing by rats. Years later, this research led to many practical applications in therapy, education, and industrial psychology. Research with no apparent practical value ultimately can be very useful. The fact that no one can predict the eventual impact of basic research leads to the conclusion that support of basic research is necessary both to advance science and to benefit society.

Behavioral research is important in many fields and has significant applications to public policy. This chapter has introduced you to the major goals and general types of research. All researchers use scientific methods, whether they are interested in basic, applied, or program evaluation questions. The themes and concepts in this chapter will be expanded in the remainder of the book. They will be the basis on which you evaluate the research of others and plan your own research projects as well.

This chapter emphasized that scientists are skeptical about what is true in the world; they insist that propositions be tested empirically. In the next two chapters, we will focus on two other characteristics of scientists. First, scientists have an intense curiosity about the world and find inspiration for ideas in many places. Second, scientists have strong ethical principles; they are committed to treating those who participate in research investigations with respect and dignity.

## Study Terms

| | |
|---|---|
| Alternative explanations | Goals of science |
| Applied research | Intuition |
| Authority | Program evaluation |
| Basic research | Skepticism |
| Covariation of cause and effect | Temporal precedence |
| Empiricism | |

## Review Questions

1. Why is it important for anyone in our society to have knowledge of research methods?
2. Why is scientific skepticism useful in furthering our knowledge of behavior? How does the scientific approach differ from other ways of gaining knowledge about behavior?
3. Provide definitions and examples of description, prediction, determination of cause, and explanation as goals of scientific research.

4. How does basic research differ from applied research?

5. Describe the characteristics of the way that science works, according to Goodstein (2000).


## Activity Questions

1. Read several editorials in your daily newspaper and identify the sources used to support the assertions and conclusions. Did the writer use intuition, appeals to authority, scientific evidence, or a combination of these? Give specific examples.

2. Imagine a debate on the following assertion: Behavioral scientists should only conduct research that has immediate practical applications. Develop arguments that support (pro) and oppose (con) the assertion.

3. Imagine a debate on the following assertion: Knowledge of research methods is unnecessary for students who intend to pursue careers in clinical and counseling psychology. Develop arguments that support (pro) and oppose (con) the assertion.

4. A newspaper headline says that "Eating Disorders May Be More Common in Warm Places"—you read the article to discover that a researcher found that the incidence of eating disorders among female students at a university in Florida was higher than at a university in Pennsylvania. Assume that this study accurately describes a difference between students at the two universities. Discuss the finding in terms of the issues of identification of cause and effect and explanation. Come back to this question after you have read the next few chapters. For more information, see Sloan, D. M. (2002). Does warm weather climate affect eating disorder pathology? *International Journal of Eating Disorders, 32,* 240–244.

5. Identify ways that you might have allowed yourself to accept beliefs or engage in practices that might have been rejected if you had engaged in scientific skepticism. For example, I continually have to remind some of my friends that a claim made in an e-mail may be a hoax or a rumor. Provide specific details of the experience(s). How might you go about investigating whether the claim is valid?

2

# Where to Start

The motivation to conduct scientific research derives from a natural curiosity about the world. Most people have their first experience with research when their curiosity leads them to ask, "I wonder what would happen if . . ." or "I wonder why . . . ," followed by an attempt to answer the question. What are the sources of inspiration for such questions? How do you find out about other people's ideas and past research? In this chapter, we will explore some sources of scientific ideas. We will also consider the nature of research reports published in professional journals.

## HYPOTHESES AND PREDICTIONS

Most research studies are attempts to test a **hypothesis** formulated by the researcher. A hypothesis is really a type of idea or question; it makes a statement about something that may be true. A hypothesis therefore is only a tentative idea or question that is waiting for evidence to support or refute it. Sometimes, hypotheses are very general and informal questions. For example, Geller, Russ, and Altomari (1986) had general questions about beer drinking among college students: How much beer is consumed in an average sitting in a college bar? How long do the students stay? Do males and females differ in their drinking? With such questions in mind, the researchers developed a procedure for collecting data to answer the questions. Research problems formulated in this way are informal hypotheses or simply questions about behavior.

Hypotheses are often stated in more specific and formal terms. Usually, such formal hypotheses state that two or more variables are related to one another. Thus, researchers might formulate hypotheses such as "crowding results in lowered performance on cognitive tasks" or "attending to more features of something to be learned will result in greater memory." Such hypotheses are formulated on the basis of past research findings and theoretical considerations. The researcher will then design a study to test the hypothesis. In the example on crowding, the researcher might place research participants in either a crowded room or an uncrowded room to work on a series of tasks and then observe their performance.

At this point, the researcher would make a specific **prediction** concerning the outcome of this experiment. Here the prediction might be that "participants in the uncrowded condition will perform better on the tasks than will participants in the crowded condition." If this prediction is confirmed by the results of the study, the hypothesis is supported. If the prediction is not confirmed, the researcher will either reject the hypothesis (and believe that crowding does not lead to poor performance) or conduct further research using different methods to study the hypothesis. It is important to note that when the results of a study confirm a prediction, the hypothesis is only *supported*, not *proven*. Researchers study the same hypothesis using a variety of methods, and each time this hypothesis is supported by a research study, our confidence that the hypothesis is correct increases.

## WHO WE STUDY: A NOTE ON TERMINOLOGY

We have been using the term *participants* to refer to the individuals who participate in research projects. An equivalent term in psychological research is *subjects*. The *American Psychological Association Publication Manual* (APA, 2001) recommends using *participants* when describing humans who take part in psychological research. You will see both terms when you read about research, and both terms will be used in this book. Other terms that you may encounter include *respondents* and *informants*. The individuals who take part in survey research are usually called *respondents*. *Informants* are the people who help researchers understand the dynamics of particular cultural and organizational settings—this term originated in anthropological and sociological research, and is now being used by psychologists as well.

## SOURCES OF IDEAS

It is not easy to say where good ideas come from. Many people are capable of coming up with worthwhile ideas but find it difficult to verbalize the process by which they are generated. Cartoonists know this—they show a brilliant idea as a lightbulb flashing on over the person's head. But where does the electricity come from? Let's consider five sources of ideas: common sense, observation of the world around us, theories, past research, and practical problems.

### Common Sense

One source of ideas that can be tested is the body of knowledge called common sense—the things we all believe to be true. Do "opposites attract" or do "birds of a feather flock together"? If you "spare the rod," do you "spoil the child"? Is a "picture worth a thousand words"? Asking questions such as these can lead to research programs studying attraction, the effects of punishment, and the role of visual images in learning and memory.

Testing a commonsense idea can be valuable because such notions don't always turn out to be correct, or research may show that the real world is much more complicated than our commonsense ideas would have it. For example, pictures can aid memory under certain circumstances, but sometimes pictures detract from learning (see Levin, 1983). Conducting research to test commonsense ideas often forces us to go beyond a commonsense theory of behavior.

### Observation of the World Around Us

Observations of personal and social events can provide many ideas for research. The curiosity sparked by your observations and experiences can lead you to ask questions about all sorts of phenomena. In fact, this type of curiosity is what drives many students to engage in their first research project.

Have you ever had the experience of storing something away in a "special place" where you were sure you could find it later (and where no one else would possibly look for it), only to later discover that you couldn't recall where you had stored it? Such an experience could lead to systematic research on whether it is a good idea to put things in special places. In fact, Winograd and Soloway (1986) conducted a series of experiments on this very topic. Their research demonstrated that people are likely to forget where something is placed when two conditions are present: (1) The location where the object is placed is judged to be highly memorable *and* (2) the location is considered a very unlikely place for the object. Thus, although it may seem to be a good idea at the time, storing something in an unusual place is generally not a good idea.

A more recent example demonstrates the diversity of ideas that can be generated by curiosity about things that happen around you. During the past few years, there has been a great deal of controversy about the effects of music lyrics, with fears that certain types of rock and rap music lead to sexual promiscuity, drug use, and violence. Some groups, such as the Parents' Music Resource Center (PMRC), would like to censor song lyrics and have persuaded record companies to place warning labels on records. There have even been congressional hearings on this topic. Some researchers have decided to conduct research to examine issues raised by this controversy. Fried (1999) suggested that the negative reaction to rap music in particular may arise because it is associated with Black music. To test this idea, Fried asked participants to read the lyrics of a folk song called "Bad Man's Blunder" that has a violent theme; the song was described as either rap or country music. Although the song is clearly not rap, the participants had a more negative reaction to the lyrics when it was described as a rap song than when it was presented as country music. The world around us is a rich source of material for scientific investigation. When psychologist Robert Levine was teaching in Brazil several years ago, he noticed that Brazilian students were much more casual about both getting to class on time and leaving afterward than were their counterparts in the United States. That observation led him to begin studying the pace of life in a variety of countries, as well as in numerous U.S. cities (Levine, 1990). Investigations such as these illustrate a point made in Chapter 1: Personal opinions and personal experiences provide insights about behavior, but scientific thinking requires us to test ideas through research.

Finally, we should mention the role of *serendipity*—sometimes the most interesting discoveries are the result of accident or sheer luck. Ivan Pavlov is best known for discovering what is called classical conditioning—a neutral stimulus (such as a tone), if paired repeatedly with an unconditioned stimulus (food) that produces a reflex response (salivation), will eventually produce the response when presented alone. Pavlov did not set out to discover classical conditioning. Instead, he was studying the digestive system in dogs by measuring their salivation when given food. He accidentally discovered that the dogs were salivating prior to the actual feeding, and then studied the ways that the stimuli preceding the feeding could produce a salivation response. Of course, such accidental discoveries are made only when viewing the world with a curious eye.

## Theories

Much research in the behavioral sciences tests theories of behavior. Theories serve two important functions in increasing our understanding of behavior. First, theories *organize and explain* a variety of specific facts or descriptions of behavior. Such facts and descriptions are not very meaningful by themselves, and so theories are needed to impose a framework on them. This framework makes the world more comprehensible by providing a few abstract concepts around which we can organize and explain a variety of behaviors. As an example, consider how Charles Darwin's theory of evolution organized and explained a variety of facts concerning the characteristics of animal species. Similarly, in psychology one theory of memory asserts that there are separate systems of short-term memory and long-term memory. This theory accounts for a number of specific observations about learning and memory, including such phenomena as the different types of memory deficits that result from a blow to the head versus damage to the hippocampus area of the brain and the rate at which a person forgets material he or she has just read.

Second, theories *generate new knowledge* by focusing our thinking so that we notice new aspects of behavior—theories guide our observations of the world. The theory generates hypotheses about behavior, and the researcher conducts studies to see whether these are correct. If the studies confirm the hypotheses, the theory is supported. As more and more evidence accumulates that is consistent with the theory, our confidence that the theory is correct grows. However, research also can reveal weaknesses in a theory and force researchers to modify the theory or develop a new, more comprehensive one.

Evolutionary theory is still helping psychologists generate hypotheses (Buss, 1998; Gaulin & McBurney, 2000). For example, evolutionary theory asserts that males and females have evolved different strategies for reproduction. All individuals have an evolutionary interest in passing their genes on to future generations. However, females have relatively few opportunities to reproduce, have a limited age range during which to reproduce, and must exert a tremendous amount of time and energy caring for their children. Males, in contrast, can reproduce at any time and have a reproductive advantage by producing as many offspring as possible. Because of these differences, the theory predicts that females and males will use different criteria for mate selection. Females will be more interested in males who can provide support for childrearing—those that are higher in status, economic resources, and dominance. Males will choose females who are younger, healthier, and more physically attractive. Research supports these predictions across a variety of cultures (Buss, 1989). Although research supports evolutionary theory, alternative theories can be developed that may better explain the same findings—theories are living and dynamic. Eagly and Wood (1999) interpreted the Buss research in terms of social structure. They argue that gender differences arise from the fact that there are male–female differences in the division of labor—males are responsible for economic welfare of the family and females are responsible for care of children—and these differences account for gender differences in mate selection preferences. Research on this exciting topic continues.

Theories are usually modified as new research defines the scope of the theory. The necessity of modifying theories is illustrated by the theory of short-term versus long-term memory mentioned previously. The original conception of the long-term memory system described long-term memory as a storehouse of permanent, fixed memories. However, research by cognitive psychologists, including Loftus (1979), has shown that memories are easily reconstructed and reinterpreted. In one study, participants watched a film of an automobile accident and later were asked to tell what they saw in the film. Loftus found that participants' memories were influenced by the way they were questioned. For example, participants who were asked whether they saw "the" broken headlight were more likely to answer yes than were participants who were asked whether they saw "a" broken headlight. Results such as these have required a more complex theory of how long-term memory operates.

## Past Research

A fourth source of ideas is past research. Becoming familiar with a body of research on a topic is perhaps the best way to generate ideas for new research. Because the results of research are published, researchers can use the body of past literature on a topic to continually refine and expand our knowledge. Virtually every study raises questions that can be addressed in subsequent research. The research may lead to an attempt to apply the findings in a different setting, to study the topic with a different age group, or to use a different methodology to replicate the results. The Geller et al. (1986) study on beer drinking reported that students who buy pitchers drink more beer than those who purchase bottles, males drink more than females, students in groups drink more than those who are alone, and females stay longer in the bar than males. Knowledge of this study and its results might lead, for example, to research on ways to reduce excess drinking by college students.

In addition, as you become familiar with the research literature on a topic, you may see inconsistencies in research results that need to be investigated, or you may want to study alternative explanations for the results. Also, what you know about one research area often can be successfully applied to another research area.

Let's look at a concrete example of a study that was designed to address methodological flaws in previous research. The study was concerned with a method of helping children who are diagnosed with autism. Childhood autism is characterized by a number of symptoms including severe impairments in language and communication ability. Recently, parents and care providers have been encouraged by a technique called "facilitated communication" that apparently allows an autistic child to communicate with others by pressing keys on a keyboard showing letters and other symbols. A facilitator holds the child's hand to facilitate the child's ability to determine which key to press. With this technique, many autistic children begin communicating their thoughts and feelings and answer questions posed to them. Most people who see facilitated communication in action regard the technique as a miraculous breakthrough.

The conclusion that facilitated communication is effective is based on a comparison of the autistic child's ability to communicate with and without the facilitator. The difference is impressive to most observers. Recall, however, that scientists are by nature skeptical. They examine all evidence carefully and ask whether claims are justified. In the case of facilitated communication, Montee, Miltenberger, and Wittrock (1995) noted that the facilitator may be unintentionally guiding the child's fingers to type meaningful sentences. In other words, the facilitator, and not the autistic individual, is controlling the communication. Montee et al. conducted a study to test this idea. In one condition, both the facilitator and the autistic child were shown a picture, and the child was asked to indicate what was shown in the picture by typing a response with the facilitator. This was done on a number of trials. In another condition, only the child saw the pictures. In a third condition, the child and facilitator were shown different pictures (but the facilitator was unaware of this fact). Consistent with the hypothesis that the facilitator is controlling the child's responses, the pictures were correctly identified only in the condition in which both saw the same pictures. Moreover, when the child and facilitator viewed different pictures, the child never made the correct response, and usually the picture the facilitator had seen was the one identified.

### Practical Problems

Research is also stimulated by practical problems that can have immediate applications. Groups of city planners and citizens might survey bicycle riders to determine the most desirable route for a city bike path, for example. On a larger scale, researchers have guided public policy by conducting research on the effects of exposure to pornographic materials, as well as other social and health issues. Much of the applied and evaluation research described in Chapter 1 addresses issues such as these.

## LIBRARY RESEARCH

Before conducting any research project, an investigator must have a thorough knowledge of previous research findings. Even if the basic idea has been formulated, a review of past studies will help the researcher clarify the idea and design the study. Thus, it is important to know how to search the literature on a topic and how to read research reports in professional journals. In this section, we will discuss only the fundamentals of conducting library research; for further information, you may refer to a more detailed guide to library research in psychology and to preparing papers that review research such as Reed and Baxter (2003) and Rosnow and Rosnow (2002).

### The Nature of Journals

If you've wandered through the periodicals section of your library, you've noticed the enormous number of professional journals. In these journals, researchers publish the results of their investigations. After a research project has been completed, the study is written as a report, which then may be submitted to the editor of an appropriate journal. The editor solicits reviews from other scientists in the same field and then decides whether the report is to be accepted for publication. Because each journal has a limited amount of space and receives many more papers than it has room to publish, most papers are rejected. Those that are accepted are published about a year later.

Most psychology journals specialize in one or two areas of human or animal behavior. Even so, the number of journals in many areas is so large that it is almost impossible for anyone to read them all. Table 2.1 lists some of the major journals in several areas of psychology; the table does not list any journals that are published only on the Internet and it does not include many journals that publish in areas closely related to psychology as well as highly specialized areas within psychology. Clearly, it would be difficult to read all of the journals listed, even if you restricted your reading to a single research area in psychology such as learning and memory. If you were seeking research on a single specific topic, it would be impractical to look at every issue of every journal in which relevant research might be published. Fortunately, you don't have to.

## Psychological Abstracts

The American Psychological Association began publishing *Psychological Abstracts,* or *Psych Abstracts,* in 1927. Until recently, students conducted literature searches manually by locating the abstracts—brief summaries—of articles in psychology and related disciplines that were published each month in *Psych Abstracts.* The print version of *Psych Abstracts* is still published. However, today you are more likely to conduct searches using computer databases that contain the abstracts. The American Psychological Association computer database system is called *PsycINFO. PsycINFO* is usually accessed via the World Wide Web, and is updated monthly. *PsycINFO* coverage is usually to 1966 but may go back to even earlier years. A related database used in some libraries is *PsycFIRST;* this contains abstracts from the past three years. The exact procedures you will use to search the *PsycINFO* systems will depend on how your library has arranged to obtain access to the database. In all cases, you will obtain a list of abstracts that are related to your particular topic of interest. You can then find and read the articles in your library. If an important article is not available in your library, ask a librarian about services to obtain articles from other libraries.

## Conducting a PsycINFO Search

The exact "look and feel" of the system you will use to search *PsycINFO* will depend on your computer system. Figure 2.1 (page 25) illustrates one Web-based system (WebSPIRS from SilverPlatter); the same *PsycINFO* database information is accessed in different ways through other systems. This screen shows the three major parts of

**TABLE 2.1** Some major journals in psychology

General

*American Psychologist** (general articles on a variety of topics)
*Contemporary Psychology** (book reviews)
*Psychological Bulletin** (literature reviews)
*Psychological Review** (theoretical articles)
*Psychological Science*
*Psychological Methods**
*Current Directions in Psychological Science*
*Psychological Science in the Public Interest*

Experimental areas of psychology

*Journal of Experimental Psychology: General**
*Journal of Experimental Psychology: Applied**
*Journal of Experimental Psychology: Learning, Memory, and Cognition**
*Journal of Experimental Psychology: Human Perception and Performance**
*Journal of Experimental Psychology: Animal Behavior Processes**
*Journal of Comparative Psychology**
*Behavioral Neuroscience**
*Bulletin of the Psychonomic Society*
*Learning and Motivation*
*Memory and Cognition*
*Cognitive Psychology*
*Cognition*
*Cognitive Science*
*Discourse Processes*
*Journal of the Experimental Analysis of Behavior*
*Animal Learning and Behavior*
*Neuropsychology**
*Emotion**
*Experimental and Clinical Psychopharmacology**

Clinical and counseling psychology

*Journal of Abnormal Psychology**
*Journal of Consulting and Clinical Psychology**
*Journal of Counseling Psychology**
*Behavior Research and Therapy*
*Journal of Clinical Psychology*
*Behavior Therapy*
*Journal of Abnormal Child Psychology*
*Journal of Social and Clinical Psychology*
*Professional Psychology: Research and Practice**

**TABLE 2.1**  Some major journals in psychology (*continued*)

___

Developmental psychology

___

*Developmental Psychology\**
*Psychology and Aging\**
*Child Development*
*Journal of Experimental Child Psychology*
*Journal of Applied Developmental Psychology*
*Developmental Review*
*Infant Behavior and Development*
*Experimental Aging Research*
*Merrill–Palmer Quarterly*

___

Personality and social psychology

___

*Journal of Personality and Social Psychology\**
*Personality and Social Psychology Bulletin*
*Journal of Experimental Social Psychology*
*Journal of Research in Personality*
*Journal of Social Issues*
*Social Psychology Quarterly*
*Journal of Applied Social Psychology*
*Basic and Applied Social Psychology*
*Journal of Social and Personal Relationships*

___

Applied areas of psychology

___

*Journal of Applied Psychology\**
*Journal of Educational Psychology\**
*Journal of Applied Behavior Analysis*
*Health Psychology\**
*Psychological Assessment\**
*Psychology, Public Policy, and Late\**
*Law and Human Behavior*
*Educational and Psychological Measurement*
*American Educational Research Journal*
*Evaluation Review*
*Evaluation and Program Planning*
*Environment and Behavior*
*Journal of Environmental Psychology*
*Journal of Consumer Research*
*Journal of Marketing Research*

___

*(continued)*

**TABLE 2.1**   Some major journals in psychology (*continued*)

Family studies and sexual behavior

*Journal of Family Psychology\**
*Journal of Marriage and the Family*
*Journal of Marital and Family Therapy*
*Journal of Sex Research*
*Journal of Sexual Behavior*
*Journal of Homosexuality*

Ethnic, gender, and cross-cultural issues

*Hispanic Journal of Behavioral Sciences*
*Journal of Black Psychology*
*Sex Roles*
*Psychology of Women Quarterly*
*Journal of Cross-Cultural Psychology*
*Cultural Diversity and Ethnic Minority Psychology\**

Some Canadian and British journals

*Canadian Journal of Experimental Psychology*
*Canadian Journal of Behavioral Science*
*British Journal of Psychology*
*British Journal of Social and Clinical Psychology*

\*Published by the American Psychological Association.

a search: you must type the topic of the search, be able to see a display of the results of the search, and be provided with options to help you with your search.

Your most important task is to specify the search terms that you want the computer to use. These are typed into an input box (in Figure 2.1, this is labeled as the Find box). How do you know what words to type in the input box? Most commonly, you will want to use standard psychological terms. The "Thesaurus of Psychological Index Terms" lists all the standard terms that are used to index the abstracts, and can be accessed directly with most *PsycINFO* systems. Suppose you are interested in the topic of test anxiety. It turns out that both *test* and *anxiety* are major descriptors in the thesaurus. If you look under *anxiety* you will see all of the related terms including *separation anxiety, social anxiety,* and *test anxiety.* While using the thesaurus, you can check any term and then request a search of that term. However, let's assume that you are using a standard search window as in Figure 2.1. When you give the command to start the search, the results of the search will be displayed.

Here is the output of one of the articles found with a search on test anxiety. I chose to display a great deal of information about the article to illustrate how information is organized in the database; usually you will choose to show less information.

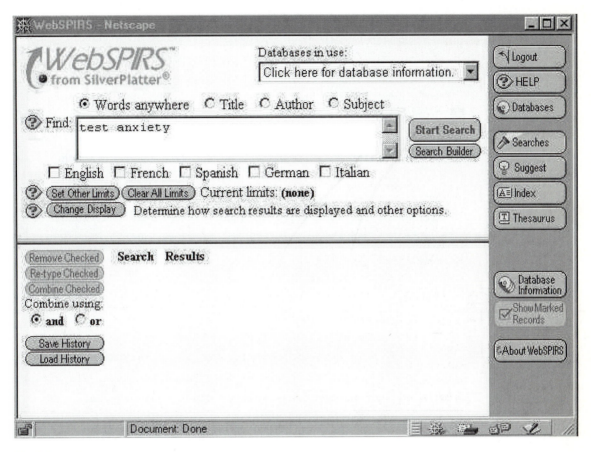

FIGURE 2.1    A *PsycINFO* user screen.

```
DOCUMENT TYPE  Journal-Article

TITLE:  Individual differences in students' retention of

knowledge and conceptual structures learned in university

and high school courses: The case of test anxiety.

AUTHOR:  Naveh-Benjamin,-Moshe; Lavi,-Hagit; McKeachie,-

Wilbert-J.; Lin,-Yi-Guang

FIRST AUTHOR AFFILIATION:  Ben-Gurion U of the Negev, Dept

of Behavioral Sciences, Beer-Sheva, Israel

SOURCE:  Applied-Cognitive-Psychology. 1997 Dec; Vol 11(6):

507-526

ISSN:  0888-4080
```

PUBLICATION YEAR:   1997

ABSTRACT:   Examined individual differences in students'
retention of knowledge several years after studying academic
material. Assessment of retention of materials as a function
of students' test anxiety can allow one to evaluate whether
high test-anxious students' original deficient academic
performance and organization of the materials are due to a
retrieval deficit or a deficit in learning and knowledge
organization. In 2 studies, 210 American students (Study 1)
and 258 Israeli students (aged 17-27 yrs; Study 2) with
different test-anxiety levels completed tasks that enabled us
to evaluate both students' levels of knowledge and their
cognitive organization of the materials. The tasks were
administered either at the end of the course, or at different
retention intervals up to 7 yrs after the end of learning.
Results indicated that whereas high test-anxious students
tested worse at the end of the courses than other students on
tests of knowledge and cognitive organization, high test-
anxious students tested at various retention intervals after
the courses performed as well as other students. The
theoretical and practical implications of these results are
discussed. ((c) 1998 APA/PsycINFO, all rights reserved)

KEY PHRASE:   test anxiety and individual differences in
retention of knowledge and conceptual structures learned in
university and high school courses, US and Israeli students

MAJOR DESCRIPTORS:   *Individual-Differences; *Retention-;
*Test-Anxiety

MINOR DESCRIPTORS:   Adulthood-; College-Students; High-
School-Students

AGE GROUP:   Adulthood

POPULATION:   Human; Male; Female

POPULATION LOCATION:   Israel; USA

PUBLICATION TYPE:   Empirical-Study

Notice that the output is organized into "fields" of information. The full
name of each field is included here; many systems allow abbreviations. You will almost always want to see the title (abbreviated as TI), author (AU), source (SO), and

abstract (AB). Note that you also have fields such as document type, a key phrase to briefly describe the article, major and minor descriptors, and age group.

When you do a simple search with a single word or a phrase such as *test anxiety*, the search yields articles that have that word or phrase anywhere in any of the fields listed. Often you will find that this produces too many articles, including articles that are not directly relevant to your interests. One way to narrow the search is to limit it to certain fields. For example, you could specify *test anxiety in TI* to limit your search to articles that had the term in the title of the article. Similarly, you could specify that the search should find only journal articles (not books or dissertations) or include participants from certain age groups.

Using the Boolean operators *AND* and *OR* and *NOT* can also help you with your searching. Suppose you want to restrict the *test anxiety in TITLE* search to college students only. You can do this by asking for *(test anxiety in TITLE) AND (college students)*. The AND forces both conditions to be true for an article to be included. The parentheses are used to separate different parts of your search specification and are useful when your searches become increasingly complicated. In fact, they could have been left out of this search but are included for illustration.

The OR operation is used to expand a search that is too narrow. Suppose you want to find articles that discuss romantic relationships on the Internet. I just searched for *Internet AND romance* and found 15 articles; changing the specification to *Internet AND (romance OR dating OR love OR attraction)* yielded 51 articles. Articles that have the term *Internet* and *any* of the other terms specified were included in the search.

The NOT operation will exclude abstracts based on a criterion you specify. The NOT operation is used when you anticipate that the search criteria will be met by some irrelevant abstracts. In the Internet example, it is possible that the term *attraction* will find research on Internet job interviews in which attraction to a particular job or job candidate is described. To exclude the term *job* from the results of the search, the following adjustment can be made: *Internet AND (romance OR dating OR love OR attraction) NOT job*. When this search was conducted, I found 47 abstracts instead of the 51 obtained previously.

Another helpful search tool is the "wildcard" asterisk (*). The asterisk stands for any set of letters in a word and so it can expand your search. Consider the word *romance* in the search above—by using *roman\**, the search will expand to include both *romance* and *romantic*. The wildcard can be very useful with the term *child\** to find *child, children, childhood,* and so on. You have to be careful when doing this, however; the *roman\** search would also find *Romania* and *romanticism*! In this case, it might be more efficient to simply add *OR romantic* to the search. These search strategies are summarized in Table 2.2.

When you complete your search, you can print the results. When you print, you can choose which of the fields to display. You probably won't need all the fields shown in the previous example. Many researchers prefer to save the results of the search on a diskette. The information can then be used with other programs such as a word processor or a citation manager. If you don't have access to a disk, you can even send the search results to your e-mail address.

**TABLE 2.2**    Some *PsychINFO* search strategies

Strategy 1: Use fields such as TI and AU
  Example: *(divorce) in TI* to require that a term appear in the title
Strategy 2: Use AND to limit search
  Example: *divorce AND child* requires both terms to be included
Strategy 3: Use OR to expand search
  Example: *divorce OR breakup* includes both terms
Strategy 4: Use NOT to exclude search terms
  Example: *shyness NOT therapy* excludes any shyness articles that have the term *therapy*
Strategy 5: Use the wildcard asterisk (*)
  Example: *child\** finds any word that begins with *child* (childhood, child's, etc.)

## Science Citation Index and Social Sciences Citation Index

Two related search resources are the *Science Citation Index* (SCI) and the *Social Sciences Citation Index* (SSCI). Both allow you to search through citation information such as the name of the author or article title. The SCI includes disciplines such as biology, chemistry, biomedicine, and pharmacology, whereas the SSCI includes social and behavioral sciences such as sociology and criminal justice. The most important feature of both resources is the ability to use the "key article" method. Here you need to first identify a "key article" on your topic, usually one published sometime in the past that is particularly relevant to your interests. You can then search for subsequent articles that cited the key article. This search will give you a bibliography of articles relevant to your topic. To provide an example of this process, I chose the following article:

> Wells, G. L., & Bradfield, A. L. (1999). Distortions in eyewitnesses' recollections: Can the postidentification feedback effect be moderated? *Psychological Science, 10,* 138–144.

When I did an article search using the SSCI, I found 10 articles that had cited the Wells and Bradfield paper since it was published in 1999. Here is one of them:

> Ghetti, S., Qin, J. J., & Goodman, G. S. (2002). False memories in children and adults: Age, distinctiveness, and subjective experience. *Developmental Psychology, 38,* 705–718.

I will now want to become familiar with this article as well as the others on the list. It may then turn out that one or more of the articles might become new "key articles" for further searches.

It is also possible to specify a "key person" to find all articles written by or citing a particular person after a given date. SCI and SSCI searches are much easier using a computer; both may be available on CD-ROM or via an Internet service.

## Literature Reviews

Articles that summarize the research in a particular area are also useful. The *Psychological Bulletin* publishes reviews of the literature in various topic areas in psychology. Each year, the *Annual Review of Psychology* publishes articles that summarize recent developments in various areas of psychology. Other disciplines have similar annual reviews.

## Other Electronic Search Resources

Your library may or may not have access to *PsycINFO* or the SCI/SSCI databases. The number of information databases that a library may purchase today is enormous; budget and other considerations determine which ones are available to you. You will need to take advantage of instructional materials that your library provides to help you learn how to best search for information available through your library. Other major databases include FirstSearch, Sociological Abstracts, MEDLINE, and ERIC (*Educational Resources Information Center*). In addition, services such as Lexis-Nexis and Factiva allow you to search general media resources such as newspapers. A reference librarian can help you use these and other resources available to you.

Some of the information resources available provide full text of articles in the database whereas others provide only abstract or citation information. For example, the American Psychological Association has developed a full-text database called *PsycARTICLES* (http://www.apa.org/psycarticles/). The articles in this database all come from journals published by APA. Other full-text article databases draw from different sources. Sometimes it is tempting to limit yourself to full-text services because it is so easy to obtain the complete article. A problem with this strategy is that you limit yourself to only those journals that are in the full-text database. It is usually a good idea to widen your search so that you are more likely to find the articles of greatest relevance to your topic. Even if the full text of the article is not available via computer, you may be able to obtain it from another library source.

## Internet Searches

The most widely available information resource is the wealth of material that is freely available on the Internet. Services such as Yahoo!, Google, About, and AltaVista allow you to search through a variety of materials stored on the Internet. The Internet is a wonderful source of information: any given search may help you find Web sites devoted to your topic, articles that people have made available to others, book reviews, and even online discussions. Although it is incredibly easy to search (just type something in a dialog box and hit the Enter key), you can improve the quality of your searches by learning: (1) the differences in the way each service finds and stores information, (2) advanced search rules including how to make searches more narrow and how to find exact phrases, and (3) ways to critically evaluate the quality of the information that you find. You also need to make sure that you carefully record the search service and search terms you used, the dates of your search, and the exact location of any Web sites that you will be using in your research; this information will be useful as you provide documentation in the papers that you prepare.

Your own library and a variety of library Web sites have information on evaluating the quality of information found on the Internet. For example, you will want to look at whether the Web site is associated with an educational institution, review the credentials of the person or organization sponsoring the site, and check on the currency of the information.

Even with the explosion of easy-to-use electronic search tools, you will probably want to also search using some "old-fashioned" methods. For example, when you find an article that is important for your research, the references at the end of the article can be used as resources to help you gain expertise about your topic.

## ANATOMY OF A RESEARCH ARTICLE

Your literature search has helped you to find research articles to read. What can you expect to find in these articles? Research articles usually have five sections: (1) an *abstract*, such as the ones found in *Psychological Abstracts*; (2) an *introduction* that explains the problem under investigation and the specific hypotheses being tested; (3) a *method* section that describes in detail the exact procedures used in the study; (4) a *results* section in which the findings are presented; and (5) a *discussion* section in which the researcher may speculate on the broader implications of the results, propose alternative explanations for the results, discuss reasons that a particular hypothesis may not have been supported by the data, and/or make suggestions for further research on the problem. In addition to the five major sections, you will find a list of all the references that were cited.

### Abstract

The abstract is a summary of the research report and typically runs no more than 120 words in length. It includes information about the hypothesis, the procedure, and the broad pattern of results. Generally, little information is abstracted from the discussion section of the paper.

### Introduction

In the introduction, the researcher outlines the problem that has been investigated. Past research and theories relevant to the problem are described in detail. The specific expectations of the researcher are noted, often as formal hypotheses. In other words, the investigator introduces the research in a logical format that shows how past research and theory are connected to the current research problem and the expected results.

## Method

The method section is divided into subsections, with the number of subsections determined by the author and dependent on the complexity of the research design. Sometimes, the first subsection presents an overview of the design to prepare the reader for the material that follows. The next subsection describes the characteristics of the participants. Were they male or female, or were both sexes used? What was the average age? How many participants were there? If the study used human participants, some mention of how participants were recruited for the study would be needed. The next subsection details the procedure used in the study. In describing any stimulus materials presented to the participants, the way the behavior of the participants was recorded, and so on, it is important that no potentially crucial detail be omitted. Such detail allows the reader to know exactly how the study was conducted, and it provides other researchers with the information necessary to replicate the study. Other subsections may be necessary to describe in detail any equipment or testing materials that were used.

## Results

In the results section, the researcher presents the findings, usually in three ways. First, there is a description in narrative form—for example, "The location of items was most likely to be forgotten when the location was both highly memorable and an unusual place for the item to be stored." Second, the results are described in statistical language. Third, the material is often depicted in tables and graphs.

The statistical terminology of the results section may appear formidable. However, lack of knowledge about the calculations isn't really a deterrent to understanding the article or the logic behind the statistics. Statistics are only a tool the researcher uses in evaluating the outcomes of the study.

## Discussion

In the discussion section, the researcher reviews the research from various perspectives. Do the results support the hypothesis? If they do, the author should give all possible explanations for the results and discuss why one explanation is superior to another. If the hypothesis has not been supported, the author should suggest potential reasons for this. What might have been wrong with the methodology, the hypothesis, or both? The researcher may also discuss how the results compare with past research results on the topic. This section may also include suggestions for possible practical applications of the research and for future research on the topic.

You should read as many research articles as possible to become familiar with the way information is presented in reports. As you read, you will develop ways of efficiently processing the information in the articles. It is usually best to read the abstract first, then skim the article to decide whether you can use the information provided. If you can, go back and read the article carefully. Note the hypotheses and theories presented in the introduction, write down anything that seems unclear or problematic in the method, and read the results in view of the material in the introduction. Be critical when you read the article; students often generate the best criticism. Most important, as you read more research on a topic, you will become more familiar with the variables being studied, the methods used to study the variables, the important theoretical issues being considered, and the problems that need to be addressed by future research. In short, you will find yourself generating your own research ideas and planning your own studies.

## Study Terms

Abstract

Discussion section

Hypothesis

Introduction section                          *Social Sciences Citation Index* (SSCI)

Literature review                             *Science Citation Index* (SCI)

Method section                                Theory

Prediction

*PsycLIT, PsycINFO, PsycFIRST*

*Psychological Abstracts*                      ## Review Questions

Results section

1. What is a hypothesis? What is the distinction between a hypothesis and a prediction?
2. What are the two functions of a theory?
3. Describe the difference in the way that past research is found when you use *PsycINFO* versus the "key article" method of the *Science Citation Index/Social Sciences Citation Index*.
4. What information does the researcher communicate in each of the sections of a research article?

## Activity Questions

1. Think of at least five "commonsense" sayings about behavior (e.g., "Spare the rod, spoil the child"; "Like father, like son"; "Absence makes the heart grow fonder"). For each, develop a hypothesis that is suggested by the saying and a prediction that follows from the hypothesis. (Based on Gardner, 1988.)

2. Choose one of the hypotheses formulated in Activity Question 1 and develop a strategy for finding research on the topic using the computer database in your library.

3. Theories serve two purposes: (1) to organize and explain observable events and (2) to generate new knowledge by guiding our way of looking at these events. Identify a consistent behavior pattern in yourself or somebody close to you (e.g., you consistently get into an argument with your sister on Friday nights). Generate two possible theories (explanations) for this occurrence (e.g., because you work long hours on Friday, you're usually stressed and exhausted when you get home; because your sister has a chemistry quiz every Friday afternoon and she's not doing well in the course, she is very irritable on Fridays). How would you gather evidence to determine which explanation might be correct? How might each explanation lead to different approaches to changing the behavior pattern, either to decrease or increase its occurrence?

# 3

# Ethical Research

E thical concerns are paramount when planning, conducting, and evaluating research. In this chapter, we will explore ethical issues in detail, and we will examine some guidelines for addressing dealing with these problems.

## MILGRAM'S OBEDIENCE EXPERIMENT

Stanley Milgram conducted a series of experiments (1963, 1964, 1965) to study the phenomenon of obedience to an authority figure. He placed an ad in the local newspaper in New Haven, Connecticut, offering to pay $4.50 to men to participate in a "scientific study of memory and learning" being conducted at Yale University. The participants reported to Milgram's laboratory at Yale, where they met a scientist dressed in a lab coat and another participant in the study, a middle-aged man named "Mr. Wallace." Mr. Wallace was actually a confederate (i.e., accomplice) of the experimenter, but the participants didn't know this. The scientist explained that the study would examine the effects of punishment on learning. One person would be a "teacher" who would administer the punishment, and the other would be the "learner." Mr. Wallace and the volunteer participant then drew slips of paper to determine who would be the teacher and who would be the learner. The drawing was rigged, however—Mr. Wallace was always the learner and the volunteer was always the teacher.

The scientist attached electrodes to Mr. Wallace and placed the teacher in front of an impressive-looking shock machine. The shock machine had a series of levers that, the individual was told, when pressed would deliver shocks to Mr. Wallace. The first lever was labeled 15 volts, the second 30 volts, the third 45 volts, and so on up to 450 volts. The levers were also labeled "Slight Shock," "Moderate Shock," and so on up to "Danger: Severe Shock," followed by red X's above 400 volts.

Mr. Wallace was instructed to learn a series of word pairs. Then he was given a test to see if he could identify which words went together. Every time Mr. Wallace made a mistake, the teacher was to deliver a shock as punishment. The first mistake was supposed to be answered by a 15-volt shock, the second by a 30-volt shock, and so on. Each time a mistake was made, the learner received a greater shock. The learner, Mr. Wallace, never actually received any shocks, but the participants in the study didn't know that. In the experiment, Mr. Wallace made mistake after mistake. When the teacher "shocked" him with about 120 volts, Mr. Wallace began screaming in pain and eventually yelled that he wanted out. What if the teacher wanted to quit? This happened—the real participants became visibly upset by the pain that Mr. Wallace seemed to be experiencing. The scientist told the teacher that he could quit but urged him to continue, using a series of verbal prods that stressed the importance of continuing the experiment.

The study purportedly was to be an experiment on memory and learning, but Milgram really was interested in learning whether participants would continue to obey the experimenter by administering ever higher levels of shock to the learner. What happened? Approximately 65 percent of the participants continued to deliver shocks all the way to 450 volts. Milgram's study received a great deal of publicity, and the results challenged many of our beliefs about our ability to re-sist authority. Milgram's study is important, and the results have implications for understanding obedience in real-life situations, such as the Holocaust in Nazi Germany and the Jonestown mass suicide (see Miller, 1986). What about the ethics of the Milgram study? How should we make decisions about whether the Milgram study or any other study is ethical?

## THE BELMONT REPORT

Current ethical guidelines for both behavioral and medical researchers have their origins in *The Belmont Report: Ethical Principles and Guidelines for the Protection of Human Subjects of Research* (National Commission for the Protection of Human Subjects of Biomedical and Behavioral Research, 1979). This report defined the principles and applications that have guided more detailed regulations and the American Psychological Association Ethics Code. The three basic ethical principles are benefi-cence, respect for persons (autonomy), and justice. The associated applications of these principles are assessment of risks and benefits, informed consent, and selection of subjects. These will guide our discussion of ethical issues in research.

## ASSESSMENT OF RISKS AND BENEFITS

The principle of **beneficence** in the *Belmont Report* refers to the need for research to maximize benefits and minimize any possible harmful effects of participation. In most decisions we make in life, we consider the relative risks (or costs) and benefits of the decision. In decisions about the ethics of research, we must calculate potential risks and benefits that are likely to result; this is called a *risk-benefit analysis*. Ethical principles require asking whether the research procedures have minimized risk to participants.

The potential risks to the participants include such factors as psychological or physical harm and loss of confidentiality; we will discuss these in detail. In addition, the cost of *not* conducting the study if in fact the proposed procedure is the only way to collect potentially valuable data can be considered (cf. Christensen, 1988). The benefits include direct benefits to the participants, such as an educational benefit, acquisition of a new skill, or treatment for a psychological or medical problem. There may also be material benefits such as a monetary payment, some sort of gift, or even the possibility of winning a prize in a raffle. Other less tangible benefits include the satisfaction gained through being part of a scientific investigation and the potential beneficial applications of the research findings (e.g., the knowledge gained through the research might improve future educational practices, psychotherapy, or social policy). As we will see, current regulations concerning the conduct of research with human participants require a risk-benefit analysis before research can be approved.

## Risks in Psychological Research

Let's return to a consideration of Milgram's research. The risk of experiencing stress and psychological harm is obvious. It is not difficult to imagine the effect of delivering intense shocks to an obviously unwilling learner. A film that Milgram made shows participants protesting, sweating, and even laughing nervously while delivering the shocks. You might ask whether subjecting people to such a stressful experiment is justified, and you might wonder whether the experience had any long-range consequences for the volunteers. For example, did participants who obeyed the experimenter feel continuing remorse or begin to see themselves as cruel, inhumane people? A defense of Milgram's study follows, but first let's consider some potentially stressful research procedures.

**Physical harm**    Procedures that could conceivably cause some physical harm to participants are rare but possible. Many medical procedures fall in this category—for example, administering a drug such as alcohol or caffeine, or depriving people of sleep for an extended period of time. The risks in such procedures require that great care be taken to make them ethically acceptable. Moreover, there would need to be clear benefits of the research that would outweigh the potential risks.

**Stress**    More common than physical stress is psychological stress. For example, participants might be told that they will receive some extremely intense electric shocks. They never actually receive the shocks; it is the fear or anxiety during the waiting period that is the variable of interest. Research by Schachter (1959) employing a procedure like this showed that the anxiety produced a desire to affiliate with others during the waiting period.

In another procedure that produces psychological stress, participants are given unfavorable feedback about their personalities or abilities. Researchers interested in self-esteem have typically given a subject a bogus test of personality or ability. The test is followed by an evaluation that lowers or raises self-esteem by indicating that the participant has an unfavorable personality trait or a low ability score.

Asking people about traumatic or unpleasant events in their lives might also cause stress for some participants. Thus, research that asks people to think about the deaths of a parent, spouse, or friend or their memories of living through a disaster could trigger a stressful reaction.

When stress is possible, it must be asked whether all safeguards have been taken to help participants in dealing with the stress. Usually there is a "debriefing" session following the study that is designed in part to deal with any potential problems that may arise during the research.

**Loss of privacy and confidentiality**    Another risk is the loss of expected privacy and confidentiality. Researchers must take care to protect the privacy of individuals. At a minimum, researchers should protect privacy by keeping all data locked in a secure place. The issue becomes particularly important when studying topics such as sexual behavior, divorce, family violence, or drug abuse; in these cases, researchers may need to ask people very sensitive questions about their private lives. It is extremely important that responses to such questions be confidential. In most cases, the responses are completely anonymous—there is no way to connect any person's identity with the data. This happens, for example, when questionnaires are administered to groups of people and no information is asked that could be used to identify an individual (such as name, Social Security number, or phone number). In other cases, such as a personal interview in which the identity of the person might be known, the researcher must carefully plan ways of coding data, storing data, and explaining the procedures to participants so that there is no question concerning the anonymity of responses.

In some research, there is a real need to be able to identify individual participants. This occurs when individuals are studied on multiple occasions over time, or when personal feedback, such as a test score, must be given. In such cases, the researcher should develop a way to identify the individuals but to separate the information about their identity from the actual data. Thus, if questionnaires or the computerized data files were seen by anyone, the data could not be linked to specific individuals.

In some cases, the risks entailed with loss of confidentiality are so great that researchers may wish to apply for a Certificate of Confidentiality from the U.S. Department of Health and Human Services. Obtaining this certificate is appropriate when the data could conceivably be the target of a legal subpoena.

Another privacy issue concerns concealed observation of behavior. In some studies, researchers make observations of behavior in public places. Observing people in shopping malls or in their cars does not seem to present any major ethical problems. However, what if a researcher wishes to observe behavior in more private settings or in ways that may violate individuals' privacy (see Wilson & Donnerstein, 1976)? For example, would it be ethical to rummage through people's trash or watch people in public restrooms? In one study, Middlemist, Knowles, and Matter (1976) measured the time to onset of urination and the duration of urination of males in restrooms at a college. The purpose of the research was to study the effect of personal space on a measure of physiological arousal (urination times). The students were observed while alone or with a confederate of the experimenter, who stood at the next stall or a more distant stall in the restroom. The presence and closeness of the confederate did have the effect of delaying urination and shortening the duration of urination. In many ways, this is an interesting study; also, the situation is one that males experience on a regular basis. However, one can question whether the invasion of privacy was justified (Koocher, 1977). The researchers can, in turn, argue that through pilot studies and discussions with potential participants they determined that ethical problems with the study were minimal (Middlemist et al., 1977). Middlemist et al. employed a method for determining whether a procedure is ethical that was first proposed by Berscheid, Baron, Dermer, and Libman (1973). Role-playing is used to gather evidence about participants' perceptions of a potential experiment. If the role-playing participants indicate that they would participate in the experiment, at least one objection to deception has been addressed.

## INFORMED CONSENT

The *Belmont Report's* principle of *respect for persons* or **autonomy** states that participants are treated as autonomous; they are capable of making deliberate decisions about whether to participate in research. The application here is **informed consent**—potential participants in a research project should be provided with all information that might influence their decision of whether to participate. Thus, research participants should be informed about the purposes of the study, the risks and benefits of participation, and their rights to refuse or terminate participation in the study. They can then freely consent or refuse to participate in the research.

### Informed Consent Form

Participants are usually provided with some type of informed consent form that contains the information that participants need to make their decision. Most commonly, the form is printed for the participant to read and sign. It is important that participants understand the information in the form. There have been cases in which the form is so technical or loaded with legal terminology that it is very unlikely that the participants fully realized what they were signing. In general, consent forms should be written in simple and straightforward language that avoids jargon and technical terminology (generally a sixth- to eighth-grade level; most word processors provide grade-level information with the grammar check feature). To make the form easier to understand, it should not be written in the first person. Instead, information should be provided as it would if the researcher were simply having a conversation with the participant. Thus, the form might say:

> *Participation in this study is voluntary. You may decline to participate without penalty.*

instead of

> *I understand that participation in this study is voluntary. I may decline to participate without penalty.*

The first statement is providing information to the participant in a straightforward way using the second person (you), whereas the second statement has a legalistic tone that may be more difficult to understand. Finally, if participants are non-English speakers, there should be a translated version of the form. Figure 3.1 provides a checklist for an informed consent form.

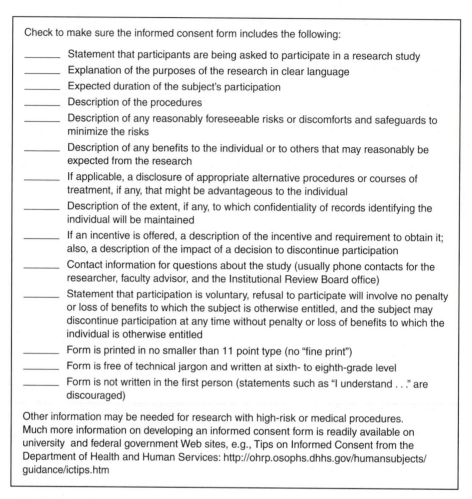

Check to make sure the informed consent form includes the following:

_____ Statement that participants are being asked to participate in a research study

_____ Explanation of the purposes of the research in clear language

_____ Expected duration of the subject's participation

_____ Description of the procedures

_____ Description of any reasonably foreseeable risks or discomforts and safeguards to minimize the risks

_____ Description of any benefits to the individual or to others that may reasonably be expected from the research

_____ If applicable, a disclosure of appropriate alternative procedures or courses of treatment, if any, that might be advantageous to the individual

_____ Description of the extent, if any, to which confidentiality of records identifying the individual will be maintained

_____ If an incentive is offered, a description of the incentive and requirement to obtain it; also, a description of the impact of a decision to discontinue participation

_____ Contact information for questions about the study (usually phone contacts for the researcher, faculty advisor, and the Institutional Review Board office)

_____ Statement that participation is voluntary, refusal to participate will involve no penalty or loss of benefits to which the subject is otherwise entitled, and the subject may discontinue participation at any time without penalty or loss of benefits to which the individual is otherwise entitled

_____ Form is printed in no smaller than 11 point type (no "fine print")

_____ Form is free of technical jargon and written at sixth- to eighth-grade level

_____ Form is not written in the first person (statements such as "I understand . . ." are discouraged)

Other information may be needed for research with high-risk or medical procedures. Much more information on developing an informed consent form is readily available on university  and federal government Web sites, e.g., Tips on Informed Consent from the Department of Health and Human Services: http://ohrp.osophs.dhhs.gov/humansubjects/guidance/ictips.htm

FIGURE 3.1
Checklist for informed consent form

### Autonomy Issues

Informed consent seems simple enough; however, there are important issues to consider. The first concerns lack of autonomy. What happens when the participants may lack the ability to make a free and informed decision to voluntarily participate? Special populations such as minors, patients in psychiatric hospitals, or adults with cognitive impairments require special precautions. When minors are asked to participate, for example, a written consent form signed by a parent or guardian is generally required in addition to agreement by the minor; this agreement by a minor is formally called *assent*. The Division of Developmental Psychology of the American Psychological Association and the Society for Research on Child Development have established their own guidelines for ethical research with children.

Coercion is another threat to autonomy. Any procedure that limits an individual's freedom to consent is potentially coercive. For example, a supervisor who asks employees to fill out a survey during a staff meeting or a professor requiring students in a class to participate in a study in order to pass the course is applying considerable pressure on potential participants. The employees may believe that the supervisor will somehow punish them if they do not participate; they also risk embarrassment if they refuse in front of co-workers. Sometimes benefits are so great that they become coercive. For example, a prisoner may believe that increased privileges or even a favorable parole decision may result from participation. Researchers must consider these issues and make sure that autonomy is preserved.

### Information Issues: Withholding Information and Deception

It may have occurred to you that providing all information about the study might be unwise. Providing too much information could potentially invalidate the results of the study; for example, researchers usually will withhold information about the hypothesis of the study or the particular condition an individual is participating in (see Sieber, 1992). It is generally acceptable to withhold information when the information would not affect the decision to participate and when the information will later be provided, usually in a debriefing session when the study is completed. Most people who volunteer for psychology research do not expect full disclosure about the study prior to participation. However, they do expect a thorough debriefing after they have completed the study. Debriefing will be described after we consider the more problematic issue of deception.

It may also have occurred to you that there are research procedures in which informed consent is not necessary or even possible. If you choose to observe the number of same-sex and mixed-sex study groups in your library, you probably don't need to announce your presence and obtain anyone's permission. If you study the content of the self-descriptions that people write for an online dating service, do you need to contact each person to include their information in your study? When planning research, it is important to make sure that you do have good reasons not to have any informed consent.

Deception occurs when there is active misrepresentation of information. The Milgram experiment illustrates two types of deception. First, there was deception about the purpose of the study. Participants in the Milgram experiment agreed to take part in a study of memory and learning but they actually took part in a study on obedience. Who could imagine that a memory and learning experiment (that title does sound tame, after all) would involve delivering high-intensity, painful electric shocks to another person? Participants in the Milgram experiment didn't know what they were letting themselves in for.

Milgram's study was conducted before informed consent was routine; however, you can imagine that Milgram's consent form would inaccurately have participants agree to be in a memory study. They would also be told that they are free to withdraw from the study at any time. Is it possible that the informed consent procedure would affect the outcome of the study? Knowledge that the research is designed to study obedience would likely alter the behavior of the participants. Few of us like to think of ourselves as obedient, and we would probably go out of our way to prove that we are not. Research indicates that providing informed consent may in fact bias participants' responses, at least in some research areas. For example, research on stressors such as noise or crowding has shown that a feeling of "control" over a stressor reduces its negative impact. If you know that you can terminate a loud, obnoxious noise, the noise produces less stress than when the noise is uncontrollable. Studies by Gardner (1978) and Dill, Gilden, Hill, and Hanslka (1982) have demonstrated that informed consent procedures do increase perceptions of control in stress experiments and therefore can affect the conclusions drawn from the research.

It is also possible that the informed consent procedure may bias the sample. In Milgram's experiment, if participants had prior knowledge that they would be asked to give severe shocks to the other person, some might have declined to be in the experiment. Therefore, we might limit our ability to generalize the results only to those "types" who agreed to participate. If this were true, anyone could say that the obedient behavior seen in the Milgram experiment occurred simply because the people who agreed to participate were sadists in the first place!

The Milgram study also illustrates a type of deception in which participants become part of a series of events staged for the purposes of the study. A confederate of the experimenter played the part of another participant in the study; Milgram created a reality for the participant in which obedience to authority could be observed. Such deception has been most common in social psychology research; it is much less frequent in areas of experimental psychology such as human perception, learning, memory, and motor performance. Even in these areas, researchers may use a cover story to make the experiment seem plausible and involving (e.g., telling participants that they are reading actual newspaper stories for a study on readability when the true purpose is to examine memory errors or organizational schemes).

The problem of deception is not limited to laboratory research. Procedures in which observers conceal their purposes, presence, or identity are also deceptive. For example, Humphreys (1970) studied the behavior of male homosexuals who frequent public restrooms (called "tearooms"). Humphreys did not participate in any homosexual activities, but he served as a lookout who would warn the others of possible intruders. In addition to observing the activities in the tearoom, Humphreys wrote down license plate numbers of tearoom visitors. Later, he obtained the addresses of the men, disguised himself, and visited their homes to interview them. Humphreys' procedure is certainly one way of finding out about homosexuality, but it employs considerable deception.

Over the years, psychologists such as Kelman (1967), Ring (1967), Rubin (1970, 1985), and Ortmann and Hertwig (1997) have criticized the use of deception. Kelman and Ortmann and Hertwig believe that any type of deception is morally unacceptable; it is simply wrong to mislead people in any way. Another objection to the use of deception is that it harms the reputation of the field. Rubin and Ring also argue that researchers sometimes devise elaborate deceptions because of the notoriety they bring—Rubin describes them as "jokers wild in the lab." Rubin pointed to a procedure in which a graduate student experimenter led participants to believe that they had broken a valuable piece of equipment. As another example, Ortmann and Hertwig describe a study in which a confederate bumped into the male participant and insulted him with a derogatory name in an attempt to elicit anger.

### Is Deception a Major Ethical Problem in Psychological Research?

Many psychologists believe that the problem of deception has been exaggerated (Bröder, 1998; Kimmel, 1998; Korn, 1998; Smith & Richardson, 1985). Bröder argues that the extreme examples of elaborate deception cited by these critics are rare. Moreover, there is evidence that the college students who participate in research do not mind deception and may in fact enjoy experiments with deception (Christensen, 1988).

Some researchers have attempted to assess the use of deception over the past several decades since the Milgram experiments in the 1960s to see if elaborate deception has indeed become less common. Because most of the concern over this type of deception arises in social psychological research, attempts to address this issue have focused on social psychology. Gross and Fleming (1982) reviewed 691 social psychological studies published in the 1960s and 1970s. Although most research in the 1970s still used deception, the deception primarily involved false cover stories.

Has the trend away from deception continued? Sieber, Iannuzzo, and Rodriguez (1995) examined the studies published in the *Journal of Personality and Social Psychology* in 1969, 1978, 1986, and 1992. The number of studies that used some form of deception decreased from 66% in 1969 to 47% in 1978 and to 32% in 1986 but increased again to 47% in 1992. The large drop in 1986 may be due to an increase that year in the number of studies on such topics as personality that require no deception to carry out. Also, informed consent was more likely to be explicitly described in 1992 than in previous years, and debriefing was more likely to be mentioned in the years after 1969. However, false cover stories are still frequently used. Korn (1997) has also concluded that use of deception is decreasing in social psychology.

There are three primary reasons for a decrease in the type of elaborate deception seen in the Milgram study. First, more researchers have become interested in cognitive variables rather than emotions and so use methods that are similar to those used by researchers in memory and cognitive psychology. Second, the general level of awareness of ethical issues as described in this chapter has led researchers to conduct studies in other ways (some alternatives to deception are described below). Third, ethics committees at universities and colleges now review proposed research more carefully so elaborate deception is likely to be approved only when the research is important and there are no alternative procedures available (ethics review boards are described later in this chapter).

## THE IMPORTANCE OF DEBRIEFING

**Debriefing** occurs after the completion of the study. It is an opportunity for the researcher to deal with issues of withholding information, deception, and potential harmful effects of participation.

If participants were deceived in any way, the researcher needs to explain why the deception was necessary. If the research altered a participant's physical or psychological state in some way—as in a study that produces stress—the researcher must make sure that the participant has "calmed down" and is comfortable about having participated. If there is a need for the participant to receive additional information or to speak with someone else about the study, the researcher should provide access to these resources. The participants should leave the experiment without any ill feelings toward the field of psychology, and they may even leave with some new insight into their own behavior or personality.

Debriefing also provides an opportunity for the researcher to explain the purpose of the study and tell participants what kinds of results are expected; the practical implications of the results may also be discussed. In some cases, researchers may contact participants later to inform them of the actual results of the study. Thus, there is both an educational and an ethical purpose of debriefing.

Is debriefing sufficient to remove any negative effects when stress and elaborate deception are involved? Let's turn again to Milgram's research. Milgram went to great lengths to provide a thorough debriefing session. Participants who were obedient were told that their behavior was normal in that they had acted no differently from most other participants. They were made aware of the strong situational pressure that was exerted on them, and efforts were made to reduce any tension they felt. Participants were assured that no shock was actually delivered, and there was a friendly reconciliation with the confederate, Mr. Wallace. Milgram also mailed a report of his research findings to the participants and at the same time asked about their reactions to the experiment. The responses showed that 84% were glad that they had participated, and 74% said they had benefited from the experience. Only 1% said they were sorry they had participated. When a psychiatrist interviewed participants a year later, no ill effects of participation could be detected. We can only conclude that debriefing did have its intended effect. Other researchers who have conducted further work on the ethics of Milgram's study reached the same conclusion (Ring, Wallston, & Corey, 1970).

Other research on debriefing has also concluded that debriefing is effective as a way of dealing with deception and other ethical issues that arise in research investigations (Smith, 1983; Smith & Richardson, 1983). However, as previously noted, deception remains a controversial issue. You may be wondering, then, whether there are alternatives to deception.

## ALTERNATIVES TO DECEPTION

After criticizing the use of deception in research, Kelman (1967) called for the development of alternative procedures. One procedure Kelman suggests is role-playing; other options include simulation studies (a variation on role-playing) and "honest" experiments.

### Role-Playing

In one **role-playing** procedure, the experimenter describes a situation to participants and then asks them how they would respond to the situation. Sometimes, participants are asked to say how they themselves would behave in the situation; other times, they are asked to predict how real participants in such a situation would behave. It isn't clear whether these two instructions produce any difference in results.

Role-playing is not generally considered to be a satisfactory alternative to deception (Freedman, 1969; Miller, 1972). One problem is that simply reading a description of a situation does not involve the participants very deeply—they are not part of a real situation. Also, because the experimenter gives the participants a complete description of the situation, the experimenter's hypothesis may become transparent to the participants. When people can figure out the hypothesis, they may try to behave in a way that is consistent with the hypothesis. Features of the experiment that may inform participants about the hypothesis are called "demand characteristics." The problem of demand characteristics is described in detail in Chapter 9.

The most serious defect of role-playing is that, no matter what results are obtained, critics can always claim that the results would have been different if the participants had been in a real situation. This criticism is based on the assumption that people aren't always able to accurately predict their own behavior or the behavior of others. This would be particularly true when undesirable behavior—such as conformity, obedience, or aggression—is involved. For example, if Milgram had used a role-playing procedure, how many people do you think would have predicted that they would be completely obedient? In fact, Milgram asked a group of psychiatrists to predict the results of his study and found that even these experts could not accurately anticipate what would happen. A similar problem would arise if people were asked to predict whether they would help someone in need. Most of us would probably overestimate our altruistic tendencies.

### Simulation Studies

A different type of role-playing involves simulation of a real-world situation. A simulation study that impressed Kelman (1967) is the Inter-Nation Simulation, in which participants role-play being leaders of nations and the researchers observe processes of negotiation, problem solving, and so on. Such simulations can create high personal involvement, as anyone who has become thoroughly engrossed in a multiuser Internet game or even Monopoly will appreciate.

Even with simulations, there may be ethical problems. A dramatic example is the Stanford Prison Experiment conducted by Zimbardo (1973; Haney & Zimbardo, 1998). Zimbardo set up a simulated prison in the basement of the psychology building at Stanford University. He then recruited college students who were paid $15 per day to play the role of either prisoner or guard for a period of two weeks. Guards were outfitted in uniform, and given sunglasses and clubs. Prisoners were assigned numbers and wore nylon stocking caps to simulate prison haircuts and reduce feelings of individuality. The participants became deeply involved in their roles, so much so that Zimbardo had to stop the simulation after 6 days because of the cruel behavior of the "guards" and the stressful reactions of the "prisoners." This was only a simulation—participants knew that they were not really prisoners or guards. Yet they became so involved in their roles that the experiment produced levels of stress that were higher than almost any other experiment one can imagine. Fortunately, the Zimbardo experiment is an unusual case—most simulation studies do not raise the ethical issues seen in this particular study.

### Honest Experiments

Rubin (1973) described what he called "honest" experimental strategies. None of these involve role-playing. The first strategy is one in which the participants are made completely aware of the purposes of the research. In a study by Byrne, Ervin, and Lamberth (1970), the researchers told college students that they were interested in the effectiveness of computer dating. They used a computer program to match male and female students who held either similar or dissimilar attitudes. Each couple had a brief date on campus, and then the researchers measured how much the members of each couple liked one another. The couples that were similar were more attracted to each other than couples that were dissimilar. The study involved neither deception nor misrepresentation of the purposes of the research.

A second honest strategy is used in situations in which programs explicitly seek to change people's behavior. Examples cited by Rubin include educational programs, health appeals, charity drives, political campaigns, and solicitations for volunteers. In such situations, people are aware that someone is trying to change their behavior. For instance, people may voluntarily expose themselves to an appeal to quit smoking. Researchers can then investigate the effectiveness of such an appeal while manipulating variables such as the amount of fear aroused (Leventhal, 1970).

Rubin also stated that many field experiments involve honest procedures. In contrast to laboratory experiments such as the Milgram study in which behavior is studied in a laboratory setting, field experiments introduce the experimental manipulation in a natural context. Rubin cites a study in which an experimenter stared at drivers of cars while they were waiting for a red light to change (Ellsworth, Carlsmith, & Henson, 1972). The drivers crossed the intersection faster than did drivers in a control condition in which no staring experimenter was present. This particular experiment does not seem particularly unethical. We have all experienced being stared at. The researchers merely applied experimental methods to systematically study this situation. Much research in field settings is indeed honest. Researchers observe the behavior of people in public places and everyday situations. However, just because an experiment is conducted in the field does not mean that no ethical issues are involved. For example, what are the ethical (and legal) implications of taking up the time of auto salespersons while posing as a customer to study different types of price offers or of exposing subway passengers to a person who collapses between stations (cf. Silverman, 1975)?

The final honest strategy discussed by Rubin involves situations in which a naturally occurring event presents an opportunity for research: "Nature, fate, government, and other unalterable forces often impose their will on people in random or nonsystematic ways." For example, researchers were able to study the effects of crowding when a shortage of student housing forced Rutgers University to assign entering students randomly to crowded and uncrowded dormitory rooms (Aiello, Baum, & Gormley, 1981). Baum, Gachtel, and Schaeffer (1983) studied the stressful effects associated with nuclear power plant disasters by comparing people who lived near the Three Mile Island nuclear plant with others who lived near an undamaged nuclear plant or a conventional coal-fired power plant. Science depends on replicability of results so it is notable that the same pattern of results was obtained following the September 11 terrorist attack (Schlenger et al., 2002). More than 2,000 adult residents of New York City, Washington, D.C., and other metropolitan areas throughout the United States completed a Posttraumatic Stress Disorder (PTSD) checklist to determine incidence of the disorder. PTSD was indicated in 11.2% of the New York residents in contrast with 2.7% of the residents of Washington and 3.6% of those living in other metropolitan areas. Such natural experiments are valuable sources of data.

## JUSTICE AND THE SELECTION OF PARTICIPANTS

The third ethical principle defined in the *Belmont Report* is termed **justice.** The principle of justice addresses issues of fairness in receiving the benefits of research as well as bearing the burdens of accepting risks. The history of medical research includes too many examples of high-risk research that was conducted with individuals selected because they were powerless and marginalized within the society. One of the most horrific is the Tuskegee Syphilis Study in which 399 poor African Americans in Alabama were not treated for syphilis in order to track the long-term effects of this disease (Reverby, 2000). This study took place from 1932 to 1972 when the details of the study were made public. The outrage over the fact that this study was done at all and that the subjects were unsuspecting African Americans spurred scientists to overhaul ethical regulations in both medical and behavioral research.

The justice principle requires researchers to address issues of equity. Any decisions to include or exclude certain people from a research study must be justified on scientific grounds. Thus, if age, ethnicity, gender, or other criteria are used to select participants, there must be a scientific rationale.

## RESEARCHER COMMITMENTS

Researchers make several implicit "contracts" with participants during the course of a study. For example, if participants agree to be present for a study at a specific time, the researcher should be there. The issue of punctuality is never mentioned by researchers, yet research participants note it when asked about the obligations of the researcher (Epstein, Suedfeld, & Silverstein, 1973). If researchers promise to send a summary of the results to participants, they should do so. If participants are to receive course credit for participation, the researcher must immediately let the instructor know that the person took part in the study. These are "little details," but they are very important in maintaining trust between participants and researchers.

## FEDERAL REGULATIONS AND THE INSTITUTIONAL REVIEW BOARD

The *Belmont Report* provided an outline for issues of research ethics. The actual rules and regulations for the protection of human research participants were issued by the U.S. Department of Health and Human Services (HHS). Under these regulations (Department of Health and Human Services, 2001), every institution that receives federal funds must have an **Institutional Review Board (IRB)** that is responsible for the review of research conducted within the institution. The IRB is a local review agency composed of at least five individuals; at least one member of the IRB must be from outside the institution. Every college and university in the United States that has federal funding has an IRB; in addition, most psychology departments have their own research review committee (Chastain & Landrum, 1999). All research conducted by faculty, students, and staff associated with the institution is reviewed in some way by the IRB. This includes research that may be conducted at another location such as a school, community agency, hospital, or via the Internet.

The federal regulations for IRB oversight of research continue to evolve. For example, all researchers must now complete educational requirements. Most colleges and universities require students and faculty to complete one or more online tutorials on research ethics to meet these requirements. You can easily find the tutorials with an Internet search.

The HHS regulations also categorized research according to the amount of risk involved in the research. This concept of risk was later incorporated into the Ethics Code of the American Psychological Association.

### Exempt Research

Research in which there is *no risk* is exempt from review. Thus, research that involves only anonymous questionnaires, surveys, and educational tests is exempt, as is naturalistic observation in public places when there is no threat to anonymity. Archival research in which the data being studied are publicly available or the participants cannot be identified is exempt as well. This type of research requires no informed consent. However, there must be an institutional mechanism to determine that the research is in fact exempt. Researchers cannot decide by themselves that research is exempt; instead, the IRB at the institution formulates a procedure to allow a researcher to apply for exempt status.

### Minimal-Risk Research

A second type of research activity is called *minimal risk*. Minimal risk means that the risks of harm to participants are no greater than risks encountered in daily life or in routine physical or psychological tests. When minimal-risk research is being conducted, elaborate safeguards are less of a concern, and approval by the IRB is routine. Some of the research activities considered minimal risk are (1) recording routine physiological data from adult participants (e.g., weighing, tests of sensory acuity, electrocardiography, electroencephalography, diagnostic echography, and voice recordings); note that this would not include recordings that might involve invasion of privacy; (2) moderate exercise by healthy volunteers; and (3) research on individual or group behavior or characteristics of individuals, such as studies of perception, cognition, game theory, or test development in which the researcher does not manipulate participants' behavior and the research will not involve stress to participants.

### Greater-Than-Minimal-Risk Research

Any research procedure that places participants at greater than minimal risk is subject to thorough review by the IRB. Complete informed consent and other safeguards may be required before approval is granted.

Researchers planning to conduct an investigation are required to submit an application to the IRB. The application requires description of risks and benefits, procedures for minimizing risk, the exact wording of the informed consent form, how participants will be debriefed, and procedures for maintaining confidentiality. Even after a project is approved, there is continuing review. If it is a long-term project, it will be reviewed at least once each year. If there are any changes in procedures, researchers are required to obtain approval from the IRB.

With the HHS regulations and review of research by the IRB, the rights and safety of human participants are well protected. We might note at this point that researchers and review board members tend to be very cautious in terms of what is considered ethical. In fact, several studies have shown that students who have participated in research studies are more lenient in their judgments of the ethics of experiments than are researchers or IRB members (Epstein et al., 1973; Smith, 1983; Sullivan & Deiker, 1973). Moreover, individuals who have taken part in research that used deception report that they did not mind the deception and evaluated the experience positively (Christensen, 1988).

## APA ETHICS CODE

Psychologists recognize the ethical issues we have discussed, and the American Psychological Association (APA) has provided leadership in formulating ethical principles and standards. The *Ethical Principles of Psychologists and Code of Conduct*—known as the *Ethics Code*—was revised in 2002 and is available at http://www.apa.org/ethics (American Psychological Association, 2002a). The preamble to the Ethics Code states:

> Psychologists are committed to increasing scientific and professional knowledge of behavior and people's understanding of themselves and others and to the use of such knowledge to improve the condition of individuals, organizations, and society. Psychologists respect and protect civil and human rights and the central importance of freedom of inquiry and expression in research, teaching, and publication. They strive to help the public in developing informed judgments and choices concerning human behavior. In doing so, they perform many roles, such as researcher, educator, diagnostician, therapist, supervisor, consultant, administrator, social interventionist, and expert witness. This Ethics Code provides a common set of principles and standards upon which psychologists build their professional and scientific work.

Five general principles relate to beneficence, responsibility, integrity, justice, and respect for the rights and dignity of others. Ten ethical standards address specific issues concerning the conduct of psychologists in teaching, research, therapy, counseling, testing, and other professional roles and responsibilities. We will be most concerned with Ethical Standard 8: Research and Publication.

## RESEARCH WITH HUMAN PARTICIPANTS

The sections of Ethical Standard 8 that most directly deal with research with human participants are:

### 8.01 Institutional approval
When institutional approval is required, psychologists provide accurate information about their research proposals and obtain approval prior to conducting the research. They conduct the research in accordance with the approved research protocol.

*8.02 Informed consent to research*

a. When obtaining informed consent as required in Standard 3.10, Informed Consent, psychologists inform participants about (1) the purpose of the research, expected duration, and procedures; (2) their right to decline to participate and to withdraw from the research once participation has begun; (3) the foreseeable consequences of declining or withdrawing; (4) reasonably foreseeable factors that may be expected to influence their willingness to participate such as potential risks, discomfort, or adverse effects; (5) any prospective research benefits; (6) limits of confidentiality; (7) incentives for participation; and (8) whom to contact for questions about the research and research participants' rights. They provide opportunity for the prospective participants to ask questions and receive answers. (See also Standards 8.03, Informed Consent for Recording Voices and Images in Research; 8.05, Dispensing With Informed Consent for Research; and 8.07, Deception in Research.)

b. Psychologists conducting intervention research involving the use of experimental treatments clarify to participants at the outset of the research (1) the experimental nature of the treatment; (2) the services that will or will not be available to the control group(s) if appropriate; (3) the means by which assignment to treatment and control groups will be made; (4) available treatment alternatives if an individual does not wish to participate in the research or wishes to withdraw once a study has begun; and (5) compensation for or monetary costs of participating including, if appropriate, whether reimbursement from the participant or a third-party payor will be sought. (See also Standard 8.02a, Informed Consent to Research.)

*8.03 Informed consent for recording voices and images in research*

Psychologists obtain informed consent from research participants prior to recording their voices or images for data collection unless (1) the research consists solely of naturalistic observations in public places, and it is not anticipated that the recording will be used in a manner that could cause personal identification or harm, or (2) the research design includes deception, and consent for the use of the recording is obtained during debriefing. (See also Standard 8.07, Deception in Research.)

*8.04 Client/patient, student, and subordinate research participants*

a. When psychologists conduct research with clients/patients, students, or subordinates as participants, psychologists take steps to protect the prospective participants from adverse consequences of declining or withdrawing from participation.

b. When research participation is a course requirement or an opportunity for extra credit, the prospective participant is given the choice of equitable alternative activities.

### 8.05 Dispensing with informed consent for research

Psychologists may dispense with informed consent only (1) where research would not reasonably be assumed to create distress or harm and involves (a) the study of normal educational practices, curricula, or classroom management methods conducted in educational settings; (b) only anonymous questionnaires, naturalistic observations, or archival research for which disclosure of responses would not place participants at risk of criminal or civil liability or damage their financial standing, employability, or reputation, and confidentiality is protected; or (c) the study of factors related to job or organization effectiveness conducted in organizational settings for which there is no risk to participants' employability, and confidentiality is protected or (2) where otherwise permitted by law or federal or institutional regulations.

### 8.06 Offering inducements for research participation

a. Psychologists make reasonable efforts to avoid offering excessive or inappropriate financial or other inducements for research participation when such inducements are likely to coerce participation.

b. When offering professional services as an inducement for research participation, psychologists clarify the nature of the services, as well as the risks, obligations, and limitations. (See also Standard 6.05, Barter With Clients/Patients.)

### 8.07 Deception in research

a. Psychologists do not conduct a study involving deception unless they have determined that the use of deceptive techniques is justified by the study's significant prospective scientific, educational, or applied value and that effective nondeceptive alternative procedures are not feasible.

b. Psychologists do not deceive prospective participants about research that is reasonably expected to cause physical pain or severe emotional distress.

c. Psychologists explain any deception that is an integral feature of the design and conduct of an experiment to participants as early as is feasible, preferably at the conclusion of their participation, but no later than at the conclusion of the data collection, and permit participants to withdraw their data. (See also Standard 8.08, Debriefing.)

### 8.08 Debriefing

a. Psychologists provide a prompt opportunity for participants to obtain appropriate information about the nature, results, and conclusions of the research, and they take reasonable steps to correct any misconceptions that participants may have of which the psychologists are aware.

b.  If scientific or humane values justify delaying or withholding this informa-
    tion, psychologists take reasonable measures to reduce the risk of harm.

c.  When psychologists become aware that research procedures have
    harmed a participant, they take reasonable steps to minimize the harm.

These standards complement the HSS regulations and the *Belmont Report.* They
stress the importance of informed consent as a fundamental part of ethical practice. However, fully informed consent may not always be possible, and deception
may sometimes be necessary. In such cases, the researcher's responsibilities to participants are increased. Obviously, decisions as to what should be considered ethical or unethical are not simple; there are no ironclad rules.

## ETHICS AND ANIMAL RESEARCH

Although this chapter has been concerned with the ethics of research with humans, you are no doubt well aware that psychologists sometimes conduct research with animals. Animals are used for a variety of reasons. The researcher can
carefully control the environmental conditions of the animals, study the same
animals over a long period, and monitor their behavior 24 hours a day if necessary. Animals are also used to test the effects of drugs and to study physiological
and genetic mechanisms underlying behavior. About 7% of the articles in *Psychological Abstracts* in 1979 studied animals (Gallup & Suarez, 1985), and data indicate that the amount of research done with animals has been steadily declining
(Thomas & Blackman, 1992). Most commonly, psychologists work with rats and
mice, and to a lesser extent, birds; according to one survey of animal research in
psychology, over 95% of the animals in research were rats, mice, and birds (see
Gallup & Suarez, 1985).

In recent years, groups opposed to animal research in medicine, psychology,
biology, and other sciences have become more vocal and militant. Animal rights
groups have staged protests at conventions of the American Psychological Association, and animal research laboratories in numerous cities have had animals
stolen by members of these groups. The groups are also lobbying for legislation
to prohibit all animal research.

Scientists argue that animal research benefits humans and point to many
discoveries that would not have been possible without animal research (Miller,
1985; Carroll & Overmier, 2001). Also, animal rights groups often exaggerate the
amount of research that involves any pain or suffering whatsoever (Coile &
Miller, 1984).

Plous (1996a, 1996b) conducted a national survey of attitudes toward the use
of animals in research and education among psychologists and psychology majors (available at http://www.apa.org/science/anguide.html). The attitudes of
both psychologists and students were quite similar. In general, there is support
for animal research: 72% of the students support such research, 18% oppose it, and
10% are unsure (the psychologists "strongly" support animal research more than
the students, however). In addition, 68% believe that animal research is necessary

for progress in psychology. Still, there is some ambivalence and uncertainty about the use of animals: When asked whether animals in psychological research are treated humanely, 12% of the students said "no" and 44% were "unsure." In addition, research involving rats or pigeons was viewed more positively than research with dogs or primates unless the research is strictly observational. Finally, females have less positive views toward animal research than males. Plous concluded that animal research in psychology will continue to be important for the field but will likely continue to decline as a proportion of the total amount of research conducted.

Animal research is indeed very important and will continue to be necessary to study many types of research questions. It is crucial to recognize that strict laws and ethical guidelines govern both research with animals and teaching procedures in which animals are used. Such regulations deal with the need for proper housing, feeding, cleanliness, and health care. They specify that the research must avoid any cruelty in the form of unnecessary pain to the animal. In addition, institutions in which animal research is carried out must have an *Institutional Animal Care and Use Committee (IACUC)* composed of at least one scientist, one veterinarian, and a community member. The IACUC is charged with reviewing animal research procedures and ensuring that all regulations are adhered to (see Holden, 1987). This section of the Ethics Code is of particular importance here:

*8.09 Humane care and use of animals in research*

  a. Psychologists acquire, care for, use, and dispose of animals in compliance with current federal, state, and local laws and regulations, and with professional standards.

  b. Psychologists trained in research methods and experienced in the care of laboratory animals supervise all procedures involving animals and are responsible for ensuring appropriate consideration of their comfort, health, and humane treatment.

  c. Psychologists ensure that all individuals under their supervision who are using animals have received instruction in research methods and in the care, maintenance, and handling of the species being used, to the extent appropriate to their role. (See also Standard 2.05, Delegation of Work to Others.)

  d. Psychologists make reasonable efforts to minimize the discomfort, infection, illness, and pain of animal subjects.

  e. Psychologists use a procedure subjecting animals to pain, stress, or privation only when an alternative procedure is unavailable and the goal is justified by its prospective scientific, educational, or applied value.

  f. Psychologists perform surgical procedures under appropriate anesthesia and follow techniques to avoid infection and minimize pain during and after surgery.

g. When it is appropriate that an animal's life be terminated, psychologists proceed rapidly, with an effort to minimize pain and in accordance with accepted procedures.

APA has also developed a more detailed *Guidelines for Ethical Conduct in the Care and Use of Animals* (American Psychological Association, 2002b). Clearly, psychologists are concerned about the welfare of animals used in research. Nonetheless, this likely will continue to be a controversial issue.

## RISKS AND BENEFITS REVISITED

You are now familiar with the ethical issues that confront researchers who study human and animal behavior. When you make decisions about research ethics, you need to consider the many factors associated with risk to the participants. Are there risks of psychological harm or loss of confidentiality? Who are the research participants? What types of deception, if any, are used in the procedure? How will informed consent be obtained? What debriefing procedures are being used? You also need to weigh the direct benefits of the research to the participants, as well as the scientific importance of the research and the educational benefits to the students who may be conducting the research for a class or degree requirement.

These are not easy decisions. Consider the study described previously in which a male confederate insults the male participant. This study, conducted by Cohen, Nisbett, Bowdle, and Schwarz (1996), compared the reactions of college students living in the northern United States with those of students living in the southern United States. The purpose was to investigate whether males in the South had developed a "culture of honor" that expects them to respond aggressively when insulted. Indeed, the students in the North had little response to the insult while the Southerners responded with heightened physiological and cognitive indicators of anger. The fact that so much violence in the world is committed by males who are often avenging some perceived insult to their honor makes this topic particularly relevant to society. Do you believe that the potential benefits of the study to society and science outweigh the risks involved in the procedure?

Obviously, an IRB reviewing this study concluded that the researchers had sufficiently minimized risks to the participants such that the benefits outweighed the costs.

If you ultimately decide that the costs outweigh the benefits, you must conclude that the study cannot be conducted in its current form. There may be alternative procedures that could be used to make it acceptable. If the benefits outweigh the costs, you will likely decide that the research should be carried out. Your calculation might differ from another person's calculation, which is precisely why having ethics review boards is such a good idea. An appropriate review of research proposals makes it highly unlikely that unethical research will be approved.

## MISREPRESENTATION

Two other elements of the Ethics Code should be noted:

### 8.10 Reporting Research Results

a. Psychologists do not fabricate data. (See also Standard 5.01a, Avoidance of False or Deceptive Statements.)

b. If psychologists discover significant errors in their published data, they take reasonable steps to correct such errors in a correction, retraction, erratum, or other appropriate publication means.

### 8.11 Plagiarism

Psychologists do not present portions of another's work or data as their own, even if the other work or data source is cited occasionally.

The fabrication of data is fraud. We must be able to believe the reported results of research; otherwise, the entire foundation of the scientific method as a means of knowledge is threatened. In fact, although fraud may occur in many fields, it probably is most serious in two areas: science and journalism. This is because science and journalism are both fields in which written reports are assumed to be accurate descriptions of actual events. There are no independent accounting agencies to check on the activities of scientists and journalists.

Instances of fraud in the field of psychology are considered to be very serious (cf. Hostetler, 1987; Riordan & Marlin, 1987), but fortunately, they are very rare (Murray, 2002). Perhaps the most famous case is that of Sir Cyril Burt, who reported that the IQ scores of identical twins reared apart were highly similar. The data were used to support the argument that genetic influences on IQ are extremely important. However, Kamin (1974) noted some irregularities in Burt's data. A number of correlations for different sets of twins were exactly the same to the third decimal place, virtually a mathematical impossibility. This observation led to the discovery that some of Burt's presumed co-workers had not in fact worked with him or had simply been fabricated. Ironically, though, Burt's "data" were close to what has been reported by other investigators who have studied the IQ scores of twins.

In most cases, fraud is detected when other scientists cannot replicate the results of a study. When many questions about the research published by Karen Ruggiero, a psychologist at the University of Texas, began to surface because of difficulties with replication, Dr. Ruggiero resigned from her position and retracted her research findings (Murray, 2002). Sometimes fraud is detected by a colleague who has worked with the researcher. For example, Stephen Breuning was guilty of faking data showing that stimulants could be used to reduce hyperactive and aggressive behavior in severely retarded children (Byrne, 1988). In this case, another researcher who had worked closely with Breuning had suspicions about the data; he then informed the federal agency that had funded the research.

The most common reason for suspecting fraud is when an important or unusual finding cannot be replicated. Fraud is not a major problem in science in part because researchers know that others will read their reports and conduct further studies, including replications. They know that their reputations and careers will be seriously damaged if other scientists conclude that the results are fraudulent. In addition, the likelihood of detection of fraud has increased in recent years as data accessibility has become more open: regulations of most funding agencies require researchers to make their data accessible to other scientists.

Why, then, do researchers sometimes commit fraud? For one thing, scientists occasionally find themselves in jobs with extreme pressure to produce impressive results. This is not a sufficient explanation, of course, because many researchers maintain high ethical standards under such pressure. Another reason is that researchers who feel a need to produce fraudulent data have an exaggerated fear of failure, as well as a great need for success and the admiration that comes with it. If you wish to explore further the dynamics of fraud, you might wish to begin with Hearnshaw's (1979) book on Sir Cyril Burt. Controversy has continued to surround the case: One edited volume is titled *Cyril Burt: Fraud or Framed?* (Macintosh, 1995). Most analyses conclude, however, that the research was fraudulent (Tucker, 1997).

We should make one final point: Allegations of fraud should not be made lightly. If you disagree with someone's results on philosophical, political, religious, or other grounds, it does not mean that they are fraudulent. Even if you cannot replicate the results, the reason may lie in aspects of the methodology of the study rather than deliberate fraud. However, the fact that fraud could be a possible explanation of results stresses the importance of careful record keeping and documentation of the procedures and results.

Plagiarism refers to misrepresenting another's work as your own. You must give proper citation of your sources. Your paper will actually be strengthened if you cite references (Harris, 2002).

We should note in conclusion that ethical guidelines and regulations are constantly evolving. The APA Ethics Code and federal, state, and local regulations may be revised periodically. Researchers need to always be aware of the most current policies and procedures. In the following chapters, we will be discussing many specific procedures for studying behavior. As you read about these procedures and apply them to research you may be interested in, remember that ethical considerations are always paramount.

## Study Terms

| | |
|---|---|
| Autonomy (*Belmont Report*) | Debriefing |
| *Belmont Report* | Deception |
| Beneficence (*Belmont Report*) | Ethics Code |
| Confidentiality | Exempt research |

Fraud

Honest experiments

IACUC

Informed consent

IRB

Justice (*Belmont Report*)

Minimal-risk research

Plagiarism

Responsibility

Risk

Risk-benefit analysis

Role-playing

Simulation studies

## Review Questions

1. Discuss the major ethical issues in behavioral research including risks, benefits, deception, debriefing, informed consent, and justice. How can researchers weigh the need to conduct research against the need for ethical procedures?

2. Why is informed consent an ethical principle? What are the potential problems with full informed consent?

3. What alternatives to deception are described in the text?

4. Summarize the principles concerning research with human participants in the APA Ethics Code.

5. What is the difference between "no risk" and "minimal-risk" research activities?

6. What is an Institutional Review Board?

7. Summarize the ethical procedures for research with animals.

8. What constitutes fraud, what are some reasons for its occurrence, and why doesn't it occur more frequently?

## Activity Questions

1. Consider the following experiment, similar to one that was conducted by Smith, Lingle, and Brock (1978). Each participant interacted for an hour with another person who was actually an accomplice. After this interaction, both persons agreed to return one week later for another session with each other. When the real participants returned, they were informed that the person they had met the week before had died. The researchers then measured reactions to the death of the person.

   a. Discuss the ethical issues raised by the experiment.

   b. Would the experiment violate the guidelines articulated in APA Ethical Standard 8 dealing with research with human participants? In what ways?

c. What alternative methods for studying this problem (reactions to death) might you suggest?

d. Would your reactions to this study be different if the participants had played with an infant and then later been told that the infant had died?

2. In a procedure described in this chapter, participants are given false feedback about an unfavorable personality trait or a low ability level. What are the ethical issues raised by this procedure? Compare your reactions to that procedure with an analogous one in which people are given false feedback that they possess a very favorable personality trait or a very high ability level.

3. A social psychologist conducts a field experiment at a local bar that is popular with college students. Interested in observing flirting techniques, the investigator instructs male and female confederates to smile and make eye contact with others at the pub for varying amounts of time (e.g., 2 seconds, 5 seconds, etc.) and varying numbers of times (e.g., once, twice, etc.). The investigator observes the responses of those receiving the gaze. What ethical considerations, if any, do you perceive in this field experiment? Is there any deception involved?

4. Should people who are observed in field experiments be debriefed? Write a paragraph supporting the pro position and another paragraph supporting the con position.

5. Dr. Alucard conducted a study to examine various aspects of the sexual behaviors of college students. The students filled out a questionnaire in a classroom on the campus; about 50 students were tested at a time. The questionnaire asked about prior experience with various sexual practices. If a student had experience, a number of other detailed questions were asked. However, if the student did not have any prior experience, he or she skipped the detailed questions and simply went on to answer another general question about a sexual experience. What ethical issues arise when conducting research such as this? Do you detect any specific problems that might arise because of the "skip" procedure used in this study?

6. Research results are not always popular, particularly when they relate to controversial social issues. Suppose you favor gun control, but find a study claiming that states with laws that allow people to carry concealed weapons have experienced drops in crime greater than comparable states without such laws. Or suppose that you believe that child sexual abuse (defined as sexual contact between a minor and an adult) inevitably leads to psychological disturbances. You then read a study of college students who reported such sexual contact; the study concludes that the psychological impact is relatively small in this population. As a final example, suppose that you either support or oppose abortion rights for women; in either case, you oppose criminal activity associated with thefts and violence. You read a study that concludes that the abortion

rights granted by the Supreme Court's 1973 *Roe v. Wade* decision is in part responsible for the dramatic drop in crime rates in the United States since 1990. How do you respond to such findings? Do you immediately decide that research opposing your views must be wrong and perhaps fraudulent? Should you pay attention to the politics of the agency that funded the study? What should you do if you can't find anything wrong with a study that does not support your views? (Note: The examples are based on actual research findings. References were not included; if you want details on the research described here, you can search using electronic resources in your library.)

---

# Studying Behavior

---

In this chapter, we will explore some of the basic issues and concepts that are necessary for understanding the scientific study of behavior. We will begin by looking at the nature of variables, including their measurement and the types of relationships among them. We will then examine general methods for studying these relationships.

## VARIABLES

A **variable** is any event, situation, behavior, or individual characteristic that varies. Examples of variables a psychologist might study include cognitive task performance, word length, spatial density, intelligence, gender, reaction time, rate of forgetting, aggression, speaker credibility, attitude change, anger, stress, age, and self-esteem. Each of these variables represents a general class within which specific instances will vary. These specific instances are called the *levels* or *values* of the variable. A variable must have two or more levels or values. For some variables, the values will have true numeric, or quantitative, properties. Suppose that task performance is a score on a 50-question cognitive test on which the values can range from a low of 0 correct to a high of 50 correct; these values have numeric properties. The values of other variables are not numeric, but instead simply identify different categories. An example is gender; the values for gender are male and female. These are different, but they do not differ in amount or quantity.

Variables can be classified into four general categories. *Situational variables* describe characteristics of a situation or environment: the length of words that you read in a book, the spatial density of a classroom, the credibility of a person who is trying to persuade you, and the number of bystanders to an emergency. *Response variables* are the responses or behaviors of individuals, such as reaction time, performance on a cognitive task, and helping a victim in an emergency. *Participant* or *subject variables* are individual differences; these are the characteristics of individuals, including gender, intelligence, and personality traits such as extraversion. Finally, *mediating variables* are psychological processes that mediate the effects of a situational variable on a particular response. As an example, Darley and Latané (1968) found that helping is less likely when there are more bystanders to an emergency. A mediating variable called diffusion of responsibility was used to explain this phenomenon (see Figure 4.1). When there are several bystanders, personal responsibility to help is diffused among all the bystanders so no single person feels much responsibility. However, when a person is the only witness to an emergency, all of the responsibility falls on that one person, thereby increasing the likelihood that the person will provide help. Thus, according to Darley and Latané, the number of bystanders affects personal responsibility, which in turn affects helping behavior.

FIGURE 4.1
Diffusion of responsibility is
a mediating variable

## OPERATIONAL DEFINITIONS OF VARIABLES

In actual research, the researcher has to decide on a method by which to study the variables of interest. It is important to know that a variable is an abstract concept that must be translated into concrete forms of observation or manipulation. Thus, a variable such as "aggression," "cognitive task performance," "amount of reward," "self-esteem," or even "word length" must be defined in terms of the specific method used to measure or manipulate it. Scientists refer to the **operational definition** of a variable—a definition of the variable in terms of the operations or techniques the researcher uses to measure or manipulate it.

Variables must be operationally defined so they can be studied empirically. A variable such as "speaker credibility" might be conceptualized as having two levels and operationally defined as a speaker described to listeners as a "Nobel Prize recipient" or as a "substitute teacher in the Central High School District." The variable of "cognitive task performance" might be defined as the number of errors detected on a proofreading task during a 10-minute period.

There also may be several levels of abstraction when studying a variable. A variable such as "word length" is concrete and easily operationalized in terms of numbers of letters or syllables, but the exact words for the study must still be selected. The concept of "stress" is very general and more abstract. When researchers study stress, they might focus on any number of stressors—noise, crowding, major health problems, job burnout, and so on. A researcher interested in stress would probably choose one stressor to study and then develop operational definitions of that specific stressor. He or she would then carry out research investigations pertaining both to the specific stressor and to the more general concept of stress. The key point is that researchers must always translate variables into specific operations to manipulate or measure them.

The task of operationally defining a variable forces scientists to discuss abstract concepts in concrete terms. The process can result in the realization that the variable is too vague to study. This realization does not necessarily indicate that the concept is meaningless, but rather that systematic research is not possible until the concept can be operationally defined. Once an operational definition is found, progress in understanding a psychological phenomenon is often dependent on the development of increasingly sophisticated technology. For example, the concept of "brain activity" is not new. The study of how brain activity is related to behavior was facilitated first by the development of electrophysiological recording techniques and more recently by brain-imaging technologies.

Operational definitions also help us communicate our ideas to others. If someone wishes to tell me about aggression, I need to know exactly what is meant by this term because there are many ways of operationally defining it. For example, aggression could be defined as (1) the number and duration of shocks delivered to another person, (2) the number of times a child punches an inflated toy clown, (3) the number of times a child fights with other children during recess, (4) homicide statistics gathered from police records, (5) a score on a personality measure of aggressiveness, or even (6) the number of times a batter is hit with a pitch during baseball games. Communication with another person will be easier if we agree on exactly what we mean when we use the term *aggression* in the context of our research.

There is rarely a single, infallible method for operationally defining a variable. A variety of methods may be available, each of which has advantages and disadvantages. Researchers must decide which one to use given the particular problem under study, the goals of the research, and other considerations such as ethics and costs. To illustrate how complex it can be to develop an operational definition of a variable, consider the choices faced by a researcher interested in studying crowding. The researcher could study the effects of crowding on college students in a carefully controlled laboratory experiment. However, the focus of the researcher's interest may be the long-term effects of crowding; if so, it might be a good idea to observe the effects of crowding on laboratory animals such as rats. The researcher could examine the long-term effects of crowding on aggression, eating, sexual behavior, and maternal behavior. But what if the researcher wants to investigate cognitive or social variables such as intellectual performance or family interaction? Here, the researcher might decide to study people who live in crowded housing and compare them to people who live in less crowded circumstances. Because no one method is perfect, complete understanding of any variable involves studying the variable using a variety of operational definitions. Several methods will be discussed throughout this book.

## RELATIONSHIPS BETWEEN VARIABLES

Much research studies the relationship between two variables. The relationship between two variables is the general way in which the different values of one variable are associated with different values of the other variable. That is, do the levels of the two variables vary systematically together? As age increases, does the amount of cooperative play increase as well? Does viewing television violence result in greater aggressiveness? Is speaker credibility related to attitude change?

Recall that some variables have true numeric values while the levels of other variables are simply different categories. This distinction will be expanded upon in Chapter 5. For the purposes of describing relationships among variables, we will begin by discussing relationships in which both variables have true numeric properties.

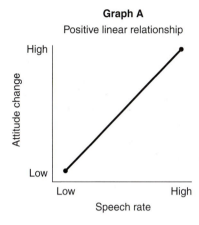

**Graph A**

Positive linear relationship

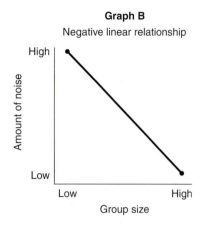

**Graph B**

Negative linear relationship

**Graph C**

Curvilinear relationship

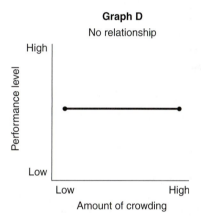

**Graph D**

No relationship

FIGURE 4.2
Four types of
relationships
between
variables

When both variables have values along a numeric scale, many different "shapes" can describe their relationship. We begin by focusing on the four most common relationships found in research: the **positive linear relationship,** the **negative linear relationship,** and the **curvilinear relationship,** and, of course, the situation in which there is *no relationship* between the variables. These relationships are best illustrated by line graphs that show the way changes in one variable are accompanied by changes in a second variable. The four graphs in Figure 4.2 show these four types of relationships.

## Positive Linear Relationship

In a positive linear relationship, increases in the values of one variable are accompanied by increases in the values of the second variable. We previously described a positive relationship between communicator credibility and persuasion; higher levels of credibility are associated with more attitude change. Consider another communicator variable, rate of speech. Are "fast talkers" more persuasive? In a study conducted by Smith and Shaffer (1991), students listened to a speech delivered at a slow (144 words per minute), intermediate (162 wpm), or fast (214 wpm) speech rate. The speaker advocated a position favoring legislation to raise the legal drinking age; the students disagreed with this position. Graph A in Figure 4.2 shows the positive linear relationship between speech rate and attitude change that was found in this study. In a graph like this, we see a horizontal and a vertical axis, termed the *x* axis and *y* axis, respectively. Values of the first variable are placed on the horizontal axis, labeled from low to high. Values of the second variable are placed on the vertical axis. Graph A shows that higher speech rates are associated with greater amounts of attitude change.

## Negative Linear Relationship

Variables can also be negatively related. In a *negative linear relationship, increases* in the values of one variable are accompanied by *decreases* in the values of the other variable. Latané, Williams, and Harkins (1979) were intrigued with reports that increasing the number of people working on a task may actually reduce group effort and productivity. The researchers designed an experiment to study this phenomenon, which they termed "social loafing." The researchers asked participants to clap and shout to make as much noise as possible. They did this alone or in groups of two, four, or six people. Graph B in Figure 4.2 illustrates the negative relationship between number of people in the group and the amount of noise made by each person. As the size of the group *increased*, the amount of noise made by each individual *decreased*. The two variables are systematically related, just as in a positive relationship; only the direction of the relationship is reversed.

## Curvilinear Relationship

In a *curvilinear relationship,* increases in the values of one variable are accompanied by both increases and decreases in the values of the other variable. In other words, the direction of the relationship changes at least once. This type of relationship is sometimes referred to as a *nonmonotonic function*. Graph C in Figure 4.2 shows a curvilinear relationship between complexity of visual stimuli and ratings of preferences for the stimuli. This particular relationship is called an inverted-U relationship. Increases in visual complexity are accompanied by increases in liking for the stimulus, but only up to a point. The relationship then becomes negative, as further increases in complexity are accompanied by *decreases* in liking for the stimulus (Vitz, 1966).

## No Relationship

When there is no relationship between the two variables, the graph is simply a flat line. Graph D in Figure 4.2 illustrates the relationship between crowding and task performance found in a study by Freedman, Klevansky, and Ehrlich (1971). Unrelated variables vary independently of one another. Increases in crowding are

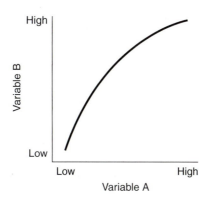

FIGURE 4.3
Positive monotonic function

not associated with any particular changes in performance; thus, a flat line describes the lack of relationship between the two variables.

These graphs illustrate several kinds of shapes; almost any shape can describe the relationship between two variables. Other relationships are described by more complicated shapes than those in Figure 4.2. For example, the positive and negative linear relationships just described are examples of a more general category of relationships described as monotonic because the relationship between the variables is always positive or always negative (it does not change directions as in the curvilinear, or nonmonotonic, relationship in Graph C). An example of a positive monotonic function that is not strictly linear is shown in Figure 4.3.

Remember that these are general patterns. Even if, in general, a positive linear relationship exists, it does not necessarily mean that everyone who scores high on one variable will also score high on the second variable. Individual deviations from the general pattern are likely. In addition to knowing the general type of relationship between two variables, it is also necessary to know the strength of the relationship. That is, we need to know the size of the correlation between the variables. Sometimes, two variables are strongly related to each other and there is little deviation from the general pattern. Other times, the two variables are not highly correlated because many individuals deviate from the general pattern. A numerical index of the strength of relationship between variables is called a **correlation coefficient.** Correlation coefficients are very important because we need to know how strongly variables are related to one another. Correlation coefficients are discussed in detail in Chapter 12.

### Relationships and Reduction of Uncertainty

When we detect a relationship between variables, we reduce uncertainty about the world by increasing our understanding of the variables we are examining. The term *uncertainty* implies that there is randomness in events; scientists refer to this as *random variability* or *error variance* in events that occur in the world. Research is aimed at reducing random variability by identifying systematic relationships between variables.

TABLE 4.1     Gender and character preference (hypothetical data)

| | | Participant gender | |
|---|---|---|---|
| | | Males | Females |
| | Mickey | 30 | 70 |
| Preference | Bugs | 70 | 30 |
| | Number of participants | 100 | 100 |

This seems complex but is much easier to see in a simple example. For this ex-ample, the variables will have no quantitative properties—we will not describe *increases* in the values of variables but rather only differences in values. Suppose you ask 200 students at your school whether they would rather be Mickey Mouse or Bugs Bunny (a silly question but play along with it). Now suppose that 100 people choose the mouse and 100 pick the rabbit (a bit unlikely but stay with me). What do you know with this information? You know only that there is variability in preferences for these cartoon characters—some people prefer Mickey and others prefer Bugs.

This variability is called *random* or *error* variance. It is called "error" only be-cause we don't understand it. If you walked up to anyone at your school and tried to guess which character the person prefers, you would just have to make a ran-dom guess—you would be right about half the time and wrong half the time. However, if we could explain the variability, it would no longer be random. How can the random variability be reduced? The answer is to see if we can identify variables that are related to preferences for the cartoon characters.

Suppose you also asked people to indicate their gender—are they male or fe-male? Now let's look at what happens when you examine whether gender is re-lated to cartoon character preference. Table 4.1 shows one possible outcome. Note that there are 100 males and 100 females in the study. The important thing, though, is that 70 of the males preferred Bugs and 70 of the females preferred Mickey. Have we reduced the random variability? We clearly have. Before you had this information, there would have been no way of predicting whether a person would be a fan of Mickey or of Bugs. Now that you have the research finding, you can predict that any female would prefer Mickey and any male would prefer Bugs. Now you will be right about 70% of the time; this is a big increase from the 50% when everything was random.

Is there still "random" variability? The answer is clearly yes. You will be wrong about 30% of the time and you don't know when you will be wrong. For unknown reasons, some males will prefer Mickey and some females will prefer Bugs. Can you reduce this "error" variability? The quest to do so motivates ad-ditional research. With further studies, you may be able to identify other vari-ables that are also related to this silly choice of cartoon characters.

This discussion underscores once again that relationships between variables are rarely perfect: there are males and females who do not fit the general pattern.

The relationship between the variables is stronger when there is less random variability—if 90% of males prefer Bugs Bunny, the relationship is much stronger (with less uncertainty or randomness). If the preference by males is 60%, the relationship is weaker.

## NONEXPERIMENTAL VERSUS EXPERIMENTAL METHODS

How can we determine whether variables are related? There are two general approaches to the study of relationships among variables, the nonexperimental method and the experimental method. With the **nonexperimental method,** relationships are studied by making observations or measures of the variables of interest. That is, behavior is observed as it occurs naturally. This may be done by asking people to describe their behavior, directly observing behavior, recording physiological responses, or even examining various public records such as census data. A relationship between variables is established when the two variables vary together. For example, in a study that will be described in Chapter 7, Steinberg and Dornbusch (1991) measured how many hours high school students worked and related this variable to grade point average. The two variables did vary together: Students who worked more hours tended to have lower grades.

The second approach to the study of relationships between variables is called the experimental method. The **experimental method** involves direct manipulation and control of variables. The researcher manipulates the first variable of interest and then observes the response. For example, Loftus (1979) used the experimental method when participants who viewed a film of an auto accident were later asked whether they saw "a" broken headlight or "the" broken headlight. The method of questioning was manipulated, and the participants' answers were then measured. With this method, the two variables do not merely vary together; one variable is introduced first to see whether it affects the second variable. This difference between the methods has important implications.

### Nonexperimental Method

Suppose a researcher is interested in the relationship between exercise and anxiety. How could this topic be studied? Using the nonexperimental method, the researcher would devise operational definitions to measure both the amount of exercise that people engage in and their level of anxiety. There could be a variety of ways of operationally defining either of these variables; for example, the researcher might simply ask people to provide self-reports of their exercise patterns and current anxiety level. The important point to remember here is that both variables are measured when using the nonexperimental method. Now suppose that the researcher collects data on exercise and anxiety from a number of people and finds that exercise is negatively related to anxiety; that is, the people who exercise more also have lower levels of anxiety. The two variables covary or correlate with each other: Observed differences in exercise are associated with

FIGURE 4.4
Causal possibilities in a
nonexperimental study

Exercise causes anxiety.            Anxiety causes exercise.

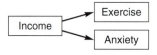

A third variable such as income is associated with both variables,
creating an apparent relationship between exercise and anxiety.

amount of anxiety. Because the nonexperimental method allows us to observe
covariation between variables, another term that is frequently used is the *corre-*
*lational method.* With this method, we examine whether the variables correlate or
vary together.

The nonexperimental method seems to be a reasonable approach to studying
relationships between variables such as exercise and anxiety. A relationship is established by finding that the two variables vary together—the variables covary or
correlate with each other. However, there is a weakness of this method when we ask
questions about cause and effect. We know the two variables are related, but what
can we say about the causal impact of one variable on the other? There are two
problems with making causal statements when the nonexperimental method was
used: (1) direction of cause and effect and (2) the third-variable problem—that is,
extraneous variables that may be causing an observed relationship (see Figure 4.4
in which arrows are used to depict causal links among variables).

**Direction of cause and effect**    The first problem is that of direction of cause
and effect. With the nonexperimental method, it is difficult to determine
which variable causes the other. In other words, it can't really be said that exercise causes a reduction in anxiety. Although there are plausible reasons for
this particular pattern of cause and effect, there are also reasons why the opposite pattern might occur. Perhaps anxiety level causes exercise, or perhaps
the experience of high anxiety interferes with the ability to exercise. The issue
here is one of temporal precedence; it is very important in making causal inferences. Knowledge of the correct direction of cause and effect in turn has
implications for applications of research findings: If exercise reduces anxiety,
then undertaking an exercise program would be a reasonable way to lower
one's anxiety. However, if anxiety causes people to stop exercising, simply forc-
ing someone to exercise is not likely to reduce the person's anxiety level.

The problem of direction of cause and effect is not the most serious drawback to the nonexperimental method, however. Scientists have pointed out, for
example, that astronomers can make accurate predictions even though they cannot manipulate variables in an experiment. In addition, the direction of cause
and effect is often not crucial because, for some pairs of variables, the causal pat-

tern may operate in both directions. For instance, there seem to be two causal patterns in the relationship between the variables of similarity and liking: (1) Similarity causes people to like each other, and (2) liking causes people to become more similar. In general, the third-variable problem is a much more serious fault of the nonexperimental method.

**The third-variable problem**   When the nonexperimental method is used, there is the danger that no direct causal relationship exists between the two variables. Exercise may not influence anxiety, and anxiety may have no causal effect on exercise. Instead, there may be a relationship between the two variables because some other variable causes both exercise *and* anxiety. This is known as the *third-variable problem*. Any number of other *third variables* (also called **confounding variables**) may be responsible for an observed relationship between two variables. In the exercise and anxiety example, one such third variable could be income level. Perhaps high income allows people more free time to exercise (and the ability to afford a health club membership!) and also lowers anxiety. If income is the determining variable, there is no direct cause-and-effect relationship between exercise and anxiety; the relationship was caused by the third variable, income level. The confounding variable is an alternative explanation for the observed relationship between the variables. Recall from Chapter 1 that the ability to rule out alternative explanations for the observed relationship between two variables is another important factor when we try to infer that one variable causes another.

As you can see, direction of cause and effect and potential third variables represent serious limitations of the nonexperimental method. Often, they are not considered in media reports of research results. For instance, a newspaper may report the results of a nonexperimental study that found a positive relationship between amount of coffee consumed and likelihood of a heart attack. Obviously, there is not necessarily a cause-and-effect relationship between the two variables. Numerous third variables (e.g., occupation, personality, or genetic predisposition) could cause both a person's coffee-drinking behavior and the likelihood of a heart attack. In sum, the results of such studies are ambiguous and should be viewed with skepticism. This topic will be considered again after describing the characteristics of the experimental method.

## Experimental Method

The experimental method reduces such ambiguity in the interpretation of results. With the experimental method, one variable is manipulated and the other is then measured. If a researcher used the experimental method to study whether exercise reduces anxiety, exercise would be manipulated—perhaps by having one group of people exercise each day for a week and another group refrain from exercise. Anxiety would then be measured. Suppose that people in the exercise group have less anxiety than the people in the no-exercise group. The researcher could now say something about the direction of cause and effect: In the experiment, exercise came first in the sequence of events. Thus, anxiety level could not influence the amount of exercise that the people engaged in.

Another characteristic of the experimental method is that it attempts to eliminate the influence of all potential confounding third variables. This is called control of extraneous variables. Such control is usually achieved by making sure that every feature of the environment except the manipulated variable is held constant. Any variable that cannot be held constant is controlled by making sure that the effects of the variable are random. Through randomization, the influence of any extraneous variables is equal in the experimental conditions. Both procedures are used to ensure that any differences between the groups are due to the manipulated variable.

**Experimental control**    With experimental control, all extraneous variables are kept constant. If a variable is held constant, it cannot be responsible for the results of the experiment. In other words, any variable that is held constant cannot be a confounding variable. In the experiment on the effect of exercise, the researcher would want to make sure that the only difference between the exercise and no-exercise groups is the exercise. For example, because people in the exercise group are removed from their daily routine to engage in exercise, the people in the no-exercise group should be removed from their daily routine as well. Otherwise, the lower anxiety in the exercise condition could have resulted from the "rest" from the daily routine rather than from the exercise.

Experimental control is accomplished by treating participants in all groups in the experiment identically; the only difference between groups is the manipulated variable. In the Loftus experiment on memory, both groups will witness the same accident, the same experimenter will ask the questions in both groups, the lighting and all other conditions will be the same, and so on. When there is a difference between the groups in reporting memory, one can be sure that the difference is the result of the method of questioning rather than of some other variable that was not held constant.

**Randomization**    Sometimes, it is difficult to keep a variable constant. The most obvious such variable is any characteristic of the participants. Consider an experiment in which half the research participants are in the exercise condition and the other half are in the no-exercise condition; the participants in the two conditions might be different on some extraneous, third variable such as income. This difference could cause an apparent relationship between exercise and anxiety. How can the researcher eliminate the influence of such extraneous variables in an experiment?

The experimental method eliminates the influence of such variables by **randomization.** Randomization ensures that the extraneous variable is just as likely to affect one experimental group as it is to affect the other group. To eliminate the influence of individual characteristics, the researcher assigns participants to the two groups in a random fashion. In actual practice, this means that assignment to groups is determined using a list of random numbers. To understand this, think of the participants in the experiment as forming a line. As each person comes to the front of the line, a random number is assigned, much like random numbers are drawn for a lottery. If the number is even, the individual is assigned to one group (e.g., exercise); if the number is odd, the subject is assigned to the other group (e.g., no exercise). By using a random assignment procedure, the researcher is confident that the characteristics of the participants in the two groups will be virtually identical. In this "lottery," for instance, people with low, medium, and high incomes will be distributed equally in the two groups. In fact, randomization ensures that the individual characteristic composition of the two groups will be virtually identical in every way. This ability to randomly assign research participants to the conditions in the experiment is an important difference between the experimental and nonexperimental methods.

To make the concept of random assignment more concrete, you might try an exercise such as the one I did with a box full of old baseball cards. The box contained cards of 50 American League players and 50 National League players. The cards were thoroughly mixed up; I then proceeded to select 32 of the cards and assign them to "groups" using the table of random numbers in Appendix C.1. As I selected each card, I used the following decision rule: If the random number is even, the player is assigned to "Group 1," and if the number is odd, the player is assigned to "Group 2." I then checked to see whether my two groups differed in terms of league representation. Group 1 had nine American League players and seven National League players, whereas Group 2 had an equal number of players from the two leagues. The two groups were virtually identical!

Any other variable that cannot be held constant is also controlled by randomization. For instance, many experiments are conducted over a period of several days or weeks, with participants arriving for the experiment at various times during each day. In such cases, the researcher uses a random order for scheduling the sequence of the various experimental conditions. This procedure prevents a situation in which one condition is scheduled during the first days of the experiment while the other is studied during later days. Similarly, participants in one group will not be studied only during the morning and the others only in the afternoon.

Direct control and randomization eliminate the influence of any extraneous variables. Thus, the experimental method allows a relatively unambiguous interpretation of the results. Any difference between groups on the observed variable can be attributed only to the influence of the manipulated variable.

## INDEPENDENT AND DEPENDENT VARIABLES

When researchers study the relationship between variables, the variables are usually conceptualized as having a cause-and-effect connection. That is, one variable is considered to be the "cause" and the other variable the "effect." Thus, speaker credibility is viewed as a cause of attitude change, while exercise is viewed as having an effect on anxiety. Researchers using both experimental and nonexperimental methods view the variables in this fashion, even though, as we have seen, there is less ambiguity about the direction of cause and effect when the experimental method is used. Researchers use the terms **independent variable** and **dependent variable** when referring to the variables being studied. The variable that is considered to be the "cause" is the independent variable, and the variable that is the "effect" is the dependent variable.

In an experiment, the manipulated variable is the independent variable, and the second variable that is measured is the dependent variable. One way to remember the distinction is to relate the terms to what happens to an individual in an experiment. The researcher devises a situation to which participants are exposed, such as watching a violent versus a nonviolent program or exercising versus not exercising. This situation is the manipulated variable; it is called the independent variable because the participant has nothing to do with its occurrence. In the next step of the experiment, the researcher measures the response to the manipulated variable. The participant is responding to what happened to him or her; the researcher assumes that what the individual does or says is caused by, or dependent on, the effect of the independent (manipulated) variable. The independent variable, then, is the variable manipulated by the experimenter, and the dependent variable is the measured behavior that is assumed to be caused by the independent variable.

When the relationship between an independent and a dependent variable is plotted in a graph, the independent variable is always placed on the horizontal axis and the dependent variable is always placed on the vertical axis. If you look back to Figure 4.2, you will see that this graphing method was used to present the four relationships. In Graph B, for example, the independent variable, "group size," is placed on the horizontal axis; the dependent variable, "amount of noise," is placed on the vertical axis.

Note that some research focuses primarily on the independent variable with the researcher studying the effect of a single independent variable on numerous behaviors. Other researchers may focus on a specific dependent variable and study how various independent variables affect that one behavior. To make this distinction more concrete, consider a study of the effect of jury size on the outcome of a trial. One researcher studying this issue might be interested in the effect of group size on a variety of behaviors, including jury decisions and risk taking among business managers. Another researcher interested solely in jury decisions might study the effects of many aspects of trials such as jury size or the judge's instructions on the behaviors of jurors. Both emphases lead to important research.

## CAUSALITY

Recall from Chapter 1 that inferences of cause and effect require three elements. First, there must be temporal precedence: The causal variable should come first in the temporal order of events and then be followed by the effect. The experimental method addresses temporal order by first manipulating the independent variable and then observing whether it has an effect on the dependent variable. In other situations, you may observe the temporal order or you may logically conclude that one order is more plausible than another. Second, there must be covariation between the two variables. Covariation is demonstrated with the experimental method when participants in an experimental condition (e.g., an exercise condition) show the effect (e.g., a reduction in anxiety) whereas participants in a control condition (e.g., no exercise) do not show the effect. This requirement may be met with a comparison of "variable present versus not present" as in exercise versus rest; it may also be met by comparisons of amounts of the variable such as a comparison of an hour versus 10 minutes of exercise. Third, there is a need to eliminate plausible alternative explanations for the observed relationship. An alternative explanation is based on the possibility that some confounding "third" variable is responsible for the observed relationship. When designing research, a great deal of attention is paid to eliminating alternative explanations. The experimental method begins by attempting to keep such variables constant through random assignment and experimental control. Other issues of control will be discussed in later chapters. The main point here is that inferences about causal relationships are stronger when there are fewer alternative explanations for the observed relationships.

Sometimes we impose even more stringent requirements before concluding that there is a causal relationship. Some philosophers, scientists, and even many students argue that a cause-and-effect relationship is proven only if the cause is both necessary *and* sufficient for the effect to occur. Suppose you have determined that reading the material for an exam is related to exam score; students who read the material score higher than students who do not read the material. To be necessary, the cause must be present for the effect to occur. To prove that reading the material is the cause of the high exam score, it must be shown that reading the material must occur to do well on the exam. To be sufficient, the cause will *always* produce the effect. To prove that reading the material is the cause, it must always result in a high exam score.

Let's analyze this situation in terms of the necessary and sufficient conditions. If we are talking about a course in which the exam is based only on material in the book, reading the book is probably necessary for a good exam score. Some students at this point say that it is possible to only attend lectures and get a good exam score without reading the book. This may be true in some classes, but it is fair to limit conditions when discussing cause-and-effect relationships.

Is reading the material sufficient to do well on the exam? That is, does reading the material always result in a high exam score? You may be thinking right now that there are many times when you read the material but did *not* excel on an exam. Reading the material is not a sufficient cause; you are most likely to retain the material when you pay attention, relate the information to other things you know, and practice recalling the material.

The "necessary *and* sufficient" requirement for establishing cause is rare in psychology. Whenever psychologists assert that there is a necessary and sufficient cause of a behavior, research soon reveals that this simply isn't so. For example, psychologists once asserted that "frustration causes aggression"; whenever frustration occurs, aggression will result, and whenever aggression occurs, frustration must be the preceding cause. This assertion was shown to be inaccurate. Frustration may lead to aggression, but other responses, such as passive withdrawal or increased effort to overcome the frustration, are possible as well. Also, aggression may result from frustration, but other events may produce aggression as well, including pain, insult, or direct attack.

Behavioral scientists are not unduly concerned with the issues of ultimate cause and effect. Rather, they are more interested in carefully describing behavior, studying how variables affect one another and theories that explain behavior. The general consensus is that there are few interesting "necessary and sufficient" causes of behavior. Instead, research on numerous variables eventually leads to an understanding of a whole "causal network" in which a number of variables are involved in complex patterns of cause and effect. This book will not focus on these difficult questions, but instead will examine the methods used to study behavior.

## CHOOSING A METHOD: ADVANTAGES OF MULTIPLE METHODS

The advantages of the experimental method for studying relationships between variables have been emphasized. However, there *are* disadvantages to experiments and many good reasons for using methods other than experiments. Let's examine some of the issues that arise when choosing a method.

### Artificiality of Experiments

In a laboratory experiment, the independent variable is manipulated within the carefully controlled confines of a laboratory. This procedure permits relatively unambiguous inferences concerning cause and effect and reduces the possibility that extraneous variables could influence the results. Laboratory experimentation is an extremely valuable way to study many problems. However, the high degree of control and the laboratory setting may sometimes create an artificial atmosphere that may limit either the questions that can be addressed or the generality of the results. For this reason, researchers may decide to use nonexperimental methods.

Another alternative is to try to conduct an experiment in a field setting. In a **field experiment,** the independent variable is manipulated in a natural setting. As in any experiment, the researcher attempts to control extraneous variables via either randomization or experimental control. As an example of a field experiment, consider Langer and Rodin's (1976) study on the effects of giving elderly nursing home residents greater control over decisions that affect their lives. One group of residents was given a great deal of responsibility for making choices concerning the operation of the nursing home; a second group was made to feel that the staff would be responsible for their care and needs. The experimenters measured dependent variables such as activity level and happiness of the residents. The results showed that the people in the increased responsibility group were more active and happy. In a follow-up study, these residents even showed greater improvements in physical health (Rodin & Langer, 1977).

Many other field experiments take place in public spaces such as street corners, shopping malls, and parking lots. Ruback and Juieng (1997) measured the amount of time drivers in a parking lot took to leave their space under two conditions: (1) when another car was waiting for the space or (2) when no other car was present. As you might expect, drivers took longer to leave when a car was waiting for the space. Apparently, the motive to protect a temporary territory is stronger than the motive to leave as quickly as possible! The advantage of the field experiment is that the independent variable is investigated in a natural context. The disadvantage is that the researcher loses the ability to directly control many aspects of the situation. The laboratory experiment permits researchers to more easily keep extraneous variables constant, thereby eliminating their influence on the outcome of the experiment. Of course, it is precisely this control that leads to the artificiality of the laboratory investigation. Fortunately, when researchers have conducted experiments in both lab and field settings, the results of the experiments are very similar (Anderson, Lindsay, & Bushman, 1999).

### Ethical and Practical Considerations

Sometimes the experimental method is not a feasible alternative because experimentation would be either unethical or impractical. Child-rearing practices would be impractical to manipulate with the experimental method, for example. Further, even if it were possible to randomly assign parents to two child-rearing conditions, such as using withdrawal of love versus physical types of punishment, the manipulation would be unethical. Instead of manipulating variables such as child-rearing techniques, researchers usually study them as they occur in natural settings. Many important research areas present similar problems—for example, studies of the effects of alcoholism, divorce and its consequences, or the impact of maternal employment on children. Such problems need to be studied, and generally the only techniques possible are nonexperimental.

When such variables are studied, people are often categorized into groups based on their experiences. When studying maternal employment, one group would consist of individuals whose mothers work outside the home and another group would consist of people whose mothers do not work. This is sometimes called an *ex post facto* design. Ex post facto means "after the fact"—the term was coined to describe research in which groups are formed on the basis of some actual difference rather than through random assignment as in an experiment. It is extremely important to study these differences. However, it is important to recognize that this is nonexperimental research because there is no random assignment to the groups.

### Participant Variables

Participant variables (also called *subject variables* and *personal attributes*) are characteristics of individuals, such as age, gender, ethnic group, nationality, birth order, personality, or marital status. These variables are by definition nonexperimental and so must be measured. For example, to study a personality characteristic such as extraversion, you might have people complete a personality test that is designed to measure this variable. Such variables may be studied in experiments along with manipulated independent variables (see Chapter 10).

### Description of Behavior

A major goal of science is to provide an accurate description of events. Thus, the goal of much research is to describe behavior; the issues that experiments address are not relevant to the primary goals of the research. A classic example of descriptive research in psychology comes from the work of Jean Piaget, who carefully observed the behavior of his own children as they matured and described in detail the changes in their ways of thinking about and responding to their environment (Piaget, 1952). Piaget's descriptions and his interpretations of his observations resulted in an important theory of cognitive development that greatly increased our understanding of this topic. Piaget's theory had a major impact on psychology that continues today (Flavell, 1996).

### Successful Predictions of Future Behavior

In many real-life situations, a major concern is to make a successful prediction about a person's future behavior—for example, success in school, ability to learn a new job, or probable interest in various major fields in college. In such circumstances, there may be no need to be concerned about issues of cause and effect. It is possible to design measures that increase the accuracy of predicting future behavior. School counselors can give tests to decide whether students should be in "enriched" classroom programs, employers can test applicants to help determine whether they should be hired, and college students can take tests that help them decide on a major. These types of measures can lead to better decisions for many people. When researchers develop measures designed to predict future behavior, they must conduct research to demonstrate that the measure does, in fact, relate to the behavior in question. This research will be discussed in Chapter 5.

### Advantages of Multiple Methods

Perhaps most important, complete understanding of any phenomenon requires study using multiple methods, both experimental and nonexperimental. No method is perfect, and no single study is definitive. To illustrate, consider a hypothesis developed by Frank and Gilovich (1988). They were intrigued by the observation that the color black represents evil and death across many cultures over time, and wondered whether this has an influence on our behavior. They noted that several professional sports teams in the National Football League and National Hockey League wear black uniforms, and hypothesized that these teams might be more aggressive than other teams in the leagues.

They first needed an operational definition of "black" and "nonblack" uniforms; they decided that a black uniform is one in which 50% or more of the uniform is black. Using this definition, five NFL and five NHL teams had black uniforms. They first asked people who had no knowledge of the NFL or NHL to view each team's uniform and then rate the teams on "malevolent" adjectives such as "mean" and "aggressive." Overall, the ratings of the black uniform teams were perceived to be more malevolent. They then compared the penalty yards of NFL black and nonblack teams and the penalty minutes of NHL teams. In both cases, black teams were assessed more penalties. But is there a causal pattern? Frank and Gilovich discovered that two NHL teams had switched uniforms from nonblack to black so they compared penalty minutes before and after the switch; consistent with the hypothesis, penalties did increase for both teams. They also looked at the penalty minutes of a third team that had changed from a nonblack color to another nonblack color, and found no change in penalty minutes. Note that none of these studies used the experimental method. In an experiment to test the hypothesis that people perceive black uniform teams as more aggressive, students watched videos of two plays from a staged football game in which the defense was wearing either black or white. Both plays included an aggressive act by the defense. On these plays, the students penalized the black uniform team more than the nonblack team. In a final experiment to see whether being on a black uniform team would increase aggressiveness, people were brought into the lab in groups of three. The groups were told they were a "team" that would be competing with another team. All members of the team were given either white or black clothing to wear for the competition; they were then asked to choose the games they would like to have for the competition. Some of the games were aggressive ("dart gun duel") and some were not ("putting contest"). As you might expect by now, the black uniform teams chose more aggressive games.

The important point here is that no study is a perfect test of a hypothesis. However, when multiple studies using multiple methods all lead us to the same conclusion, our confidence in the findings and our understanding of the phenomenon are greatly increased.

## EVALUATING RESEARCH: THREE VALIDITIES

*Validity* refers to "truth" and the accurate representation of information. Research can be described and evaluated in terms of three types of validity: construct validity, internal validity, and external validity. Each gives us a different perspective on any particular research investigation.

### Construct Validity

**Construct validity** refers to the adequacy of the operational definition of variables: Does the operational definition of a variable actually reflect the true theoretical meaning of the variable? Many variables are abstract "constructs" such as social anxiety, speaker credibility, or social loafing. A social anxiety measure must be developed to assess the theoretical construct; this is, of course, an operational definition of the variable. The measure has construct validity if it measures the social anxiety construct and not some other variable such as dominance. Similarly, a manipulation of speaker credibility with low and high credibility speakers must manipulate credibility and not something else such as attractiveness. Because variables can be measured and manipulated in a variety of ways, there is never a perfect operational definition of a variable. Over time, many researchers will use multiple methods to operationally define any variable. This topic will be addressed further in subsequent chapters.

### Internal Validity

**Internal validity** refers to the ability to draw conclusions about causal relationships from our data. A study has high internal validity when strong inferences can be made that one variable caused changes in the other variable. We have seen that strong causal inferences can be made more easily when the experimental method is used. Internal validity is increased when the considerations of cause and effect that were previously discussed can be applied to the research.

### External Validity

Finally, the **external validity** of a study is the extent to which the results can be generalized to other populations and settings. Can the results be replicated with other operational definitions of the variables, with different participants, in other settings? In this chapter, concerns over the artificiality of laboratory experiments were addressed; this is an issue of external validity. Note that the goal of high internal validity may sometimes conflict with the goal of external validity. Field experiments represent one way that researchers try to increase the external validity of their experiments. The issue of external validity is a complex one that will be discussed more fully in Chapter 14.

At this point, you may be wondering how researchers select a methodology to study a problem. A variety of methods are available, each with advantages and disadvantages. Researchers select the method that best enables them to address the questions they wish to answer. No method is inherently superior to another. Rather, the choice of method is made after considering the problem under investigation, ethics, cost and time constraints, and issues associated with the three types of validity. In the remainder of this book, many specific methods will be discussed, all of which are useful under different circumstances. In fact, all are necessary to understand the wide variety of behaviors that are of interest to behavioral scientists. Complete understanding of any problem or issue requires research using a variety of methodological approaches.

## Study Terms

Confounding

Confounding variables

Construct validity

Correlation coefficient

Curvilinear relationship

Dependent variable

Experimental control

Experimental method

External validity

Field experiment

Independent variable

Internal validity

Mediating variable

Necessary cause

Negative linear relationship

Nonexperimental method (correlational method)

Operational definition

Participant (subject) variable

Positive linear relationship

Randomization

Response variable

Situational variable

Sufficient cause

Third-variable problem

Variable

## Review Questions

1. What is a variable? List at least five different variables, and then specify the levels of each variable.

2. Define "operational definition" of a variable. Give at least two operational definitions of the variables you thought of in the previous review question.

3. Distinguish among positive linear, negative linear, and curvilinear relationships.

4. What is the difference between the nonexperimental method and the experimental method?

5. What is the difference between an independent variable and a dependent variable?

6. Distinguish between laboratory and field experiments.

7. What is meant by the problem of direction of cause and effect and the third-variable problem?

8. How do direct experimental control and randomization influence the possible effects of extraneous variables?

9. What are some reasons for using the nonexperimental method to study relationships between variables?

10. Describe the three elements for inferring causation.

11. What is meant by a "necessary and sufficient" cause?

*Activity Questions* _____

1. Males and females may differ in their approaches to helping others. For example, males may be more likely to help a person having car trouble, and females may be more likely to bring dinner to a sick friend. Develop two operational definitions for the concept of helping behavior, one that emphasizes the "male style" and the other the "female style." How might the use of one or the other lead to different conclusions from experimental results regarding who helps more, males or females? What does this tell you about the importance of operational definitions?

2. You observe that classmates who get good grades tend to sit toward the front of the classroom, while those who receive poorer grades tend to sit toward the back. What are three possible cause-and-effect relationships for this nonexperimental observation?

3. Consider the hypothesis that stress at work causes family conflict at home.
   a. What type of relationship is proposed (e.g., positive linear, negative linear)?
   b. Graph the proposed relationship.
   c. Identify the independent variable and the dependent variable in the statement of the hypothesis.
   d. How might you investigate the hypothesis using the experimental method?
   e. How might you investigate the hypothesis using the nonexperimental method (recognizing the problems of determining cause and effect)?
   f. What factors might you consider in deciding whether to use the experimental or nonexperimental method to study the relationship between work stress and family conflict?

4. Identify the independent and dependent variables in the following descriptions of experiments:
   a. Students watched a cartoon either alone or with others and then rated how funny they found the cartoon to be.
   b. A comprehension test was given to students after they had studied textbook material either in silence or with the television turned on.
   c. Some elementary school teachers were told that a child's parents were college graduates, and other teachers were told that the child's parents had not finished high school; they then rated the child's academic potential.
   d. Workers at a company were assigned to one of two conditions: One group completed a stress management training program; another group of workers did not participate in the training. The number of sick days taken by these workers was examined for the two subsequent months.

5. A few years ago, newspapers reported a finding that Americans who have a glass of wine a day are healthier than those who have no wine (or who have a lot of wine or other alcohol). What are some plausible alternative explanations for this finding; that is, what variables other than wine could explain the finding? (Hint: What sorts of people in the United States are most likely to have a glass of wine with dinner?)

6. The limitations of nonexperimental research were dramatically brought to the attention of the public by the results of an experiment on the effects of postmenopausal hormone replacement therapy (part of a larger study known as the Women's Health Initiative). An experiment is called a clinical trial in medical research. In the clinical trial, participants were randomly assigned to receive either the hormone replacement therapy or a placebo (no hormones). The hormone replacement therapy consisted of estrogen plus progestin. In 2002, the investigators concluded that women taking the hormone replacement therapy had a higher incidence of heart disease than did women in the placebo (no hormone) condition. At that point, they stopped the experiment and informed both the participants and the public that they should talk with their physicians about the advisability of this therapy. The finding dramatically contrasted with the results of nonexperimental research in which women taking hormones had a lower incidence of heart disease; in these studies, researchers compared women who were already taking the hormones with women not taking hormones. Why do you think the results were different with the experimental research and the nonexperimental research?

# Measurement Concepts

We learn about behavior through careful measurement. As we discussed in Chapter 4, behavior can be measured in many ways. The most common measurement strategy is to ask people to tell you about themselves: How many times have you argued with your spouse in the past week? How would you rate your overall happiness? How much did you like your partner in this experiment? Of course, you can also directly observe behaviors. How many errors did someone make on a task? Will people that you approach in a shopping mall give you change for a dollar? How many times did a person smile during an interview? Physiological and neurological responses can be measured as well. How much did heart rate change while working on the problems? Did muscle tension increase during the interview? There is an endless supply of fascinating behaviors that can be studied. We will describe various methods of measuring variables at several points in subsequent chapters. In this chapter, however, we explore the technical aspects of measurement. We need to consider reliability, validity, and reactivity of measures. We will also consider scales of measurement.

## RELIABILITY OF MEASURES

**Reliability** refers to the consistency or stability of a measure of behavior. Your everyday definition of reliability is quite close to the scientific definition. For example, you might say that Professor Fuentes is "reliable" because she begins class exactly at 10 A.M. each day; in contrast, Professor Fine might be called "unreliable" because, while she sometimes begins class exactly on the hour, on any given day she may appear anytime between 10 and 10:20 A.M.

Similarly, a reliable measure of a psychological variable such as intelligence will yield the same result each time you administer the intelligence test to the same person. The test would be unreliable if it measured the same person as average one week, low the next, and bright the next. Put simply, a reliable measure does not fluctuate from one reading to the next. If the measure does fluctuate, there is error in the measurement device.

A more formal way of understanding reliability is to use the concepts of true score and measurement error. Any measure that you make can be thought of as comprising two components: (1) a **true score,** which is the real score on the variable, and (2) **measurement error.** An unreliable measure of intelligence contains considerable measurement error and so does not provide an accurate indication of an individual's true intelligence. In contrast, a reliable measure of intelligence—one that contains little measurement error—will yield an identical (or nearly identical) intelligence score each time the same individual is measured.

To illustrate the concept of reliability further, imagine that you know someone whose "true" intelligence score is 100. Now suppose that you administer an unreliable intelligence test to this person each week for a year. After the year, you calculate the person's average score on the test based on the 52 scores you obtained. Now suppose that you test another friend who also has a true

FIGURE 5.1
Comparing data of a reliable and unreliable measure

intelligence score of 100; however, this time you administer a highly reliable test. Again, you calculate the average score. What might your data look like? Typical data are shown in Figure 5.1. In each case, the average score is 100. However, scores on the unreliable test range from 85 to 115, whereas scores on the reliable test range from 97 to 103. The *measurement error* in the unreliable test is revealed in the greater variability shown by the person who took the unreliable test.

When conducting research, you can measure each person only once; you can't give the measure 50 or 100 times to discover a true score. Thus, it is very important that you use a reliable measure. Your single administration of the measure should closely reflect the person's true score.

The importance of reliability is obvious. An unreliable measure of length would be useless in building a table; an unreliable measure of a variable such as intelligence is equally useless in studying that variable. Researchers cannot use unreliable measures to systematically study variables or the relationships among variables. Trying to study behavior using unreliable measures is a waste of time because the results will be unstable and unable to be replicated.

Reliability is most likely to be achieved when researchers use careful measurement procedures. In some research areas, this might involve carefully training observers to record behavior; in other areas, it might mean paying close attention to the way questions are phrased or the way recording electrodes are placed on the body to measure physiological reactions.

How can we assess reliability? We cannot directly observe the true score and error components of an actual score on the measure. However, we can assess the stability of measures using correlation coefficients. Recall from Chapter 4 that a correlation coefficient is a number that tells us how strongly two variables are related to each other. There are several ways of calculating correlation coefficients; the most common correlation coefficient when discussing reliability is the **Pear-**

**son product-moment correlation coefficient.** The Pearson correlation coefficient (symbolized as $r$) can range from 0.00 to +1.00 and 0.00 to −1.00. A correlation of 0.00 tells us that the two variables are not related at all. The closer a correlation is to 1.00, either +1.00 or −1.00, the stronger is the relationship. The positive and negative signs provide information about the direction of the relationship. When the correlation coefficient is positive (a "plus" sign), there is a positive linear relationship—high scores on one variable are associated with high scores on the second variable. A negative linear relationship is indicated by a "minus" sign—high scores on one variable are associated with low scores on the second variable. The Pearson correlation coefficient will be discussed further in Chapter 12.

To assess the reliability of a measure, we will need to obtain at least two scores on the measure from many individuals. If the measure is reliable, the two scores should be very similar; a Pearson correlation coefficient that relates the two scores should be a high positive correlation. When you read about reliability, the correlation will usually be called a *reliability coefficient*. Let's examine specific methods of assessing reliability.

## Test-Retest Reliability

**Test-retest reliability** is assessed by measuring the same individuals at two points in time. For example, the reliability of a test of intelligence could be assessed by giving the measure to a group of people on one day and again a week later. We would then have two scores for each person, and a correlation coefficient could be calculated to determine the relationship between the test score and the retest score. Recall that high reliability is indicated by a high correlation coefficient showing that the two scores are very similar. If many people have very similar scores, we conclude that the measure reflects true scores rather than measurement error. It is difficult to say how high the correlation should be before we accept the measure as reliable, but for most measures the reliability coefficient should probably be at least .80.

Given that test-retest reliability involves administering the same test twice, the correlation might be artificially high because the individuals remember how they responded the first time. Alternate forms reliability is sometimes used to avoid this problem. Alternate forms reliability involves administering two different forms of the same test to the same individuals at two points in time.

Intelligence is a variable that can be expected to stay relatively constant over time; thus, we expect the test-retest reliability for intelligence to be very high. However, some variables may be expected to change from one test period to the next. For example, a mood scale designed to measure a person's current mood state is a measure that might easily change from one test period to another and so test-retest reliability might not be appropriate. On a more practical level, obtaining two measures from the same people at two points in time may sometimes be difficult. To address these issues, researchers have devised methods to assess reliability without two separate assessments.

### Internal Consistency Reliability

It is possible to assess reliability by measuring individuals at only one point in time. We can do this because most psychological measures are made up of a number of different questions, called items. An intelligence test might have 100 items, a measure of extraversion might have 15 items, or a multiple-choice examination in a class might have 50 items. A person's test score would be based on the total of his or her responses on all items. In the class, an exam consists of a number of questions about the material, and the total score is the number of correct answers. An extraversion measure might ask people to agree or disagree with items such as "I enjoy the stimulation of a lively party." An individual's extraversion score is obtained by finding the total number of such items that are endorsed.

**Internal consistency reliability** is the assessment of reliability using responses at only one point in time. Because all items measure the same variable, they should yield similar or consistent results. One indicator of internal consistency is **split-half reliability;** this is the correlation of an individual's total score on one half of the test with the total score on the other half. The two halves are created by randomly dividing the items into two parts. The actual calculation of a split-half reliability coefficient is a bit more complicated because the final measure will include items from both halves. Thus, the combined measure will have more items and will be more reliable than either half by itself. This fact must be taken into account when calculating the reliability coefficient; consult a text on psychological measurement for technical procedures if you need to perform the calculations.

Another internal consistency indicator of reliability is called **Cronbach's alpha.** Here the researcher calculates the correlation of each item with every other item. A large number of correlation coefficients are produced; you would only want to do this with a computer! The value of *alpha* is the average of all the correlation coefficients. It is also possible to examine the correlation of each item score with the total score based on all items. Such item-total correlations and Cronbach's *alpha* are very informative because they provide information about each individual item. Items that do not correlate with the other items can be eliminated from the measure to increase reliability.

### Interrater Reliability

In some research, raters observe behaviors and make ratings or judgments. To do this, a rater uses instructions for making judgments about the behaviors—for example, by rating whether a behavior of a child on a playground is aggressive and how aggressive is the behavior. You could have one rater make judgments about aggression, but the single observations of one rater might be unreliable. The solution to this problem is to use at least two raters who observe the same behavior. **Interrater reliability** is the extent to which raters agree in their observations. Thus, if two raters are judging whether behaviors are aggressive, high interrater reliability is obtained when most of the observations result in the same judgment. A commonly used indicator of interrater reliability is called *Cohen's Kappa*.

## Reliability and Accuracy of Measures

Reliability is clearly important when researchers develop measures of behavior. Reliability is not the only characteristic of a measure and the only thing that researchers worry about. Reliability tells us about measurement error but it does not tell us about whether we have a good measure of the variable of interest. To use a silly example, suppose I want to measure intelligence. The measure I develop looks remarkably like the device that is used to measure shoe size at my local shoe store. I ask you to place your foot in the device and I use the gauge to measure your intelligence. There are numbers that provide a scale of intelligence so I can immediately assess a person's intelligence level. Will these numbers result in a reliable measure of intelligence? The answer is that they will! Consider what a test-retest reliability coefficient would be. If I administer the "foot intelligence scale" on Monday, it will be almost the same the following Monday; the test-retest reliability is high. But is this an accurate measure of intelligence? Obviously, the scores have nothing to do with intelligence; just because I labeled that device as an intelligence test does not mean that it is a good measure of intelligence.

Let's consider a less silly example. Suppose your neighborhood gas station pump puts the same amount of gas in your car every time you purchase a gallon (or liter) of fuel; the gas pump gauge is reliable. However, the issue of accuracy is still open. The only way you can know about accuracy of the pump is to compare the gallon (or liter) you receive with some standard measure of a gallon. In fact, states have inspectors responsible for comparing the amount that the pump says is a gallon with an exact gallon measure. A pump with a gauge that does not deliver what it says must be repaired or replaced. This difference between the reliability and accuracy of measures leads us to a consideration of the validity of measures.

## CONSTRUCT VALIDITY OF MEASURES

If something is valid, it is "true" in the sense that it is supported by available evidence. The amount of gasoline that the gauge indicates should match some standard measure of liquid volume; a measure of a personality characteristic such as shyness should be an accurate indicator of that trait. Recall from Chapter 4 that **construct validity** refers to the adequacy of the operational definition of variables. To what extent does the operational definition of a variable actually reflect the true theoretical meaning of the variable? In terms of measurement, construct validity is a question of whether the measure that is employed actually measures the construct it is intended to measure. Applicants for some jobs are required to take a Clerical Ability Test; this measure is supposed to predict an individual's clerical ability. The validity of such a test is determined by whether it actually does measure this ability. A measure of shyness is an operational definition of the shyness variable; the validity of this measure is determined by whether it does measure this construct.

---

**Face Validity**

    The content of the measure appears to reflect the construct being measured.

**Criterion-Oriented Validity**

    Scores on the measure are related to a criterion (an indicator of the construct).

    **Types of criterion-oriented validity**

| | |
|---|---|
| **Predictive validity** | Scores on the measure predict behavior on a criterion. |
| **Concurrent validity** | People in groups known to differ on the construct score differently on the measure. |
| **Convergent validity** | Scores on the measure are related to other measures of the same construct. |
| **Discriminant validity** | Scores on the measure are *not* related to other measures that are theoretically different. |

---

**FIGURE 5.2**
Indicators of construct validity of a measure

### Indicators of Construct Validity

How do we know that a measure is valid? Ways that we can assess validity are summarized in Figure 5.2. The simplest way to argue that a measure is valid is to suggest that the measure appears to accurately assess the intended variable. This is called **face validity**—the evidence for validity is that the measure appears "on the face of it" to measure what it is supposed to measure. Face validity is not very sophisticated; it involves only a judgment of whether, given the theoretical definition of the variable, the content of the measure appears to actually measure the variable. That is, do the procedures used to measure the variable appear to be an accurate operational definition of the theoretical variable? Thus, a measure of a variable such as shyness will usually appear to measure that variable. A measure of shyness called the Shy Q (Bortnik, Henderson, & Zimbardo, 2002) includes items such as "I often feel insecure in social situations" but does not include an item such as "I learned to ride a bicycle at an early age"—the first item appears to be more closely related to shyness than does the second one.

    However, face validity is not sufficient to conclude that a measure is in fact valid. Appearance is not a very good indicator of accuracy. Some very poor measures may have face validity; for example, most personality measures that appear in popular magazines typically have several questions that look reasonable but often don't tell you anything meaningful. The interpretations of the scores may make for fun reading, but there is no empirical evidence to support the conclusions that are drawn in the article. In addition, many good measures of variables do not have obvious face validity. For example, is it obvious that rapid eye movement during sleep is a measure of dream occurrence? Instead of relying on face validity, researchers assess validity by conducting research with the measure.

Construct validity research examines the relationship between scores on the measure and some criterion—this has been termed **criterion-oriented validity** by Trochim (2000). A researcher makes a prediction, based on the theory underlying the construct, of how performance on the measure will relate to another variable called a criterion. There are four types of criterion-related research approaches that differ in the type of criterion that is employed: predictive validity, concurrent validity, convergent validity, and discriminant validity (Trochim, 2000). These are related to one another because all are ways of demonstrating the construct validity of a measure.

## Predictive Validity

**Predictive validity** is the extent to which the measure allows you to predict behaviors that it should predict. Thus, with predictive validity, the criterion is some future behavior. For some measures, the nature of the criterion will be obvious. A Clerical Ability Test is intended to provide a fast way to predict future performance in a clerical position. Similarly, many college students take the Graduate Record Exam (GRE), which was developed to predict success in graduate programs, or the Law School Admission Test (LSAT) developed to predict success in law school. The construct validity of such measures is demonstrated when scores on the measure do predict the future behaviors. For example, predictive validity of the LSAT is demonstrated when research shows that people who score high on the test do better in law school than people who score low on the test (i.e., there is a positive relationship between the test score and grades in law school). The measure can be used to advise people on whether they will be successful in law school or to select applicants for a law school.

For other types of variables, the predictions are less obvious. If you have a measure of shyness, you can make predictions about how scores on the measure will relate to various behaviors. For example, your theory of shyness might predict that shyness scores will be related to the amount of anxiety that people will exhibit when they describe themselves to a stranger. If this prediction turns out to be correct, your confidence in the validity of the measure is increased. However, confirmation of a single prediction would never be used as the sole evidence for the construct validity of a measure of a variable such as shyness. Rather, the validity of the measure is built up over time as numerous studies investigate the theory of the particular construct being measured. Further, measures of variables usually have a limited life span. As research findings accumulate, researchers refine the measure and sometimes develop new measures that make better predictions. This process leads to better measures and fuller understanding of the underlying variable being studied.

### Concurrent Validity

The criterion for **concurrent validity** research is whether two or more groups of people differ on the measure in expected ways. Returning to the shyness measure example, your theory of shyness might lead you to expect that salespersons whose job requires making "cold calls" to potential customers would score lower on your shyness scale than salespersons in positions that require dealing only with people who have made the effort to contact the company to potentially make a purchase.

### Convergent Validity

Any given measure is a particular operational definition of the variable being measured. Often there will be other operational definitions—other measures—of the same or similar constructs. **Convergent validity** is the extent to which scores on the measure in question are related to scores on other measures of the same construct or similar constructs. Measures of similar constructs should "converge"—for example, one measure of shyness should correlate highly with another shyness measure or a measure of a similar construct such as social anxiety. In actual research on a shyness scale, the convergent validity of the Shy Q was demonstrated by showing that Shy Q scores were highly correlated (.77) with a scale called the Fear of Negative Evaluation (Bortnik et al., 2002).

### Discriminant Validity

**Discriminant validity** is demonstrated when the measure is *not* related to variables with which it should not be related. The measure should discriminate between the construct being measured and other unrelated constructs. In research on the discriminant validity of their shyness measure, Bortnik et al. (2002) found no relationship between Shy Q scores and several conceptually unrelated interpersonal values such as valuing forcefulness with others.

The Sensation Seeking Scale (Zuckerman, 1979) is an excellent illustration of construct validity research in which multiple studies support predictions made by a theory. Zuckerman's research was stimulated by a psychological theory of optimal levels of physiological arousal. The theory states that people have a need to maintain an optimal level of arousal. When arousal is too low, people will be motivated to do things to increase arousal; when arousal is too high, individuals will attempt to reduce arousal. The theory helps to explain many behaviors, such as the hallucinations and other disturbances that people experience when they are placed in sensory deprivation environments. Zuckerman decided to study this theory by focusing on individual differences; he asked why some people consistently seem to seek out novel or arousing sensations (e.g., parachuting, listening to loud music, driving in car races) while other people avoid arousing sensations.

The Sensation Seeking Scale was developed to study such individual differences in personality. The scale itself includes items intended to measure thrill seeking, susceptibility to boredom, and other aspects of sensation seeking. The reliability of the scale was assessed, of course. After determining that the scale was reliable, construct validity research could begin. Over a period of many years, research by Zuckerman and others demonstrated predictive validity: People who score high on the scale do in fact behave differently from people who score low. High sensation seekers engage in more dangerous activities, drive faster, and prefer less intellectual activities, for example. Other research with the Sensation Seeking Scale examined how the measure is related to other similar and different personality constructs. Work on the Sensation Seeking Scale has ultimately led to research on the biological basis for sensation seeking, such as identifying what brain mechanisms are responsible for arousal needs and whether the trait has a genetic basis. Zuckerman's research illustrates a systematic program of research on the validity of a measure of a psychological construct.

## REACTIVITY OF MEASURES

A potential problem when measuring behavior is **reactivity.** A measure is said to be reactive if awareness of being measured changes an individual's behavior. A reactive measure tells what the person is like when he or she is aware of being observed, but it doesn't tell how the person would behave under natural circumstances. Simply having various devices such as electrodes and blood pressure cuffs attached to your body may change the physiological responses being recorded. Knowing that a researcher is observing you or recording your behavior on tape might change the way you behave. Measures of behavior vary in terms of their potential reactivity. There are also ways to minimize reactivity, such as allowing time for individuals to become used to the presence of the observer or the recording equipment.

A book by Webb, Campbell, Schwartz, Sechrest, and Grove (1981) has drawn attention to a number of measures that are called *nonreactive* or *unobtrusive*. Many such measures involve clever ways of indirectly recording a variable. For example, an unobtrusive measure of preferences for paintings in an art museum is the frequency with which tiles around each painting must be replaced—the most popular paintings are the ones with the most tile wear. Levine's (1990) study on the pace of life in cities, mentioned in Chapter 2, used indirect measures such as the accuracy of bank clocks and the speed of processing standard requests at post offices to measure pace of life. Some of the measures described by Webb et al. (1981) are simply humorous. For instance, in 1872, Sir Francis Galton studied the efficacy of prayer in producing long life. Galton wondered whether British royalty, who were frequently the recipients of prayers by the populace, lived longer than other people. He checked death records and found that members of royal families actually led shorter lives than other people, such as men of literature and science. The book by Webb and his colleagues is a rich source of such nonreactive measures. More important, it draws attention to the problem of reactivity and sensitizes researchers to the need to reduce reactivity whenever possible. We will return to this issue at several points in this book.

## VARIABLES AND MEASUREMENT SCALES

Every variable that is studied must be operationally defined. The operational definition is the specific method used to manipulate or measure the variable (see Chapter 4). There must be at least two values or levels of the variable. In Chapter 4, we mentioned that the values may be quantitatively different or they may reflect categorical differences. In actuality, the world is a bit more complex. The levels can be conceptualized as a scale that uses one of four kinds of measurement scales: nominal, ordinal, interval, and ratio.

### Nominal Scales

**Nominal scales** have no numerical or quantitative properties. Instead, categories or groups simply differ from one another (sometimes nominal variables are called "categorical" variables). An obvious example is the variable of gender. A person is classified as either male or female. Being male does not imply a greater amount of "sexness" than being female; the two levels are merely different. This is called a nominal scale because we simply assign names to different categories. Another example is the classification of undergraduates according to major. A psychology major would not be entitled to a higher number than a history major, for instance. Even if you were to assign numbers to the different categories, the numbers would be meaningless, except for identification.

In an experiment, the independent variable is often a nominal or categorical variable. For example, Punnett (1986) studied a variable that can be called "type of motivation." Workers were motivated with either a specific, difficult performance goal or a vague goal to "do your best." The goal-setting variable is clearly nominal because the two levels are merely different; the goals have no numerical properties. Punnett found that the specific goal produced higher performance than the vague goal.

### Ordinal Scales

**Ordinal scales** allow us to rank order the levels of the variable being studied. Instead of having categories that are simply different, as in a nominal scale, the categories can be ordered from first to last. One example of an ordinal scale is provided by the movie rating system used in the television section of my local newspaper. Movies on TV are given one, two, three, or four checks, based on these descriptions:

| | | | | |
|---|---|---|---|---|
| √ | √ | √ | √ | New or old, a classic |
| √ | √ | √ | | First-rate |
| √ | √ | | | Flawed; may have moments |
| √ | | | | Desperation time |

The rating system is not a nominal scale because the number of checks is meaningful in terms of a continuum of quality. However, the checks allow us only to rank order the movies. A four-check movie is better than a three-check movie; a three-check movie is better than a two-check movie; and so on. Although we have this quantitative information about the movies, we cannot say that the difference between a one-check and a two-check movie is always the same or that it is equal to the difference between a two-check and a three-check movie. No particular value is attached to the intervals between the numbers used in the rating scale.

### Interval and Ratio Scales

In an **interval scale,** the difference between the numbers on the scale is meaningful. Specifically, the intervals between the numbers are equal in size. The difference between 1 and 2 on the scale, for example, is the same as the difference between 2 and 3. Interval scales generally have five or more quantitative levels.

A household thermometer (Fahrenheit or Celsius) measures temperature on an interval scale. The difference in temperature between 40° and 50° is equal to the difference between 70° and 80°. However, there is no absolute zero on the scale that would indicate the absence of temperature. The zero on any interval scale is only an arbitrary reference point. Without an absolute zero point on interval scales, we cannot form ratios of the numbers. That is, we cannot say that one number on the scale represents twice as much (or three times as much, and so forth) temperature as another number. You cannot say, for example, that 60° is twice as warm as 30°.

An example of an interval scale in the behavioral sciences might be a personality measure of a trait such as extraversion. If the measurement is an interval scale, we cannot make a statement such as "the person who scored 20 is twice as extraverted as the person who scored 10" because there is no absolute zero point that indicates an absence of the trait being measured.

**Ratio scales** do have an absolute zero point that indicates the absence of the variable being measured. Examples include many physical measures, such as length, weight, or time. With a ratio scale, such statements as "a person who weighs 220 pounds weighs twice as much as a person who weighs 110 pounds" or "participants in the experimental group responded twice as fast as participants in the control group" are possible.

Ratio scales are used in the behavioral sciences when variables that involve physical measures are being studied—particularly time measures such as reaction time, rate of responding, and duration of response. However, many variables in the behavioral sciences are less precise and so use nominal, ordinal, or interval scale measures. It should also be noted that the statistical tests for interval and ratio scales are the same.

### The Importance of the Measurement Scales

When you read about the operational definitions of variables, you'll recognize the levels of the variable in terms of these types of scales. The conclusions one draws about the meaning of a particular score on a variable depend on which type of scale was used. With interval and ratio scales, you can make quantitative distinctions that allow you to talk about amounts of the variable. With nominal scales, there is no quantitative information. To illustrate, suppose you are studying perceptions of physical attractiveness. In an experiment, you might show participants pictures of people with different characteristics such as their waist-to-hip ratio (waist size divided by hip size); this variable has been studied extensively by Singh (1993). How should you measure the participants' physical attractiveness judgments? You could use a nominal scale such as:

_____ Not Attractive _____ Attractive

These scale values allow participants to state whether they find the person attractive or not, but do not allow you to know about the amount of attractiveness. As an alternative, you could use a scale that asks participants to rate amount of attractiveness:

Very Unattractive ____ ____ ____ ____ ____ ____ ____ Very Attractive

This rating scale provides you with quantitative information about amount of attractiveness because you can assign numeric values to each of the response options on the scale; in this case, the values would range from 1 to 7. A major finding of Singh's research is that males rate females with a .70 waist-to-hip ratio as most attractive. Singh interprets this finding in terms of evolutionary theory—this ratio presumably is a signal of reproductive capacity.

The scale that is used also determines the types of statistics that are appropriate when the results of a study are analyzed. For now, we do not need to worry about statistical analysis. However, we will return to this point in Chapter 12.

We are now ready to consider methods for measuring behavior. A variety of observational methods are described in Chapter 6. We will then focus on questionnaires and interviews in Chapter 7.

## Study Terms

| | |
|---|---|
| Concurrent validity | Face validity |
| Construct validity | Internal consistency reliability |
| Convergent validity | Interrater reliability |
| Criterion-oriented validity | Interval scale |
| Criterion variable | Item-total correlation |
| Cronbach's *alpha* | Measurement error |
| Discriminant validity | Nominal scale |

Ordinal scale

Pearson product-moment correlation coefficient

Predictive validity

Ratio scale

Reactivity

Reliability

Split-half reliability

Test-retest reliability

True score

## Review Questions

1. What is meant by the reliability of a measure? Distinguish between true score and measurement error.

2. Describe the methods of determining the reliability of a measure.

3. Discuss the concept of construct validity. Distinguish between convergent and discriminant validity.

4. What is meant by criterion-oriented validity?

5. Why isn't face validity sufficient to establish the validity of a measure?

6. What is a reactive measure?

7. Distinguish between nominal, ordinal, interval, and ratio scales.

## Activity Questions

1. Find a reference book on psychological measurement such as the one by Robinson, Shaver, and Wrightsman (1991) or do a library search on construct validity. Identify a measure that interests you and describe the reliability and validity research reported for this measure.

2. Here are a number of references to variables. For each, identify whether a nominal, ordinal, interval, or ratio scale is being used:

   a. The temperatures in cities throughout the country that are listed in most newspapers.

   b. The birth weights of babies who were born at Wilshire General Hospital last week.

   c. The number of hours you spent studying each day during the past week.

   d. The amount of the tip left after each meal at a restaurant during a 3-hour period.

   e. The number of votes received by the Republican and Democratic candidates for Congress in your district in the 2000 election.

   f. The brand listed third in a consumer magazine's ranking of DVD players.

g. Connecticut was voted the number one team in the poll of sports-writers, and Kansas was number two.

h. Your friend's score on an intelligence test is 109.

i. The wall color in my office is yellow and the boss's office is white.

j. The type of programming on each radio station in your city (e.g., KPSY plays jazz, KSOC is talk radio).

3. Take a personality test on the Internet (you can find such tests using Internet search engines). Based on the information provided, what can you conclude about reliability, construct validity, and reactivity?

4. Think of an important characteristic that you would look for in a potential romantic partner, such as humorous, intelligent, attractive, hardworking, religious, and so on. How might you measure that characteristic? Describe two methods that you might use to assess construct validity.

# Observing Behavior

The crux of nonexperimental research is that behavior is observed or measured. Because behavior is so varied and occurs in so many settings, social scientists have developed many ways of conducting nonexperimental research. We will explore a variety of approaches, including observing behavior in natural settings, asking people to describe their behavior (self-report), and examining existing records of behavior, such as census data or hospital records. Because so much nonexperimental research involves surveys using questionnaires or interviews, we cover the topic of survey research in a separate chapter. Before we describe these methods in detail, it will be helpful to understand the distinction between quantitative and qualitative methods of describing behavior.

## QUANTITATIVE AND QUALITATIVE APPROACHES

Observational methods can be broadly classified as primarily quantitative or qualitative. To understand the distinction, imagine that you are interested in describing the ways that the lives of teenagers are affected by working. You might take a quantitative approach by developing a questionnaire that you would ask a sample of teenagers to complete. You could ask about the number of hours they work, the type of work they do, their levels of stress, their school grades, and their use of drugs. After assigning numerical values to the responses, you could subject the data to a quantitative, statistical analysis. A quantitative description of the results would focus on such things as the percentage of teenagers who work and the way this percentage varies by age. Some of the results of this type of survey are described in Chapter 7.

Suppose, instead, that you take a qualitative approach to describing behavior. You might conduct a series of focus groups in which you gather together groups of 8–10 teenagers and engage them in a discussion about their perceptions and experiences with the world of work. You would ask the teenagers to tell you about the topic using their own words and cognitive frameworks. To record the focus group discussions, you might use a video- or audiotape recorder and have a transcript prepared later, or you might have observers take detailed notes during the discussions. A qualitative description of the findings would focus on the themes that emerge from the discussions and the manner in which the teenagers conceptualized the issues. Such description is qualitative because it is expressed in nonnumerical terms using language and images.

Other methods, both qualitative and quantitative, could also be used to study teenage employment. Keep in mind the distinction between quantitative and qualitative approaches to describing behavior as you read about other specific observational methods discussed in this chapter. Both approaches are valuable and provide us with different ways of understanding.

# NATURALISTIC OBSERVATION

Naturalistic observation is sometimes called *field work* or simply *field observation* (see Lofland & Lofland, 1995). In a **naturalistic observation** study, the researcher makes observations in a particular natural setting (the field) over an extended period of time, using a variety of techniques to collect information. The report includes these observations and the researcher's interpretations of the findings. This research approach has roots in anthropology and the study of animal behavior and is currently widely used in the social sciences to study many phenomena in all types of social and organizational settings.

Sylvia Scribner's (1997) research on "practical thinking" is a good example of naturalistic observation research in psychology. Scribner studied ways that people in a variety of occupations make decisions and solve problems. She describes the process of this research: ". . . my colleagues and I have driven around on a 3 a.m. milk route, helped cashiers total their receipts and watched machine operators logging in their production for the day . . . we made detailed records of how people were going about performing their jobs. We collected copies of all written materials they read or produced—everything from notes scribbled on brown paper bags to computer print-outs. We photographed devices in their working environment that required them to process other types of symbolic information—thermometers, gauges, scales, measurement instruments of all kinds" (Scribner, 1997, p. 223). One aspect of thinking that Scribner studied was the way that workers make mathematical calculations. She found that milk truck drivers and other workers make complex calculations that depend on their acquired knowledge. For example, a delivery invoice might require the driver to multiply 32 quarts of milk by .68 per quart. To arrive at the answer, drivers use knowledge acquired on the job about how many quarts are in a case and the cost of a case; thus, they multiply 2 cases of milk by 10.88 per case. In general, the workers that Scribner observed employed complex but very efficient strategies to solve problems at work. More important, the strategies used could often not be predicted from formal models of problem solving.

A researcher uses naturalistic observation when he or she wants to describe and understand how people in a social or cultural setting live, work, and experience the setting. If you want to know about bars as a social setting, for example, you need to visit one or more bars over an extended period of time, talk to people, observe interactions, and become accepted as a "regular" (cf. Cavan, 1966). If you want to know how people persuade or influence others, you can get a job as a car salesperson or take an encyclopedia sales training course (cf. Cialdini, 1988). If you are interested in how people become part of some social group (e.g., marijuana users, prostitutes, a particular religious cult), you can arrange to meet members of the group to interview them about their experiences (cf. Becker, 1963, on marijuana users). Researchers who have studied what it is really like to be a patient in a mental hospital have had themselves admitted as patients (cf. Rosenhan, 1973). Of course, you might not want to do any of these things; however, if these questions interest you, the written reports of these researchers make for fascinating reading.

### Description and Interpretation of Data

Naturalistic observation demands that researchers immerse themselves in the situation. The field researcher observes everything—the setting, the patterns of personal relationships, people's reactions to events, and so on. The goal is to provide a complete and accurate picture rather than to test hypotheses formed prior to the study. To achieve this goal, the researcher must keep detailed field notes—that is, write or dictate on a regular basis (at least once each day) everything that has happened. Field researchers uses a variety of techniques to gather information: observing people and events, interviewing key "informants" to provide inside information, talking to people about their lives, and examining documents produced in the setting, such as newspapers, newsletters, or memos. In addition to taking detailed field notes, researchers conducting naturalistic observation usually use audio- and videotape recordings.

The researcher's first goal is to describe the setting, events, and persons observed. The second, equally important goal is to analyze what was observed. The researcher must interpret what occurred, essentially generating hypotheses that help explain the data and make them understandable. Such an analysis is done by building a coherent structure to describe the observations. The final report, while sensitive to the chronological order of events, is usually organized around the structure developed by the researcher. Specific examples of events that occurred during observation are used to support the researcher's interpretations.

A good naturalistic observation report will support the analysis by using multiple confirmations. For example, similar events may occur several times, similar information may be reported by two or more people, and several different events may occur that all support the same conclusion.

The data in naturalistic observation studies are primarily *qualitative* in nature; that is, they are the descriptions of the observations themselves rather than *quantitative* statistical summaries. Such qualitative descriptions are often richer and closer to the phenomenon being studied than are statistical representations. However, there is no reason that quantitative data cannot be gathered in a naturalistic observation study. If circumstances allow it, data can be gathered on income, family size, education levels, and other easily quantifiable variables. Such data can be reported and interpreted along with qualitative data gathered from interviews and direct observations.

### Issues in Naturalistic Observation

**Participation and concealment**     Two related issues facing the researcher are whether to be a participant or nonparticipant in the social setting and whether to conceal his or her purposes from the other people in the setting. Do you become an active participant in the group or do you observe from the outside? Do you conceal your purposes or even your presence, or do you openly let people know what you are doing?

A nonparticipant observer is an outsider who does not become an active part of the setting. In contrast, a participant observer assumes an active, insider role.

Because participant observation allows the researcher to observe the setting from the inside, he or she may be able to experience events in the same way as natural participants. Friendships and other experiences of the participant observer may yield valuable data. A potential problem with participant observation, however, is that the observer may lose the objectivity necessary to conduct scientific observation. Remaining objective may be especially difficult when the researcher already belongs to the group being studied (e.g., a researcher who belongs to Parents Without Partners and who undertakes a study of that group). Remember that naturalistic observation requires accurate description and objective interpretation with no prior hypotheses. If a researcher has some prior reason to either criticize people in the setting or give a glowing report of a particular group, the observations will likely be biased and the conclusions will lack objectivity.

Should the researcher remain concealed or be open about the research purposes? Concealed observation may be preferable because the presence of the observer may influence and alter the behavior of those being observed. Imagine how a nonconcealed observer might alter the behavior of high school students in many situations at a school. Thus, concealed observation is less reactive than nonconcealed observation because people are not aware that their behaviors are being observed and recorded. Still, nonconcealed observation may be preferable from an ethical viewpoint: Consider the invasion of privacy when researchers hid under beds in dormitory rooms to discover what college students talk about (Henle & Hubbell, 1938)! Also, people often quickly become used to the observer and behave naturally in the observer's presence. Two well-known examples of nonconcealed observation are provided by television. In the 1999 PBS documentary series "An American Love Story" and in MTV's "Real World," people living together were filmed over an extended period of time. Many viewers of these series are surprised to see how quickly people forget about the cameras and spontaneously reveal many private aspects of their lives.

The decision of whether to conceal one's purpose or presence depends on both ethical concerns and the nature of the particular group and setting being studied. Sometimes a participant observer is nonconcealed to certain members of the group, who give the researcher permission to be part of the group as a concealed observer. Often a concealed observer decides to say nothing directly about his or her purposes but will completely disclose the goals of the research if asked by anyone. Nonparticipant observers are also not concealed when they gain permission to "hang out" in a setting or use interview techniques to gather information (e.g., in Becker's study of marijuana users, some of the people who were interviewed first introduced Becker to their network of friends who were also marijuana users). In actuality, then, there are degrees of participation and concealment: A nonparticipant observer may not become a member of the group, for example, but may over time become accepted as a friend or simply part of the ongoing activities of the group. In sum, researchers who use naturalistic observation to study behavior must carefully determine what their role in the setting will be.

**Defining the scope of the observation**    A researcher employing naturalistic observation may want to study *everything* about a setting. However, this may not be possible, simply because a setting and the questions one might ask about it are so complex. Thus, researchers often must limit the scope of their observations to behaviors that are relevant to the central issues of the study. We previously mentioned Cialdini's interest in social influence in settings such as car dealerships. In this case, Cialdini might focus only on sales techniques and ignore such things as management practices and relationships among salespersons.

**Limits of naturalistic observation**    Naturalistic observation obviously cannot be used to study all issues or phenomena. The approach is most useful when investigating complex social settings both to understand the settings and to develop theories based on the observations. It is less useful for studying well-defined hypotheses under precisely specified conditions.

Field research is also very difficult to do (cf. Green & Wallaf, 1981). Unlike a typical laboratory experiment, field research data collection cannot always be scheduled at a convenient time and place. In fact, field research can be extremely time-consuming, often placing the researcher in an unfamiliar setting for extended periods. Also, in experimental research, the procedures are well defined and the same for each participant, and the data analysis is planned in advance. In naturalistic observation research, however, there is an ever-changing pattern of events, some important and some unimportant; the researcher must record them all and remain flexible in order to adjust to them as research progresses. Finally, the process of analysis that follows the completion of the research is not simple. The researcher must repeatedly sort through the data to develop hypotheses to explain the data, and then make sure all data are consistent with the hypotheses.

If some of the observations are not consistent, the researcher does more analysis. Judd, Smith, and Kidder (1991) emphasize the importance of **negative case analysis.** A negative case is an observation that does not fit the explanatory structure devised by the researcher. When a researcher finds a negative case, he or she revises the hypothesis and again examines all the data to make sure that they are consistent with the new hypothesis. The researcher may even collect additional data in order to examine more closely the circumstances that led to the negative case. Although naturalistic observation research is a difficult and challenging scientific procedure, it yields invaluable knowledge when done well.

## SYSTEMATIC OBSERVATION

**Systematic observation** refers to the careful observation of one or more specific behaviors in a particular setting. This research approach is much less global than naturalistic observation research. The researcher is interested in only a few very specific behaviors, the observations are quantifiable, and the researcher frequently has developed prior hypotheses about the behaviors.

For example, Bakeman and Brownlee (1980; also see Bakeman & Gottman, 1986) were interested in the social behavior of young children. Three-year-olds were videotaped in a room in a "free play" situation. Each child was taped for 100 minutes; observers viewed the videotapes and coded each child's behavior every 15 seconds, using the following coding system:

*Unoccupied:* Child is not doing anything in particular or is simply watching other children.

*Solitary play:* Child plays alone with toys but is not interested in or affected by the activities of other children.

*Together:* Child is with other children but is not occupied with any particular activity.

*Parallel play:* Child plays beside other children with similar toys but does not play with the others.

*Group play:* Child plays with other children, including sharing toys or participating in organized play activities as part of a group of children.

Bakeman and Brownlee were particularly interested in the sequence or order in which the different behaviors were engaged in by the children. They found, for example, that the children rarely went from being unoccupied to engaging in parallel play. However, they frequently went from parallel to group play, indicating that parallel play is a transition state in which children decide whether to go ahead and interact in a group situation.

## Coding Systems

Numerous behaviors can be studied using systematic observation. The researcher must decide which behaviors are of interest, choose a setting in which the behaviors can be observed, and most important, develop a **coding system,** such as the one described, to measure the behaviors. Sometimes the researcher develops the coding system to fit the needs of the particular study. Coding systems should be as simple as possible, allowing observers to easily categorize behaviors. The need for simplicity is especially important when observers are coding live behaviors rather than viewing videotapes that can be reviewed or even coded on a frame-by-frame basis. An example of a simple coding system comes from a study by Barton, Baltes, and Orzech (1980) in which nursing home residents and staff were observed. Only five categories were used: (1) resident independent behavior (e.g., doing something by oneself, such as grooming), (2) resident dependent behavior (asking for help), (3) staff independence-supporting behavior (praise or encouragement for independence), (4) staff dependency-supportive behavior (giving assistance or encouraging taking assistance), and (5) other, unrelated behaviors of both residents and staff. Their results illustrate one of the problems of care facilities: Staff perceive themselves as "care providers" and so most frequently engage in dependency-supportive behaviors. Does this behavior lead to greater dependency by the residents and perhaps a loss of feelings of control? If so, the consequences may be serious: Recall the Rodin and Langer (1977) experiment discussed in Chapter 4, in which feelings of control led to greater happiness and general well-being among nursing home residents.

Sometimes researchers can use coding systems that have been developed by others. For example, the Family Interaction Coding System (FICS; see Patterson & Moore, 1979) consists of 29 categories of interaction; these are grouped as aversive (hostility), prosocial (helping), and general activities. Most of the research using the FICS has centered on how children's aversive behaviors are learned and maintained in a family. Another coding system is SYMLOG, the System for the Multiple Level Observation of Groups (Bales & Cohen, 1979). SYMLOG provides a way of coding interactions of individuals in groups on three major dimensions: unfriendly-friendly, emotionally expressive-instrumentally controlled, and submissive-dominant. A major advantage of using a previously developed coding system is that a body of research already exists in which the system has proven useful, and training materials are usually available.

### Methodological Issues

**Equipment**    We should briefly mention several methodological issues in systematic observation. The first concerns equipment. You can directly observe behavior and code it at the same time; for example, you could directly observe and record the behavior of children in a classroom or couples interacting on campus using paper-and-pencil measures. However, it is becoming more common to use videotape equipment to make such observations. Video recorders have the advantage of providing a permanent record of the behavior observed that can be coded later. Your observations can be coded on a clipboard; and a stopwatch is sometimes useful for recording the duration of events. Alternatively, computer-based recording devices can be used to code the observed behaviors, as well as to keep track of their duration.

**Reactivity**    A second issue is **reactivity**—the possibility that the presence of the observer will affect people's behaviors (see Chapter 5). As noted previously, reactivity can be reduced by concealed observation. The use of one-way mirrors and hidden microphones or cameras can conceal the presence of an observer. Alternatively, reactivity can be reduced by allowing enough time for people to become used to the presence of the observer and any recording equipment.

**Reliability**    Recall from Chapter 5 that reliability refers to the degree to which a measurement reflects a true score rather than a measurement error. Reliable measures are stable, consistent, and precise. When conducting systematic observation, two or more raters are usually used to code behavior. Reliability is indicated by a high agreement among the raters. Very high levels of agreement are reported in virtually all published research using systematic observation (generally 80% agreement or higher). For some large-scale research programs in which many observers will be employed over a period of years, observers are first trained using videotapes, and their observations during training are checked for agreement with previous observers (cf. Bakeman & Gottman, 1986).

**Sampling**   Finally, sampling of behaviors should be mentioned. For many research questions, samples of behavior taken over a long period provide more accurate and useful data than single, short observations. Consider a study on television viewing in homes (Anderson, Lorch, Field, Collins, & Nathan, 1986). The researchers wanted to know how members of families watch TV. They could have studied short periods of TV watching, perhaps during a single evening; however, such data can be distorted by short-term trends—time of day, a particular show, or the variations in family activities that influence TV viewing. A better method of addressing the question is to observe TV viewing over time, which is exactly what the researchers did. Video recorders and cameras were installed in the homes of 99 families; the equipment was set to record in a time-lapse mode whenever the TV was turned on. Using this method, almost 5,000 hours of TV viewing were recorded. Because coding this much data would be time-consuming, to analyze the data Anderson et al. sampled a segment of TV viewing every 55 minutes. Among other things, they found that no one is watching the TV 15% of the time and that TV viewing increases up to age 10 and then begins to decrease.

## CASE STUDIES

A **case study** provides a description of an individual. This individual is usually a person, but it may also be a setting such as a business, school, or neighborhood. A naturalistic observation study is sometimes called a case study, and in fact the naturalistic observation and case study approaches sometimes overlap. We have included case studies as a separate category in this chapter because case studies do not necessarily involve naturalistic observation. Instead, the case study may be a description of a patient by a clinical psychologist or a historical account of an event such as a model school that failed. A **psychobiography** is a type of case study in which a researcher applies psychological theory to explain the life of an individual, usually an important historical figure (cf. Elms, 1994). Thus, case studies may use such techniques as library research and telephone interviews with persons familiar with the case but no direct observation at all (cf. Yin, 1994).

Depending on the purpose of the investigation, the case study may present the individual's history, symptoms, characteristic behaviors, reactions to situations, or responses to treatment. Typically, a case study is done when an individual possesses a particularly rare, unusual, or noteworthy condition. One famous case study involved a man with an amazing ability to recall information (Luria, 1968). The man, called "S.," could remember long lists and passages with ease, apparently using mental imagery for his memory abilities. Luria also described some of the drawbacks of S.'s ability. For example, he frequently had difficulty concentrating because mental images would spontaneously appear and interfere with his thinking. Another case study example concerns language development; it was provided by "Genie," a child who was kept isolated in her room, tied to a chair, and never spoken to until she was discovered at the age of 13½ (Curtiss, 1977). Genie, of course, lacked any language skills. Her case provided psychologists and linguists with the opportunity to attempt to teach her language skills and discover which skills could be learned. Apparently, Genie was able to acquire some rudimentary language skills, such as forming childlike sentences, but she never developed full language abilities.

A recent example illustrates the way that individuals with particular types of brain damage can allow researchers to test hypotheses (Stone, Cosmides, Tooby, Kroll, & Knight, 2002). The individual in question, R.M., had extensive limbic system damage. The researchers were interested in studying the ability to detect cheaters in social exchange relationships. Social exchange is at the core of our relationships: One person provides goods or services for another person in exchange for some other resource. Stone et al. were seeking evidence that social exchange can evolve in a species only when there is a biological mechanism for detecting cheaters; that is, those who do not reciprocate by fulfilling their end of the bargain. R.M. completed two types of reasoning problems. One type involved detecting violations of social exchange rules (e.g., you must fulfill a requirement if you receive a particular benefit); the other type focused on nonsocial precautionary action rules (e.g., you must take this precaution if you engage in a particular hazardous behavior). Individuals with no brain injury do equally well on both types of measures. However, R.M. performed very poorly on the social exchange problems but did well on the precautionary problems, as well as other general measures of cognitive ability. This finding supports the hypothesis that our ability to engage in social exchange relationships is grounded in the development of a biological mechanism that differs from general cognitive abilities.

Case studies are valuable in informing us of conditions that are rare or unusual and thus providing unique data about some psychological phenomenon, such as memory, language, or social exchange. Insights gained through a case study may also lead to the development of hypotheses that can be tested using other methods.

## ARCHIVAL RESEARCH

**Archival research** involves using previously compiled information to answer research questions. The researcher does not actually collect the original data. Instead, he or she analyzes existing data such as statistics that are part of public records (e.g., number of divorce petitions filed), reports of anthropologists, the content of letters to the editor, or information contained in computer databases. Judd, Smith, and Kidder (1991) distinguish among three types of archival research data: statistical records, survey archives, and written records.

## Statistical Records

Statistical records are collected by many public and private organizations. The U.S. Census Bureau maintains the most extensive set of statistical records available to researchers for analysis. There are also numerous less obvious ones, including public health statistics and test score records kept by testing organizations such as the Educational Testing Service.

The sport of baseball is known for the extensive records that are kept on virtually every aspect of every game ever played. These statistics are available to anyone who wants to examine them. Reifman, Larrick, and Fein (1991) used two sources of archival data, baseball statistics and daily temperature, to study the relationship between heat and aggression. They examined all daytime major league games played in outdoor stadiums over a 3-year period to record the number of batters hit by a pitch. Hitting the batter is the measure of aggression. They also looked at the temperature on each day of the games. The results showed a clear link between temperature and aggression. More batters were hit on days when the temperature was above 90° (Fahrenheit) than when it was in the 80s. The number was lower still when temperatures were below 80°.

Public records can also be used as sources of archival data. For example, Gwaltney-Gibbs (1986) used marriage license applications in one Oregon county in 1970 and 1980 to study changing patterns of premarital cohabitation. She found that only 13% of the couples used the same address on the application in 1970 but that 53% gave the same address in 1980. She was also able to relate cohabitation to other variables such as age and race. The findings were interpreted as support for the notion that premarital cohabitation has become a new step in patterns of courtship leading to marriage. Another example of the use of public records to study the relationship between temperature and aggression is research by Anderson and Anderson (1984) that demonstrated a relationship between temperature and violent crime statistics in two U.S. cities. Data on both variables are readily available from agencies that keep these statistics.

## Survey Archives

Survey archives consist of data from surveys that are stored on computers and available to researchers who wish to analyze them. Major polling organizations make many of their surveys available. Also, many universities are part of the Inter-university Consortium for Political and Social Research (ICPSR), which makes survey archive data available. One very useful data set is the General Social Survey, a series of surveys funded by the National Science Foundation and intended as a resource for social scientists (Russell & Megaard, 1988). Each survey includes over 200 questions covering a range of topics such as attitudes, life satisfaction, health, religion, education, age, gender, and race. Survey archives are now becoming available via the Internet at sites that enable researchers to analyze the data online. Survey archives are extremely important because most researchers do not have the financial resources to conduct surveys of randomly selected national samples; the archives allow them to access such samples to test their ideas.

### Written and Mass Communication Records

Written records are documents such as diaries and letters that have been preserved by historical societies, ethnographies of other cultures written by anthropologists, and public documents as diverse as speeches by politicians or bulletin board messages left by Internet users. Mass communication records include books, magazine articles, movies, television programs, and newspapers.

As an example of archival research using such records, Schoeneman and Rubanowitz (1985) studied "Dear Abby" and "Ann Landers" letters published in newspapers. The researchers were interested in the causes people gave for problems they wrote about in their letters. Letters were coded according to whether the writers were discussing themselves or other people and whether the causes discussed in the letters were internal (caused by the person's own actions or personality) or external (caused by some situation external to the person). When people discussed themselves, the causes of the problems were primarily external, but when other people were described, more of the problems were seen as internally caused (also see Fischer, Schoeneman, & Rubanowitz, 1987).

Archival data may also be used in cross-cultural research to examine aspects of social structure that differ from society to society. A variable such as the presence versus absence of monogamous marital relationships cannot be studied in a single society. In North America, for example, monogamy is the norm and bigamy is illegal. By looking at a number of cultures, some monogamous and some not, we can increase our understanding of the reasons that one system or the other comes to be preferred. This method was adopted in a study by Rosenblatt and Cozby (1972) on the role of freedom of choice in mate selection. Some societies have considerable restrictions on whom one can marry; other societies give great freedom of choice to young people in deciding on a spouse. In the study, anthropologists' descriptions (called *ethnographies*) of a number of societies were used to rate the societies as being either low or high in terms of freedom of choice of spouse. The ethnographies also provided information on a number of other variables. The results indicated that when there is freedom of choice of spouse, romantic love and sexual attraction are important bases for mate selection, but that greater antagonism also is present in the interactions among young males and females. The Rosenblatt and Cozby study used the Human Relations Area Files (HRAF), a resource available in many university libraries, to obtain information from the ethnographies. The HRAF consists of anthropologists' descriptions of many cultures, which have been organized according to categories such as courtship and marriage customs, and child-rearing practices. Thus, it is relatively easy to find specific information from many societies by using the HRAF.

## Content Analysis of Documents

**Content analysis** is the systematic analysis of existing documents such as the ones described in this section (see Weber, 1990). Like systematic observation, content analysis requires researchers to devise coding systems that raters can use to quantify the information in the documents. Sometimes the coding is quite simple and straightforward; for example, it is easy to code whether the addresses of the bride and groom on marriage license applications are the same or different. More often, the researcher must define categories in order to code the information. In the Rosenblatt and Cozby cross-cultural study, raters had to read the ethnographic information and determine whether each culture was low or high on freedom of choice of spouse. Raters were trained to use the coding system, and interrater reliability coefficients were computed to ensure that there was high agreement among the raters. Similar procedures would be used in studies examining archival documents such as speeches, magazine articles, television shows, and letters.

The use of archival data allows researchers to study interesting questions, some of which could not be studied in any other way. Archival data are a valuable supplement to more traditional data collection methods. There are at least two major problems with the use of archival data, however. First, the desired records may be difficult to obtain: They may be placed in long-forgotten storage places, or they may have been destroyed. Second, we can never be completely sure of the accuracy of information collected by someone else.

## DESCRIBING PERSONALITY AND INDIVIDUAL DIFFERENCES

How do we study personality? How do we observe a personality characteristic such as extraversion? As we noted in Chapter 4, extraversion and other personality variables are theoretical constructs that cannot be directly observed. Researchers devise measures to assess personality. A topic this complex requires both quantitative and qualitative approaches. A major area of psychology has been the development of quantitative measures of individual differences in psychological attributes such as intelligence, self-esteem, extraversion, and depression. For example, Costa and McCrae (1985) developed the NEO Personality Inventory (NEO-PI) to measure five major dimensions of personality: neuroticism, extraversion, openness to experience, agreeableness, and conscientiousness. Other tests focus on very specific characteristics of a person, such as "sensation-seeking," "social anxiety," and "loving style." Still other measures focus on clinical diagnosis (e.g., MMPI-II), helping people decide on possible careers (e.g., Vocational Interest Inventory), and screening applicants for jobs through administration of a variety of measures.

An important area of personality research studies the way that personality characteristics are related to a person's behavior and interactions with others. For example, you might want to study how individuals who are categorized as introverted or extraverted recall material read under distracting versus quiet conditions. We will explore research designs that address such issues in Chapter 8.

Psychologists study many individual difference attributes in addition to personality. They study interests and aptitudes related to career choices and job performance, for example. The field of psychological testing and assessment focuses on developing accurate measures of psychological characteristics and conducting research that uses the measures to help us better understand human behavior.

It is usually wise to use existing measures of psychological characteristics rather than develop your own. Existing measures have reliability and validity data and you can compare your findings with prior research that uses the measure. Sources of information about psychological tests that have been developed include the *Mental Measurements Yearbook* (Conoley & Kramer, 1989) and *Test Critiques* (Keyser & Sweetland, 1991). These reference books are published periodically and contain descriptions and evaluations of many psychological tests.

Although most attempts to understand personality in recent years have been quantitative, qualitative approaches to understanding personality are being used increasingly as an alternative to quantitative research. For example, researchers are focusing on narrative accounts of life histories to gain insights into the ways that personalities develop and are influenced by both common and unique, idiosyncratic life events (Baumeister & Newman, 1994; Josselson & Lieblich, 1993). These accounts may come from various sources such as interviews and autobiographical writings. The accounts may be relatively unfocused, or they may target particular parts of one's life such as personal relationships. Most important, such qualitative analyses may yield data that are difficult to obtain with traditional personality measures, challenge traditional theories of personality, and lead to a more complete understanding of human behavior.

This chapter has provided you with a great deal of information about important qualitative and quantitative observational methods that can be used to study a variety of questions about behavior. In the next chapter, we will explore a very common way of finding out about human behavior—simply asking people to use self-reports to tell us about themselves.

## Study Terms

Archival research

Case study

Coding system

Content analysis

Naturalistic observation

Negative case analysis

Participant observation

Psychobiography

Reactivity

Systematic observation

## Review Questions

1. What is naturalistic observation? How does a researcher collect data when conducting naturalistic observation research?
2. Why are the data in naturalistic observation research primarily qualitative?
3. Distinguish between participant and nonparticipant observation; between concealed and nonconcealed observation.
4. What is systematic observation? Why are the data from systematic observation primarily quantitative?
5. What is a coding system? What are some important considerations when developing a coding system?
6. What is a case study? When are case studies used? What is a psychobiography?
7. What is archival research? What are the major sources of archival data?
8. What is content analysis?

## Activity Questions

1. Some questions are more readily answered using quantitative techniques, and others are best addressed through qualitative techniques or a combination of both approaches. Suppose you are interested in how a parent's alcoholism affects the life of an adolescent. Develop a research question best answered using quantitative techniques and another research question better suited to qualitative techniques. A quantitative question is, "Are adolescents with alcoholic parents more likely to have criminal records?" and a qualitative question is, "What issues do alcoholic parents introduce in their adolescent's peer relationships?"
2. Devise a simple coding system to do a content analysis of print advertisements in popular magazines. Apply the system to an issue of a magazine and describe your findings.

Overall, how do you feel about your future?

☑ very opimistic
☐ somewhat optimistic
☐ somewhat pessimistic
☐ very pessimistic

# Asking People About Themselves: Survey Research

Survey research employs questionnaires and interviews to ask people to provide information about themselves—their attitudes and beliefs, demographics (age, gender, income, marital status, and so on) and other facts, and past or intended future behaviors. This chapter will explore methods of designing and conducting surveys, including sampling techniques.

## WHY CONDUCT SURVEYS?

During the past few weeks, I have read numerous stories about survey findings in my local newspaper. One was a survey of California voters to measure their preference for the two candidates for governor. Another was a nationwide survey asking adults about their current thoughts and emotions regarding the events of September 11, 2001. A nationwide survey of teenagers reported their experiences with violence. I also encountered surveys at work. My department surveyed recent graduates of the master's degree program to ask about their employment and perceptions of their educational experience in the program. A student administered a questionnaire to victims of domestic violence living at two local shelters to measure their experiences with police. Closer to home, my wife purchased a new car a few weeks ago and received a survey from the manufacturer asking about her satisfaction with the dealer and car quality. Surveys are clearly a common and important method of studying behavior.

Surveys provide us with a methodology for asking people to tell us about themselves. They have become extremely important as society demands data about issues rather than only intuition and anecdotes. My department needs data from graduates to help determine changes that should be made to the curriculum. Auto companies want data from buyers to assess and improve product quality and customer satisfaction. Without collecting such data, we are totally dependent upon stories we might hear or letters that a graduate or customer might write. Other surveys can be important for making public policy decisions by lawmakers and public agencies. In basic research, many important variables,

FIGURE 7.1

Relationship between
hours of work and
grade point average

*Source:* "Negative Correlates
of Part-time Employment
During Adolescence," by
L. Steinberg and S. M.
Dornbusch, 1991, *Develop-
mental Psychology, 27,*
pp. 303–313. Copyright
© 1991 by the American
Psychological Association.
Reprinted by permission.

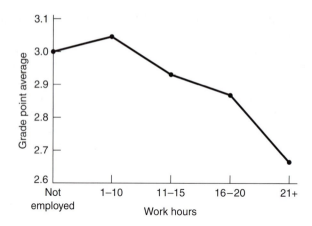

including attitudes, current emotional states, and self-reports of behaviors, are
most easily studied using questionnaires or interviews.

We often think of survey data providing a "snapshot" of how people think and
behave at a given point in time. However, the survey method is also an important
way for researchers to study relationships among variables and ways that attitudes
and behaviors change over time. For example, Steinberg and Dornbusch (1991) examined the relationship between the number of hours that high school students
work and variables such as grade point average, drug and alcohol use, and psycho-
somatic distress. The sample consisted of 3,989 students in grades 10–12 at nine
high schools in California and Wisconsin. The researchers found that "long work
hours during the school year are associated with lower investment and performance in school, greater psychological and somatic distress, drug and alcohol use,
delinquency, and autonomy from parents" (Steinberg & Dornbusch, 1991, p. 304).
Figure 7.1 shows a typical finding: There are some positive aspects of working fewer
than 10 hours per week (as opposed to not being employed); however, increasingly
negative effects are associated with longer work hours.

Survey research is also important as a complement to experimental research
findings. Recall from Chapter 2 that Winograd and Soloway (1986) conducted
experiments on the conditions that lead to forgetting where we place something.
To study this topic using survey methods, Brown and Rahhal (1994) asked both
younger and older adults about their actual experiences when they hid something and later forgot its location. They reported that older adults take longer
than younger adults to find the object, older adults hide objects from potential
thieves, whereas younger people hide things from friends and relatives. Interestingly, most lost objects are eventually found, usually by accident in a location
that had been searched previously. This research illustrates a point made in previous chapters that multiple methods are needed to understand any behavior.

An assumption that underlies the use of questionnaires and interviews is
that people are willing and able to provide truthful and accurate answers. Re-

searchers have addressed this issue by studying possible biases in the way people respond. A **response set** is a tendency to respond to all questions from a particular perspective rather than to provide answers that are directly related to the questions. Thus, response sets can affect the usefulness of data obtained from self-reports. The most common response set is called social desirability, or "faking good." The social desirability response set leads the individual to answer in the most socially acceptable way—the way that "most people" are perceived to respond or the way that would reflect most favorably on the person. Social desirability can be a problem in many research areas, but it is probably most acute when the question concerns a sensitive topic such as violent or aggressive behavior, substance abuse, or sexual practices. However, it should not be assumed that people consistently misrepresent themselves. Jourard (1969) suggested that people are most likely to lie when they don't trust the researcher. If the researcher openly and honestly communicates the purposes and uses of the research, promises to provide feedback about the results, and assures confidentiality, then the participants can reasonably be expected to give honest responses.

We turn now to the major considerations in survey research: constructing the questions that are asked, the methods for presenting the questions, and sampling of the individuals taking part in the research.

## CONSTRUCTING QUESTIONS TO ASK

A great deal of thought must be given to writing questions for questionnaires and interviews. This section describes some of the most important factors to consider when constructing questions.

### Defining the Research Objectives

When constructing questions for a survey, the first thing the researcher must do is explicitly determine the research objectives: What is it that he or she wishes to know? The survey questions must be tied to the research questions that are being addressed. Too often, surveys get out of hand when researchers begin to ask any question that comes to mind about a topic without considering exactly what useful information will be gained by doing so. This process will usually require the researcher to decide on the type of questions to ask. As noted previously, there are three general types of survey questions (Judd, Smith, & Kidder, 1991).

**Attitudes and beliefs**    Questions about attitudes and beliefs focus on the ways that people evaluate and think about issues. Should more money be spent on mental health services? Are you satisfied with the way that police responded to your call? How do you evaluate this instructor?

**Facts and demographics**    Factual questions ask people to indicate things they know about themselves and their situation. In most studies, asking some demographic information is necessary to adequately describe your sample. Age and gender are typically asked. Depending on the topic of the study, questions on such information as ethnicity, income, marital status, employment status, and number of children might be included. Obviously, if you are interested in making comparisons among groups, such as males and females, you must ask the relevant information about group membership. It is unwise to ask such questions if you have no real reason to use the information, however.

Other factual information you might ask will depend on the topic of your survey. Each year, *Consumer Reports* magazine asks me to tell them about the repairs that have been necessary on many of the products that I own, such as my car and dishwasher. Factual questions about illnesses and other medical information would be asked in a survey of health and quality of life.

**Behaviors**    Other survey questions can focus on past behaviors or intended future behaviors. How many times last week did you exercise for 20 minutes or longer? How many children do you plan to have? Have you ever been so depressed that you called in sick to work?

### Question Wording

A great deal of care is necessary to write the very best questions for a survey. Cognitive psychologists have identified a number of potential problems with question wording (see Graesser, Kennedy, Wiemer-Hastings, & Ottati, 1999). Many of the problems stem from a difficulty with understanding the question, including (a) unfamiliar technical terms, (b) vague or imprecise terms, (c) ungrammatical sentence structure, (d) phrasing that overloads working memory, and (e) embedding the question with misleading information. Here is a question that illustrates some of the problems identified by Graesser et al.:

> Did your mother, father, full-blooded sisters, full-blooded brothers, daughters, or sons ever have a heart attack or myocardial infarction?

There is memory overload because of the length of the question and the need to keep track of all those relatives while reading the question, and the respondent must worry about two different diagnoses with regard to each relative. Further, the term *myocardial infarction* may be unfamiliar to most people. How do you write questions to avoid such problems? The following items are important to consider when you are writing questions.

**Simplicity**    The questions asked in a survey should be relatively simple. People should be able to easily understand and respond to the questions. Avoid jargon and technical terms that people won't understand. Sometimes, however, you have to make the question a bit more complex to make it easier to understand. Usually this occurs when you need to define a term or describe an issue prior to asking the question. Thus, before asking whether someone approves of Proposition J, you will probably want to provide a brief description of the content of this ballot measure.

**Double-barreled questions**    Avoid "double-barreled" questions that ask two things at once. A question such as "Should senior citizens be given more money for recreation centers and food assistance programs?" is difficult to answer because it taps two potentially very different attitudes. If you are interested in both issues, ask two questions.

**Loaded questions**    A loaded question is written to lead people to respond in one way. For example, the questions "Do you favor eliminating the wasteful excesses in the public school budget?" and "Do you favor reducing the public school budget?" will likely elicit different answers. Or consider that men are less likely to say they have "raped" someone than that they have "forced sex"; similarly, women are less likely to say they have been raped than forced to have unwanted sex (Koss, 1992). Questions that include emotionally charged words such as *rape, waste, immoral, ungodly,* or *dangerous* may influence the way that people respond and thus lead to biased conclusions.

**Negative wording**    Avoid phrasing questions with negatives. This question is phrased negatively: "The city should not approve the proposed women's shelter." Agreement with this question means disagreement with the proposal. This phrasing can confuse people and result in inaccurate answers. A better format would be: "The city should approve the proposed women's shelter."

**"Yea-saying" and "nay-saying"**    When you ask several questions about a topic, there is a possibility that a respondent will employ a response set to agree or disagree with all the questions. Such a tendency is referred to as **"yea-saying"** or **"nay-saying."** The problem here is that the respondent may in fact be expressing true agreement, but alternatively may simply be agreeing with anything you say. One way to detect this response set is to word the questions so that consistent agreement is unlikely. For example, a study of family communication patterns might ask people how much they agree with the following statements: "The members of my family spend a lot of time together" and "I spend most of my weekends with friends." Similarly, a measure of loneliness (e.g., Russell, Peplau, & Cutrona, 1980) will phrase some questions so that agreement means the respondent is lonely ("I feel isolated from others") and others with the meaning reversed so that disagreement indicates loneliness (e.g., "I feel part of a group of friends"). Although it is possible that someone could legitimately agree with both items, consistently agreeing or disagreeing with a set of related questions phrased in both standard and reversed formats is an indicator that the individual is "yea-saying" or "nay-saying."

Graesser and his colleagues have developed a computer program called *QUAID* (Question Understanding Aid) that analyzes question wording. Researchers can try out their questions online at the QUAID Web site (http://mnemosyne.csl.psyc.memphis.edu/quaid).

## RESPONSES TO QUESTIONS

### Closed- Versus Open-Ended Questions

Questions may be either closed- or open-ended. With closed-ended questions, a limited number of response alternatives are given; with open-ended questions, respondents are free to answer in any way they like. Thus, you could ask a person: "What is the most important thing for children to prepare them for life?" followed by a list of answers from which to choose (a closed-ended question) or you could leave this question open-ended for the person to provide the answer.

Using closed-ended questions is a more structured approach; they are easier to code and the response alternatives are the same for everyone. Open-ended questions require time to categorize and code the responses and are therefore more costly. Sometimes a respondent's response cannot be categorized at all because the response doesn't make sense or the person couldn't think of an answer. Still, an open-ended question can yield valuable insights into what people are thinking. Open-ended questions are most useful when the researcher needs to know what people are thinking and how they naturally view their world; closed-ended questions are more likely to be used when the dimensions of the variables are well defined.

Schwarz (1999) points out that the two approaches can sometimes lead to different conclusions. He cites the results of a survey question about preparing children for life. When "To think for themselves" was one alternative in a closed-ended list, 62% chose this option; however, only 5% gave this answer when the open-ended format was used. This finding points to the need to have a good understanding of the topic when asking closed-ended questions.

### Number of Response Alternatives

With closed-ended questions, there are a fixed number of response alternatives. In public opinion surveys, a simple "yes or no" or "agree or disagree" dichotomy is often sufficient. In more basic research, it is often preferable to have a sufficient number of alternatives to allow people to express themselves—for example, a 5- or 7-point scale ranging from "strongly agree to strongly disagree" or "very positive to very negative." Such a scale might appear as follows:

Strongly agree ____ ____ ____ ____ ____ ____ ____ Strongly disagree

### Rating Scales

Rating scales such as the one just shown are very common in many areas of research. Rating scales ask people to provide "how much" judgments on any number of dimensions—amount of agreement, liking, or confidence, for example. Rating scales can have many different formats. The format that is used depends on factors such as the topic being investigated. Perhaps the best way to gain an understanding of the variety of formats is simply to look at a few examples. The simplest and most direct scale presents people with five or seven response alternatives with the endpoints on the scale labeled to define the extremes. For example,

Students at the university should be required to pass a comprehensive examination to graduate.

Strongly agree ____ ____ ____ ____ ____ ____ ____ Strongly disagree

How confident are you that the defendant is guilty of attempted murder?

Not at all confident _____ _____ _____ _____ _____ Very confident

**Graphic rating scale**    A graphic rating scale requires a mark along a continuous 100-millimeter line that is anchored with descriptions at each end.

How would you rate the movie you just saw?

Not very enjoyable _____ Very enjoyable

A ruler is then placed on the line to obtain the score on a scale that ranges from 0 to 100.

**Semantic differential scale**    The semantic differential scale is a measure of the meaning of concepts that was developed by Osgood and his associates (Osgood, Suci, & Tannenbaum, 1957). Respondents rate any concept—persons, objects, behaviors, ideas—on a series of bipolar adjectives using 7-point scales.

*Smoking Cigarettes*

| Good | ____ : ____ : ____ : ____ : ____ : ____ : ____ | Bad |
| Strong | ____ : ____ : ____ : ____ : ____ : ____ : ____ | Weak |
| Active | ____ : ____ : ____ : ____ : ____ : ____ : ____ | Passive |

Research on the semantic differential shows that virtually anything can be measured using this technique. Ratings of specific things (marijuana), places (the student center), people (the governor, accountants), ideas (abortion, tax reduction), and behaviors (attending church, using public transit) can be obtained. A large body of research shows that the concepts are rated along three basic dimensions: the first and most important is *evaluation* (e.g., adjectives such as good–bad, wise–foolish, kind–cruel); the second is *activity* (active–passive, slow–fast, excitable–calm); and the third is *potency* (weak–strong, hard–soft, large–small).

**Nonverbal scale for children**    Young children may not understand the types of scales we've just described, but they are able to give ratings. For example, you could ask children to point to the face that shows how they feel about a toy:

Point to the face that shows how you feel about the toy.

### Labeling Response Alternatives

The examples thus far have labeled only the endpoints on the rating scale. Respondents decide the meaning of the other response alternatives. This is a reasonable approach, and people are usually able to use such scales without difficulty. Sometimes researchers need to provide labels to more clearly define the meaning of each alternative. Here is a fairly standard alternative to the agree-disagree scale shown previously:

| Strongly Agree | Agree | Undecided | Disagree | Strongly Disagree |
| --- | --- | --- | --- | --- |

This type of scale assumes that the middle alternative is a "neutral" point halfway between the endpoints. Sometimes, however, a perfectly balanced scale may not be possible or desirable. Consider a scale asking a college professor to rate a student for a job or graduate program. This particular scale asks for comparative ratings of students:

In comparison with other graduates, how would you rate this student's potential for success?

| Lower 50 % | Upper 50% | Upper 25% | Upper 10% | Upper 5% |
| --- | --- | --- | --- | --- |

Notice that most of the alternatives are asking people to make a rating in terms of the top 25% of students. This is done because students who apply for such programs tend to be very bright and motivated, and so professors rate them favorably. The wording of the alternatives attempts to force the raters to make finer distinctions among generally very good students.

Labeling alternatives is particularly interesting when asking about the frequency of a behavior. For example, you might ask, "How often do you exercise for at least 20 minutes?" What kind of scale should you use to let people answer this question? You could list (1) never, (2) rarely, (3) sometimes, (4) frequently. These terms convey your meaning but they are vague. Here is another set of alternatives, similar to ones described by Schwarz (1999):

_____ less than twice a week

_____ about twice a week

_____ about four times a week

_____ about six times a week

_____ at least once each day

A different scale might be:

_____ less than once per month

_____ about once a month

_____ about once every two weeks

_____ about once a week

_____ more than once per week

Schwarz (1999) calls the first scale a high-frequency scale because most alternatives indicate a high frequency of exercise. The other scale is referred to as low frequency. Schwarz points out that the labels should be chosen carefully because people may interpret the meaning of the scale differently, depending on the labels used. If you were actually asking the exercise question, you might decide on alternatives different from the ones described here. Moreover, your choice should be influenced by factors such as the population you are studying. If you are studying people who generally exercise a lot, you will be more likely to use a higher-frequency scale than you would if you were studying people who generally don't exercise a great deal.

## FINALIZING THE QUESTIONNAIRE

### Formatting the Questionnaire

A written questionnaire itself should appear attractive and professional. It should be neatly typed and free of spelling errors. People should find it easy to identify the questions and the response alternatives to the questions. Leave enough space between questions so people don't become confused when reading the questionnaire. If you have a particular scale format, such as a 5-point rating scale, use it consistently. Don't change from 5- to 4- to 7-point scales, for example.

It is also a good idea to carefully consider the sequence in which you will ask your questions. In general, it is best to ask the most interesting and important questions first to capture the attention of your respondents and motivate them to complete the survey. Roberson and Sundstrom (1990) obtained the highest return rates in an employee attitude survey when important questions were presented first and demographic questions were asked last. In addition, it is a good idea to group questions together when they address a similar theme or topic. Doing so will make your survey appear more professional, and your respondents are more likely to take it seriously.

### Refining Questions

Before actually administering the survey, it is a good idea to give the questions to a small group of people and have them "think aloud" while answering them. The participants might be chosen from the population being studied, or they could be friends or colleagues who can give reasonable responses to the questions. For the "think aloud" procedure, you will need to ask the individuals to tell you how they interpret each question and how they respond to the response alternatives. This procedure can provide valuable information that you can use to improve the questions. (The importance of pilot studies such as this is discussed further in Chapter 9.)

## ADMINISTERING SURVEYS

There are two ways to administer surveys. One is to use a written questionnaire. Respondents read the questions and indicate their responses on a form. The other way is to use an interview format. An interviewer asks the questions and records the responses in a personal verbal interaction. Both questionnaires and interviews can be presented to respondents in several ways. Let's examine the various methods of administering surveys.

### Questionnaires

With questionnaires, the questions are presented in written format and the respondents write their answers. There are several positive features of using questionnaires. First, they are generally less costly than interviews. They also allow the respondent to be completely anonymous as long as no identifying information (e.g., name, Social Security or driver's license number) is asked. However, questionnaires require that the respondents be able to read and understand the questions. In addition, many people find it boring to sit by themselves reading questions and then providing answers; thus, there may be a problem of motivation. Questionnaires can be administered in person to groups or individuals, through the mail, on the Internet, and with other technologies.

**Personal administration to groups or individuals**    Often researchers are able to distribute questionnaires to groups or individuals. This might be a college class, parents attending a school meeting, people attending a new employee orientation, or individual students waiting for an appointment with an advisor. An advantage of this approach is that you have a captive audience that is likely to complete the questionnaire once they start it. Also, the researcher is present so people can ask questions if necessary.

Mail surveys    Surveys can be mailed to individuals at a home or business address. This is a very inexpensive way of contacting the people who were selected for the sample. However, the mail format is a drawback because of potentially low response rates: The questionnaire can easily be placed aside and forgotten among all the other tasks that people must attend to at home and work. Even if people start to fill out the questionnaire, something may happen to distract them, or they may become bored and simply throw the form in the trash. Some of the methods for increasing response rates are described later in this chapter. Another drawback is that no one is present to help if the person becomes confused or has a question about something.

Internet surveys    It is very easy to design a questionnaire for administration on the Internet. Both open- and closed-ended questions can be written and presented to respondents. After the questionnaire is completed, the responses are immediately sent to the researcher. One of the first problems to consider is how to sample people. Most commonly, surveys are listed on search engines so people who are interested in a topic can discover that someone is interested in collecting data. Some of the major polling organizations are building a database of people interested in participating in surveys. Every time they conduct a survey, they select a sample from the database and send an e-mail invitation to participate. The Internet is also making it easier to obtain samples of people with particular characteristics. There are all sorts of Internet special interest groups for people with a particular illness or of a particular age, marital status, or occupational group. They use newsgroups, e-mail discussions, bulletin boards, and chat rooms to exchange ideas and information. Researchers can ask people who use these resources to volunteer for surveys. One concern about Internet data collection is whether the results will be at all similar to what might be found using traditional methods. Although research on this topic is not extensive, data indicate that Internet results are in fact comparable (Krantz, Ballard, & Scher, 1997; Stanton, 1998).

One problem with Internet data is that ultimately there is an ambiguity about the characteristics of the individuals providing information for the study. To meet ethical guidelines, the researcher will usually state that only persons 18 years of age or older are eligible; yet how is that controlled? People may also misrepresent their age, gender, or ethnicity. We simply do not know if this is a major problem. However, for most research topics it is unlikely that people will go to the trouble of misrepresenting themselves on the Internet to a greater extent than they would with any other method of collecting data.

Other technologies    Researchers are taking advantage of new technologies to assist with the collection of data. An interesting application is seen in studies aimed at sampling people's behaviors and emotions over an extended period of time. The usual approach would be to ask people to provide retrospective accounts of their behaviors or emotions (e.g., how often have you felt angry during the last week?). With pagers, cell phones, and other wireless communication devices, it is possible to contact people at various times and ask them to provide an immediate report of their current activities and emotional reactions. Feldman Barrett & Barrett (2001) refer to this as "computerized experience-sampling." Responses might be provided on a paper questionnaire to be turned in later, or some other technology might be used such as a series of questions administered via Touch-Tone phone or a program running on a personal digital assistant.

### Interviews

The fact that an interview involves an interaction between people has important implications. First, people are often more likely to agree to answer questions for a real person than to answer a mailed questionnaire. Good interviewers become quite skilled in convincing people to participate. Thus, response rates tend to be higher when interviews are used. The interviewer and respondent often establish a rapport that helps motivate the person to answer all the questions and complete the survey. People are more likely to leave questions unanswered on a written questionnaire than in an interview. An important advantage of an interview is that the interviewer can clarify any problems the person might have in understanding questions. Further, an interviewer can ask follow-up questions if needed to help clarify answers.

One potential problem in interviews is called **interviewer bias.** This term describes all of the biases that can arise from the fact that the interviewer is a unique human being interacting with another human. Thus, one potential problem is that the interviewer could subtly bias the respondent's answers by inadvertently showing approval or disapproval of certain answers. Or, if there are several interviewers, each could possess different characteristics (e.g., level of physical attractiveness, age, or race) that might influence the way respondents answer. Another problem is that interviewers may have expectations that could lead them to "see what they are looking for" in the respondents' answers. Such expectations could bias their interpretations of responses or lead them to probe further for an answer from certain respondents but not from others—for example, when questioning whites but not people from other groups or when testing boys but not girls. Careful screening and training of interviewers help to limit such biases.

We can now examine three methods of conducting interviews: face-to-face, telephone, and focus groups.

**Face-to-face interviews**    Face-to-face interviews require that the interviewer and respondent meet to conduct the interview. Usually the interviewer travels to the person's home or office, although sometimes the respondent goes to the interviewer's office. Such interviews tend to be quite expensive and time-consuming. Therefore, they are most likely to be used when the sample size is fairly small and there are clear benefits to a face-to-face interaction.

**Telephone interviews**    Almost all interviews for large-scale surveys are done via telephone. Telephone interviews are less expensive than face-to-face interviews, and they allow data to be collected relatively quickly because many interviewers can work on the same survey at once. Also, computerized telephone survey techniques lower the cost of telephone surveys by reducing labor and data analysis costs. With a computer-assisted telephone interview (CATI) system, the interviewer's questions are prompted on the computer screen, and the data are entered directly into the computer for analysis.

**Focus group interviews**    A focus group is an interview with a group of about 6 to 10 individuals brought together for a period of usually 2–3 hours. Virtually any topic can be explored in a focus group. Often the group members are selected because they have a particular knowledge or interest in the topic. Because the focus group requires people to both spend time and incur some costs traveling to the focus group location, there is usually some sort of monetary or gift incentive to participate.

The questions tend to be open-ended and they are asked of the whole group. An advantage here is that group interaction is possible: People can respond to one another, and one comment can trigger a variety of responses. The interviewer must be skilled in working with groups both to facilitate communication and to deal with problems that may arise, such as one or two persons trying to dominate the discussion or hostility between group members. The group discussion is usually recorded and may be transcribed. The tapes and transcripts are then analyzed to find themes and areas of group consensus and disagreement. Sometimes the transcripts are analyzed with a computer program to search for certain words and phrases. Researchers usually prefer to conduct at least two or three discussion groups on a given topic to make sure that the information gathered is not unique to one group of people. However, because each focus group is time-consuming and costly and provides a great deal of information, researchers don't do very many such groups on any one topic.

## SURVEY DESIGNS TO STUDY CHANGES OVER TIME

Surveys most frequently study people at one point in time. On many occasions, however, researchers wish to make comparisons over time. For example, my local newspaper hires a firm to conduct an annual random survey of county residents. Because the questions are the same each year, it is possible to track changes over time in such variables as satisfaction with the area, attitudes toward the school system, and perceived major problems facing the county. Similarly, a large number of new freshman students are surveyed each year at colleges throughout the United States to study changes in the composition, attitudes, and aspirations of this group (Astin, 1987). Often researchers will test hypotheses concerning how behavior may change over time. For example, Sebald (1986) compared surveys of teenagers in 1963, 1976, and 1982. The survey questions asked about whom the teenagers seek advice from on a variety of issues. The primary finding was that seeking advice from peers rather than from parents increased from 1963 to 1976 but that this peer orientation decreased from 1976 to 1982.

Another way to study changes over time is to conduct a **panel study** in which the same people are surveyed at two or more points in time. In a "two-wave" panel study, people are surveyed at two points in time; in a "three-wave" panel study, there are three surveys; and so on. Panel studies are particularly important when the research question addresses the relationship between one variable at "time one" and another variable at some later "time two." For example, Hill, Rubin, and Peplau (1976) surveyed dating couples to study variables such as attitude similarity. The same people were surveyed later to determine whether they were still in the dating relationship and, if so, how satisfied they were. The results showed that attitude similarity, measured at time one, is a predictor of how long the dating relationship will last.

## SAMPLING FROM A POPULATION

Most research projects involve **sampling** participants from a population of interest. The **population** is composed of all individuals of interest to the researcher. One population of interest in a large public opinion poll, for instance, might be all eligible voters in the United States. This implies that the population of interest does not include people under the age of 18, convicted felons, visitors from other countries, and anyone else not eligible to vote. You might conduct a survey in which your population consists of all students at your college or university. With enough time and money, a survey researcher could conceivably contact everyone in the population. The United States attempts to do this every 10 years with an official census of the entire population. With a relatively small population, you might find it easy to study the entire population.

In most cases, however, studying the entire population would be a massive undertaking. Fortunately, it can be avoided by selecting a sample from the population of interest. With proper sampling, we can use information obtained from the participants (or "respondents") who were sampled to precisely estimate characteristics of the population as a whole. Statistical theory allows us to infer what the population is like, based on data obtained from a sample (the logic underlying what is called *statistical significance* will be addressed in Chapter 13).

### Confidence Intervals

When researchers make inferences about populations, they do so with a certain degree of confidence. Here is a statement that you might see when you read the results of a survey: "The results from the survey are accurate within 3 percentage points, using a 95% level of confidence." What does this tell you? Suppose you asked students to tell you whether they prefer to study at home or at school, and the survey results indicate that 61% prefer to study at home. You now know that the actual population value is probably between 58% and 64%. This is called a **confidence interval**—you can have 95% confidence that the true population value lies within this interval around the obtained sample result. Your best estimate of the population value is the sample value. However, because you have only a sample and not the entire population, your result may be in error. The confidence interval gives you information about the likely amount of the error. The formal term for this error is *sampling error* although you are probably more familiar with the term *margin of error.* Recall that the concept of measurement error was discussed in Chapter 5: When you measure a single individual on a variable, the obtained score may deviate from the true score because of measurement error. Similarly, when you study one sample, the obtained result may deviate from the true population value because of sampling error.

The surveys you often read about in newspapers and the previous example deal with percentages. What about questions that ask for more quantitative information? The logic in this instance is very much the same. For example, if you also ask students to report how many hours and minutes they studied during the previous day, you might find that the average amount of time was 76 minutes. A confidence interval could then be calculated based on the size of the sample; for example, the 95% confidence interval is 76 minutes plus or minus 10 minutes. It is highly likely that the true population value lies within the interval of 66 to 86 minutes. The topic of confidence intervals is discussed again in Chapter 13.

## Sample Size

It is important to note that a larger sample size will reduce the size of the confidence interval. Although the size of the interval is determined by several factors, the most important is sample size. Larger samples are more likely to yield data that accurately reflect the true population value. This statement should make intuitive sense to you; a sample of 200 people from your school should yield more accurate data about your school than a sample of 25 people.

How large should the sample be? The sample size can be determined using a mathematical formula that takes into account the size of the confidence interval and the size of the population you are studying. Table 7.1 shows the sample size needed for a sample percentage to be accurate within plus or minus 3%, 5%, and 10%, given a 95% level of confidence. Note first that you need a larger sample size for increased accuracy. With a population size of 10,000, you need a sample of 370 for 5% accuracy; the needed sample size increases to 964 for 3% accuracy. It is also important to note that sample size is *not* a constant percentage of the population size. Many people believe that proper sampling requires a certain percentage of the population; these people often complain about survey results when they discover that a survey of an entire state was done with "only" 700 or 1,000 people. However, you can see in the table that the needed sample size does not change much even as the population size increases from 5,000 to 100,000 or more. As Fowler (1984) notes, "a sample of 150 people will describe a population of 1,500 or 15 million with virtually the same degree of accuracy . . ." (p. 41).

TABLE 7.1    Sample size and precision of population estimates (95% confidence level)

| Size of population | Precision of Estimate | | |
|---|---|---|---|
| | ±3% | ±5% | ±10% |
| 2,000 | 696 | 322 | 92 |
| 5,000 | 879 | 357 | 94 |
| 10,000 | 964 | 370 | 95 |
| 50,000 | 1,045 | 381 | 96 |
| 100,000 | 1,056 | 383 | 96 |
| Over 100,000 | 1,067 | 384 | 96 |

*Note:* The sample sizes were calculated using conservative assumptions about the nature of the true population values.

## SAMPLING TECHNIQUES

There are two basic techniques for sampling individuals from a population: probability sampling and nonprobability sampling. In **probability sampling,** each member of the population has a specifiable probability of being chosen. Probability sampling is very important when you want to make precise statements about a specific population on the basis of the results of your survey. In **nonprobability sampling,** we don't know the probability of any particular member of the population being chosen. Although this approach is not as sophisticated as probability sampling, we shall see that nonprobability sampling is quite common and useful in many circumstances.

### Probability Sampling

Simple random sampling    With **simple random sampling,** every member of the population has an equal probability of being selected for the sample. If the population has 1,000 members, each has one chance out of a thousand of being selected. Suppose you want to sample students who attend your school. A list of all students would be needed; from that list, students would be chosen at random to form the sample.

When conducting telephone interviews, researchers commonly have a computer randomly generate a list of telephone numbers with the dialing prefixes used for residences in the city or area being studied. This will produce a random sample of the population because most residences have telephones (if many people do not have phones, the sample would be biased). Some companies will even provide researchers with a list of telephone numbers for a survey in which the phone numbers of businesses and numbers that phone companies do not use have been removed. You might note that this procedure results in a random sample of households rather than individuals. Survey researchers use other procedures when it is important to select one person at random from the household.

**Stratified random sampling**    A somewhat more complicated procedure is **stratified random sampling.** The population is divided into subgroups (or strata), and random sampling techniques are then used to select sample members from each stratum. Any number of dimensions could be used to divide the population, but the dimension (or dimensions) chosen should be relevant to the problem under study. For instance, a survey of sexual attitudes might stratify on the basis of age, gender, and amount of education because these factors are related to sexual attitudes. Stratification on the basis of height or hair color would be ridiculous.

Stratified random sampling has the advantage of a built-in assurance that the sample will accurately reflect the numerical composition of the various subgroups. This kind of accuracy is particularly important when some subgroups represent very small percentages of the population. For instance, if African Americans make up 5% of a city of 100,000, a simple random sample of 100 people might not include any African Americans; a stratified random sample would include five African Americans chosen randomly from the population. In practice, when it is important to represent a small group within a population, researchers will "oversample" that group to ensure that a representative sample of the group is surveyed; a large enough sample must be obtained to be able to make inferences about the population. Thus, if your campus has a distribution of students similar to the city described here and you need to compare attitudes of African Americans and Whites, you will need to sample a large percentage of the African American students and only a small percentage of the White students to obtain a reasonable number of respondents from each group.

**Cluster sampling**    It might have occurred to you that obtaining a list of all members of a population might be difficult. What if officials at your school decide that you cannot have access to a list of all students? What if you want to study a population that has no list of members, such as people who work in county health care agencies? In such situations, a technique called **cluster sampling** can be used. Rather than randomly sampling from a list of individuals, the researcher can identify "clusters" of individuals and then sample from these clusters. After the clusters are chosen, all individuals in each cluster are included in the sample. For example, you might conduct the survey of students using cluster sampling by identifying all classes being taught—the classes are the clusters of students. You could then randomly sample from this list of classes and have all members of the chosen classes complete your survey (making sure, of course, that no one completes the survey twice).

Most often, use of cluster sampling requires a series of samples from larger to smaller clusters—a "multistage" approach. For example, a researcher interested in studying county health care agencies might first randomly determine a number of states to sample and then randomly sample counties from each state chosen. The researcher would then go to the health care agencies in each of these counties and study the people who work in them. Note that the main advantage of cluster sampling is that the researcher does not have to sample from lists of individuals to obtain a truly random sample of individuals.

### Nonprobability Sampling

In contrast, nonprobability sampling techniques are quite arbitrary. A population may be defined, but little effort is expended to ensure that the sample accurately represents the population. However, among other things, nonprobability samples are cheap and convenient. Two types of nonprobability sampling are haphazard sampling and quota sampling.

Haphazard sampling     One form of nonprobability sampling is **haphazard sampling** or "convenience" sampling. Haphazard sampling could be called a "take-them-where-you-find-them" method of obtaining participants. Thus, you would select a sample of students from your school in any way that is convenient. You might stand in front of the student union at 9 A.M., ask people who sit around you in your classes to participate, or visit a couple of fraternity and sorority houses. Unfortunately, such procedures are likely to introduce biases into the sample so that the sample may not be an accurate representation of the population of all students. Thus, if you selected your sample from students walking by the student union at 11 A.M., your sample excludes students who don't frequent this location, and it may also eliminate afternoon and evening students. On my own campus, this sample would differ from the population of all students by being younger, working fewer hours, and being more likely to belong to a fraternity or sorority. Sample biases such as these limit your ability to use your sample data to estimate the actual population values. Your results may not generalize to your intended population but instead may describe only the biased sample that you obtained.

Quota sampling     Another form of nonprobability sampling is **quota sampling.** A researcher who uses this technique chooses a sample that reflects the numerical composition of various subgroups in the population. Thus, quota sampling is similar to the stratified sampling procedure previously described; however, random sampling does not occur when you use quota sampling. To illustrate, suppose you want to ensure that your sample of students includes 19% freshmen, 23% sophomores, 26% juniors, 22% seniors, and 10% graduate students because these are the percentages of the classes in the total population. A quota sampling technique would make sure you have these percentages, but you would still collect your data using haphazard techniques. If you didn't get enough graduate students in front of the student union, perhaps you could go to a graduate class to complete the sample. Although quota sampling is a bit more sophisticated than haphazard sampling, the problem remains that no restrictions are placed on how individuals in the various subgroups are chosen. The sample does reflect the numerical composition of the whole population of interest, but respondents within each subgroup are selected in a haphazard manner.

## EVALUATING SAMPLES

Samples should be representative of the population from which they are drawn. A completely unbiased sample is one that is highly representative of the population. How do you create a completely unbiased sample? First, you would randomly sample from a population that contains *all* individuals in the population. Second, you would contact and obtain completed responses from *all* individuals selected to be in the sample. Such standards are rarely achieved. Even if random sampling is used, there can be bias from two sources: the sampling frame used and poor response rates. Moreover, even though nonprobability samples have more potential sources of bias than probability samples, there are many reasons why they are used and should be evaluated positively.

### Sampling Frame

The **sampling frame** is the *actual* population of individuals (or clusters) from which a random sample will be drawn. Rarely will this perfectly coincide with the population of interest—some biases will be introduced. If you define your population as "residents in my city," the sampling frame may be a list of telephone numbers that you will use to contact residents between 5 P.M. and 9 P.M. This sampling frame excludes persons who do not have telephones or whose schedule prevents them from being at home when you are making calls. Also, if you are using the telephone directory to obtain numbers, you will exclude persons who have unlisted numbers. As another example, suppose you want to know what doctors think about the portrayal of the medical profession on television. A reasonable sampling frame would be all doctors listed in your telephone directory. Immediately you can see that you have limited your sample to a particular geographical area. More important, you have also limited the sample to doctors who have private practices—doctors who work in clinics and hospitals have been excluded. When evaluating the results of the survey, you need to consider how well the sampling frame matches the population of interest. Often the biases introduced are quite minor; however, they could be consequential.

### Response Rate

The **response rate** in a survey is simply the percentage of people in the sample who actually completed the survey. Thus, if you mail 1,000 questionnaires to a random sample of adults in your community and 500 are completed and returned to you, the response rate is 50%. Response rate is important because it indicates how much bias there might be in the final sample of respondents.

Nonrespondents may differ from respondents in any number of ways including age, income, marital status, and education. The lower the response rate, the greater the likelihood that such biases may distort the findings and in turn limit the ability to generalize the findings to the population of interest.

In general, mail surveys have lower response rates than telephone surveys. With both methods, however, steps can be taken to maximize response rates. With mail surveys, an explanatory postcard or letter can be sent a week or so prior to mailing the survey. Follow-up reminders and even second mailings of the questionnaire are often effective in increasing response rates. It often helps to have a personally stamped return envelope rather than a business reply envelope. Even the look of the cover page of the questionnaire can be important (Dillman, 2000). With telephone surveys, respondents who aren't home can be called again and people who can't be interviewed today can be scheduled for a call at a more convenient time. Sometimes an incentive may be necessary to increase response rates. Such incentives can include cash, a gift, or a gift certificate for agreeing to participate. A crisp dollar bill "thank you" can be included with a mailed questionnaire. Another incentive is a chance to win a drawing for a prize. Finally, researchers should attempt to convince people that the survey's purposes are important and their participation will be a valuable contribution.

### Reasons for Using Convenience Samples

Much of the research in psychology uses nonprobability sampling techniques to obtain participants for either surveys or experiments. The advantage of these techniques is that the investigator can obtain research participants without spending a great deal of money or time on selecting the sample. For example, it is common practice to select participants from students in introductory psychology classes. Often, these students are required to participate in studies being conducted by faculty and their students; the introductory psychology students can then choose which studies they wish to participate in.

Even in studies that do not use college students, the sample is often based on convenience rather than concern for obtaining a random sample. One of my colleagues studies children, but they are almost always from one particular elementary school. You can guess that this is because my colleague has established a good relationship with the teachers and administrators; thus, obtaining permission to conduct the research is fairly easy. Even though the sample is somewhat biased because it includes only children from one neighborhood that has certain social and economic characteristics, my colleague is not terribly concerned.

Why aren't researchers more worried about obtaining random samples for their research? The most important reason is that the research is being conducted to study relationships between variables rather than to accurately estimate population values. In the study of high school students cited previously (Steinberg & Dornbusch, 1991), the sample included only high school students in California and Wisconsin. The sample data provide information on the average hours that these students work and their average use of alcohol. However, the researchers were not interested in giving a precise estimate of the number of hours that teenagers in the entire United States work; they were more interested in whether the number of hours that teenagers work is related to variables such as grade point average and alcohol use.

These issues will be explored further in Chapter 14. For now, it is also important to recognize that some nonprobability samples are more representative than others. The sample studied by Steinberg and Dornbusch appears to be highly representative of U.S. teenagers in general; even though the students came from only two states, they are from different geographical areas and several different high schools. Introductory psychology students are fairly representative of college students in general, and most college student samples are fairly representative of young adults. There aren't many obvious biases, particularly if you are studying basic psychological processes. Other samples might be much less representative of an intended population. Not long ago, a public affairs program on my local public television station asked viewers to dial a telephone number or send e-mail to vote for or against a gun control measure being considered by the legislature; the following evening, the program announced that almost 90% of the respondents opposed the measure. The sampling problems here are obvious: Groups opposed to gun control could immediately contact members to urge them to vote, and there were no limits on how many times someone could respond. In fact, the show received about 100 times more votes than it usually receives when it does such surveys. It is likely, then, that this sample was not at all representative of the population of the city or even viewers of the program.

You now have a great deal of information about methods for asking people about themselves. If you engage in this type of research, you will often need to design your own questions by following the guidelines described in this chapter and consulting sources such as Judd et al. (1991) and Converse and Presser (1986). However, you can also adapt questions and entire questionnaires that have been used in previous research. For example, Greenfield (1999) studied the new phenomenon of Internet addiction by adapting questions from a large body of existing research on addiction to gambling. Consider using previously developed questions, particularly if they have proven useful in other studies (make sure you don't violate any copyrights, however). A variety of measures of social, political, and occupational attitudes developed by others have been compiled by Robinson and his colleagues (Robinson, Athanasiou, & Head, 1969; Robinson, Rusk, & Head, 1968; Robinson, Shaver, & Wrightsman, 1991).

We noted in Chapter 4 that both nonexperimental and experimental research methods are necessary to fully understand behavior. The previous chapters have focused on nonexperimental approaches. In the next chapter, we begin a detailed description of experimental research design.

## Study Terms

| | |
|---|---|
| CATI | Population |
| Closed-ended questions | Probability sampling |
| Cluster sampling | Quota sampling |
| Confidence interval | Random sample |
| Face-to-face interview | Rating scale |
| Focus group | Response rate |
| Graphic rating scale | Response set |
| Group survey administration | Sampling |
| Haphazard (convenience) sampling | Sampling error |
| High-frequency scale | Sampling frame |
| Internet survey | Semantic differential scale |
| Interviewer bias | Simple random sampling |
| Mail survey | Stratified random sampling |
| Nonprobability sampling | Survey research |
| Open-ended questions | Telephone interview |
| Panel study | Yea-saying and nay-saying response set |

## Review Questions

1. What is a survey? Describe some research questions you might address with a survey.

2. Distinguish between probability and nonprobability sampling techniques. What are the implications of each?

3. Distinguish between haphazard and quota sampling.

4. Distinguish between simple random, stratified random, and cluster sampling.

5. Why don't researchers who want to test hypotheses about the relationships between variables worry a great deal about random sampling?

6. What are the advantages and disadvantages of using questionnaires versus interviews in a survey?

7. Distinguish between the different questionnaire, interview, and Internet survey administration methods.

8. What are some factors to take into consideration when constructing questions for surveys (including both questions and response alternatives)?

9. Define interviewer bias.

10. What is a social desirability response set?
11. How does sample size affect the interpretation of survey results?

## Activity Questions

1. In the Steinberg and Dornbusch (1991) study on teenage employment (see Figure 7.1), longer work hours were associated with lower grade point averages. Can you conclude that working longer hours *causes* lower grades? Why or why not? How might you expand the scope of this investigation through a panel study?

2. Select a topic for a survey. Write at least five closed-ended questions that you might include in the survey. For each question, write one "good" version and one "poor" version. For each poor question, state what elements make it poor and why the good version is an improvement.

3. Suppose you want to know how many books in a bookstore have only male authors, only female authors, or both male and female authors (the "bookstore" in this case might be a large retail store, the textbook section of your college bookstore, or all the books in the stacks of your library). Because there are thousands of books in the store, you decide to study a sample of the books rather than examine every book there. Describe a possible sampling procedure using a nonprobability sampling technique. Then describe how you might sample books using a probability sampling technique. Now speculate on the ways that the outcomes of your research might differ using the two techniques.

# Experimental Design

In the experimental method, all extraneous variables are controlled. Suppose you want to test the hypothesis that crowding impairs cognitive performance. To do this, you might put one group of people in a crowded room and another group in an uncrowded room. The participants in each of the groups would then complete the same cognitive tasks. Now suppose that the people in the crowded group do not perform as well on the cognitive tests as those in the uncrowded condition. Can the difference in test scores be attributed to the difference in crowding? Yes, *if* there is no other difference between the groups. However, what if the crowded group was tested in a room with no windows but the uncrowded group was tested in a room that did have windows—for example, they were in two different rooms in a high school? In that case, it would be impossible to know whether the poor scores of the participants in the crowded group were due to the crowding or to the lack of windows.

## CONFOUNDING AND INTERNAL VALIDITY

Recall from Chapter 4 that the experimental method has the advantage of allowing a relatively unambiguous interpretation of results. The researcher manipulates the independent variable to create groups that differ in the *levels* of the variable and then compares the groups in terms of their scores on the dependent variable. All other variables are kept constant, either through direct *experimental control* or through *randomization*. If the scores of the groups are different, the researcher can conclude that the independent variable caused the results because the only difference between the groups is the manipulated variable.

Although the task of designing an experiment is logically elegant and exquisitely simple, you should be aware of possible pitfalls. In the hypothetical crowding experiment just described, the variables of crowding and window presence are confounded. The window variable was not kept constant. A **confounding variable** is a variable that varies along with the independent variable; confounding occurs when the effects of two independent variables are intertwined so you cannot determine which of the variables is responsible for the observed effect. If the window variable had been held constant, the presence or absence of windows might have affected performance, but the effect of the windows would have been identical in both conditions. Thus, the presence of windows would not be a factor to consider when interpreting the difference between the crowded and uncrowded groups.

In short, both rooms in the crowding experiment should have had windows or both should have been windowless. Because one room had windows and one room did not, any difference in the dependent variable (test scores) cannot be attributed solely to the independent variable (crowding). An alternative explanation can be offered: The difference in test scores may have been caused, at least in part, by the window variable.

Good experimental design involves eliminating possible confounding that results in alternative explanations. A researcher can claim that the independent variable caused the results only by eliminating competing, alternative explanations. When the results of an experiment can confidently be attributed to the effect of the independent variable, the experiment is said to have **internal validity** (see Chapter 4). To achieve internal validity, the researcher must design and conduct the experiment so that only the independent variable can be the cause of the results.

This chapter will focus on true experimental designs that provide the highest degree of internal validity. In Chapter 11, we will turn to an examination of quasi-experimental designs that lack the crucial element of random assignment while at the same time attempting to allow us to infer that an independent variable had an effect on a dependent variable.

## BASIC EXPERIMENTS

The simplest possible experimental design has two variables: the independent variable and the dependent variable. The independent variable has two levels: an experimental group and a control group. Researchers must make every effort to ensure that the only difference between the two groups is the manipulated variable. Remember, the experimental method involves control over extraneous variables, through either keeping such variables constant (experimental control) or using randomization to make sure that any extraneous variables will affect both groups equally. The basic, simple experimental design can take one of two forms: a posttest-only design or a pretest-posttest design.

### Posttest-Only Design

A researcher using a **posttest-only design** must (1) obtain two equivalent groups of participants, (2) introduce the independent variable, and (3) measure the effect of the independent variable on the dependent variable. The design looks like this:

Thus, the first step is to choose the participants and assign them to the two groups. The procedures used must achieve equivalent groups to eliminate any potential **selection differences:** The people selected to be in the conditions cannot differ in any systematic way. The groups can be made equivalent by randomly assigning participants to the two conditions or by having the same participants participate in both conditions. The R in the diagram means that participants were randomly assigned to the two groups.

Next, the researcher must choose two levels of the independent variable, such as an experimental group that receives a treatment and a control group that does not. Thus, a researcher might study the effect of reward on motivation by offering a reward to one group of children before they play a game and offering no reward to children in the control group. A study testing the effect of a treatment method for reducing smoking could compare a group that receives the treatment with a control group that does not. Another approach would be to use two different amounts of the independent variable—that is, to use more reward in one group than the other or to compare the effects of different amounts of relaxation training designed to help people quit smoking (e.g., 1 hour of training compared with 10 hours). Either of these approaches would provide a basis for comparison of the two groups.

Finally, the effect of the independent variable is measured. The same measurement procedure is used for both groups, so that comparison of the two groups is possible. Because the groups were equivalent to begin with and there were no confounding variables, any difference between the groups on the dependent variable must be attributed to the effect of the independent variable. The result is an experimental design that has internal validity. In actuality, a statistical significance test would be used to assess the difference between the groups. However, we don't need to be concerned with statistics at this point. An experiment must be well designed, and confounding variables must be eliminated. If not, the results are useless, and statistics will be of no help at all.

### Pretest-Posttest Design

The only difference between the posttest-only design and the **pretest-posttest design** is that in the latter a pretest is given before the experimental manipulation is introduced. This design makes it possible to ascertain that the groups were, in fact, equivalent at the beginning of the experiment. However, this precaution is usually not necessary if participants have been randomly assigned to the two groups. With a sufficiently large sample of participants, random assignment will produce groups that are virtually identical in all respects.

You are probably wondering how many participants are needed in each group to make sure that random assignment has made the groups equivalent. The larger the sample, the less likelihood there is that the groups will differ in any systematic way prior to the manipulation of the independent variable. At the same time, there is an increasing likelihood that any difference between the groups on the dependent variable is due to the effect of the independent variable. There are formal procedures for determining the sample size needed to detect a statistically significant effect, but as a rule of thumb you will probably need a minimum of 20 to 30 participants per condition. In some areas of research, many more participants may be necessary. Further issues in determining the number of participants needed for an experiment are described in Chapter 13.

### Advantages and Disadvantages of the Two Designs

Each design has advantages and disadvantages that influence the decision whether to include or omit a pretest. The first decision factor concerns the equivalence of the groups in the experiment. Although randomization is likely to produce equivalent groups, it is possible that, with small sample sizes, the groups will not be equal. Thus, a pretest enables the researcher to assess whether the groups were in fact equivalent to begin with.

Sometimes, a pretest is necessary to select the participants in the experiment. A researcher might need to give a pretest to find the lowest or highest scorers on a smoking measure, a math anxiety test, or a prejudice measure. Once identified, the participants would be randomly assigned to the experimental and control groups. Also, the researcher who uses a pretest can measure the extent of change in each individual. If a smoking reduction program appears to be effective for some individuals but not others, attempts can be made to find out why.

A pretest is also necessary whenever there is a possibility that participants will drop out of the experiment; this is most likely to occur in a study that lasts over a long time period. The dropout factor in experiments is called **mortality.** People may drop out for reasons unrelated to the experimental manipulation, such as illness; sometimes, however, mortality is related to the experimental manipulation. Even if the groups are equivalent to begin with, different mortality rates can make them nonequivalent. How might mortality affect a treatment program designed to reduce smoking? One possibility is that the heaviest smokers in the experimental group might leave the program. Therefore, when the posttest is given, only the light smokers would remain, so that a comparison of the experimental and control groups would show less smoking in the experimental group even if the program had no effect. In this way, mortality becomes an alternative explanation for the results. Use of a pretest enables you to assess the effects of mortality; you can look at the pretest scores of the dropouts and know whether mortality affected the final results. With the pretest, it is possible to examine whether mortality is a plausible alternative explanation.

Thus, pretests may offer some advantages in the experimental design. One disadvantage of a pretest, however, is that it may be time-consuming and awkward to administer in the context of the particular experimental procedures being used. Perhaps most important, a pretest can sensitize participants to what you are studying, enabling them to figure out your hypothesis. They may then react differently to the manipulation than they would have without the pretest. When a pretest affects the way participants react to the manipulation, it is very difficult to generalize the results to people who have not received a pretest. That is, the independent variable may not have an effect in the real world, where pretests are rarely given. We will examine this issue more fully in Chapter 14.

If awareness of the pretest is a problem, the pretest can be disguised. One way to do this is by administering it in a completely different situation with a different experimenter. Another approach is to embed the pretest in a set of irrelevant measures so it is not obvious that the researcher is interested in a particular topic.

TABLE 8.1     Solomon four-group design

| | Independent Variable | |
| --- | --- | --- |
| Pretest condition | Control group | Experimental group |
| No pretest (posttest only) | | |
| Pretest and posttest | | |

*Note:* If there is no pretest effect, the posttest mean scores in the two control group conditions will be equal, and the two experimental posttest means will be equal as well. If there is a pretest effect, the pattern of results will differ in the posttest only and the pretest plus posttest conditions.

It is also possible to assess directly the impact of the pretest with a combination of both the posttest-only and the pretest-posttest design. In this design, half the participants receive only the posttest, and the other half receive both the pretest and the posttest (see Table 8.1). This is formally called a *Solomon four-group design.* With this design, the effect of the pretest can be directly assessed—if there is no impact of the pretest, the posttest scores will be the same in the two control groups (with and without the pretest) and in the two experimental groups. Two possible outcomes of a Solomon four-group design are shown in Figure 8.1. The top graph illustrates an outcome in which the results are the same with or without a pretest. The other graph shows an outcome in which there is a difference between the experimental and control groups when there is a pretest, but there is no difference when there is no pretest. The Solomon four-group design will be discussed further in Chapter 14. Finally, concealed observation of behavior could be employed in a pretest although ethical concerns would have to be addressed to do this. When reading about an experiment in which a pretest-posttest design was used, you should try to determine whether the pretest may have created a problem for interpreting the results.

## ASSIGNING PARTICIPANTS TO EXPERIMENTAL CONDITIONS

Recall that there are two basic ways of assigning participants to experimental conditions. In one procedure, participants are randomly assigned to the various conditions so that each participates in only one group. This is called an **independent groups design.** In the other procedure, participants are in all conditions. In the simplest experiment, for example, each participant is assigned to both levels of the independent variable. This is called a **repeated measures design** because each participant is measured after receiving each level of the independent variable. In the next two sections, we will examine each of these designs in detail.

FIGURE 8.1
Examples of outcomes of
Solomon four-group
design

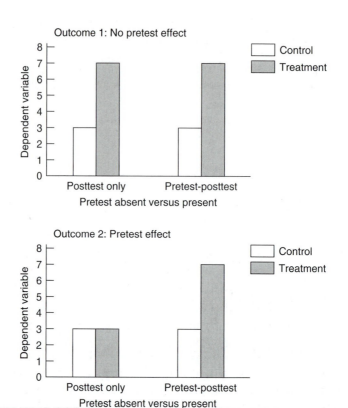

Outcome 1: No pretest effect

Outcome 2: Pretest effect

## INDEPENDENT GROUPS DESIGN

In an independent groups design, different participants are assigned to each of the conditions using *random assignment*. This means that the decision to assign an individual to a particular condition is completely random and beyond the control of the researcher. For example, you could ask for the participant's month of birth and assign to one group for odd months and the other group for even months. In practice, researchers usually use a sequence of random numbers to determine assignment. A table of random numbers and instructions for using it are shown in Appendix C. The table is made up of a series of the digits 0–99 that were arranged randomly by a computer. The researcher can use the arrangement of the numbers in the table to determine which group each participant will be assigned to. Random assignment will prevent any systematic biases, and the groups will be equivalent in terms of participant characteristics such as income, intelligence, age, or political attitudes. In this way, participant differences cannot be an explanation for results of the experiment. As we noted in Chapter 4, in an experiment on the effects of exercise on anxiety, anxiety being lower in the exercise group than in the no-exercise group cannot be explained by saying that people in the groups are somehow different on characteristics such as income, education, or personality.

An alternative procedure is to have the *same* individuals participate in all of the groups. This is called a repeated measures experimental design.

## REPEATED MEASURES DESIGN

Consider an experiment investigating the relationship between the meaningfulness of material and the learning of that material. In an independent groups design, one group of participants is given highly meaningful material to learn and another group receives less meaningful material. In a repeated measures design, the same individuals will participate in both conditions. Thus, participants might first read low-meaningful material and take a recall test to measure learning; the same participants would then read high-meaningful material and take the recall test. You can see why this is called a repeated measures design; participants are repeatedly measured on the dependent variable after being in each condition of the experiment.

### Advantages and Disadvantages of Repeated Measures Design

The repeated measures design has several advantages. An obvious one is that fewer research participants are needed because each individual participates in all conditions. When participants are scarce or when it is costly to run each individual in the experiment, a repeated measures design may be preferred. In much research on perception, for instance, extensive training of participants is necessary before the actual experiment can begin. Such research often involves only a few individuals who participate in all conditions of the experiment.

An additional advantage of repeated measures designs is that they are extremely sensitive to finding statistically significant differences between groups. This is because we have data from the same people in both conditions. To illustrate why this is important, consider possible data from the recall experiment. Using an independent groups design, the first three participants in the high-meaningful condition had scores of 68, 81, and 92. The first three participants in the low-meaningful condition had scores of 64, 78, and 85. If you calculated an average score for each condition, you would find that the average recall was a bit higher when the material was more meaningful. However, there is a lot of variability in the scores in both groups. You certainly are not finding that everyone in the high-meaningful condition has high recall and everyone in the other condition has low recall. The reason for this variability is that people differ—there are individual differences in recall abilities so there is a range of scores in both conditions. This is part of "random error" in the scores that we cannot explain.

However, if the same scores were obtained from the first three participants in a repeated measures design, the conclusions would be much different. Let's line up the recall scores for the two conditions:

|  | *High meaning* | *Low meaning* | *Difference* |
|---|---|---|---|
| Participant 1 | 68 | 64 | +4 |
| Participant 2 | 81 | 78 | +3 |
| Participant 3 | 92 | 85 | +7 |

With a repeated measures design, the individual differences can be seen and explained. It is true that some people score higher than others because of individual differences in recall abilities, but now you can much more clearly see the effect of the independent variable on recall scores. It is much easier to separate the systematic individual differences from the effect of the independent variable: Scores are higher for every participant in the high-meaningful condition. As a result, we are much more likely to detect an effect of the independent variable on the dependent variable.

The major problem with a repeated measures design stems from the fact that the different conditions must be presented in a particular sequence. Suppose that there is greater recall in the high-meaningful condition. Although this result could be caused by the manipulation of the meaningfulness variable, the result could also simply be an **order effect**—the order of presenting the treatments affects the dependent variable. Thus, greater recall in the high-meaningful condition could be attributed to the fact that the high-meaningful task came second in the order of presentation of the conditions. Performance on the second task might improve merely because of the practice gained on the first task.

There are several types of order effects. Order effects that are associated simply with the passage of time include practice effects and fatigue effects. A *practice effect* is an improvement in performance as a result of repeated practice with a task. A *fatigue effect* is a deterioration in performance as the research participant becomes tired, bored, or distracted. Time-related order effects are possible whenever there is a sequence of tasks to perform. For example, suppose you ask a child to play a video game for 30-minute periods under different conditions each time (e.g., different rewards for good performance or different amounts of distraction). The child playing the game for the first time might show a practice effect with scores improving over time, but the child who is familiar with the game might show a fatigue effect, with scores deteriorating as boredom or fatigue sets in.

Other types of order effects occur when the effect of the first treatment carries over to influence the response to the second treatment. For example, a *contrast effect* occurs when the response to the second condition in the experiment is altered because the two conditions are contrasted to one another. Suppose the independent variable is severity of a crime. After reading about the less severe crime, the more severe one might seem much worse to participants than it normally would. In addition, reading about the severe crime might subsequently cause participants to view the less severe crime as much milder than they normally would.

There are two approaches to dealing with such problems. The first is to employ counterbalancing techniques. The second is to devise a procedure in which the interval between conditions is long enough to minimize the influence of the first condition on the second.

### Counterbalancing

**Complete counterbalancing**    In a repeated measures design, it is very important to counterbalance the order of the conditions. With complete **counterbalancing,** all possible orders of presentation are included in the experiment. In the example of a study on learning high- and low-meaningful material, half of the participants would be randomly assigned to the low-high order, and the other half would be assigned to the high-low order. This design is illustrated as follows:

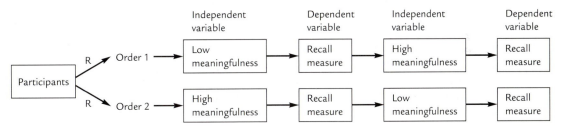

By counterbalancing the order of conditions, it is possible to determine the extent to which order is influencing the results. In the hypothetical memory study, you would know whether the greater recall in the high-meaningful condition is consistent for both orders; you would also know the extent to which a practice effect is responsible for the results.

Counterbalancing principles can be extended to experiments with three or more groups. With three groups, there are 6 possible orders ($3! = 3 \times 2 \times 1 = 6$); with four groups, the number of possible orders increases to 24 ($4! = 4 \times 3 \times 2 \times 1 = 24$); you would need a minimum of 24 participants to represent each order, and you would need 48 participants to have only two participants per order. Imagine the number of orders possible in an experiment by Shepard and Metzler (1971). In their basic experimental paradigm, each participant is shown a three-dimensional object along with the same figure rotated at one of 10 different angles ranging from 0 degrees to 180 degrees (see the sample objects illustrated in Figure 8.2). Each time, the participant presses a button when it is determined that the two figures are the same or different. The dependent variable is reaction time—the amount of time it takes to decide whether the figures are the same or different. The results show that reaction time becomes longer as the angle of rotation increases away from the original. In this experiment with 10 conditions, there are 3,628,800 possible orders! Fortunately, there are alternatives

FIGURE 8.2
Three-dimensional figures

FIGURE 8.3
A Latin square with four conditions
*Note:* The four conditions were randomly
given the letter designations. A = 60 degrees,
B = 0 degrees, C = 180 degrees, and D = 120
degrees. Each row represents a different order
of running the conditions.

Order of conditions

|  | 1 | 2 | 3 | 4 |
|---|---|---|---|---|
| Row 1 | A (60) | B (0) | D (120) | C (180) |
| Row 2 | B (0) | C (180) | A (60) | D (120) |
| Row 3 | C (180) | D (120) | B (0) | A (60) |
| Row 4 | D (120) | A (60) | C (180) | B (0) |

to complete counterbalancing that still allow researchers to draw valid conclusions about the effect of the independent variable.

**Latin squares**     A technique to control for order effects without having all
possible orders is to construct a **Latin square:** a limited set of orders constructed to ensure that (1) each condition appears at each ordinal position
and (2) each condition precedes and follows each condition one time. Using a
Latin square to determine order controls for most order effects without having to include all possible orders. Suppose you replicated the Shepard and
Metzler (1971) study using only 4 of the 10 rotations: 0, 60, 120, and 180 degrees. A Latin square for these four conditions is shown in Figure 8.3. Each
row in the square is one of the orders of the conditions (the conditions are labeled A, B, C, and D). The number of orders in a Latin square is equal to the
number of conditions; thus, if there are four conditions, there are four orders.
When you conduct your study using the Latin square to determine order, you
need at least 1 participant per row. Usually, you will have 2 or more participants per row; the number of participants run in each order must be equal.
The procedures for constructing Latin squares with any number of conditions
are provided in Appendix D.

**Randomized blocks**    In many areas of research that use repeated measures designs, the basic experimental procedure is repeated many times. For example, the 10 rotations in the Shepard and Metzler study might be repeated numerous times using different original figures. Each repetition of the basic experiment is called a *block of trials*. To control for order effects when there are many such blocks of trials, the order of presentation can be randomly determined each time.

We should note that, in an experiment in which individuals are tested over a series of trials, as in many learning studies, "trials" is a repeated measures variable. In this situation, counterbalancing is not an issue; in fact, the order effect of changes in performance over trials is of interest to the researcher.

### Time Interval Between Treatments

In addition to counterbalancing the order of treatments, researchers need to carefully determine the time interval between presentation of treatments and possible activities between them. A rest period may counteract a fatigue effect; attending to an unrelated task between treatments may reduce the possibility of a contrast effect. If the treatment is the administration of a drug that takes time to wear off, the interval between treatments may have to be a day or more. Wilson, Ellinwood, Mathew, and Johnson (1994) examined the effects of three doses of marijuana on cognitive and motor task performance. Each participant was tested before and after smoking a marijuana cigarette. Because of the time necessary for the effects of the drug to wear off, the three conditions were run on separate days. A similar long time interval would be needed with procedures that produce emotional changes such as heightened anxiety or anger. You may have noted that introduction of an extended time interval may create a separate problem: Participants will have to commit to the experiment for a longer period of time. This can make it more difficult to recruit volunteers, and if the study extends over 2 or more days, some participants may not return.

### Choosing Between Independent Groups and Repeated Measures Designs

Repeated measures designs have two major advantages over independent groups designs: (1) a reduction in the number of participants required to complete the experiment and (2) greater control over participant differences and thus greater ability to detect an effect of the independent variable. As noted previously, in certain areas of research, these advantages are very important. However, the disadvantages of repeated measures designs and the need to take precautions to deal with these are usually sufficient reasons for researchers to use independent groups designs.

A very different consideration in whether to use a repeated measures design concerns generalization to conditions in the "real world." Greenwald (1976) has pointed out that in actual everyday situations, we sometimes encounter independent variables in an independent groups fashion: We encounter only one condition without a contrasting comparison. However, some independent variables are most frequently encountered in a repeated measures fashion: Both conditions appear, and our responses occur in the context of exposure to both levels of the independent variable. Thus, for example, if you are interested in how characteristics of a defendant affect jurors, an independent groups design may be most appropriate because actual jurors focus on a single defendant in a trial. However, if you are interested in the effects of characteristics of a job applicant on employers, a repeated measures design would be reasonable because employers typically consider several applicants at once. Whether or not to use an independent groups or repeated measures design may be partially determined by these generalization issues.

Finally, any experimental procedure that produces a relatively permanent change in an individual cannot be used in a repeated measures design. Examples include a surgical procedure such as a brain lesion or a psychotherapy treatment.

## MATCHED PAIRS DESIGN

A somewhat more complicated method of assigning participants to conditions in an experiment is called a **matched pairs design.** Instead of simply randomly assigning participants to groups, the goal is to first match people on a participant characteristic. The matching variable will be either the dependent measure or a variable that is strongly related to the dependent variable. For example, in a learning experiment, participants might be matched on the basis of scores on a cognitive ability measure. If cognitive ability is not related to the dependent measure, however, matching would be a waste of time. The goal is to achieve the same equivalency of groups that is achieved with a repeated measures design without the necessity of having the same participants in both conditions.

When using a matched pairs design, the first step is to obtain a measure of the matching variable from each individual. The participants are then rank ordered from highest to lowest based on their scores on the matching variable. Now the researcher can form matched pairs that are approximately equal on the characteristic (the highest two participants form the first pair, the next two form the second pair, and so on). Finally, the members of each pair are randomly assigned to the conditions in the experiment.

A matched pairs design ensures that the groups are equivalent (on the matching variable) prior to introduction of the independent variable manipulation. This assurance could be particularly important with small sample sizes because random assignment procedures are more likely to produce equivalent groups as the sample size increases. Matching, then, is most likely to be used when only a few participants are available or when it is very costly to run large numbers of individuals in the experiment.

These advantages result in a greater ability to detect a statistically significant effect of the independent variable because it is possible to account for individual differences in responses to the independent variable just as we saw with a repeated measures design.

These issues of variability and statistical significance are discussed further in Chapter 13 and Appendix B. The main point here is that matching on a variable makes it more likely that a statistically significant difference between groups will be found in an experiment. However, matching procedures can be costly and time-consuming because they require measuring participants on the matching variable prior to the experiment. Such efforts are worthwhile only when the matching variable is strongly related to the dependent measure and you know that the relationship exists prior to conducting your study. For these reasons, matched pairs is not a commonly used design.

A compromise technique avoids the problems of matching while maintaining some of its statistical advantages. Rather than obtaining data on the subject variable (e.g., intelligence scores) in advance to establish matched pairs, the simple random assignment design is used, but time is allotted to collect data on the subject variable. Although these data are collected "after the fact," they can be used in the statistical analysis of the results. You may have seen research that reports the use of "analysis of covariance" or refers to a variable such as intelligence as a "covariate." Here, a statistical technique called **analysis of covariance** statistically controls for the correlation between the subject variable and the dependent variable in the experiment. This procedure removes the error variance that results from the fact that variability in scores on the dependent variable is due in part to the effect of the subject variable. Analysis of covariance theory and procedures are beyond the scope of this book. However, after you have familiarized yourself with the simpler statistical methods described in Chapter 12 and Appendix B, you will be ready to use techniques such as these.

## DEVELOPMENTAL RESEARCH DESIGNS

Developmental psychologists often study the ways that individuals change as a function of age. A researcher might test a theory concerning changes in reasoning ability as children grow older, the age at which self-awareness develops in young children, or the global values people have as they move from adolescence through old age. In all cases, the major variable is age. Developmental researchers face an interesting choice in designing their studies because there are two general methods for studying individuals of different ages: the cross-sectional method and the longitudinal method. You will see that the cross-sectional method shares similarities with the independent groups design whereas the longitudinal method is similar to the repeated measures design. We will also examine a hybrid approach called the sequential method. The three approaches are illustrated in Figure 8.4.

### Cross-Sectional Method

In a study using the **cross-sectional method,** persons of different ages are studied at only one point in time. Suppose you are interested in examining how the ability to learn a computer application changes as people grow older. Using the

**Cross-sectional method**

|  | Year of birth (cohort) | Time 1: 2000 |
|---|---|---|
| Group 1: | 1945 | 55 years old |
| Group 2: | 1940 | 60 years old |
| Group 3: | 1935 | 65 years old |

**Longitudinal method**

|  | Year of birth (cohort) | Time 1: 2000 | Time 2: 2005 | Time 3: 2010 |
|---|---|---|---|---|
| Group 1: | 1945 | 55 years old ⟶ | 60 years old ⟶ | 65 years old |

**Sequential method**

|  | Year of birth (cohort) | Time 1: 2000 | Time 2: 2005 | Time 3: 2010 |
|---|---|---|---|---|
| Group 1: | 1945 | 55 years old ⟶ | 60 years old ⟶ | 65 years old |
| Group 2: | 1935 | 65 years old ⟶ | 70 years old ⟶ | 75 years old |

FIGURE 8.4
Three designs for developmental research

cross-sectional method, you might study people who are currently 20, 30, 40, and 50 years of age. The participants in your study would be given the same computer learning task, and you would compare the groups on their performance.

*Longitudinal Method*

In the **longitudinal method,** the same group of people is observed at different points in time as they grow older. Perhaps the most famous longitudinal study is the Terman Life Cycle Study that was begun by Stanford psychologist Lewis Terman in 1921. Terman studied 1,528 California schoolchildren who had intelligence test scores of at least 135. The participants, who called themselves "Termites," were initially measured on numerous aspects of their cognitive and social development in 1921 and 1922. Terman and his colleagues continued studying the Termites during their childhood and adolescence and throughout their adult lives (cf. Terman, 1925; Terman & Oden, 1947, 1959). Terman's successors at Stanford continue to track the Termites until each one dies. The study has provided a rich description of the lives of highly intelligent individuals and disconfirmed many negative stereotypes of high intelligence—for example, the Termites were very well adjusted both socially and emotionally. The data have now been archived for use by other researchers. Friedman et al. (1995) used the Terman data to study social and health practice factors associated with age at death. One intriguing finding was that the personality dimension of "conscientiousness" is related to longevity.

Most longitudinal investigations do not take on the proportions of the Terman study in which individuals were studied over a lifetime, but any study that attempts to compare the same individuals at different ages is using the longitudinal method. Caspi, for example, conducted a 15-year longitudinal study in which New Zealand children were tested at ages 3 and 18. Among the many findings from this study is one that showed that temperaments at age 3 are related to personality traits at age 18—for example, "undercontrolled" children were impulsive and aggressive adults (Caspi & Silva, 1995). Other longitudinal studies often span fewer numbers of years—e.g., an 8-year study that demonstrated the positive effects of day care in a sample of Swedish children (Broberg, Wessels, Lamb, & Hwang, 1997).

### Comparison of Longitudinal and Cross-Sectional Methods

The cross-sectional method is much more common than the longitudinal method primarily because it is less expensive and immediately yields useful results. Note that, with a longitudinal design, it would take 30 years to study the same group of individuals from age 20 to 50, but with a cross-sectional design, comparisons of different age groups can be obtained relatively quickly.

There are, however, some disadvantages to cross-sectional designs. Most important, the researcher must infer that differences among age groups are due to the developmental variable of age. The developmental change is not observed directly among the same group of people, but rather is based on comparisons among different cohorts of individuals. You can think of a **cohort** as a group of people born at about the same time, exposed to the same events in a society, and influenced by the same demographic trends such as divorce rates and family size. If you think about the hairstyles of people you know who are in their 30s, 40s, 50s, and 60s, you will immediately recognize the importance of cohort effects! More crucially, differences among cohorts reflect different economic and political conditions in society, different music and arts, different educational systems, and different child-rearing practices. In a cross-sectional study, a difference among groups of different ages may reflect developmental age changes; however, the differences may result from cohort effects (Schaie, 1986).

To illustrate this issue, let's return to our hypothetical study on learning to use computers. Suppose you found that age is associated with a decrease in ability such that the people in the 50-year-old group score lower on the learning measure than the 40-year-olds, and so on. Should you conclude that the ability to learn to use a computer application decreases with age? That may be an accurate conclusion; alternatively, the differences could be due to a cohort effect: The older people had less experience with computers while growing up. The key point here is that the cross-sectional method confounds age and cohort effects.

(Review the discussion of confounding and internal validity at the beginning of this chapter.) Finally, you should note that cohort effects are most likely to be a problem when the researcher is examining age effects across a wide range of ages (e.g., adolescents through older adults).

The only way to conclusively study changes that occur as people grow older is to use a longitudinal design. Also, longitudinal research is the best way to study how scores on a variable at one age are related to another variable at a later age. For example, if a researcher wants to study how the home environment of children at age 5 is related to school achievement at age 13, a longitudinal study provides the best data. The alternative in this case would be to study 13-year-olds and ask them or their parents about the earlier home environment; this *retrospective* approach has its own problems when one considers the difficulty of remembering events in the distant past.

Thus, the longitudinal approach, despite being expensive and difficult, has definite advantages. However, there is one major problem: Over the course of a longitudinal study, people may move, die, or lose interest in the study. Researchers who conduct longitudinal studies become adept at convincing people to continue, often travel anywhere to collect more data, and compare test scores of people who drop out with those who stay to provide better analyses of their results. In sum, a researcher shouldn't embark on a longitudinal study without considerable resources and a great deal of patience and energy!

### Sequential Method

A compromise between the longitudinal and cross-sectional methods is to use the **sequential method.** This method, along with the cross-sectional and longitudinal method, is illustrated in Figure 8.4. In the figure, the goal of the study is to minimally compare 55- and 65-year-olds. The first phase of the sequential method begins with the cross-sectional method; for example, you could study groups of 55- and 65-year-olds. These individuals are then studied using the longitudinal method with each individual tested at least one more time. This method takes fewer years to complete than a longitudinal study, and the researcher reaps immediate rewards because data on the different age groups are available in the first year of the study.

You now have a fundamental understanding of the design of experiments. In the next chapter, we will consider issues that arise when you decide how to actually conduct an experiment.

### Study Terms

Analysis of covariance

Cohort

Confounding Variable

Contrast effect

Counterbalancing

Cross-sectional method

Fatigue effect

Independent groups design

Internal validity

Latin square

Longitudinal method

Matched pairs design

Mortality

Order effect

Posttest-only design

Practice effect

Pretest-posttest design

Random assignment

Randomized blocks

Repeated measures design

Selection differences

Sequential method

## Review Questions

1. What is confounding of variables?
2. What is meant by the internal validity of an experiment?
3. How do the two true experimental designs eliminate the problem of selection differences?
4. Distinguish between the posttest-only design and the pretest-posttest design. What are the advantages and disadvantages of each?
5. When would a researcher decide to use the matched pairs design? What would be the advantage of this design?
6. What is a repeated measures design? What are the advantages of using a repeated measures design? What are the disadvantages?
7. What are some of the ways of dealing with the problems of a repeated measures design?
8. The procedure used to obtain your sample (i.e., random or nonrandom sampling) is not the same as the procedure for assigning participants to conditions; distinguish between random sampling and random assignment.
9. Distinguish between longitudinal, cross-sectional, and sequential methods.
10. What is a cohort effect?

## Activity Questions

1. Design an experiment to test the hypothesis that single-gender math classes are beneficial to adolescent females. Operationally define both the independent and dependent variables. Your experiment should have two groups and use the matched pairs procedure. Make a good case for your selection of the matching variable. In addition, defend your choice of either a posttest-only design or a pretest-posttest design.
2. Design a repeated measures experiment that investigates the effect of report presentation style on the grade received for the report. Use two

levels of the independent variable: a "professional style" presentation (high-quality paper, consistent use of margins and fonts, carefully constructed tables and charts) and a "nonprofessional style" (average-quality paper, frequent changes in the margins and fonts, tables and charts lacking proper labels). Discuss the necessity for using counterbalancing. Create a table illustrating the experimental design.

3. Professor Foley conducted a cola taste test. Each participant in the experiment first tasted 2 ounces of Coca-Cola, then 2 ounces of Pepsi, and finally 2 ounces of RC Cola. A rating of the cola's flavor was made after each taste. What are the potential problems with this experimental design and the procedures used? Revise the design and procedures to address these problems. You may wish to consider several alternatives and think about the advantages and disadvantages of each.

4. Dr. Cardenas studied political attitudes among different groups of 20-, 40-, and 60-year-olds. Political attitudes were found to be most conservative in the age-60 group and least conservative in the age-20 group.

   a. What type of method was used in this study?

   b. Can you conclude that people become more politically conservative as they get older? Why or why not?

   c. Propose alternative ways of studying this topic.

# 9

# Conducting Experiments

The previous chapters have laid the foundation for planning a research investigation. In this chapter, we will focus on some very practical aspects of conducting research. How do you select the research participants? What should you consider when deciding how to manipulate an independent variable? What should you worry about when you measure a variable? What do you do when the study is completed?

## SELECTING RESEARCH PARTICIPANTS

The focus of your study may be children, college students, schizophrenics, rats, pigeons, rabbits, primates, or even cockroaches or flatworms; in all cases, the participants or subjects must somehow be selected. The method used to select participants has implications for generalizing the research results.

Recall from Chapter 7 that most research projects involve sampling research participants from a population of interest. The population is composed of all of the individuals of interest to the researcher. Samples may be drawn from the population using probability sampling or nonprobability sampling techniques. When it is important to accurately describe the population, you must use probability sampling. This is why probability sampling is so crucial when conducting scientific polls. Much research, however, is more interested in testing hypotheses about behavior. Here, the focus of the study is the relationships between the variables being studied and testing predictions derived from theories of behavior. In such cases, the participants may be found in the easiest way possible using nonprobability haphazard or "convenience" sampling methods. You may ask students in introductory psychology classes to participate, knock on doors in your dorm to find people to be tested, or choose a class in which to test children simply because you know the teacher. Nothing is wrong with such methods as long as you recognize that they affect the ability to generalize your results to some larger population. The issue of generalizing results is discussed in Chapter 14; despite the problems of generalizing results based upon convenient haphazard samples, ample evidence supports the view that we *can* generalize findings to other populations and situations.

You will also need to determine your sample size. How many participants will you need in your study? In general, increasing your sample size increases the likelihood that your results will be statistically significant because larger samples provide more accurate estimates of population values (see Table 7.1). Most researchers pay attention to the sample sizes in the research area being studied and select a sample size that is typical for studies in the area. A more formal approach to selecting a sample size is discussed in Chapter 13.

## MANIPULATING THE INDEPENDENT VARIABLE

To manipulate an independent variable, you have to construct an operational definition of the variable (see Chapter 4). That is, you must turn a conceptual variable into a set of operations—specific instructions, events, and stimuli to be presented to the research participants. In addition, the independent and dependent variables must be introduced within the context of the total experimental setting. This has been called "setting the stage" (Aronson, Brewer, & Carlsmith, 1985).

## Setting the Stage

In setting the stage, you usually have to do two things: provide the participants with the informed consent information needed for your study and explain to participants why the experiment is being conducted. Sometimes, the rationale given is completely truthful, although only rarely will you want to tell participants the actual hypothesis. For example, you might say that you are conducting an experiment on memory when, in fact, you are studying a specific aspect of memory (your independent variable). If participants know what you are studying, they may try to confirm the hypothesis, or they may try to look good by behaving in the most socially acceptable way. If you find that deception is necessary, you have a special obligation to address the deception when you debrief the participants at the conclusion of the experiment.

There are no clear-cut rules for setting the stage, except that the experimental setting must seem plausible to the participants, nor are there any clear-cut rules for translating conceptual variables into specific operations. Exactly how the variable is manipulated depends on the variable and the cost, practicality, and ethics of the procedures being considered.

## Types of Manipulations

**Straightforward manipulations**     Researchers are usually able to manipulate a variable with relative simplicity by presenting written, verbal, or visual material to the participants. Such *straightforward* manipulations manipulate variables with instructions and stimulus presentations. Stimuli may be presented verbally, in written form, via videotape, or with a computer. Let's look at a few examples.

Labranche, Helweg-Larsen, Byrd, and Choquette (1997) studied the impact of health promotion brochures by asking women to read a brochure on breast self-examinations. In one condition, the brochure included only text; in the other condition, pictures depicting breast self-examination were added to the brochure. Participants' responses to the two brochures depended on their level of comfort with sexual materials. One question asked about whether the woman believed she could properly perform a breast self-examination. Women who were uncomfortable with sexual materials were less sure about their ability when they read the brochure with pictures than when they read the text-only brochure. The type of brochure did not affect the women who were comfortable with sexual materials.

Studies on jury decisions often ask participants to read a description of a jury trial in which a crucial piece of information is varied. Bornstein (1998) studied the effect of the severity of injury on product liability judgments. Participants read about a case in which a woman taking birth-control pills had been diagnosed with cancer. In a low-severity condition, the cancer was detected early, one ovary was removed, the woman could still have children, and future prognosis was good. In the high-severity condition, the cancer was detected late, both ovaries were removed so pregnancy would not be possible, and the future prognosis was poor. The evidence on whether the pills could be responsible for the cancer was the same in both conditions; thus, product liability judgments should be the same in both conditions. Nevertheless, the severity information affected liability judgments: The pill manufacturer was found liable by 40% of the participants in the high-severity condition versus 21% in the low-severity condition.

Most memory research relies on straightforward manipulations. For example, Coltheart and Langdon (1998) displayed lists of words to participants and later measured recall. The word lists differed on phonological similarity: Some lists had words that sounded similar, such as *cat, map,* and *pat,* and other lists had dissimilar words such as *mop, pen,* and *cow.* They found that lists with dissimilar words are recalled more accurately. In a more complex memory study, Reeve and Aggleton (1998) presented a script of a future episode of a British soap opera called *The Archers* to both fans ("experts") and people unfamiliar with the show. In one condition, the script was typical of an actual episode of the program—the Archers visit a livestock market. In the other condition, the script was atypical—the Archers visit a boat show. The characters and basic structure of the show were identical in the two conditions. After reading the script, the participants were given a measure of retention of the details of the episode. They found that being an expert aided retention only when the story was a typical one. In the atypical condition, both fans and nonfans had equal retention. Reeve and Aggleton concluded that the benefits of being an expert are very limited.

As a final example of a straightforward manipulation, consider a study by Petty, Cacioppo, and Goldman (1981) on the effect of communicator credibility and personal involvement on attitude change. The participants were college seniors who read about the reasons that a comprehensive examination should be required for graduation from their university. To manipulate credibility, the arguments were said to be written by either a professor of education at Princeton University or a junior at a local college. The researchers also manipulated personal involvement by telling the students that the examination was being considered for implementation either that year (thus affecting the individuals participating in the study) or 10 years later. Participants in the low-involvement condition changed their attitudes more if the communicator was high in credibility, but the credibility of the communicator did not make a difference when the participants were highly involved.

You will find that most manipulations of independent variables in many areas of research are straightforward. Researchers vary the difficulty of material to be learned, motivation levels, the way questions are asked, characteristics of people to be judged, and a variety of other factors in a straightforward manner.

**Staged manipulations**    Other manipulations are less straightforward. Sometimes, it is necessary to stage events that occur during the experiment in order to manipulate the independent variable successfully. When this occurs, the manipulation is called a *staged* or *event manipulation.*

Staged manipulations are most frequently used for two reasons. First, the researcher may be trying to create some psychological state in the participants, such as frustration, anger, or a temporary lowering of self-esteem; second, a staged manipulation may be necessary to simulate some situation that occurs in the real world. For example, Fazio, Cooper, Dayson, and Johnson (1981) studied cognitive performance under conditions of multiple task demands. Participants in one condition spent 10 minutes proofreading a manuscript; participants in the other condition performed the same proofreading task but were interrupted by the experimenter from time to time and asked to go to another room to perform other tasks. These conditions simulate common real-world work environments.

Staged manipulations frequently employ a **confederate** (sometimes termed an "accomplice"). Usually, the confederate appears to be another participant in an experiment but is actually part of the manipulation (we discussed the use of confederates in Chapter 3). A confederate may be useful to create a particular social situation. For example, in a study on aggression, the confederate and the participant both report to the experiment and are told to wait in a room for the experiment to begin. During the waiting period, the confederate insults the participant in an "anger" condition but does not insult the participant in a "no-anger" condition. The experimenter then enters and informs the two individuals that they will be interacting in a particular situation; the situation is designed so the actual participant can deliver a noxious stimulus to the confederate, such as a loud noise or a foul odor. The amount of noise or odor delivered is the measure of aggression; the researcher compares the amount given in the anger and no-anger conditions.

The classic Asch (1956) conformity experiment provides another example of how confederates may be used. Asch gathered people into groups and asked them to respond to a line judgment task such as the one in Figure 9.1. Which of the three test lines matches the standard? Although this appears to be a simple task, Asch made it more interesting by having the confederates announce the same incorrect judgment prior to asking the actual participant; this procedure was repeated over a number of trials with different line judgments. Asch was able to demonstrate how easy it is to produce conformity—participants conformed to the unanimous majority on many of the trials even though the correct answer was clear. Finally, confederates may be used in field experiments as well as laboratory research. For example, Baron studied helping behavior by having an accomplice pose as a shopper at a mall who asks actual shoppers for change (Baron, 1997).

Staged manipulations demand a great deal of ingenuity and even some acting ability. They are used to involve the participants in an ongoing social situation, which the individuals perceive not as an experiment but as a real experience. Researchers assume that the result will be natural behavior that truly reflects the feelings and intentions of the participants. However, such procedures allow for a great deal of subtle interpersonal communication that is hard to put into words; this may make it difficult for other researchers to replicate the experiment. Also, a complex manipulation is difficult to interpret. If many things happened during the experiment, what *one* thing was responsible for the results? In

**FIGURE 9.1**
Example of the Asch line judgment task

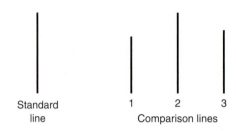

Standard
line

1      2      3
Comparison lines

general, it is easier to interpret results when the manipulation is relatively straightforward. However, the nature of the variable you are studying sometimes demands complicated procedures.

### Strength of the Manipulation

The simplest experimental design has two levels of the independent variable. In planning the experiment, the researcher has to choose these levels. A general principle to follow is to make the manipulation as strong as possible. A strong manipulation maximizes the differences between the two groups and increases the chances that the independent variable will have a statistically significant effect on the dependent variable.

To illustrate, suppose you think that there is a positive linear relationship between attitude similarity and liking ("birds of a feather flock together"). In conducting the experiment, you could arrange for participants to encounter another person, a confederate. In one group, the confederate and the participant would share similar attitudes; in the other group, the confederate and the participant would be dissimilar. Similarity, then, is the independent variable, and liking is the dependent variable. Now you have to decide on the amount of similarity. Figure 9.2 shows the hypothesized relationship between attitude similarity and liking at 10 different levels of similarity. Level 1 represents the least amount of similarity with no common attitudes, and level 10 the greatest (all attitudes are similar). To achieve the strongest manipulation, the participants in one group would encounter a confederate of level 1 similarity and those in the other group would encounter a confederate of level 10 similarity. This would result in the greatest difference in the liking means—a 9-point difference. A weaker manipulation—using levels 4 and 7, for example—would result in a smaller mean difference.

A strong manipulation is particularly important in the early stages of research, when the researcher is most interested in demonstrating that a relationship does, in fact, exist. If the early experiments reveal a relationship between the variables, subsequent research can systematically manipulate the other levels of the independent variable to provide a more detailed picture of the relationship.

The principle of using the strongest manipulation possible should be tempered by at least two considerations. First, the strongest possible manipulation may involve a situation that rarely, if ever, occurs in the real world. For example, an extremely strong crowding manipulation might involve placing so many peo-

FIGURE 9.2
Relationship between attitude similarity and liking

ple in a room that no one could move—a manipulation that might significantly affect a variety of behaviors. However, we wouldn't know if the results were similar to those occurring in more common, less crowded situations such as many classrooms or offices.

A second consideration is ethics: A manipulation should be as strong as possible within the bounds of ethics. A strong manipulation of fear or anxiety, for example, might not be possible because of the potential physical and psychological harm to participants.

### Cost of the Manipulation

Cost is another factor in the decision about how to manipulate the independent variable. Researchers who have limited monetary resources may not be able to afford expensive equipment, salaries for confederates, or payments to participants in long-term experiments. Also, a manipulation in which participants must be run individually requires more of the researcher's time than a manipulation that allows running many individuals in a single setting. In this respect, a manipulation that uses straightforward presentation of written or verbal material is less costly than a complex, staged, experimental manipulation. Some government and private agencies offer grants for research; because much research is costly, continued public support of these agencies is very important.

## MEASURING THE DEPENDENT VARIABLE

In previous chapters, we have discussed various aspects of measuring variables including reliability, validity, and reactivity of measures, observational methods, and the development of self-report measures for questionnaires and interviews. In this chapter, we will focus on measurement considerations that are particularly relevant to experimental research.

*Types of Measures*

The dependent variable in most experiments is one of three general types: self-report, behavioral, or physiological.

**Self-report measures**    Self-reports can be used to measure attitudes, liking for someone, judgments about someone's personality characteristics, intended behaviors, emotional states, attributions about why someone performed well or poorly on a task, confidence in one's judgments, and many other aspects of human thought and behavior. Rating scales with descriptive anchors (endpoints) are most commonly used. For example, the Labranche et al. (1997) study described earlier asked women to respond on a 7-point scale after they read the brochure:

> *I feel I could properly give myself a breast self-examination.*
>
> Strongly _____ _____ _____ _____ _____ _____ _____ Strongly
> disagree                                                agree

**Behavioral measures**    Behavioral measures are direct observations of behaviors. As with self-reports, measurements of an almost endless number of behaviors are possible. Sometimes, the researcher may record whether or not a given behavior occurs—for example, whether or not an individual responds to a request for help, makes an error on a test, or chooses to engage in one activity rather than another. Often, the researcher must decide whether to record the number of times a behavior occurs in a given time period—the *rate* of a behavior; how quickly a response occurs after a stimulus—a *reaction time;* or how long a behavior lasts—a measure of *duration*. The decision of which aspect of behavior to measure depends on which is most theoretically relevant for the study of a particular problem or which measure logically follows from the independent variable manipulation.

Sometimes, the nature of the variable being studied requires either a self-report or a behavioral measure. A measure of helping behavior is almost by definition a behavioral measure, whereas a measure of perception of the personality characteristics of someone will employ a self-report measure. For many variables, however, both self-reports and behavioral measures could be appropriate. Thus, liking or attraction could be measured on a rating scale or with a behavioral measure of the distance two people place between themselves or the amount of time they spend looking into each other's eyes. When both options are possible, a series of studies may be conducted to study the effects of an independent variable on both types of measures.

**Physiological measures**    Physiological measures are recordings of responses of the body. Many such responses are available; examples include the **galvanic skin response** (GSR), **electromyogram** (EMG), and **electroencephalogram** (EEG). The GSR is a measure of general emotional arousal and anxiety; it measures the electrical conductance of the skin, which changes when sweating occurs. The EMG measures muscle tension and is frequently used as a measure of tension or stress. The EEG is a measure of electrical activity of brain cells. It can be used to record general brain arousal as a response to different situations, activity in different parts of the brain as learning occurs, or brain activity during different stages of sleep.

The GSR, EMG, and EEG have long been used as physiological indicators of important psychological variables. Many other physiological measures are available, including temperature, heart rate, and information that can be gathered from blood or urine analysis (see Cacioppo & Tassinary, 1990). In recent years, magnetic resonance imaging (MRI) has become an increasingly important tool for researchers in behavioral neuroscience. An MRI provides an image of the brain structure of an individual. It allows scientists to compare the brain structure of individuals with a particular condition (e.g., a cognitive impairment, schizophrenia, or attention deficit hyperactivity disorder) with the brain structure of those without the condition. In addition, what is termed **functional MRI** (*fMRI*) allows researchers to scan areas of the brain while a research participant performs a physical or cognitive task. The data provide evidence for what brain processes are involved in these tasks. For example, a researcher can see which areas of the brain are most active when performing different memory tasks.

### Sensitivity of the Dependent Variable

The dependent variable should be sensitive enough to detect differences between groups. A measure of liking that asks, "Do you like this person?" with a simple "yes" or "no" response alternative is less sensitive than one that asks, "How much do you like this person?" on a 5- or 7-point scale. With the first measure, people may tend to be nice and say yes even if they have some negative feelings about the person. The second measure allows for a gradation of liking; such a scale would make it easier to detect differences in amount of liking.

The issue of **sensitivity** is particularly important when measuring human performance. Memory can be measured using recall, recognition, or reaction time; cognitive task performance might be measured by examining speed or number of errors during a proofreading task; physical performance can be measured through various motor tasks. Such tasks vary in their difficulty. Sometimes a task is so easy that everyone does well regardless of the conditions that are manipulated by the independent variable. This results in what is called a **ceiling effect**—the independent variable appears to have no effect on the dependent measure only because participants quickly reach the maximum performance level. The opposite problem occurs when a task is so difficult that hardly anyone can perform well; this is called a **floor effect.**

The need to consider sensitivity of measures is nicely illustrated in the Freedman et al. (1971) study of crowding mentioned in Chapter 4. The study examined the effect of crowding on various measures of cognitive task performance and found that crowding did not impair performance. You could conclude that crowding has no effect on performance; however, it is also possible that the measures were either too easy or too difficult to detect an effect of crowding. In fact, subsequent research showed that the tasks may have been too easy; when participants were asked to perform more complex tasks, crowding did result in lower performance (Paulus, Annis, Seta, Schkade, & Matthews, 1976).

## Multiple Measures

It is often desirable to measure more than one dependent variable. One reason to use multiple measures stems from the fact that a variable can be measured in a variety of concrete ways (recall the discussion of operational definitions in Chapter 4). In a study on health-related behaviors, for example, researchers measured the number of work days missed because of ill health, the number of doctor visits, and the use of aspirin and tranquilizers (Matteson & Ivancevich, 1983). Physiological measures might have been taken as well. If the independent variable has the same effect on several measures of the same dependent variable, our confidence in the results is increased. It is also useful to know whether the same independent variable affects some measures but not others. For example, an independent variable designed to affect liking might have an effect on some measures of liking (e.g., desirability as a person to work with) but not others (e.g., desirability as a dating partner). Researchers also may be interested in studying the effects of an independent variable on several different behaviors. For example, an experiment on the effects of a new classroom management technique might examine academic performance, interaction rates among classmates, and teacher satisfaction.

When you have more than one dependent measure, the question of *order* arises. Does it matter which measures are made first? Is it possible that the results for a particular measure will be different if the measure comes early rather than later? The issue is similar to the order effects that were discussed in Chapter 8 in the context of repeated measures designs. Perhaps responding to the first measures will somehow affect responses on the later measures; or perhaps the first measures are attended to more closely than later measures. There are two possible ways of responding to this issue. If it appears that the problem is serious, the order of presenting the measures can be counterbalanced using the counterbalancing techniques described in Chapter 8. Often there are no indications from previous research that order is a serious problem. In this case, the prudent response is to present the most important measures first and the less important ones later. With this approach, order will not be a problem in interpreting the results on the most important dependent variables. Even though order may be a potential problem for some of the measures, the overall impact on the study is minimized.

Making multiple measurements in a single experiment is valuable when it is feasible to do so. However, it may be necessary to conduct a series of experiments to explore the effects of an independent variable on various behaviors.

## Cost of Measures

Another consideration is cost—some measures may be more costly than others. Paper-and-pencil self-report measures are generally inexpensive; measures that require trained observers or elaborate equipment can become quite costly. A researcher studying nonverbal behavior, for example, might have to use a video camera to record each participant's behaviors in a situation. Two or more observers would then have to view the tapes to code behaviors such as eye contact, smiling, or self-touching (two observers are needed to ensure that the observations are reliable). Thus, there would be expenses for both equipment and personnel. Physiological recording devices are also expensive. Researchers need resources from the university or outside agencies to carry out such research.

## Ethics

Ethical concerns are always important. Researchers must be extremely careful about potential invasion of privacy and must always ensure that confidentiality issues have been addressed.

## ADDITIONAL CONTROLS

The basic experimental design has two groups: in the simplest case, an experimental group that receives the manipulation and a control group that does not. Use of a control group makes it possible to eliminate a variety of alternative explanations based on history, maturation, statistical regression, and so on. Sometimes additional control procedures may be necessary to address other types of alternative explanations. Two general control issues concern expectancies on the part of both the participants in the experiment and the experimenters.

### Controlling for Participant Expectations

**Demand characteristics**    We noted previously that experimenters do not wish to inform participants about the specific hypotheses being studied or the exact purpose of the research. The reason for this lies in the problem of **demand characteristics** (Orne, 1962). A demand characteristic is any feature of an experiment that might inform participants of the purpose of the study. The concern is that when participants form expectations about the hypothesis of the study, they will then do whatever is necessary to confirm the hypothesis; this, of course, assumes they are motivated to be cooperative. Orne conducted research to demonstrate that people are in fact cooperative. For example, he asked participants to add numbers on a sheet of paper; when they had finished, they picked up a card from a large stack for further instructions. Each instruction card said to tear the sheet into 32 pieces and to go to the next page of numbers. The participants continued this ridiculous task for several hours with no protest or questioning! Although you can probably think of situations in which the individuals would try to be uncooperative, Orne's conception of the cooperative participants seems to be generally correct.

One way to control for demand characteristics is to use deception—to make participants think that the experiment is studying one thing when actually it is studying something else. The experimenter may devise elaborate cover stories to explain the purpose of the study and to disguise what is really being studied. The researcher may also attempt to disguise the dependent measure by using an unobtrusive measure or by placing the measure among a set of unrelated **filler items** on a questionnaire. Another approach is simply to assess whether demand characteristics are a problem by asking participants about their perceptions of the purpose of the research. It may be that participants do not have an accurate view of the purpose of the study; or if some individuals do guess the hypotheses of the study, their data may be analyzed separately.

Demand characteristics may be eliminated when people are not aware that an experiment is taking place or that their behavior is being observed. Thus, experiments conducted in field settings and observational research in which the observer is concealed or unobtrusive measures are used minimize the problem of demand characteristics.

Placebo groups    A special kind of participant expectation arises in research on the effects of drugs. Consider an experiment that is investigating whether a drug such as Prozac reduces depression. One group of people diagnosed as depressive receives the drug and the other group does not. Now suppose that the drug group shows an improvement. We do not know whether the improvement was caused by the properties of the drug or by the expectations about the effect of the drug—what is called a *placebo effect*. In other words, just administering a pill or an injection may be sufficient to cause an observed improvement in behavior. To control for this possibility, a **placebo group** can be added. Participants in the placebo group receive a pill or injection containing an inert, harmless substance; they do not receive the drug given to members of the experimental group. If the improvement results from the active properties of the drug, the participants in the experimental group should show greater improvement than those in the placebo group. If the placebo group improves as much as the experimental group, the improvement is a placebo effect.

Sometimes, participants' expectations are the primary focus of an investigation. For example, Marlatt and Rohsenow (1980) conducted research to determine which behavioral effects of alcohol are due to alcohol itself as opposed to the psychological impact of believing one is drinking alcohol. The experimental design to examine these effects had four groups: (1) expect no alcohol–receive no alcohol, (2) expect no alcohol–receive alcohol, (3) expect alcohol–receive no alcohol, and (4) expect alcohol–receive alcohol. This design is called a *balanced placebo design*. Marlatt and Rohsenow's research suggests that the belief that one has consumed alcohol is a more important determinant of behavior than the alcohol itself. That is, people who believed they had consumed alcohol (Groups 3 and 4) behaved very similarly, although those in Group 3 were not actually given any alcohol.

In some areas of research, the use of placebo control groups has ethical implications. Suppose you are studying a treatment that does have a positive effect on people (for example, by reducing migraine headaches or alleviating symptoms of depression). It is important to use careful experimental procedures to make sure that the treatment does have an impact and that alternative explanations for the effect, including a placebo effect, are eliminated. However, it is also important to help those people who are in the control conditions. Participants in the control conditions may be given the treatment as soon as they have completed their part in the study.

Placebo effects are real and must seriously be studied in many areas of research. There is currently a great deal of research and debate on the extent to which any beneficial effects of antidepressant medications such as Prozac are due to placebo effects (e.g., Kirsch, Moore, Scoboria, & Nicholls, 2002).

## Controlling for Experimenter Expectations

Experimenters are usually aware of the purpose of the study and thus may develop expectations about how participants should respond. These expectations can in turn bias the results. This general problem is called **experimenter bias** or **expectancy effects** (Rosenthal, 1966, 1967, 1969).

Expectancy effects may occur whenever the experimenter knows which condition the participants are in. There are two potential sources of experimenter bias. First, the experimenter might unintentionally treat participants differently in the various conditions of the study. For example, certain words might be emphasized when reading instructions to one group but not the other, or the experimenter might smile more when interacting with people in one of the conditions. The second source of bias can occur when experimenters record the behaviors of the participants; there may be subtle differences in the way the experimenter interprets and records the behaviors.

**Research on expectancy effects**    Expectancy effects have been studied in a variety of ways. Perhaps the earliest demonstration of the problem is the case of Clever Hans, a horse whose alleged brilliance was revealed by Pfungst (1911) to be an illusion. Robert Rosenthal describes Clever Hans:

> Hans, it will be remembered, was the clever horse who could solve problems of mathematics and musical harmony with equal skill and grace, simply by tapping out the answers with his hoof. A committee of eminent experts testified that Hans, whose owner made no profit from his horse's talents, was receiving no cues from his questioners. Of course, Pfungst later showed that this was not so, that tiny head and eye movements were Hans' signals to begin and to end his tapping. When Hans was asked a question, the questioner looked at Hans' hoof, quite naturally so, for that was the way for him to determine whether Hans' answer was correct. Then, it was discovered that when Hans approached the correct number of taps, the questioner would inadvertently move his head or eyes upward—just enough that Hans could

discriminate the cue, but not enough that even trained animal observers or psychologists could see it.[1]

If a clever horse can respond to subtle cues, it is reasonable to suppose that clever humans can too. In fact, research has shown that experimenter expectancies can be communicated to humans by both verbal and nonverbal means (Duncan, Rosenberg, & Finklestein, 1969; Jones & Cooper, 1971). An example of more systematic research on expectancy effects is a study by Rosenthal (1966). In this experiment, graduate students trained rats that were described as coming from either "maze bright" or "maze dull" genetic strains. The animals actually came from the same strain and had been randomly assigned to the bright and dull categories; however, the "bright" rats *did* perform better than the "dull" rats. Subtle differences in the ways the students treated the rats or recorded their behavior must have caused this result. A generalization of this particular finding is called "teacher expectancy." Research has shown that telling a teacher that a pupil will bloom intellectually over the next year results in an increase in the pupil's IQ score (Rosenthal & Jacobson, 1968). In short, teachers' expectations can influence students' performance.

The problem of expectations influencing ratings of behavior is nicely illustrated in an experiment by Langer and Abelson (1974). Clinical psychologists were shown a videotape of an interview in which the person interviewed was described as either an applicant for a job or a patient; in reality, all saw the same tape. The psychologists later rated the person as more "disturbed" when they thought the person was a patient than when the person was described as a job applicant.

**Solutions to the expectancy problem**     Clearly, experimenter expectations can influence the outcomes of research investigations. How can this problem be solved? Fortunately, there are a number of ways of minimizing expectancy effects. First, experimenters should be well trained and should practice behaving consistently with all participants. The benefit of training was illustrated in the Langer and Abelson study with clinical psychologists. The bias of rating the "patient" as disturbed was much less among behavior-oriented therapists than among traditional ones. Presumably, the training of the behavior-oriented therapists led them to focus more on the actual behavior of the person, so they were less influenced by expectations stemming from the label of "patient."

Another solution is to run all conditions simultaneously so that the experimenter's behavior is the same for all participants. This solution is feasible only under certain circumstances, however, such as when the study can be carried out with the use of printed materials or the experimenter's instructions to participants are the same for everyone.

1. From Rosenthal, R. (1967). Convert communication in the psychological experiment. *Psychological Bulletin, 67,* 356–367. Copyright 1967 by the American Psychological Association. Reprinted by permission.

Expectancy effects are also minimized when the procedures are automated. As noted previously, it may be possible to manipulate independent variables and record responses using computers; with automated procedures, the experimenter's expectations are unlikely to influence the results.

A final solution is to use experimenters who are unaware of the hypothesis being investigated. In these cases, the person conducting the study or making observations is blind regarding what is being studied or which condition the participant is in. This procedure originated in drug research using placebo groups. In a *single-blind* experiment, the participant is unaware of whether a placebo or the actual drug is being administered; in a *double-blind* experiment, neither the participant nor the experimenter knows whether the placebo or actual treatment is being given. To use a procedure in which the experimenter or observer is unaware of either the hypothesis or the group the participant is in, you must hire other people to conduct the experiment and make observations.

Because researchers are aware of the problem of expectancy effects, solutions such as the ones just described are usually incorporated into the procedures of the study. If a study does have a potential problem of expectancy effects, researchers are bound to notice and will attempt to replicate the experiment with procedures that control for them. The procedures used in scientific research must be precisely defined so they can be replicated by others. This allows other researchers to build on previous research. It is also a self-correcting mechanism that ensures that methodological flaws will be discovered. The importance of replication will be discussed further in Chapter 14.

## ADDITIONAL CONSIDERATIONS

So far, we have discussed several of the factors that a researcher considers when planning a study. Actually conducting the study and analyzing the results is a time-consuming process. Before beginning the research, the investigator wants to be as sure as possible that everything will be done right. And once the study has been designed, there are some additional procedures that will improve it.

### Research Proposals

After putting considerable thought into planning the study, the researcher writes a research proposal. The proposal will have a literature review that provides a background for the study. The intent is to clearly explain why the research is being done—what questions the research is designed to answer. The details of the procedures that will be used to test the idea are then given. The plans for analysis of the data are also provided. A research proposal is very similar to the introduction and method sections of a journal article.

Such proposals must be included in applications for research grants; ethics review committees require some type of proposal as well (see Chapter 3 for more information on Institutional Review Boards). Preparing a proposal is a good idea in planning any research project. Simply putting your thoughts on paper helps to organize and systematize ideas. In addition, you can show the proposal to friends, colleagues, professors, and other interested parties who can provide useful feedback about the adequacy of your procedures. They may see problems that you didn't recognize, or they may offer ways of improving the study.

### Pilot Studies

When the researcher has finally decided on all the specific aspects of the procedure, it is possible to conduct a **pilot study** in which the researcher does a "trial run" with a small number of participants. The pilot study will reveal whether participants understand the instructions, whether the total experimental setting seems plausible, whether any confusing questions are being asked, and so on.

Sometimes participants in the pilot study are questioned in detail about the experience following the experiment. Another method is to use the "think aloud" protocol (described in Chapter 7) in which the participants in the pilot study are instructed to verbalize their thoughts about everything that is happening during the study. Such procedures provide the researcher with an opportunity to make any necessary changes in the procedure before doing the entire study. Also, a pilot study allows the experimenters who are collecting the data to become comfortable with their roles and to standardize their procedures.

### Manipulation Checks

A **manipulation check** is an attempt to directly measure whether the independent variable manipulation has the intended effect on the participants. Manipulation checks provide evidence for the construct validity of the manipulation (construct validity was discussed in Chapter 4). If you are manipulating anxiety, for example, a manipulation check will tell you whether participants in the high-anxiety group really were more anxious than those in the low-anxiety condition. The manipulation check might involve a self-report of anxiety, a behavioral measure (such as number of arm and hand movements), or a physiological measure. All manipulation checks, then, ask whether the independent variable manipulation was in fact a successful operationalization of the conceptual variable being studied. Consider, for example, a manipulation of physical attractiveness as an independent variable. In an experiment, participants respond to someone who is supposed to be perceived as attractive or unattractive. The manipulation check in this case would determine whether participants do rate the highly attractive person as more physically attractive.

Manipulation checks are particularly useful in the pilot study to decide whether the independent variable manipulation is in fact having the intended effect. If the independent variable is not effective, the procedures can be changed. However, it is also important to conduct a manipulation check in the actual experiment. Because a manipulation check in the actual experiment might distract participants or inform them about the purpose of the experiment, it is usually wise to position the administration of the manipulation check measure near the end of the experiment; in most cases, this would be after measuring the dependent variables and prior to the debriefing session.

A manipulation check has two advantages. First, if the check shows that your manipulation was not effective, you have saved the expense of running the actual experiment. You can turn your attention to changing the manipulation to make it more effective. For instance, if the manipulation check shows that neither the low- nor the high-anxiety group was very anxious, you could change your procedures to increase the anxiety in the high-anxiety condition.

Second, a manipulation check is advantageous if you get nonsignificant results—that is, if the results indicate that no relationship exists between the independent and dependent variables. A manipulation check can identify whether the nonsignificant results are due to a problem in manipulating the independent variable. If your manipulation is not successful, it is only reasonable that you will obtain nonsignificant results. If both groups are equally anxious after you manipulate anxiety, anxiety can't have any effect on the dependent measure. What if the check shows that the manipulation was successful, but you still get nonsignificant results? Then you know at least that the results were not due to a problem with the manipulation; the reason for not finding a relationship lies elsewhere. Perhaps you had a poor dependent measure, or perhaps there really is no relationship between the variables.

### Debriefing

The importance of debriefing was discussed in Chapter 3 in the context of ethical considerations. After all the data are collected, a debriefing session is usually held. This is an opportunity for the researcher to interact with the participants to discuss the ethical and educational implications of the study.

The debriefing session can also provide an opportunity to learn more about what participants were thinking during the experiment. Researchers can ask participants what they believed to be the purpose of the experiment, how they interpreted the independent variable manipulation, and what they were thinking when they responded to the dependent measures. Such information can prove useful in interpreting the results and planning future studies.

Finally, researchers may ask the participants to refrain from discussing the study with others. Such requests are typically made when more people will be participating and they may talk with one another in classes or residence halls. People who have already participated are aware of the general purposes and procedures; it is important that these individuals not provide expectancies about the study to potential future participants.

## ANALYZING AND INTERPRETING RESULTS

After the data have been collected, the next step is to analyze them. Statistical analyses of the data are carried out to allow the researcher to examine and interpret the pattern of results obtained in the study. The statistical analysis helps the researcher decide whether there really is a relationship between the independent and dependent variables; the logic underlying the use of statistical tests is discussed in Chapter 13. It is not the purpose of this book to teach statistical methods; however, the calculations involved in several statistical tests are provided in Appendix B.

## COMMUNICATING RESEARCH TO OTHERS

The final step is to write a report that details why you conducted the research, how you obtained the participants, what procedures you used, and what you found. A description of how to write such reports is included in Appendix A. After you have written the report, what do you do with it? How do you communicate the findings to others? Research findings are most often submitted as journal articles or as papers to be read at scientific meetings. In either case, the submitted paper is evaluated by two or more knowledgeable reviewers who decide whether the paper is acceptable for publication or presentation at the meeting.

### Professional Meetings

Meetings sponsored by professional associations are important opportunities for researchers to present their findings to other researchers and the public. National and regional professional associations such as the American Psychological Association (APA) and the American Psychological Society (APS) hold annual meetings at which psychologists and psychology students present their own research and learn about the latest research being done by their colleagues. Sometimes, verbal presentations are delivered to an audience. However, poster sessions are more common; here, researchers display posters that summarize the research and are available to discuss the research with others.

### Journal Articles

As we noted in Chapter 2, there are many journals in which research papers are published. Nevertheless, the number of journals is small compared to the number of reports written; thus, it is not easy to publish research. When a researcher submits a paper to a journal, two or more reviewers read the paper and recommend acceptance (often with the stipulation that revisions be made) or rejection. This process is called *peer review* and it is very important in making sure that research has careful external review before it is published. As many as 90% of papers submitted to the more prestigious journals are rejected. Many rejected papers are submitted to other journals and eventually accepted for publication, but much research is never published. This is not necessarily bad; it simply means that selection processes separate high-quality research from that of lesser quality.

Many of the decisions that must be made when planning an experiment were described in this chapter. The discussion focused on experiments that use the simplest experimental design with a single independent variable. In the next chapter, more complex experimental designs are described.

## Study Terms

Behavioral measure

Ceiling effect

Confederate

Debriefing

Demand characteristics

Double-blind procedure

Electroencephalogram

Electromyogram

Expectancy effects (experimenter bias)

Filler items

Floor effect

Functional MRI

Galvanic skin response

Manipulation check

Manipulation strength

MRI

Physiological measure

Pilot study

Placebo group

Self-report measure

Sensitivity

Single-blind procedure

Staged manipulation

Straightforward manipulation

## Review Questions

1. Distinguish between staged and straightforward manipulations of an independent variable.
2. Distinguish between the general types of dependent variables.
3. What is meant by the sensitivity of a measure? What are ceiling and floor effects?
4. Discuss the ways that computers can be used in conducting an experiment.
5. What are demand characteristics? Describe ways to minimize demand characteristics.
6. What is the reason for a placebo group?
7. What are experimenter expectancy effects? What are some solutions to the experimenter bias problem?
8. What methods can be used to debug an experiment?
9. What is a pilot study?

10. What is a manipulation check? How does it help the researcher interpret the results of an experiment?

11. What does a researcher do with the findings after completing a research project?

## Activity Questions

1. Dr. Turk studied the relationship between age and reading comprehension, specifically predicting that older people will show lower comprehension than younger ones. Turk was particularly interested in comprehension of material that is available in the general press. Groups of participants who were 20, 30, 40, and 50 years of age read a chapter from a book by physicist Stephen W. Hawking (1988) entitled *A Brief History of Time: From the Big Bang to Black Holes* (the book was on the best-seller list at the time). After reading the chapter, participants were given a comprehension measure. The results showed that there was no relationship between age and comprehension scores; all age groups had equally low comprehension scores. Why do you think no relationship was found? Identify at least two possible reasons.

2. Recall the experiment on facilitated communication by children with autism that was described in Chapter 2 (Montee, Miltenberger, & Wittrock, 1995). Interpret the findings of that study in terms of experimenter expectancy effects.

3. Your lab group has been assigned the task of designing an experiment to investigate the effect of time spent studying on a recall task. Thus far, your group has come up with the following plan: "Participants will be randomly assigned to two groups. Individuals in one group will study a list of 5 words for 5 minutes, and those in the other group will study the same list for 7 minutes. Immediately after studying, the participants will read a list of 10 words and circle those that appeared on the original study list." Refine this experiment, giving specific reasons for any changes.

4. If you were investigating variables that affect helping behavior, would you be more likely to use a straightforward or staged manipulation? Why?

5. Design an experiment using a staged manipulation to test the hypothesis that when people are in a good mood, they are more likely to contribute to a charitable cause. Include a manipulation check in your design.

6. In a pilot study, Dr. Mori conducted a manipulation check and found no significant difference between the experimental conditions. Should she continue with the experiment? What should she do next? Explain your recommendations for Dr. Mori.

7. Write a debriefing statement that you would read to participants in the Asch study.

# 10

# Complex Experimental Designs

T hus far we have focused primarily on the simplest experimental design in which one independent variable is manipulated with two levels and one dependent variable is measured. This simple design allows us to examine important aspects of research, such as internal validity and procedures for assigning participants to conditions. However, researchers often investigate problems that demand more complicated designs. These complex experimental designs are the subject of this chapter.

## INCREASING THE NUMBER OF LEVELS OF AN INDEPENDENT VARIABLE

In the simplest experimental design, there are only two levels of the independent variable. However, a researcher might want to design an experiment with three or more levels for several reasons. First, a design with only two levels of the independent variable cannot provide very much information about the exact form of the relationship between the independent and dependent variables. For example, Figure 10.1 shows the outcome of a hypothetical experiment on the relationship between motivation and performance on a motor task. The solid line describes the results when there are only two levels—no reward for good performance and $4.00 promised for high performance. Because there are only two levels, the relationship can be described only with a straight line. We do not know what the relationship would be if other amounts were included as levels of the independent variable. The broken line in Figure 10.1 shows the results when $1.00, $2.00, and $3.00 are also included. This result is a more accurate description of the relationship between amount of reward promised and performance. In the hypothetical experiment, the amount of reward is very effective in increasing performance up to a point, after which only modest increases in performance accompany increases in reward. Thus, the relationship is a monotonic

FIGURE 10.1
Results of a hypothetical experiment: linear versus positive monotonic functions

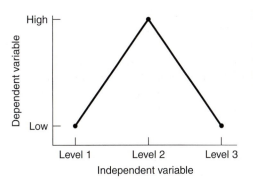

**FIGURE 10.2**
An inverted-U curvilinear relationship

*Note:* At least three levels of the independent variable are required to show curvilinear relationships.

positive relationship rather than a strictly linear relationship (see Chapter 4). An experiment with only two levels cannot yield such exact information.

Recall from Chapter 4 that variables are sometimes related in a curvilinear or nonmonotonic fashion; that is, the direction of relationship changes. Figure 10.2 shows an example of a curvilinear relationship; this particular form of curvilinear relationship is called an *inverted-U*. An experimental design with only two levels of the independent variable cannot detect curvilinear relationships between variables. If a curvilinear relationship is predicted, at least three levels must be used. As Figure 10.2 shows, if only levels 1 and 3 of the independent variable had been used, no relationship between the variables would have been detected. Many such curvilinear relationships exist in psychology. The relationship between fear arousal and attitude change is one example. Increasing the amount of fear aroused by a persuasive message increases attitude change up to a moderate level of fear; further increases in fear arousal actually reduce attitude change.

Finally, researchers frequently are interested in comparing more than two groups. Suppose you want to know whether playing with an animal has beneficial effects on nursing home residents. You could have two conditions, such as a no-animal control group and a group in which a dog is brought in for play each day. However, you might also be interested in knowing the effect of a cat and a bird and so you could add these two groups to your study. Or you might be interested in comparing the effect of a large versus a small dog in addition to a no-animal control condition. In an actual study on stress reduction techniques by Bruning and Frew (1987), employees were randomly assigned to one of four groups: exercise, management skills training, meditation, and a no-treatment control. In this study, all three techniques led to decreases in blood pressure and pulse rate.

## INCREASING THE NUMBER OF INDEPENDENT VARIABLES: FACTORIAL DESIGNS

Researchers often manipulate more than one independent variable in a single experiment. Typically, two or three independent variables are operating simultaneously. This type of experimental design is a closer approximation of real-world conditions, in which independent variables do not exist by themselves. Researchers recognize that in any given situation a number of variables are operating to affect behavior, so they design experiments with more than one independent variable.

**Factorial designs** are designs with more than one independent variable (or *factor*). In a factorial design, all levels of each independent variable are combined with all levels of the other independent variables. The simplest factorial design—known as a 2 × 2 (two by two) factorial design—has two independent variables, each having two levels.

An experiment by Smith and Ellsworth (1987) illustrates a 2 × 2 factorial design. Smith and Ellsworth studied the effects of asking misleading questions on the accuracy of eyewitness testimony. Participants in the experiment first viewed a videotape of a robbery and then were asked questions about what they saw. One independent variable was the type of question—misleading or unbiased. The second independent variable was the questioner's knowledge of the crime: The person asking the questions had either viewed the tape only once (a "naive" questioner) or had seen the tape a number of times (a "knowledgeable" questioner).

This 2 × 2 design results in four experimental conditions: (1) knowledgeable questioner–misleading questions, (2) knowledgeable questioner–unbiased questions, (3) naive questioner–misleading questions, and (4) naive questioner–unbiased questions. A 2 × 2 design always has four groups. The general format for describing factorial designs is

$$\frac{\text{Number of levels}}{\text{of first IV}} \times \frac{\text{Number of levels}}{\text{of second IV}} \times \frac{\text{Number of levels}}{\text{of third IV}}$$

and so on. A design with two independent variables, one having two levels and the other having three levels, is a 2 × 3 factorial design; there are six conditions in the experiment. A 3 × 3 design has nine conditions.

### Interpretation of Factorial Designs

Factorial designs yield two kinds of information. The first is information about the effect of each independent variable taken by itself: the **main effect** of an independent variable. In a design with two independent variables, there are two main effects—one for each independent variable. The second type of information is called an **interaction.** If there is an interaction between two independent variables, the effect of one independent variable depends on the particular level of the other variable. In other words, the effect that an independent variable has on the dependent variable depends on the level of the other independent variable. Interactions are a new source of information that cannot be obtained in a simple experimental design in which only one independent variable is manipulated.

To illustrate main effects and interactions, we can look at the results of the Smith and Ellsworth study on accuracy of eyewitness testimony. Table 10.1 illustrates a common method of presenting outcomes for the various groups in a factorial design. The number in each cell represents the mean percent of errors made in the four conditions.

TABLE 10.1     2 × 2 factorial design: Results of the eyewitness testimony experiment

| Questioneer type (independent variable B) | Type of question (independent variable A) | | Overall means (main effect of B) |
|---|---|---|---|
| | Unbiased | Misleading | |
| Knowledge | 13 | 41 | 27.0 |
| Naive | 13 | 18 | 15.5 |
| Overall means (main effect of A) | 13.0 | 29.5 | |

**Main effects**     A main effect is the effect each variable has by itself. The main effect of independent variable A, type of question, is the overall effect of the variable on the dependent measure. Similarly, the main effect of independent variable B, type of questioner, is the effect of the different types of questions on accuracy of recall.

The main effect of each independent variable is the overall relationship between the independent variable and the dependent variable. For independent variable A, is there a relationship between type of question and recall errors? We can find out by looking at the overall means in the unbiased and misleading question conditions. These means are shown in the margins of Table 10.1. The overall percent of errors made by participants in the misleading questions condition is 29.5, and the error percent in the unbiased question condition is 13.0. These overall main effect means are obtained by averaging across all participants in each group, irrespective of the type of questioner (knowledgeable or naive). Note that the overall mean of 29.5 in the misleading question condition is the average of 41 in the knowledgeable–misleading group and 18 in the naive–misleading group (this calculation assumes equal numbers of participants in each group). You can see that, overall, more errors are made when the questions are misleading than when they are unbiased. Statistical tests would enable us to determine whether this is a significant main effect.

The main effect for independent variable B (questioner type) is the overall relationship between that independent variable, by itself, and the dependent variable. You can see in Table 10.1 that the overall score in the knowledgeable questioner condition is 27.0, and the overall score in the naive questioner group is 15.5. Thus, in general, more errors result when the questioner is knowledgeable.

**Interactions**     These main effects tell us that, overall, there are more errors when the questioner is knowledgeable and when the questions are misleading. There is also the possibility that an interaction exists; if so, the main effects of the independent variables must be qualified. This is because an interaction between independent variables indicates that the effect of one independent

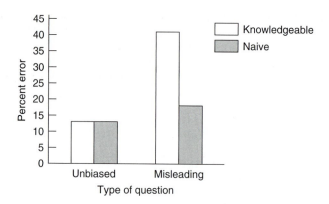

variable is different at different levels of the other independent variable. That
is, an interaction tells us that the effect of one independent variable depends
on the particular level of the other.

We can see an interaction in the results of the Smith and Ellsworth study.
The effect of the type of question is different depending on whether the questioner is knowledgeable or naive. When the questioner is knowledgeable, misleading questions result in more errors (41% in the misleading question
condition versus 13% in the unbiased condition). However, when the questioner
is naive, the type of question has little effect (18% for misleading questions and
13% for unbiased questions). Thus, the relationship between type of question
and recall errors is best understood by considering both independent variables:
We must consider whether the questions are misleading *and* whether the questioner is knowledgeable or naive.

Interactions can be seen easily when the means for all conditions are presented in a graph. Figure 10.3 shows a bar graph of the results of the eyewitness
testimony experiment. Note that all four means have been graphed. Two bars
compare the types of questioner in the unbiased question condition; the same
comparison is shown for the misleading question condition. You can see that
questioner knowledge is not a factor when an unbiased question is asked; however, when the question is misleading, the knowledgeable questioner has a
greater ability to create bias than does the naive questioner.

The concept of interaction is a relatively simple one that you probably use all
the time. When we say "it depends," we are usually indicating that some sort of
interaction is operating—it depends on some other variable. Suppose, for example, that a friend has asked you if you want to go to a movie. Whether you go may
reflect an interaction between two variables: (1) Is an exam coming up? and
(2) who stars in the movie? If there is an exam coming up, you won't go under
any circumstance. If you do not have an exam to worry about, your decision will
depend on whether you like the person in the movie; that is, you will go only if
a favorite star is in the movie.

You might try graphing the movie example in the same way we graphed the eyewitness testimony example in Figure 10.3. The dependent variable (going to the movie) is always placed on the vertical axis. One independent variable is placed on the horizontal axis. Bars are then drawn to represent each of the levels of the other independent variable. Graphing the results in this manner is a useful method of visualizing interactions in a factorial design.

### Factorial Designs With Manipulated and Nonmanipulated Variables

One common type of factorial design includes both experimental (manipulated) and nonexperimental (measured or nonmanipulated) variables. These designs— sometimes called **IV × PV designs** (i.e., independent variable by participant variable)—allow researchers to investigate how different types of individuals (i.e., participants) respond to the same manipulated variable. These "participant variables" are personal attributes such as gender, age, ethnic group, personality characteristics, and clinical diagnostic category. You will sometimes see participant variables described as subject variables or attribute variables. This is only a difference of terminology.

The simplest IV × PV design includes one manipulated independent variable that has at least two levels and one participant variable with at least two levels. The two levels of the subject variable might be two different age groups, groups of low and high scorers on a personality measure, or groups of males and females. An example of this design is a study by Furnham, Gunter, and Peterson (1994). Do you ever try to study when there is a distraction such as a television program? Furnham et al. showed that the ability to study with such a distraction depends on whether you are more extraverted or introverted. The manipulated variable was distraction. College students read material in silence and within hearing range of a TV drama. Thus, a repeated measures design was used and the order of the conditions was counterbalanced. After they read the material, the students completed a reading comprehension measure. The participant variable was extraversion: Participants completed a measure of extraversion and then were classified as extraverts or introverts. The results are shown in Figure 10.4. There was a main effect of distraction and an interaction.

Overall, students had higher comprehension scores when they studied in silence. In addition, there was an interaction between extraversion and distraction. Without a distraction, the performance of extraverts and introverts was almost the same. However, extraverts performed better than introverts when the TV was on. If you are an extravert, be more understanding when your introverted friends want things quiet when studying!

Factorial designs with both manipulated independent variables and participant variables offer a very appealing method for investigating many interesting research questions. Such experiments recognize that full understanding of behavior requires knowledge of both situational variables and the personal attributes of individuals.

FIGURE 10.4
Interaction in IV × PV design

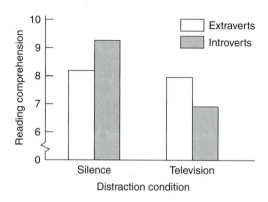

### Interactions and Moderator Variables

In many research studies, interactions are discussed in terms of the operation of a **moderator variable.** A moderator variable influences the relationship between two other variables (Baron & Kenny, 1986). In the jury study, we can begin with a general statement of the relationship between the type of question and recall errors, e.g., *misleading questions result in more errors than do unbiased questions.* What if we then make a qualifying statement that the type of questioner influences this relationship: *Misleading questions result in more errors only when the questioner is believed to be knowledgeable; no increase in errors will occur when the questioner is naive.* The questioner variable is a moderator variable because it *moderates* the relationship between the other variables. Moderator variables may be particular situations, as in the jury study by Smith and Ellsworth (1987), or they may be characteristics of people, as in the study on studying by extraverts and introverts.

### Outcomes of a 2 × 2 Factorial Design

A 2 × 2 factorial design has two independent variables, each with two levels. When analyzing the results, there are several possibilities: (1) There may or may not be a significant main effect for independent variable A, (2) there may or may not be a significant main effect for independent variable B, and (3) there may or may not be a significant interaction between the independent variables.

Figure 10.5 illustrates the eight possible outcomes in a 2 × 2 factorial design. For each outcome, the means are given and then graphed using bar graphs. The means that are given in the figure are idealized examples; such perfect outcomes rarely occur in actual research. Nevertheless, you should study the graphs to determine for yourself why, in each case, there is or is not a main effect for A, a main effect for B, and an A × B interaction.

The first four graphs illustrate outcomes in which there is no A × B interaction, and the last four graphs depict outcomes in which there is an interaction.

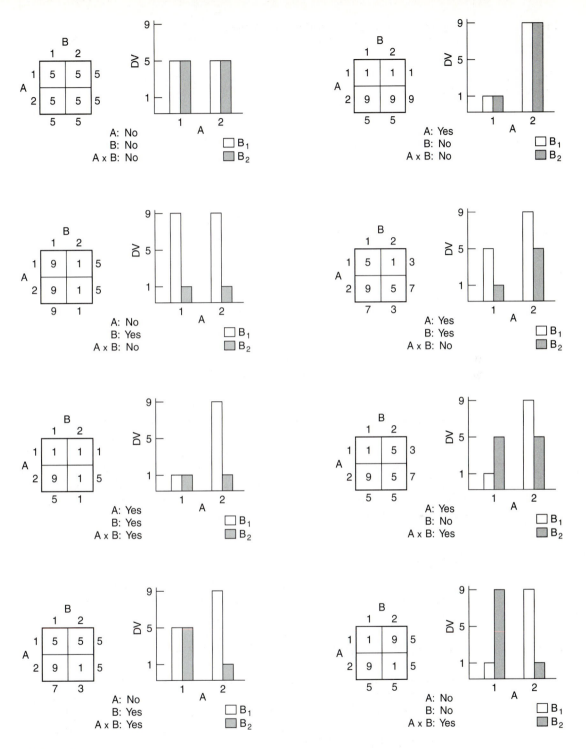

FIGURE 10.5
Outcomes of a factorial design with two independent variables

When there is a statistically significant interaction, you need to carefully examine the means to understand why the interaction occurred. In some cases, there is a strong relationship between the first independent variable and the dependent variable at one level of the second independent variable; however, there is no relationship or a weak relationship at the other level of the second independent variable. In other studies, the interaction may indicate that an independent variable has opposite effects on the dependent variable, depending on the level of the second independent variable. This pattern is shown in the last graph in Figure 10.5.

The independent and dependent variables in the figure do not have concrete variable labels. As an exercise, interpret each of the graphs using actual variables from three different hypothetical experiments. This works best if you draw the graphs, including labels for the variables, on a separate sheet of paper for each experiment:

Hypothetical experiment 1: Effect of age of defendant and type of substance use during an offense on months of sentence. A male, age 20 or 50, was found guilty of causing a traffic accident while under the influence of either alcohol or marijuana.

Independent variable A: Type of Offense—Alcohol versus Marijuana

Independent variable B: Age of Defendant—20 versus 50 years of age

Dependent variable: Months of sentence (range from 0 to 10 months)

Hypothetical experiment 2: Effect of gender and violence on recall of advertising. Participants (males and females) viewed a video on a computer screen that was either violent or not violent. They were then asked to read print ads for eight different products over the next 3 minutes. The dependent variable was the number of ads correctly recalled.

Independent variable A: Exposure to Violence: Nonviolent versus Violent Video

Independent variable B: Participant Gender: Male versus Female

Dependent variable: Number of ads recalled (range from 0 to 8)

Hypothetical experiment 3: Devise your own experiment with two independent variables and one dependent variable.

### Interactions and Simple Main Effects

A procedure called analysis of variance is used to assess the statistical significance of the main effects and the interaction in a factorial design. When there is a significant interaction, there is a need to statistically evaluate the individual means. If you take a look at Figure 10.3 once again, you see a clear interaction. When there is a significant interaction, the next step is to look at the **simple main effects.** A simple main effect analysis examines mean differences at *each level* of the independent variable. Recall that the main effect of an independent variable averages across the levels of the other independent variable; with simple main effects, the results are analyzed as if we had separate experiments at each level of the other independent variable.

**Simple main effect of type of questioner**    In Figure 10.3, we can look at the simple main effect of type of questioner. This will tell us whether the difference between the knowledgeable and naive questioner is significant when the question is (1) unbiased and (2) misleading. In this case, the simple main effect of type of question is significant when the question is misleading (means of 41 versus 18), but the simple main effect of question type is not significant when the question is unbiased (means of 13 and 13).

**Simple main effect of type of question**    We could also examine the simple main effect of type of question; here, we would compare the two questions when the questioner is (1) knowledgeable and (2) naive. The simple main effect that you will be most interested in will depend on the predictions that you made when you designed the study. The exact statistical procedures do not concern us; the point here is that the pattern of results with all the means must be examined when there is a significant interaction in a factorial design.

### Assignment Procedures and Factorial Designs

The considerations of assigning participants to conditions that were discussed in Chapter 8 can be generalized to factorial designs. There are two basic ways of assigning participants to conditions: (1) In an independent groups design, different participants are assigned to each of the conditions in the study; (2) in a repeated measures design, the *same* individuals participate in all conditions in the study. These two types of assignment procedures have implications for the number of participants necessary to complete the experiment. We can illustrate this fact by looking at a 2 × 2 factorial design. The design can be completely independent groups, completely repeated measures, or a **mixed factorial design**— that is, a combination of the two.

**Independent groups**    In a 2 × 2 factorial design, there are four conditions. If we want a completely independent groups design, a different group of participants will be assigned to each of the four conditions. The Smith and Ellsworth (1987) study on eyewitness testimony and the Petty, Cacioppo, and Goldman (1981) study on the effect of communicator credibility and personal involvement on attitude change that was described in Chapter 9 illustrate factorial designs with different individuals in each of the conditions. Suppose that you have planned a 2 × 2 design and want to have 10 participants in each condition; you will need a total of 40 *different* participants, as shown in the first table in Figure 10.6.

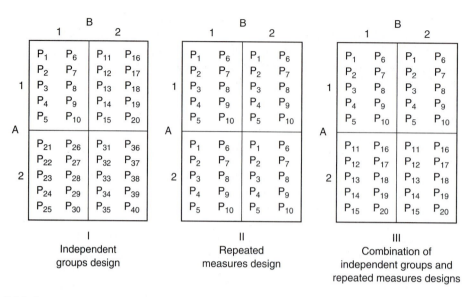

**FIGURE 10.6**
Number of participants required to have 10 observations in each condition

**Repeated measures**    In a completely repeated measures procedure, the same individuals will participate in *all* conditions. Suppose you have planned a study on the effects of marijuana similar to the one by Wilson, Ellinwood, Mathew, and Johnson (1994) that was described in Chapter 8: One factor is marijuana (marijuana treatment versus placebo control) and the other factor is task difficulty (easy versus difficult). In a 2 × 2 completely repeated measures design, each individual would participate in all of the conditions by completing both easy and difficult tasks under both marijuana treatment conditions. If you wanted 10 participants in each condition, a total of 10 subjects would be needed, as illustrated in the second table in Figure 10.6. This design offers considerable savings in the number of participants required. In deciding whether to use a completely repeated measures assignment procedure, however, the researcher would have to consider the disadvantages of repeated measures designs.

**Mixed factorial design using combined assignment**    The Furnham, Gunter, and Peterson (1994) study on television distraction and extraversion illustrates the use of both independent groups and repeated measures procedures in a mixed factorial design. The participant variable, extraversion, is an independent groups variable. Distraction is a repeated measures variable; all participants studied with both distraction and silence. The third table in Figure 10.6 shows the number of participants needed to have 10 per condition in a 2 × 2 mixed factorial design. In this table, independent variable A is an independent groups variable. Ten participants are assigned to level 1 of this independent variable, and another 10 participants are assigned to level 2. Independent variable B is a repeated measures variable, however. The 10 participants assigned to $A_1$ receive both levels of independent variable B. Similarly, the other 10 participants assigned to $A_2$ receive both levels of the B variable. Thus, a total of 20 participants are required.

### Increasing the Number of Levels of an Independent Variable

The 2 × 2 is the simplest factorial design. With this basic design, the researcher can arrange experiments that are more and more complex. One way to increase complexity is to increase the number of levels of one or more of the independent variables. A 2 × 3 design, for example, contains two independent variables: Independent variable A has two levels, and independent variable B has three levels. Thus, the 2 × 3 design has six conditions. Table 10.2 shows a 2 × 3 factorial design with the independent variables of task difficulty (easy, hard) and anxiety level (low, moderate, high). The dependent variable is performance on the task. The numbers in each of the six cells of the design indicate the mean performance score of the group. The overall means in the margins show the main effects of each of the independent variables. The results in Table 10.2 indicate a main effect of task difficulty because the *overall* performance score in the easy-task group is higher than the hard-task mean. However, there is no main effect of anxiety because the mean performance score is the same in each of the three anxiety groups. Is there an interaction between task difficulty and anxiety? Note that increasing the amount of anxiety has the effect of increasing performance on the easy task but *decreasing* performance on the hard task. The effect of anxiety is different, depending on whether the task is easy or hard; thus, there is an interaction.

  This interaction can be easily seen in a graph. The previous figures in this chapter have been bar graphs. Figure 10.7 is a line graph. The data in a bar graph

**TABLE 10.2**    2 × 3 factorial design

| Task difficulty | Anxiety level | | | Overall means (main effect) |
|---|---|---|---|---|
| | Low | Moderate | High | |
| Easy | 4 | 7 | 10 | 7.0 |
| Hard | 7 | 4 | 1 | 4.0 |
| Overall means (main effect) | 5.5 | 5.5 | 5.5 | |

FIGURE 10.7
Line graph of date from 3
(anxiety level) × 2 (task
difficulty) factorial design

and a line graph can be the same but the visual representation differs somewhat. Lines are drawn instead of bars to show the findings for each independent variable. In Figure 10.7, one line shows the effect of anxiety for the easy task
and a second line represents the effect of anxiety for the difficult task. Line
graphs are used when the independent variable represented on the horizontal
axis is quantitative. The levels of the independent variable are increasing
amounts of the variable.

### Increasing the Number of Independent Variables in a Factorial Design

We can also increase the number of variables in the design. A 2 × 2 × 2 factorial
design contains three variables, each with two levels. Thus, there are eight conditions in this design. In a 2 × 2 × 3 design, there are 12 conditions; in a 2 × 2
× 2 × 2 design, there are 16. The rule for constructing factorial designs remains
the same throughout.

A 2 × 2 × 2 factorial design is constructed in Table 10.3. The independent
variables are (1) instruction method (lecture, discussion), (2) class size (10, 40),
and (3) student gender (male, female). Note that gender is a nonmanipulated
variable and the other two variables are manipulated variables. The dependent
variable is performance on a standard test.

Notice that the 2 × 2 × 2 design can be seen as two 2 × 2 designs, one for
the males and another for the females. The design yields main effects for each of
the three independent variables. For example, the overall mean for the lecture
method is obtained by considering all participants who experience the lecture
method, irrespective of class size or gender. Similarly, the discussion method
mean is derived from all participants in this condition. The *two* means are then
compared to see whether there is a significant main effect: Is one method superior to the other *overall?*

**TABLE 10.3**    2 × 2 × 2 factorial design

| Instruction method | Class size | |
|---|---|---|
| | 10 | 40 |
| | Male | |
| Lecture | | |
| Discussion | | |
| | Female | |
| Lecture | | |
| Discussion | | |

The design also allows us to look at interactions. In the 2 × 2 × 2 design, we can look at the interaction between (1) method and class size, (2) method and gender, and (3) class size and gender. We can also look at a three-way interaction that involves all three independent variables. Here, we want to determine whether the nature of the interaction between two of the variables differs depending on the particular level of the other variable. Three-way interactions are rather complicated; fortunately, you will not encounter too many of these in your explorations of behavioral science research.

Sometimes students are tempted to include in a study as many independent variables as they can think of. A problem with this is that the design may become needlessly complex and require enormous numbers of participants. The design previously discussed had 8 groups; a 2 × 2 × 2 × 2 design has 16 groups; adding yet another independent variable with two levels means that 32 groups would be required. Also, when there are more than three or four independent variables, many of the particular conditions that are produced by the combination of so many variables do not make sense or could not occur under natural circumstances.

The designs described thus far all use the same logic for determining that the independent variable did in fact cause a change on the dependent variable measure. In the next chapter, we will consider alternative designs that use somewhat different procedures for examining the relationship between independent and dependent variables.

## Study Terms

Factorial design

Interaction

IV × PV design

Main effect

Mixed factorial design

Moderator variable

Simple main effect

## Review Questions

1. Why would a researcher have more than two levels of the independent variable in an experiment?
2. What is a factorial design? Why would a researcher use a factorial design?
3. What are main effects in a factorial design? What is an interaction?
4. Describe an IV × PV factorial design.
5. Identify the number of conditions in a factorial design on the basis of knowing the number of independent variables and the number of levels of each independent variable.

## Activity Questions

1. In a study by Chaiken and Pliner (1987), research participants read an "eating diary" of either a male or female stimulus person. The information in the diary indicated that the person ate either large meals or small meals. After reading this information, participants rated the person's femininity and masculinity.

   a. Identify the design of this experiment.

   b. How many conditions are in the experiment?

   c. Identify the independent variable(s) and dependent variable(s).

   d. Is there a participant variable in this experiment? If so, identify it. If not, can you suggest a participant variable that might be included?

2. Chaiken and Pliner reported the following mean femininity ratings (higher numbers indicate greater femininity): male–small meals (2.02), male–large meals (2.05), female–small meals (3.90), and female–large meals (2.82). Assume there are equal numbers of participants in each condition.

   a. Are there any main effects?

   b. Is there an interaction?

   c. Graph the means.

   d. Describe the results in a brief paragraph.

3. Using recent psychology journals, find an example of a 2 × 2 independent groups design. Identify each factor and the levels of each factor. Find another experiment that exemplifies a two-factor design using repeated measures for one or more variables; identify whether it is a completely repeated measures procedure or a mixed factorial design. Identify each factor and the levels of each factor. Was there an interaction? If so, describe the interaction.

4. Assume that you want 15 participants in each condition of your experiment that uses a 3 × 3 factorial design. How many *different* participants do you need for (a) a completely independent groups assignment, (b) a completely repeated measures assignment, and (c) a mixed factorial design with both independent groups assignment and repeated measures variables?

# 11

# Quasi-Experimental and Single Case Experimental Designs

In the classic experimental design described in Chapter 8, participants are randomly assigned to the independent variable conditions, and a dependent variable is measured. The responses on the dependent measure are then compared to determine whether the independent variable had an effect. Because all other variables are held constant, differences on the dependent variable must be due to the effect of the independent variable. This design has high internal validity—we are very confident that the independent variable caused the observed responses on the dependent variable. You will frequently encounter this experimental design when you explore research in the behavioral sciences. However, other research designs have been devised to address special research problems. This chapter focuses on quasi-experimental and single case research designs—research approaches that present interesting challenges to determining internal validity.

As we noted in Chapter 1, researchers frequently investigate applied research questions and conduct evaluation research. Quasi-experimental designs emerged from the need to conduct applied research in settings in which the control features of true experimental designs cannot be achieved. In a **quasi-experimental design,** there is a need to assess the impact of an independent variable on a dependent variable. However, causal inference is much more difficult because quasi-experiments lack all the control features of true experiments. In this chapter, we will examine several quasi-experimental designs that might be used in situations in which a true experiment is not possible. Although quasi-experimental designs can be used to study many research problems, it is helpful to consider them in the context of program evaluation research.

## PROGRAM EVALUATION

**Program evaluation** was briefly described in Chapter 1. This is research on programs that are proposed and implemented to achieve some positive effect on a group of individuals. Such programs may be implemented in schools, work settings, or entire communities. In schools, an example is the DARE (Drug Abuse Resistance Education) program designed to reduce drug use. This program is conducted in conjunction with local police departments and has become extremely popular since it was developed in the early 1980s. Program evaluation applies the many research approaches to investigate these types of programs.

Donald Campbell (1969) urged a culture of evaluation in which all such programs are honestly evaluated to determine whether they are effective. Thus, the initial focus of evaluation research was "outcome evaluation": Did the program result in the positive outcome for which it was designed (e.g., reductions in drug abuse, higher grades, lower absenteeism, or lower recidivism)? However, as the field of program evaluation has progressed since Campbell's 1969 paper, evaluation research has become concerned with much more than outcome evaluation (Rossi, Freeman, & Lipsey, 1999).

**FIGURE 11.1**
Phases of program evaluation research

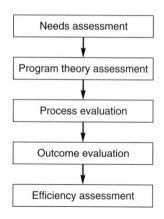

Rossi et al. (1999) identify five types of evaluations; each attempts to answer a different question about the program. These are depicted in Figure 11.1 as the five phases of the evaluation process. The first is the evaluation of need. *Needs assessment* studies ask whether there are, in fact, problems that need to be addressed in a target population. For example, is there drug abuse by children and adolescents in the community? If so, what types of drugs are being used? What services do homeless individuals need most? Do repeat juvenile offenders have particular personal and family problems that could be addressed by an intervention program? Once a need has been established, programs can be planned to address the need. The data for the needs assessment may come from surveys, interviews, and statistical data maintained by public health, criminal justice, and other agencies.

The second type of program evaluation question addresses program theory. After identifying needs, a program can be designed to address them. Rossi et al. (1999) emphasize that the program must be based on valid assumptions about the causes of the problems and the rationale of the proposed program. The *assessment of program theory* may involve the collaboration of researchers, service providers, and prospective clients of the program to determine that the proposed program does in fact address the needs of the target population in appropriate ways. Rossi et al. describe a study that assessed the needs of homeless men and women in New York City (Herman, Struening, & Barrow, 1994). The most important overall needs were help with finding a place to live, finding a job, and improving job skills. Men in particular needed help with drinking or drug problems, handling money, and getting along with others. Women were more likely to need help with health and medical problems. A program designed to address these needs should take this information into account and have a rationale for how homeless individuals will in fact benefit from the program.

The third type of program evaluation question is *process evaluation* or program monitoring. When the program is under way, the evaluation researcher monitors it to determine whether it is reaching the target population, whether it is attracting enough clients, and whether the staff is providing the planned services. Sometimes, the staff has not received adequate training, or the services are being offered in a location that is undesirable or difficult to find. In sum, the researcher wants assurance that the program is doing what it is supposed to do. This research is extremely important because we would not want to conclude that a program itself is ineffective if, in fact, it is the *implementation* of the program that is not working. Such research may involve questionnaires and interviews, observational studies, and analysis of records kept by program staff.

The fourth question concerns *outcome evaluation* or impact assessment: Are the intended outcomes of the program being realized? Is the goal—to reduce drug use, increase literacy, decrease repeat offenses by juveniles, or provide job skills—being achieved? To determine this, the evaluation researcher must devise a way of measuring the outcome and then study the impact of the program on the outcome measure. We need to know what participants of the program are like, and we need to know what they would be like if they had not completed the program. Ideally, a true experimental design with random assignment to conditions would be carried out to answer questions about outcomes. However, other research approaches, such as the quasi-experimental and single case designs described in this chapter, are very useful ways of assessing the impact of an intervention program.

The final program evaluation question addresses *efficiency assessment*. Once it is shown that a program does have its intended effect, researchers must determine whether it is "worth it." The cost of the program must be weighed against its benefits. Also, the researchers must determine whether the resources used to implement the program might be put to some better use.

As noted, evaluation research may be conducted with all of the methodological approaches discussed in previous chapters: surveys, naturalistic observation, and true experiments. However, this research often must be conducted in settings and under circumstances in which a true experimental design cannot be implemented. In such situations, an alternative to a true experimental design must be used. One alternative is a quasi-experimental design. Here we will look only at some of the more commonly used quasi-experimental designs. For more detailed discussions, see Campbell (1968, 1969); Shadish, Cook, and Campbell (2002); and Campbell and Stanley (1966). We will then examine single case designs that can be used in program evaluation and many other research areas.

## QUASI-EXPERIMENTAL DESIGNS

### One-Group Posttest-Only Design

Suppose you want to investigate whether sitting close to a stranger will cause the stranger to move away. You might try sitting next to a number of strangers and measure the number of seconds that elapse before they leave. Your design would look like this:

Now suppose that the average amount of time before the people leave is 9.6 seconds. Unfortunately, this finding is not interpretable. You don't know whether they would have stayed longer if you had not sat down or whether they would have stayed for 9.6 seconds anyway. It is even possible that they would have left sooner if you had not sat down—perhaps they liked you!

This **one-group posttest-only design**—called a "one-shot case study" by Campbell and Stanley (1966)—lacks a crucial element of a true experiment: a control or comparison group. There must be some sort of comparison condition to enable you to interpret your results. The one-group posttest-only design with its missing comparison group has serious deficiencies in the context of designing an internally valid experiment that will allow us to draw causal inferences about the effect of an independent variable on a dependent variable.

You might wonder whether this design is ever used. In fact, you may see this type of design used as evidence for the effectiveness of a program. For example, employees in a company might participate in a 4-hour information session on emergency procedures. At the conclusion of the program, they complete a knowledge test on which their average score is 90%. This result is then used to conclude that the program is successfully educating employees. The problem, of course, is that the score may have been equal, lower, or even higher without the program. The reason why results such as these are sometimes accepted is because we may have an implicit idea of how a control group would perform. Unfortunately, we need that comparison data.

### One-Group Pretest-Posttest Design

One way to obtain a comparison is to measure participants before the manipulation (a pretest) and again afterward (a posttest). An index of change from the pretest to the posttest could then be computed. Although this **one-group pretest-posttest design** sounds fine, there are some major problems with it.

To illustrate, suppose you wanted to test the hypothesis that a relaxation training program will result in a reduction in cigarette smoking. Using the one-group pretest-posttest design, you would select a group of people who smoke, administer a measure of smoking, have them go through relaxation training, and then re-administer the smoking measure. Your design would look like this:

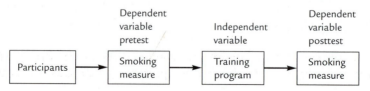

If you did find a reduction in smoking, you could not assume that the result was due to the relaxation training program. This design has failed to take into account several alternative explanations: history, maturation, testing, instrument decay, and regression toward the mean.

**History**    *History* refers to any event that occurs between the first and second measurements but is not part of the manipulation. Any such event is confounded with the manipulation. For example, suppose that a famous person dies of lung cancer during the time between the first and second measures. This event, and not the relaxation training, could be responsible for a reduction in smoking. Admittedly, the celebrity death example is dramatic and perhaps unlikely. However, **history effects** can be caused by virtually any confounding event that occurs at the same time as the experimental manipulation.

**Maturation**    People change over time. In a brief period they become bored, fatigued, perhaps wiser, and certainly hungrier; over a longer period, children become more coordinated and analytical. Any changes that occur systematically over time are called **maturation effects.** Maturation could be a problem in the smoking reduction example if people generally become more concerned about health as they get older. Any such time-related factor might result in a change from the pretest to the posttest. If this happens, you might mistakenly attribute the change to the treatment rather than to maturation.

**Testing**    Testing becomes a problem if simply taking the pretest changes the participant's behavior. For example, the smoking measure might require people to keep a diary in which they note every cigarette smoked during the day. Simply keeping track of smoking might be sufficient to cause a reduction in the number of cigarettes a person smokes. Thus, the reduction found on the posttest could be the result of taking the pretest rather than of the program itself. In other contexts, taking a pretest may sensitize people to the purpose of the experiment or make them more adept at a skill being tested. Again, the experiment would not have internal validity.

**Instrument decay**    Sometimes, the basic characteristics of the measuring instrument change over time; this is called **instrument decay.** Consider sources of instrument decay when human observers are used to measure behavior: Over time, an observer may gain skill, become fatigued, or change the standards on which observations are based. In our example on smoking, participants might be highly motivated to record all cigarettes smoked during the pretest when the task is new and interesting, but by the time the posttest is given they may be tired of the task and sometimes forget to record a cigarette. Such instrument decay would lead to an apparent reduction in cigarette smoking.

**Regression toward the mean**    Sometimes called *statistical regression,* **regression toward the mean** is likely to occur whenever participants are selected because they score extremely high or low on some variable. When they are tested again, their scores tend to change in the direction of the mean. Extremely high scores are likely to become lower (closer to the mean), and extremely low scores are likely to become higher (again, closer to the mean).

Regression toward the mean would be a problem in the smoking experiment if participants were selected because they were initially found to be extremely heavy smokers. By choosing people for the program who scored highest on the pretest, the researcher may have selected many participants who were, for whatever reason, smoking much more than usual at the particular time the measure was administered. Those people who were smoking much more than usual will likely be smoking less when their smoking is measured again. If we then compare the overall amount of smoking before and after the program, it will appear that people are smoking less. The alternative explanation is that the smoking reduction is due to statistical regression rather than the effect of the program.

Regression toward the mean will occur whenever you gather a set of extreme scores taken at one time and compare them with scores taken at another point in time. The problem is actually rooted in the reliability of the measure. Recall from Chapter 5 that any given measure reflects a true score plus measurement error. If there is perfect reliability, the two measures will be the same (if nothing happens to lower or raise the scores). If the measure of smoking is perfectly reliable, a person who reports smoking 20 cigarettes today will report smoking 20 cigarettes two weeks from now. However, if the two measures are not perfectly reliable and there is measurement error, most scores will be close to the true score but some will be higher and some will be lower. Thus, one smoker with a true score of 20 cigarettes per day might sometimes smoke 5 and sometimes 35; however, most of the time, the number is closer to 20 than the extremes. Another smoker might have a true score of 35 but on occasion smokes as few as 20 and as many as 50; again, most of the time, the number is closer to the true score than to the extremes. Now suppose you select two people who said they smoked 35 cigarettes on the previous day, and that both of these people are included in the group—you picked the first person on a very unusual day and the second person on a very ordinary day. When you measure these people two weeks later, the first person is probably going to report smoking close to 20 cigarettes and the second person close to 35. If you average the two, it will appear that there is an overall reduction in smoking.

What if the measure were perfectly reliable? In this case, the person with a true score of 20 cigarettes would always report this amount and therefore would not be included in the heavy smoker (35+) group at all. Only people with true scores of 35 or more would be in the group and any reduction in smoking would be due to the treatment program. The point here is that regression toward the mean is a problem if there is measurement error.

Statistical regression occurs when we try to explain events in the "real world" as well. Sports columnists often refer to the hex that awaits an athlete who appears on the cover of *Sports Illustrated*. The performances of a number of athletes have dropped considerably after they were the subjects of *Sports Illustrated* cover stories. Although these cover stories might cause the lower performance (perhaps the notoriety results in nervousness and reduced concentration), statistical regression is also a likely explanation. An athlete is selected for the cover of the magazine because he or she is performing at an exceptionally high level; the principle of regression toward the mean states that very high performance is likely to deteriorate. We would know this for sure if *Sports Illustrated* also did cover stories on athletes who were in a slump and this became a good omen for them!

All these problems can be eliminated by the use of an appropriate control group. A group that does not receive the experimental treatment provides an adequate control for the effects of history, statistical regression, and so on. For example, outside historical events would have the same effect on both the experimental and the control groups. If the experimental group differs from the control group on the dependent measure administered after the manipulation, the difference between the two groups can be attributed to the effect of the experimental manipulation.

In forming a control group, the participants in the experimental condition and the control condition must be equivalent. If participants in the two groups differ *before* the manipulation, they will probably differ *after* the manipulation as well. The next design illustrates this problem.

### Nonequivalent Control Group Design

The **nonequivalent control group design** employs a separate control group, but the participants in the two conditions—the experimental group and the control group—are not equivalent. The differences become a confounding variable that provides an alternative explanation for the results. This problem, called **selection differences,** usually occurs when participants who form the two groups in the experiment are chosen from existing natural groups. If the relaxation training program is studied with the nonequivalent control group design, the design will look like this:

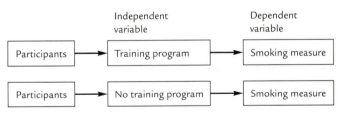

The participants in the first group are given the smoking frequency measure after completing the relaxation training. The people in the second group do not participate in any program. In this design, the researcher does not have any control over which participants are in each group. Suppose, for example, that the study is conducted in a division of a large company. All of the employees who smoke are identified and recruited to participate in the training program. The people who volunteer for the program are in the experimental group, and the people in the control group are simply the smokers who did not sign up for the training. The problem of selection differences arises because smokers who choose to participate may differ in some important way from those who do not. For instance, they may already be light smokers compared to the others and more confident that a program can help them. If so, any difference between the groups on the smoking measure would reflect preexisting differences rather than the effect of the relaxation training.

It is important to note that the problem of selection differences arises in this design even when the researcher apparently has successfully manipulated the independent variable using two similar groups. For example, a researcher might have all smokers in the engineering division of a company participate in the relaxation training program and smokers who work in the marketing division serve as a control group. The problem here, of course, is that the smokers in the two divisions may have differed in smoking patterns *prior* to the relaxation program.

### Nonequivalent Control Group Pretest-Posttest Design

The nonequivalent control group posttest-only design can be greatly improved if a pretest is given. When this is done, we have a **nonequivalent control group pretest-posttest design,** one of the most useful quasi-experimental designs. It can be diagrammed as follows:

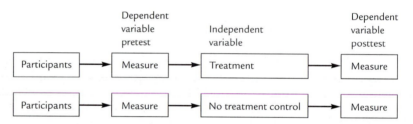

This is not a true experimental design because assignment to groups is not random; the two groups may not be equivalent. We have the advantage, however, of knowing the pretest scores. Thus, we can see whether the groups were the same on the pretest. Even if the groups are not equivalent, we can look at *changes* in scores from the pretest to the posttest. If the independent variable has an effect, the experimental group should show a greater change than the control group (see Kenny, 1979). Strategies for statistical analysis of such change scores are discussed by Trochim (2000).

Joy, Kimball, and Zabrack (1986) used a nonequivalent control group pretest-posttest design to study the effect of television on children's aggressive behavior. A Canadian town that had not had television reception until 1974 was the focus of the study (this town was dubbed "Notel" by Joy et al.). Both before and after the introduction of television in Notel, the researchers measured children's physical and verbal aggression. At the same time, they measured aggression in two similar towns, one that received only a single Canadian station ("Unitel") and one that received both Canadian and U.S. networks ("Multitel"). Thus, it was possible to compare the change in aggression in Notel with that in

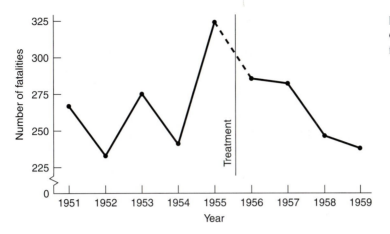

FIGURE 11.2
Connecticut traffic
fatalities, 1951–1959

the control communities of Unitel and Multitel. The results of the study showed that there was a greater increase in aggression in Notel than in either Unitel or Multitel.

## Interrupted Time Series Design

Campbell (1969) discusses at length the evaluation of one specific legal reform: the 1955 crackdown on speeding in Connecticut. Although seemingly an event in the distant past, the example is still a good illustration of an important methodological issue. The crackdown was instituted after a record high number of traffic fatalities occurred in 1955. The easiest way to evaluate this reform is to compare the number of traffic fatalities in 1955 (before the crackdown) with the number of fatalities in 1956 (after the crackdown). Indeed, there was a reduction in the number of traffic deaths, from 324 in 1955 to 284 in 1956. This single comparison is really a one-group pretest-posttest design with all of that design's problems of internal validity; there are many other reasons that traffic deaths might have declined. One alternative is to use an **interrupted time series design** that would examine the traffic fatality rates over an extended period of time, both before and after the reform was instituted. Figure 11.2 shows this information for the years 1951–1959. Campbell (1969) argues that the drop from 1955 to 1956 does not look particularly impressive, given the great fluctuations in previous years, but there is a steady downward trend in fatalities after the crackdown. Even here, however, Campbell sees a problem in interpretation. The drop could be due to statistical regression: Because 1955 was a record high year, the probability is that there would have been a drop anyway. Still, the data for the years extending before and after the crackdown allow for a less ambiguous interpretation than would be possible with data for only 1955 and 1956.

**FIGURE 11.3**
Control series design comparing Connecticut traffic fatality rate (solid line) with the fatality rate of four comparable states (dashed line)

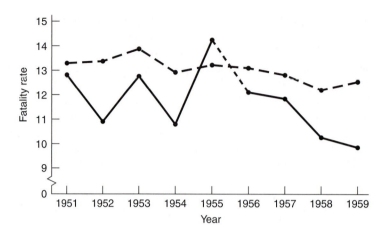

### Control Series Design

One way to improve the interrupted time series design is to find some kind of control group—a **control series design.** In the Connecticut speeding crack-down, this was possible because other states had not instituted the reform. Figure 11.3 shows the same data on traffic fatalities in Connecticut plus the fatality figures of four comparable states during the same years. The fact that the fatality rates in the control states remained relatively constant while those in Connecticut consistently declined led Campbell to conclude that the crackdown did indeed have some effect.

You may be wondering about the evaluation of the DARE program. Many researchers have, in fact, conducted outcome evaluation studies using quasi-experimental designs to examine both short-term and long-term effects. Most studies compare students in schools that have DARE programs with students from schools that do not. The general conclusion is that DARE has very small effects on the participants (cf. Ennett, Tobler, Ringwalt, & Flewelling, 1994). Moreover, studies that have examined long-term effects conclude that there are no long-term benefits of the program (Rosenbaum & Hanson, 1998); for example, college students who had participated in DARE as a child or teenager had the same amount of substance use as students never exposed to the program (Thombs, 2000).

## SINGLE CASE EXPERIMENTAL DESIGNS

**Single case experimental designs** have traditionally been called *single-subject* designs, but now the terms used are *single case* (Barlow & Hersen, 1984; Shadish et al., 2002) and *single participant* (Morgan & Morgan, 2001). These designs have a historical tradition of application within the context of research on reinforcement. It can be traced to the work of B. F. Skinner (1953) on reinforcement schedules, and it is often seen in applied and clinical settings when behavior modification techniques are used (Kazdin, 2001). However, the techniques and logic of single case experiments can be readily applied to other research areas as well.

Single case experiments were developed from a need to determine whether an experimental manipulation had an effect on a single research participant. In a single case design, the subject's behavior is measured over time during a **baseline** control period. The manipulation is then introduced during a treatment period, and the subject's behavior continues to be observed. A change in the subject's behavior from baseline to treatment periods is evidence for the effectiveness of the manipulation. The problem, however, is that there could be many explanations for the change other than the experimental treatment (i.e., alternative explanations). For example, some other event may have coincided with the introduction of the treatment. The single case designs described in the following sections address this problem.

## Reversal Designs

As noted, the basic issue in single case experiments is how to determine that the manipulation of the independent variable had an effect. One method is to demonstrate the reversibility of the manipulation. A simple **reversal design** takes the following form:

A (baseline period) → B (treatment period) → A (baseline period)

This design, called an ABA design, requires that behavior be observed during the baseline control (A) period and again during the treatment (B) period, and also during a second baseline (A) period after the experimental treatment has been removed. (Sometimes this is called a *withdrawal design,* in recognition of the fact that the treatment is removed or withdrawn.) For example, the effect of a reinforcement procedure on a child's academic performance could be assessed with an ABA design. The number of correct homework problems could be measured each day during the baseline. A reinforcement treatment procedure would then be introduced in which the child received stars for correct problems; the stars could be accumulated and exchanged for toys or candy. Later, this treatment would be discontinued during the second baseline (A) period. Hypothetical data from such an experiment are shown in Figure 11.4. The fact that behavior changed when the treatment was introduced and reversed when the treatment was withdrawn is evidence for its effectiveness.

Figure 11.4 depicts a treatment that had a relatively dramatic impact on behavior. Some treatments do produce an immediate change in behavior, but many other variables may require a longer time to show an impact. Dermer and Hoch (1999) point out that single case designs are appropriate for these variables by maintaining a long treatment period.

The ABA design can be greatly improved by extending it to an ABAB design, in which the experimental treatment is introduced a second time, or even to an ABABAB design that allows the effect of the treatment to be tested

FIGURE 11.4
Hypothetical data from
ABA reversal design

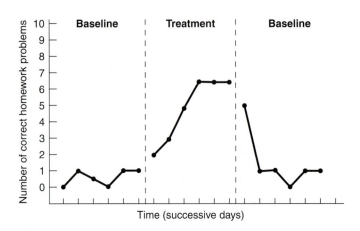

a third time. This is done to address two problems with the ABA reversal design. First, a single reversal is not extremely powerful evidence for the effectiveness of the treatment. The observed reversal might have been due to a random fluctuation in the child's behavior; perhaps the treatment happened to coincide with some other event, such as the child's upcoming birthday, that caused the change (and the post-birthday reversal). These possibilities are much less likely if the treatment has been shown to have an effect two or more times; random or coincidental events are unlikely to be responsible for both reversals. The second problem is ethical. As Barlow and Hersen (1984) point out, it doesn't seem right to end the design with the withdrawal of a treatment that may be very beneficial for the participant. Using an ABAB design provides the opportunity to observe a second reversal when the treatment is introduced again. The sequence ends with the treatment rather than the withdrawal of the treatment.

A control group also may be used in a reversal design. For example, one group of researchers used reinforcement to increase ridership on a campus bus system (Everett, Hayward, & Meyers, 1974). Riders were counted on two different buses for 36 days. The experimental manipulation consisted of giving a token to each rider on one of the specially marked buses; the tokens could be exchanged for goods and services at local stores. No tokens were used on the control bus. An ABA design was used. The first 16 days were a baseline period, and during this phase, ridership on each bus was about 250 people per day. The experimental manipulation was introduced on days 17–24. During this period, ridership on the experimental bus was about 400 per day; there was no change in ridership on the control bus. The token system was discontinued on day 25, and ridership was monitored on both buses through day 36. Ridership on the experimental bus returned to baseline levels during this period and was no longer greater than ridership on the control bus.

## Multiple Baseline Designs

It may have occurred to you that a reversal of some behaviors may be impossible or unethical. For example, it would be unethical to reverse treatment that reduces dangerous or illegal behaviors, such as indecent exposure or alcoholism, even if the possibility exists that a second introduction of the treatment might result in another change. Other treatments might produce a long-lasting change in behavior that is not reversible. In such cases, multiple measures over time can be made before and after the manipulation. If the manipulation is effective, a change in behavior will be immediately observed, and the change will continue to be reflected in further measures of the behavior. In a **multiple baseline design,** the effectiveness of the treatment is demonstrated when a behavior changes only after the manipulation is introduced. To demonstrate the effectiveness of the treatment, such a change must be observed under *multiple* circumstances to rule out the possibility that other events were responsible.

There are several variations of the multiple baseline design (Barlow & Hersen, 1984). In the multiple baseline *across subjects,* the behavior of several subjects is measured over time; for each subject, though, the manipulation is introduced at a different point in time. Figure 11.5 shows data from a hypothetical smoking reduction experiment with 3 subjects. Note that introduction of the manipulation was followed by a change in behavior for each subject. However, because this change occurred across individuals and the manipulation was introduced at a different time for each subject, we can rule out explanations based on chance, historical events, and so on.

In a multiple baseline *across behaviors,* several different behaviors of a single subject are measured over time. At different times, the same manipulation is applied to each of the behaviors. For example, a reward system could be instituted to increase the socializing, grooming, and reading behaviors of a psychiatric patient. The reward system would be applied to each of these behaviors at different times. Demonstrating that each behavior increased when the reward system was applied would be evidence for the effectiveness of the manipulation.

The third variation is the multiple baseline *across situations,* in which the same behavior is measured in different settings, such as at home and at work. Again, a manipulation is introduced at a different time in each setting, with the expectation that a change in the behavior in each situation will occur only after the manipulation.

## Replications in Single Case Designs

The procedures for use with a single subject can, of course, be replicated with other subjects, greatly enhancing the generalizability of the results. Usually, reports of research that employs single case experimental procedures do present the results from several subjects (and often in several settings). The tradition in single case research has been to present the results from each subject individually rather than group data and to present overall means. Sidman (1960), a leading spokesperson for this tradition, has pointed out that grouping the data from

FIGURE 11.5
Hypothetical data
from multiple baseline
design across
subjects

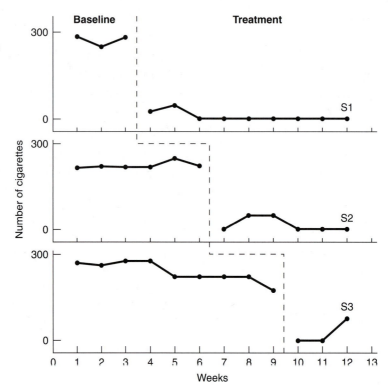

a number of subjects by using group means can sometimes give a misleading picture of individual responses to the manipulation. For example, the manipulation may be effective in changing the behavior of some subjects but not others. This was true in a study of seat belt use (Berry & Geller, 1991). Different seat belt signal conditions were studied (e.g., a second signal that would come on if the subject did not buckle up after an initial signal). Among 13 subjects, 6 always used their seat belt irrespective of the condition, and 3 never used their seat belt. For the other 4 subjects, the signal conditions did have an effect. Because the emphasis of the study was on the individual subject, the pattern of results was quickly revealed.

Single case designs are useful for studying many research problems and should be considered as a powerful alternative to more traditional research designs. They can be especially valuable for someone who is applying some change technique in a natural environment—for example, a teacher who is trying a new technique in the classroom. In addition, complex statistical analyses are not required for single case designs.

We have now described most of the major approaches to designing research. In the next two chapters, we consider methods of analyzing research data.

## Study Terms

Baseline

Control series design

Efficiency assessment

History effects

Instrument decay

Interrupted time series design

Maturation effects

Multiple baseline design

Needs assessment

Nonequivalent control group design

Nonequivalent control group pretest-posttest design

One-group posttest-only design

One-group pretest-posttest design

Outcome evaluation

Process evaluation

Program evaluation

Program theory assessment

Quasi-experimental design

Regression toward the mean

Reversal design

Selection differences

Single case experiment

Statistical regression (regression toward the mean)

Testing effects

## Review Questions

1. Describe what a program evaluation researcher's goals would be when addressing each of the five types of evaluation research questions.

2. Why might a researcher use a quasi-experimental design rather than a true experimental design?

3. Describe the threats to internal validity discussed in the text: history, maturation, testing, instrument decay, regression toward the mean, and selection differences.

4. Why does having a control group eliminate the problems associated with the one-group pretest-posttest design?

5. Describe the nonequivalent control group pretest-posttest design. Why is this a quasi-experimental design rather than a true experiment?

6. Describe the interrupted time series and the control series designs. What are the strengths of the control series design as compared to the interrupted time series design?

7. What is a reversal design? Why is an ABAB design superior to an ABA design?

8. What is meant by *baseline* in a single case design?

9. What is a multiple baseline design? Why is it used? Distinguish between multiple baseline designs across subjects, across behaviors, and across situations.

## Activity Questions

1. Dr. Smith learned that one sorority on campus had purchased several Macintosh computers and another sorority had purchased several Windows-based computers. Dr. Smith was interested in whether the type of computer affects the quality of students' papers and so went to each of the sorority houses to collect samples of papers from the members. Two graduate students in the English department then rated the quality of the papers. Dr. Smith found that the quality of the papers was higher in one sorority than in the other. What are the independent and dependent variables in this study? Identify the type of design that Dr. Smith used. What variables are confounded with the independent variable? Design a true experiment that would address Dr. Smith's original question.

2. Gilovich (1991) described an incident that he read about during a visit to Israel. A very large number of deaths had occurred during a brief time period in one region of the country. A group of rabbis attributed the deaths to a recent change in religious practice that allowed women to attend funerals. Women were immediately forbidden from attending funerals in that region, and the number of deaths subsequently decreased. How would you explain this phenomenon?

3. The captain of each precinct of a metropolitan police department selected two officers to participate in a program designed to reduce prejudice by increasing sensitivity to racial and ethnic group differences and community issues. The training program took place every Friday morning for 3 months. At the first and last meetings, the officers completed a measure of prejudice. To assess the effectiveness of the program, the average prejudice score at the first meeting was compared with the average score at the last meeting; it was found that the average score was in fact lower following the training program. What type of design is this? What specific problems arise if you try to conclude that the training program was responsible for the reduction in prejudice?

4. A student club is trying to decide whether to implement a peer tutoring program for students who are enrolled in the statistics class in your department. Club members who have completed the statistics class would offer to provide tutoring to students currently enrolled in the class. You decide to take the lessons of program evaluation seriously, and so you develop a strategy to conduct evaluation research.

   a. How would you measure whether there is a need for such a program?

   b. Briefly describe how you might implement a tutoring program. How would you monitor the program?

   c. Propose a quasi-experimental design to evaluate whether the program is effective.

   d. How might you determine the economic efficiency of such a program?

5. Many elementary schools have implemented a daily "sustained silent reading" period during which students, faculty, and staff spend 15–20 minutes silently reading a book of their choice. Advocates of this policy claim that the activity encourages pleasure reading outside the required silent reading time. Design a nonequivalent control group pretest-posttest quasi-experiment to test this claim. Include a well-reasoned dependent measure as well.

6. For the preceding situation, discuss the advantages and disadvantages of using a quasi-experimental design in contrast to conducting a true experiment.

7. Your dog gets lonely while you are at work and consequently engages in destructive activities such as pulling down curtains or strewing waste-basket contents all over the floor. You decide that playing a radio while you are gone might help. How might you determine whether this "treatment" is effective?

8. Your best friend frequently suffers from severe headaches. You've noticed that your friend consumes a great deal of diet cola, and so you consider the hypothesis that the artificial sweetener in the cola is responsible for the headaches. Devise a way to test your hypothesis using a single case design. What do you expect to find if your hypothesis is correct? If you obtain the expected results, what do you conclude about the effect of the artificial sweetener on headaches?

# 12

# Understanding Research Results: Description and Correlation

S tatistics help us understand the data collected in research investigations. There are two reasons for using statistics. First, statistics are used to describe the data. Second, statistics are used to make inferences, on the basis of sample data, about a population. We examine descriptive statistics and correlation in this chapter; inferential statistics are discussed in Chapter 13. The focus is on the underlying logic and general procedures for making statistical decisions. Specific calculations for a variety of statistics are provided in Appendix B.

## SCALES OF MEASUREMENT: A REVIEW

Before looking at any statistics, we need to review the concept of scales of measurement. Whenever a variable is studied, there is an operational definition of the variable and there must be two or more levels of the variable. Recall from Chapter 5 that the levels of the variable can be described using one of four scales of measurement: nominal, ordinal, interval, and ratio. The scale used determines the types of statistics that are appropriate when the results of a study are analyzed. Also recall that the meaning of a particular score on a variable depends on which type of scale was used when the variable was measured or manipulated.

The levels of nominal scale variables have no numerical, quantitative properties. The levels are simply different categories or groups. Most independent variables in experiments are nominal, for example, as in an experiment that compares behavioral and cognitive therapies for depression. Variables such as gender, eye color, hand dominance, birth order, and marital status are nominal scale variables; left-handed and right-handed people are simply different.

Variables with ordinal scale levels involve minimal quantitative distinctions. We can rank order the levels of the variable being studied from lowest to highest. The clearest example of an ordinal scale is one that asks people to make rank-ordered judgments. For example, you might ask people to rank the most important problems facing your state today. If education is ranked first, health care second, and crime third, you know the order but you do not know how strongly people feel about the problems. Education and health care may be very close together in seriousness with crime a distant third; the intervals between each of the problems are probably not equal.

Interval and ratio scale variables have much more detailed quantitative properties. With an interval scale variable, the intervals between the levels are equal in size. The difference between 1 and 2 on the scale, for example, is the same as the difference between 2 and 3. Interval scales generally have five or more quantitative levels. You might ask people to rate their mood on a 7-point scale ranging from a "very negative" to a "very positive" mood. There is no absolute zero point that indicates an "absence" of mood.

In the behavioral sciences, it is often difficult to know precisely whether an ordinal or an interval scale is being used. However, it is often useful to assume that the variable is being measured on an interval scale because interval scales allow for more sophisticated statistical treatments than do ordinal scales. Of course, if the measure is a rank ordering (for example, a rank ordering of students in a class on the basis of popularity), an ordinal scale clearly is being used.

Ratio scale variables have both equal intervals and an absolute zero point that indicates the absence of the variable being measured. Time, weight, length, and other physical measures are the best examples of ratio scales. Interval and ratio scale variables are conceptually different; however, the statistical procedures used to analyze data with such variables are identical. An important implication of interval and ratio scales is that data can be summarized using the mean, or arithmetic average. It is possible to provide a number that reflects the mean amount of a variable—for example, the "average mood of people who won a contest was 5.1" or the "mean weight of the men completing the weight loss program was 187.7."

## ANALYZING THE RESULTS OF RESEARCH INVESTIGATIONS

Scales of measurement have important implications for the way that the results of research investigations are described and analyzed. Most research focuses on the study of relationships between variables. Depending on the way that the variables are studied, there are three basic ways of describing the results: (1) comparing group percentages, (2) correlating scores of individuals on two variables, and (3) comparing group means.

### Comparing Group Percentages

Suppose you want to know whether males and females differ in their interest in travel. In your study, you ask males and females whether they like or dislike travel. To describe your results, you will need to calculate the percentage of females who like to travel and compare this with the percentage of males who like to travel. Suppose you tested 50 females and 50 males and found that 40 of the females and 30 of the males indicated that they like to travel. In describing your findings, you would report that 80% of the females like to travel in comparison to 60% of the males. Thus, a relationship between the gender and travel variables appears to exist. Note that we are focusing on percentages because the travel variable is nominal: Liking and disliking are simply two different categories. After describing your data, the next step would be to perform a statistical analysis to determine whether there is a statistically significant difference between the males and females. Statistical significance is discussed in Chapter 13; statistical analysis procedures are described in Appendix B.

### Correlating Individual Scores

A second type of analysis is needed when you do not have distinct groups of subjects. Instead, individuals are measured on two variables, and each variable has a range of numerical values. Later in this chapter, we will consider an analysis of data on the relationship between location in a classroom and grades in the class: Do people who sit near the front receive higher grades?

## Comparing Group Means

Much research is designed to compare the mean responses of participants in two or more groups. For example, in an experiment designed to study the effect of exposure to an aggressive adult, children in one group might observe an adult "model" behaving aggressively while children in a control group do not. Each child then plays alone for 10 minutes in a room containing a number of toys, while observers record the number of times the child behaves aggressively during play. Aggression is a ratio scale variable because there are equal intervals and a true zero on the scale.

In this case, you would be interested in comparing the mean number of aggressive acts by children in the two conditions to determine whether the children who observed the model were more aggressive than the children in the control condition. Hypothetical data from such an experiment in which there were 10 children in each condition are shown in Table 12.1; the scores in the table represent the number of aggressive acts by each child. In this case, the mean aggression score in the model group is 5.20 and the mean score in the no-model condition is 3.10. In the next chapter, we will conduct a statistical test to determine whether this difference is statistically significant.

For all types of data, it is important to understand your results by carefully describing the data collected. We begin by constructing frequency distributions.

TABLE 12.1    Scores on aggression measure in a hypothetical experiment on modeling and aggression

| Model group | No-model group |
|:-----------:|:--------------:|
| 3 | 1 |
| 4 | 2 |
| 5 | 2 |
| 5 | 3 |
| 5 | 3 |
| 5 | 3 |
| 6 | 4 |
| 6 | 4 |
| 6 | 4 |
| 7 | 5 |
| $\Sigma X = 52$ | $\Sigma X = 31$ |
| $\bar{X} = 5.20$ | $\bar{X} = 3.10$ |
| $s^2 = 1.289$ | $s^2 = 1.433$ |
| $s = 1.135$ | $s = 1.197$ |
| $n = 10$ | $n = 10$ |

## FREQUENCY DISTRIBUTIONS

When analyzing results, it is useful to start by constructing a frequency distribution of the data. A **frequency distribution** indicates the number of individuals that receive each possible score on a variable. Frequency distributions of exam scores are familiar to most college students—they tell how many students received a given score on the exam. Along with the number of individuals associated with each response or score, it is useful to examine the percentage associated with this number.

### Graphing Frequency Distributions

It is often useful to graphically depict frequency distributions. Let's examine several types of graphs: pie chart, bar graph, and frequency polygon.

Pie charts   **Pie charts** divide a whole circle or "pie" into "slices" that represent relative percentages. Figure 12.1 shows a pie chart (in this case, a three-dimensional pie chart) showing a frequency distribution in which 70% of people like to travel and 30% dislike travel. Because there are two pieces of information to graph, there are two slices in this pie. Pie charts are particularly useful when representing nominal scale information. In the figure, the number of people who chose each response has been converted to a percentage—the simple number could have been displayed instead, of course.

Bar graphs   **Bar graphs** use a separate and distinct bar for each piece of information. Figure 12.2 represents the same information about travel using a bar graph. In this graph, the *x* or horizontal axis shows the two possible responses. The *y* or vertical axis shows the number who chose each response, and so the length of each bar represents the number of people who responded to the "like" and "dislike" options.

Frequency polygons   **Frequency polygons** use a line to represent frequencies. This is most useful when the data represent interval or ratio scales as in the modeling and aggression data shown in Table 12.1. Here we have a clear numeric scale of the number of aggressive acts during the observation period. Figure 12.3 graphs the data from the hypothetical experiment using two fre-

**FIGURE 12.1**
Pie chart

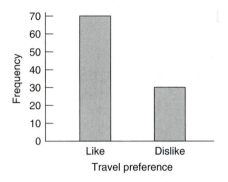

**FIGURE 12.2**
Bar graph displaying data obtained in two groups

**FIGURE 12.3**
Frequency polygons illustrating the distributions of scores in Table 12.1

Note: Each frequency polygon is anchored at scores that were not obtained by anyone (0 and 6 in the no-model group; 2 and 8 in the model group).

quency polygons—one for each group. The solid line represents the no-model group, and the dotted line stands for the model group.

What can you discover by examining frequency distributions? First, you can directly observe how your participants responded. You can see what scores are most frequent and you can look at the shape of the distribution of scores. You can tell whether there are any "outliers"—scores that are unusual, unexpected, or very different from the scores of other participants. In an experiment, you can compare the distribution of scores in the groups.

## DESCRIPTIVE STATISTICS

In addition to examining the distribution of scores, you can calculate descriptive statistics. **Descriptive statistics** allow researchers to make precise statements about the data. Two statistics are needed to describe the data. A single number can be used to describe the central tendency, or how participants scored overall. Another number describes the variability, or how widely the distribution of scores is spread. These two numbers summarize the information contained in a frequency distribution.

## Central Tendency

A **central tendency** statistic tells us what the sample as a whole, or on the average, is like. There are three measures of central tendency—the mean, the median, and the mode. The **mean** of a set of scores is obtained by adding all the scores and dividing by the number of scores. It is symbolized as $\overline{X}$, and in scientific reports, it is abbreviated as $M$. The mean is an appropriate indicator of central tendency only when scores are measured on an interval or ratio scale, because the actual values of the numbers are used in calculating the statistic. In Table 12.1, the mean score for the no-model group is 3.10 and for the model group is 5.20. Note that the Greek letter $\Sigma$ (sigma) in Table 12.1 is statistical notation for summing a set of numbers. Thus, $\Sigma X$ is shorthand for "sum of the values in a set of scores."

The **median** is the score that divides the group in half (with 50% scoring below and 50% scoring above the median). In scientific reports, the median is abbreviated as $Mdn$. The median is appropriate when scores are on an ordinal scale because it takes into account only the rank order of the scores. It is also useful with interval and ratio scale variables, however. The median for the no-model group is 3 and for the model group is 5.

The **mode** is the most frequent score. The mode is the only measure of central tendency that is appropriate if a nominal scale is used. The mode does not use the actual values on the scale, but simply indicates the most frequently occurring value. There are two modal values for the no-model group—3 and 4 occur equally frequently. The mode for the model group is 5.

The median or mode can be a better indicator of central tendency than the mean if a few unusual scores bias the mean. For example, the median family income of a county or state is usually a better measure of central tendency than the mean family income. Because a relatively small number of individuals have extremely high incomes, using the mean would make it appear that the "average" person makes more money than is actually the case.

## Variability

We can also determine how much **variability** exists in a set of scores. A measure of variability is a number that characterizes the amount of spread in a distribution of scores. One such measure is the **standard deviation,** symbolized as $s$, which indicates the average deviation of scores from the mean. In scientific reports, it is abbreviated as $SD$. The standard deviation is derived by first calculating the **variance,** symbolized as $s^2$ (the standard deviation is the square root of the variance). The standard deviation of a set of scores is small when most people have similar scores close to the mean. The standard deviation becomes larger as more people have scores that lie further from the mean value. For the model group, the standard deviation is 1.135, which tells us that most scores in that condition lie 1.135 units above and below the mean—that is, between 4.065 and 6.335. Thus, the mean and the standard deviation provide a great deal of information about the distribution. Note that, as with the mean, the calculation of the standard deviation uses the actual values of the scores; thus, the standard deviation is appropriate only for interval and ratio scale variables.

FIGURE 12.4
Graph of the results of the modeling experiment

Another measure of variability is the *range,* which is simply the difference between the highest score and the lowest score. The range for both the model and no-model groups is 4.

## GRAPHING RELATIONSHIPS

Graphing relationships between variables was discussed briefly in Chapter 4. A common way to graph relationships between variables is to use a bar graph or a line graph. Figure 12.4 is a bar graph depicting the means for the model and no-model groups. The levels of the independent variable (no-model and model) are represented on the horizontal *x* axis, and the dependent variable values are shown on the vertical *y* axis. For each group, a point is placed along the *y* axis that represents the mean for the groups, and a bar is drawn to visually represent the mean value. Bar graphs are used when the values on the *x* axis are nominal categories (e.g., a no-model and a model condition). Line graphs are used when the values on the *x* axis are numeric (e.g., number of hours that teenagers work, as shown in Figure 7.1). In this case, a line is drawn to connect the data points to represent the relationship between the variables.

It is interesting to note a common trick that is sometimes used by scientists and all too commonly used by advertisers. The trick is to exaggerate the distance between points on the measurement scale to make the results appear more dramatic than they really are. Suppose, for example, that a cola company (cola A) conducts a taste test that shows 52% of the participants prefer cola A and 48% prefer cola B. How should the cola company present these results? The two bar graphs in Figure 12.5 show the most honest method, as well as one that is considerably more dramatic. It is always wise to look carefully at the numbers on the scales depicted in graphs.

## CORRELATION COEFFICIENTS: DESCRIBING THE STRENGTH OF RELATIONSHIPS

It is important to know whether a relationship between variables is relatively weak or strong. A **correlation coefficient** is a statistic that describes how strongly variables are related to one another. You are probably most familiar with the **Pearson product-moment correlation coefficient,** which is used when both variables have

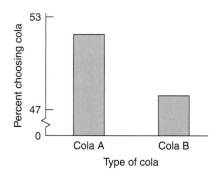

FIGURE 12.5
Two ways to graph the same data

interval or ratio scale properties. The Pearson product-moment correlation coefficient is called the Pearson *r*. Values of a Pearson *r* can range from 0.00 to $\pm 1.00$. Thus, the Pearson *r* provides information about the strength of the relationship and the direction of the relationship. A correlation of 0.00 indicates that there is no relationship between the variables. The nearer a correlation is to 1.00 (plus or minus), the stronger is the relationship. Indeed, a 1.00 correlation is sometimes called a perfect relationship because the two variables go together in a perfect fashion. The sign of the Pearson *r* tells us about the direction of the relationship; that is, whether there is a positive relationship or a negative relationship between the variables.

Data from studies examining similarities of intelligence test scores among siblings illustrate the connection between the magnitude of a correlation coefficient and the strength of a relationship. The relationship between scores of identical twins is very strong (correlation of .86), demonstrating a strong similarity of test scores in these pairs of individuals. The correlation for fraternal twins reared together is less strong, with a correlation of .60. The correlation among nontwin siblings raised together is .47, and the correlation among nontwin siblings reared apart is .24 (cf. Bouchard & McGue, 1981).

There are many different types of correlation coefficients. Each coefficient is calculated somewhat differently depending on the measurement scale that applies to the two variables. As noted, the Pearson *r* correlation coefficient is appropriate when the values of both variables are on an interval or ratio scale. We will now focus on the details of the Pearson product-moment correlation coefficient.

### Pearson r Correlation Coefficient

To calculate a correlation coefficient, we need to obtain pairs of observations from each subject. Thus, each individual has two scores, one on each of the variables. Table 12.2 shows fictitious data for 10 students measured on the variables

TABLE 12.2    Pairs of scores for 10 participants on seating pattern and exam scores (fictitious data)

| Subject identification number | Seating | Exam score |
|:---:|:---:|:---:|
| 01 | 2 | 95 |
| 02 | 5 | 50 |
| 03 | 1 | 85 |
| 04 | 4 | 75 |
| 05 | 3 | 75 |
| 06 | 5 | 60 |
| 07 | 2 | 80 |
| 08 | 3 | 70 |
| 09 | 1 | 90 |
| 10 | 4 | 70 |

of classroom seating pattern and exam grade. Students in the first row receive a seating score of 1, those in the second row receive a 2, and so on. Once we have made our observations, we can see whether the two variables are related. Do the variables go together in a systematic fashion?

The Pearson $r$ provides two types of information about the relationship between the variables. The first is the strength of the relationship; the second is the direction of the relationship. As noted previously, the values of $r$ can range from 0.00 to $\pm 1.00$. The absolute size of $r$ is the coefficient that indicates the strength of the relationship. A value of 0.00 indicates that there is no relationship. The nearer $r$ is to 1.00 (plus or minus), the stronger is the relationship. The plus and minus signs indicate whether there is a positive linear or negative linear relationship between the two variables. It is important to remember that it is the size of the correlation coefficient, not the sign, that indicates the strength of the relationship. Thus, a correlation coefficient of $-.54$ indicates a stronger relationship than does a coefficient of $+.45$.

The data in Table 12.2 can be visualized in a *scatterplot* in which each pair of scores is plotted as a single point in a diagram. Figure 12.6 shows two scatterplots. The values of the first variable are depicted on the $x$ axis, and the values of the second variable are shown on the $y$ axis. These scatterplots show a perfect positive relationship ($+1.00$) and a perfect negative relationship ($-1.00$). You can easily see why these are perfect relationships: The scores on the two variables fall on a straight line that is on the diagonal of the diagram. Each person's score on one variable goes perfectly with his or her score on the other variable. If we know an individual's score on one of the variables, we can predict exactly what his or her score will be on the other variable. Such "perfect" relationships are rarely if ever observed in actuality.

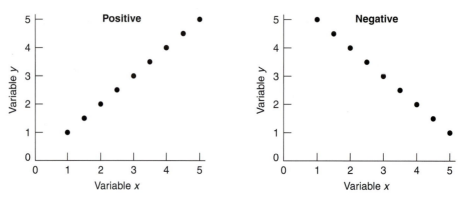

FIGURE 12.6
Scatterplots of perfect (±1.00) relationships

The scatterplots in Figure 12.7 show patterns of correlation you are more likely to encounter in exploring research findings. The first diagram shows pairs of scores with a positive correlation of +.65; the second diagram shows a negative relationship, −.77. The data points in these two scatterplots reveal a general pattern of either a positive or negative relationship, but the relationships are not perfect. You can make a general prediction in the first diagram, for instance, that the higher the score on one variable, the higher the score on the second variable. However, if you know a person's score on the first variable, you cannot perfectly predict what that person's score will be on the second variable. To confirm this, take a look at value 1 on variable $x$ (the horizontal axis) in the positive scatterplot. Looking up, you will see that two individuals had a score of 1. One of these had a score of 1 on variable $y$ (the vertical axis), and the other had a score of 3. The data points do not fall on the perfect diagonal. Instead, there is a variation (scatter) from the perfect diagonal line.

The third diagram shows a scatterplot in which there is absolutely no correlation ($r = 0.00$). The points fall all over the diagram in a completely random pattern. Thus, scores on variable $x$ are not related to scores on variable $y$.

The fourth diagram has been left blank so that you can plot the scores from the data in Table 12.2. The $x$ (horizontal) axis has been labeled for the seating pattern variable, and the $y$ (vertical) axis for the exam score variable. To complete the scatterplot, you will need to plot the 10 pairs of scores. For each individual in the sample, find the score on the seating pattern variable; then go up until you reach that person's exam score. A point placed there will describe the score on both variables. There will be 10 points on the finished scatterplot.

The correlation coefficient calculated from these data shows a negative relationship between the variables ($r = -.88$). In other words, as the seating distance from the front of the class increases, the exam score decreases. Although these data are fictitious, the negative relationship is consistent with actual research findings (Brooks & Rebata, 1991).

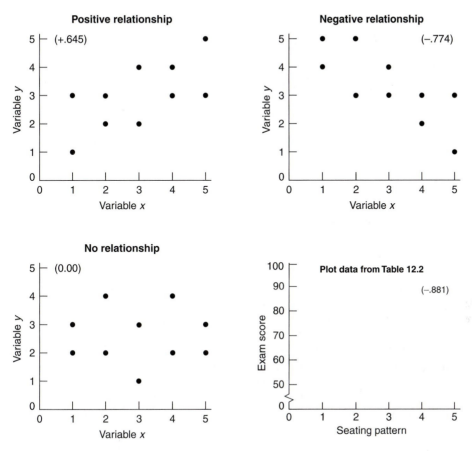

**FIGURE 12.7**
Scatterplots depicting patterns of correlation

## Important Considerations

**Restriction of range** It is important that the researcher sample from the full range of possible values of both variables. If the range of possible values is restricted, the magnitude of the correlation coefficient is reduced. For example, if the range of seating pattern scores is restricted to the first two rows, you will not get an accurate picture of the relationship between seating pattern and exam score. In fact, when only scores of students sitting in the first two rows are considered, the correlation between the two variables is exactly 0.00. With a restricted range, there is restricted variability in the scores and thus less variability that can be explained.

The problem of restriction of range occurs when the individuals in your sample are very similar or *homogenous* on the variable you are studying. If you are studying age as a variable, for instance, testing only 6- and 7-year-olds will reduce

FIGURE 12.8
Scatterplot of a curvilinear
relationship (Pearson
product-moment correlation
coefficient = 0.00)

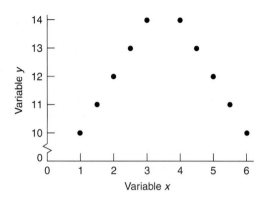

your chances of finding age effects. Likewise, trying to study the correlates of intelligence will be almost impossible if everyone in your sample is very similar in intelligence (e.g., the senior class of a prestigious private college).

**Curvilinear relationship**    The Pearson product-moment correlation coefficient ($r$) is designed to detect only linear relationships. If the relationship is curvilinear, as in the scatterplot shown in Figure 12.8, the correlation coefficient will not indicate the existence of a relationship. The Pearson $r$ correlation coefficient calculated from these data is exactly 0.00, even though the two variables clearly are related.

When the relationship is curvilinear, another type of correlation coefficient must be used to determine the strength of the relationship. Because a relationship may be curvilinear, it is important to construct a scatterplot in addition to looking at the magnitude of the correlation coefficient. The scatterplot is valuable because it gives a visual indication of the shape of the relationship. Computer programs for statistical analysis will usually display scatterplots and can show you how well the data fit to a linear or curvilinear relationship.

## EFFECT SIZE

We have been describing the Pearson $r$ correlation coefficient as the appropriate way to describe the relationship between two variables with interval or ratio scale properties. Researchers want to be able to describe the strength of relationship between variables in all studies. **Effect size** is a general term that refers to the strength of association between variables. The Pearson $r$ correlation coefficient is one indicator of effect size; it indicates the strength of the linear association between two variables. In an experiment with two or more treatment conditions, some other types of correlation coefficients can be calculated to indicate the magnitude of the effect of the independent variable on the dependent variable. For example, in our experiment on the effects of witnessing an aggressive model on children's aggressive behavior, we compared the means of two groups. In addition to knowing the means, it is valuable to know the effect size. An effect size correlation coefficient can be calculated for the modeling and aggression experiment. In this case, the effect size correlation value is .68. As with all correlation coefficients, the values of this effect size correlation can range from 0.00 to 1.00 (we don't need to worry about the direction of relationship so plus and minus values are not used). The formula used for calculating the correlation is discussed in Chapter 13.

The advantage of reporting effect size is that it provides us with a scale of values that is consistent across all types of studies. The values range from 0.00 to 1.00, irrespective of the variables used, the particular research design selected, or the number of participants studied. You might be wondering what correlation coefficients should be considered indicative of small, medium, and large effects. A general guide is that correlations near .15 (about .10 to .20) are considered small, those near .30 are medium, and correlations above .40 are large.

It is sometimes preferable to report the squared value of a correlation coefficient; instead of $r$, you will see $r^2$. Thus, if the obtained $r = .50$, the reported $r^2 = .25$. Why transform the value of $r$? This reason is that the transformation changes the obtained $r$ to a percentage. The percentage value represents the percent of variance in one variable that is accounted for by the second variable. The range of $r^2$ values can range from 0.00 (0%) to 1.00 (100%). The $r^2$ value is sometimes referred to as the percent of shared variance between the two variables. What does this mean exactly? Recall the concept of variability in a set of scores— if you measured the weight of a random sample of American adults, you would observe variability in that weights would range from relatively low weights to relatively high weights. If you are studying factors that contribute to people's weight, you would want to examine the relationship between weights and scores on the contributing variable. One such variable might be gender: In actuality, the correlation between gender and weight is about .70 (with males weighing more than females). That means that 49% (squaring .70) of the variability in the weights is accounted for by variability in gender. You know a lot about how to "explain" the variability in the weights but there is still 51% of the variability that is not accounted for. This variability might be accounted for by other variables, such as the weights of the biological mother and father, prenatal stress, diet, and exercise. In an ideal world, you could account for 100% of the variability in weights if you had enough information on all other variables that contribute to people's weights: Each variable would make an incremental contribution until all the variability is accounted for.

## STATISTICAL SIGNIFICANCE

The emphasis in this chapter has been on *describing* the data obtained in a study. After describing the data, you will usually want to make a decision concerning the statistical significance of the results. Is the difference between the means of the model and no-model groups a statistically significant difference? This is largely a matter of inferring whether the results will hold up if the experiment is repeated several times, each time with a new sample of research participants. Inferential statistics are used to determine whether we can, in fact, make statements that the results reflect what would happen if we were to conduct the experiment over and over again with multiple samples. Statistical significance is discussed in Chapter 13. The remainder of this chapter focuses on additional topics of correlation.

## REGRESSION EQUATIONS

**Regression equations** are calculations used to predict a person's score on one variable when that person's score on another variable is already known. They are essentially "prediction equations" that are based on known information about the relationship between the two variables. For example, after discovering that seating pattern and exam score are related, a regression equation may be calculated that predicts anyone's exam score based only on information about where the person sits in the class. The general form of a regression equation is

$$Y = a + bX$$

where $Y$ is the score we wish to predict, $X$ is the known score, $a$ is a constant, and $b$ is a weighting adjustment factor that is multiplied by $X$ (it is the slope of the line created with this equation). In our seating–exam score example, the following regression equation is calculated from the data:

$$Y = 99 + (-8)X$$

Thus, if we know a person's score on $X$ (seating), we can insert that into the equation and predict what that person's score on $Y$ (exam score) will be. If the person's $X$ score is 2 (by sitting in the second row), we can predict that $Y = 99 + (-16)$, or that the person's exam score will be 83. Through the use of regression equations such as these, colleges can use SAT scores to predict college grades.

When researchers are interested in predicting some future behavior (called the *criterion variable*) on the basis of a person's score on some other variable (called the *predictor variable*), it is first necessary to demonstrate that there is a reasonably high correlation between the criterion and predictor variables. The regression equation then provides the method for making predictions on the basis of the predictor variable score only.

## MULTIPLE CORRELATION

Thus far we have focused on the correlation between two variables at a time. Researchers recognize that a number of different variables may be related to a given behavior (this is the same point noted above in the discussion of factors that contribute to weight). A technique called **multiple correlation** is used to combine a number of predictor variables to increase the accuracy of prediction of a given criterion or outcome variable.

A multiple correlation (symbolized as $R$ to distinguish it from the simple $r$) is the correlation between a combined set of predictor variables and a single criterion variable. Taking all of the predictor variables into account usually permits greater accuracy of prediction than if any single predictor is considered alone. For example, applicants to graduate school in psychology could be evaluated on a combined set of predictor variables using multiple correlation. The predictor variables might be (1) college grades, (2) scores on the Graduate Record Exam Aptitude Test, (3) scores on the Graduate Record Exam Psychology Test, and (4) favorability of letters of recommendation. No one of these factors is a perfect predictor of success in graduate school, but this combination of variables can yield a more accurate prediction. The multiple correlation is usually higher than the correlation between any one of the predictor variables and the criterion or outcome variable.

In actual practice, predictions would be made with an extension of the regression equation technique discussed previously. A multiple regression equation can be calculated that takes the following form:

$$Y = a + b_1X_1 + b_2X_2 + \ldots + b_nX_n$$

where $Y$ is the criterion variable, $X_1$ to $X_n$ are the predictor variables, $a$ is a constant, and $b_1$ to $b_n$ are weights that are multiplied by scores on the predictor variables. For example, a regression equation for graduate school admissions would be:

Predicted grade point average $= a + b_1$ (college grades)

$\qquad\qquad\qquad + b_2$ (score on GRE Aptitude Test)

$\qquad\qquad\qquad + b_3$ (score on GRE Psychology Test)

$\qquad\qquad\qquad + b_4$ (favorability of recommendation letters)

Researchers use multiple regression to study basic research topics. For example, Ajzen and Fishbein (1980) developed a model called the "theory of reasoned action" that uses multiple correlation and regression to predict specific behavioral intentions (e.g., to attend church on Sunday, buy a certain product, or join an alcohol recovery program) on the basis of two predictor variables. These are (1) attitude toward the behavior and (2) perceived normative pressure to engage in the behavior. Attitude is one's own evaluation of the behavior, and normative pressure comes from other people such as parents and friends. In one study, these researchers demonstrated that the multiple correlation between intention to buy a brand of beer and the combined predictors of attitude and norm was .79. The regression equation was as follows:

Intention $= .76$(attitude) $+ .27$(norm)

This equation is somewhat different from those described previously. In basic research, you are not interested in predicting an exact score (such as an exam score or GPA), and so the mathematical calculations can assume that all variables are measured on the same scale. When this is done, the weighting factor reflects the magnitude of the correlation between the criterion variable and each predictor variable. In the beer purchase example, the weight for the attitude predictor is higher than the weight for the norm predictor; this shows that, in this case, attitudes are more important as a predictor of intention than are norms. However, for other behaviors, it may be found that attitudes are less important than norms.

It is also possible to visualize the regression equation. In the beer purchase example, the relationships among variables could be diagrammed as follows:

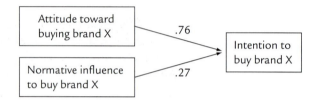

You should note the squared multiple correlation coefficient ($R^2$) is interpreted in much the same way as the squared correlation coefficient ($r^2$). That is, $R^2$ tells you the percentage of variability in the criterion variable that is accounted for by the combined set of predictor variables. Again, this value will be higher than any of the single predictors by themselves.

## PARTIAL CORRELATION AND THE THIRD-VARIABLE PROBLEM

Researchers face the third-variable problem in nonexperimental research when some uncontrolled third variable may be responsible for the relationship between the two variables of interest. The problem doesn't exist in experimental research, because all extraneous variables are controlled either by keeping the variables constant or by using randomization. A technique called **partial correlation** provides a way of statistically controlling third variables. A partial correlation is a correlation between the two variables of interest, with the influence of the third variable removed from, or "partialed out of," the original correlation.

Suppose a researcher finds that the correlation between residential crowding and performance on a test is −.50; increasing crowding is associated with lower scores. The researcher suspects that a third variable may be operating. Social class, for example, could influence both crowding and performance. The use of partial correlations involves measuring subjects on the

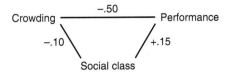

FIGURE 12.9
Two partial correlations between crowding and performance

third variable in addition to the two primary variables. Thus, the researcher has to measure participants on all the variables: crowding, performance, and social class.

When a partial correlation between crowding and performance, with social class partialed out, is calculated, we can determine whether the original correlation is substantially reduced. Is our original correlation of −.50 lowered very much when the influence of social class is removed? Figure 12.9 shows two different partial correlations—in both, there is a −.50 correlation between crowding and performance. However, the first partial correlation drops to −.09 when social class is statistically controlled, and the second partial correlation remains high even when the influence of social class is removed. The outcome of the partial correlation depends on the magnitude of the correlations between the third variable and the two variables of primary interest.

## STRUCTURAL MODELS

Recent advances in statistical theory and methods have resulted in techniques for testing **structural models** of relationships among variables using the nonexperimental method. Although these methods are beyond the scope of this book, you should be aware that they exist (see Loehlin, 1998; Maruyama, 1998). A structural model is an expected pattern of relationships among a set of variables. The proposed pattern is based on a theory of how the variables are causally related to one another. This research approach is called *structural modeling* or *structural equation modeling*, because the techniques really allow researchers to test how well obtained data fit a theoretical "structural model" that describes the relationships among variables (also, the mathematical operations underlying the technique are based on structural equations).

The diagram on attitudes and intentions shown previously is a very simple structural model. A somewhat more complex model based on the same theory of reasoned action is shown in Figure 12.10. Vincent, Peplau, and Hill (1998) studied the career aspirations and gender role attitudes of 105 young women (average

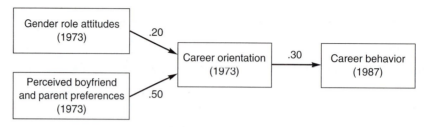

FIGURE 12.10
Structural model based on data from Vincent, Peplau, and Hill (1998)

age of 21 years) in 1973. At that time, they measured three variables: (1) gender role attitudes or how positively the women valued "traditional" women's roles in society, (2) perceived preferences of parents and boyfriends to follow "traditional" career paths, and (3) career orientation. The career orientation measure asked the women to describe their plans or intentions for the future—would they be primarily mothers and homemakers or did they perceive themselves as involved in full-time careers outside the home? The researchers were able to contact the same women in 1987 to measure their actual life career paths.

Arrows leading from one variable to another depict obtained paths that relate the variables in the model; the arrows indicate a proposed causal sequence suggested by the theory of reasoned action. Note that actual behavior has been added to the model; behavioral intention directly influences actual behavior. The coefficients are similar to the weights derived in the regression equations described previously. They indicate strength of a relationship on our familiar 0.00 to 1.00 scale. Both gender role attitudes and perceived preferences of parents and boyfriends are related to career intentions. The normative pressure from parents and boyfriends has a stronger impact than attitudes. Career orientation in 1973 was in turn related to actual career behavior in 1987. Vincent et al. used structural equation modeling techniques to show that the obtained data did in fact closely fit the model shown in Figure 12.10.

An older but related tool for exploring relationships among variables is called **path analysis.** Path analysis is used primarily to explore possible relationships among variables, while structural equation modeling is used to test how well data fit a theoretical model that has been developed, or to compare how well several competing models fit the obtained data. In both cases, this type of research leads to better understanding of the complex networks of relationships among variables.

In the next chapter we turn from description of data to making decisions about statistical significance. These two topics are of course related. The topic of effect size that was described in this chapter is also very important when evaluating statistical significance.

## Study Terms

Bar graph
Central tendency
Correlation coefficient
Criterion variable
Descriptive statistics
Effect size
Frequency distribution
Frequency polygons
Interval scales
Mean
Median
Mode
Multiple correlation
Nominal scales
Ordinal scales

Partial correlation
Path analysis
Pearson product-moment correlation coefficient
Pie chart
Predictor variable
Ratio scales
Regression equations
Restriction of range
Scatterplot
Standard deviation
Statistical significance
Structural models
Variability
Variance

## Review Questions

1. Distinguish between comparing percentages, comparing means, and correlating scores.
2. What is a frequency distribution?
3. Distinguish between a pie chart, bar graph, and frequency polygon. Construct one of each.
4. What is a measure of central tendency? Distinguish between the mean, median, and mode.
5. What is a measure of variability? Distinguish between the standard deviation and the range.
6. What is a correlation coefficient? What do the size and sign of the correlation coefficient tell us about the relationship between variables?
7. What is a scatterplot?
8. What happens when a scatterplot shows the relationship to be curvilinear?
9. What is the difference between a correlation coefficient/effect size and the correlational method?
10. What is a regression equation? How might an employer use a regression equation?

11. How does multiple correlation increase accuracy of prediction?

12. What is the purpose of partial correlation?

13. When a structural model is diagrammed, what information is conveyed by the arrows leading from one variable to another?

## Activity Questions

1. Your favorite newspaper or newsmagazine is a rich source of descriptive statistics on a variety of topics. Examine the past week's newspapers and any newsmagazines in your home; describe at least five instances of actual data presented. These can include surveys, experiments, business data, and even sports information.

2. Hill (1990) studied the correlations between final exam score in an introductory sociology course and several other variables such as number of absences. The following Pearson $r$ correlation coefficients with final exam score were obtained:

| Overall college GPA | .72 |
| Number of absences | −.51 |
| Hours spent studying on weekdays | −.11 (not significant) |
| Hours spent studying on weekends | .31 |

Describe each correlation and draw graphs depicting the general shape of each relationship. Why might hours spent studying on weekends be correlated with grades but weekday studying not be?

3. Ask 20 students on campus how many units they are carrying this term, as well as how many hours per week they work in paid employment. Create a frequency distribution and find the mean for each data set. Construct a scatterplot showing the relationship between class load and hours per week employed. Does there appear to be a relationship between the variables? (Note: If there might be a restriction of range problem on your campus because few students work or most students take about the same number of units, ask different questions, such as the number of hours spent studying and watching television each week.)

4. Prior to the start of the school year, Mrs. King reviewed the cumulative folders of the students in her fourth-grade class. She found that the standard deviation of the students' scores on the reading readiness test was exactly 0.00. What information does this provide her? How might that information prove useful?

# 13

# Understanding Research Results: Statistical Inference

I n the previous chapter, we examined ways of describing the results of a study. In addition to descriptive statistics, researchers are interested in inferential statistics. We need to infer whether the results that were obtained in a particular study would still occur if the study were repeated over and over again. In this chapter, we examine methods for doing so.

## SAMPLES AND POPULATIONS

Inferential statistics are necessary because the results of a given study are based on data obtained from a single sample of research participants. Researchers rarely, if ever, study entire populations; their findings are based on sample data. In addition to describing the sample data, we want to make statements about populations. Would the results hold up if the experiment were conducted repeatedly, each time with a new sample?

In the hypothetical experiment described in Chapter 12 (see Table 12.1), mean aggression scores were obtained in model and no-model conditions. These means are different: Children who observe an aggressive model subsequently behave more aggressively than children who don't see the model. **Inferential statistics** are used to determine whether we can, in fact, make statements that the results reflect what would happen if we were to conduct the experiment again and again with multiple samples. In essence, we are asking whether we can infer that the difference in the sample means shown in Table 12.1 reflects a true difference in the population means.

Recall our discussion of this issue in Chapter 7 when the topic of survey data was discussed. A sample of people in your state might tell you that 57% prefer the Democratic candidate for an office and that 43% favor the Republican candidate. The report then says that these results are accurate to within 3 percentage points, with a 95% confidence level. This means that the researchers are very confident that, if they were able to study the entire population rather than a sample, the actual percentage who preferred the Democratic candidate would be between 60% and 54% and the percentage preferring the Republican would be between 46% and 40%. In this case, the researcher could predict with a great deal of certainty that the Democratic candidate will win because there is no overlap in the projected population values.

Inferential statistics allow us to arrive at such conclusions on the basis of sample data. In our study with the model and no-model conditions, are we confident that the means are sufficiently different to infer that the difference would be obtained in an entire population?

## INFERENTIAL STATISTICS

Much of the previous discussion of experimental design centered on the importance of ensuring that the groups are equivalent in every way except the independent variable manipulation. Equivalence of groups is achieved by experimentally controlling all other variables or by randomization. The assumption is that if the groups are equivalent, any differences in the dependent variable must be due to the effect of the independent variable.

This assumption is usually valid. However, it is also true that the difference between any two groups will almost never be zero. In other words, there will be some difference in the sample means, even when all of the principles of experimental design are utilized. This happens because we are dealing with samples rather than populations. Random or chance error will be responsible for some difference in the means even if the independent variable had no effect on the dependent variable.

The point is that the difference in the sample means reflects any true difference in the population means (i.e., the effect of the independent variable) plus any random error. Inferential statistics allow researchers to make inferences about the true difference in the population on the basis of the sample data. Specifically, inferential statistics give the probability that the difference between means reflects random error rather than a real difference.

## NULL AND RESEARCH HYPOTHESES

Statistical inference begins with a statement of the null hypothesis and a research (or alternative) hypothesis. The **null hypothesis** is simply that the population means are equal—the observed difference is due to random error. The **research hypothesis** is that the population means are, in fact, not equal. The null hypothesis states that the independent variable had no effect; the research hypothesis states that the independent variable did have an effect. In the aggression modeling experiment, the null and research hypotheses are:

$H_0$ (null hypothesis): The population mean of the no-model group is equal to the population mean of the model group.

$H_1$ (research hypothesis): The population mean of the no-model group is not equal to the population mean of the model group.

The logic of the null hypothesis is this: If we can determine that the null hypothesis is incorrect, then we accept the research hypothesis as correct. Acceptance of the research hypothesis means that the independent variable had an effect on the dependent variable.

The null hypothesis is used because it is a very precise statement—the population means are exactly equal. This permits us to know precisely the probability of the outcome of the study occurring if the null hypothesis is correct. Such precision isn't possible with the research hypothesis, so we infer that the research hypothesis is correct only by rejecting the null hypothesis. The null hypothesis is rejected when there is a very low probability that the obtained results could be due to random error. This is what is meant by **statistical significance:** A significant result is one that has a very low probability of occurring if the population means are equal. More simply, significance indicates that there is a low probability that the difference between the obtained sample means was due to random error. Significance, then, is a matter of probability.

## PROBABILITY AND SAMPLING DISTRIBUTIONS

**Probability** is the likelihood of the occurrence of some event or outcome. We all use probabilities frequently in everyday life. For example, if you say that there is a high probability that you will get an A in this course, you mean that this outcome is likely to occur. Your probability statement is based on specific information, such as your grades on examinations. The weather forecaster says there is a 10% chance of rain today; this means that the likelihood of rain is very low. A gambler gauges the probability that a particular horse will win a race on the basis of the past records of that horse.

Probability in statistical inference is used in much the same way. We want to specify the probability that an event (in this case, a difference between means in the sample) will occur if there is no difference in the population. The question is: What is the probability of obtaining this result if only random error is operating? If this probability is very low, we reject the possibility that only random or chance error is responsible for the obtained difference in means.

### Probability: The Case of ESP

The use of probability in statistical inference can be understood intuitively from a simple example. Suppose that a friend claims to have ESP (extrasensory perception) ability. You decide to test your friend with a set of five cards commonly used in ESP research; a different symbol is presented on each card. In the ESP test, you look at each card and think about the symbol, and your friend tells you which symbol you are thinking about. In your actual experiment, you have 10 trials; each of the five cards is presented two times in a random order. Your task is to know whether your friend's answers reflect random error (guessing) or whether they indicate that something more than random error is occurring. The null hypothesis in your study is that only random error is operating. The research hypothesis is that the number of correct answers shows more than random or chance guessing. (Note, however, that accepting the research hypothesis could mean that your friend has ESP ability, but it could also mean that the cards were marked, that you had somehow cued your friend when thinking about the symbols, and so on.)

You can easily determine the number of correct answers to expect if the null hypothesis is correct. Just by guessing, one out of five answers (20%) should be correct. On 10 trials, two correct answers are expected under the null hypothesis. If, in the actual experiment, more (or less) than two correct answers are obtained, would you conclude that the obtained data reflect random error or something more than merely random guessing?

Suppose that your friend gets three correct. Then you would probably conclude that only guessing is involved, because you would recognize that there is a high probability that there would be three correct answers *even though only two correct are expected under the null hypothesis.* You expect that exactly two answers in 10 trials would be correct in the long run, if you conducted this experiment with this subject over and over again. However, small deviations away from the expected two are highly likely in a sample of 10 trials.

Suppose, though, that your friend gets seven correct. You might conclude that the results indicate more than random error in this one sample of 10 observations. This conclusion would be based on your intuitive judgment that an outcome of 70% correct when only 20% is expected is very unlikely. At this point, you would decide to reject the null hypothesis and state that the result is significant. A significant result is one that is very unlikely if the null hypothesis is correct.

How unlikely does a result have to be before we decide it is significant? A decision rule is determined prior to collecting the data. The probability required for significance is called the *alpha level.* The most common alpha level probability used is .05. The outcome of the study is considered significant when there is a .05 or less probability of obtaining the results; that is, there are only 5 chances out of 100 that the results were due to random error in one sample from the population. If it is very unlikely that random error is responsible for the obtained results, the null hypothesis is rejected.

## Sampling Distributions

You may have been able to judge intuitively that obtaining seven correct on the 10 trials is very unlikely. Fortunately, we don't have to rely on intuition to determine the probabilities of different outcomes. Table 13.1 shows the probability of actually obtaining each of the possible outcomes in the ESP experiment with 10 trials and a null hypothesis expectation of 20% correct. An outcome of two correct answers has the highest probability of occurrence. Also, as intuition would suggest, an outcome of three correct is highly probable, but an outcome of seven correct is highly unlikely.

The probabilities shown in Table 13.1 were derived from a probability distribution called the *binomial distribution;* all statistical significance decisions are based on probability distributions such as this one. Such distributions are called *sampling distributions.* The sampling distribution is based on the assumption that the null hypothesis is true; in the ESP example, the null hypothesis is that the person is only

TABLE 13.1    Exact probability of each possible outcome of the ESP experiment with 10 trials

| Number of correct answers | Probability |
|:---:|:---:|
| 10 | .00000+ |
| 9 | .00000+ |
| 8 | .00007 |
| 7 | .00079 |
| 6 | .00551 |
| 5 | .02642 |
| 4 | .08808 |
| 3 | .20133 |
| 2 | .30199 |
| 1 | .26844 |
| 0 | .10737 |

guessing and should therefore get 20% correct. Such a distribution assumes that if you were to conduct the study with the same number of observations over and over again, the most frequent finding would be 20%. However, because of the random error possible in each sample, there is a certain probability associated with other outcomes. Outcomes that are close to the expected null hypothesis value of 20% are very likely. However, outcomes further from the expected result are less and less likely if the null hypothesis is correct. When your obtained results are highly unlikely if you are, in fact, sampling from the distribution specified by the null hypothesis, you conclude that the null hypothesis is incorrect. Instead of concluding that your sample results reflect a random deviation from the long-run expectation of 20%, you decide that the null hypothesis is incorrect. That is, you conclude that you have not sampled from the sampling distribution specified by the null hypothesis. Instead, in the case of the ESP example, you decide that your data are from a different sampling distribution in which, if you were to test the person repeatedly, most of the outcomes would be near your obtained result of seven correct answers.

All statistical tests rely on sampling distributions to determine the probability that the results are consistent with the null hypothesis. When it is highly unlikely that the null hypothesis is correct (usually a .05 probability or less), the researcher decides to reject the null hypothesis and therefore to accept the research hypothesis.

## Sample Size

The ESP example also illustrates the importance of sample size—the total number of observations—on determinations of statistical significance. Suppose you had tested your friend on 100 trials instead of 10 and had observed 30 correct answers. Just as you had expected 2 correct answers in 10 trials, you would now expect 20 of 100 answers to be correct. However, 30 out of 100 has a much lower likelihood of occurrence than 3 out of 10. This is because, with more observations sampled, you are more likely to obtain an accurate estimate of the true population value. Thus, as the size of your sample increases, you are more confident that your outcome is actually different from the null hypothesis expectation.

## EXAMPLE: THE *t* AND *F* TESTS

Different statistical tests allow us to use probability to decide whether to reject the null hypothesis. In this section, we will examine the *t*-test and the *F* test. The *t*-test is most commonly used to examine whether two groups are significantly different from each other. In the hypothetical experiment on the effect of a model on aggression, a *t*-test is appropriate because we are asking whether the mean of the no-model group differs from the mean of the model group. The *F* test is a more general statistical test that can be used to ask whether there is a difference among three or more groups or to evaluate the results of factorial designs (discussed in Chapter 10).

To use a statistical test, you must first specify the null hypothesis and the research hypothesis that you are evaluating. The null and research hypotheses for the modeling experiment were described previously. You must also specify the significance level that you will use to decide whether to reject the null hypothesis; this is the alpha level. As noted, researchers generally use a significance level of .05.

### t-*Test*

The sampling distribution of all possible values of *t* is shown in Figure 13.1. (This particular distribution is for the sample size we used in the hypothetical experiment on modeling and aggression; the sample size was 20 with 10 participants in each group.) This sampling distribution has a mean of 0 and a standard deviation of 1. It reflects all the possible outcomes we could expect if we compare the means of two groups *and* the null hypothesis is correct.

To use this distribution to evaluate our data, we need to calculate a value of *t* from the obtained data and evaluate the obtained *t* in terms of the sampling distribution of *t* that is based on the null hypothesis. If the obtained *t* has a low probability of occurrence (.05 or less), then the null hypothesis is rejected.

The *t* value is a ratio of two aspects of the data, the difference between the group means and the variability within groups. The ratio may be described as follows:

$$t = \frac{\text{group difference}}{\text{within-group variability}}$$

The group difference is simply the difference between your obtained means; under the null hypothesis, you expect this difference to be zero. The value of *t* increases as the difference between your obtained sample means increases. Note that the sampling distribution of *t* assumes that there is no difference in the population means; thus, the expected value of *t* under the null hypothesis is zero.

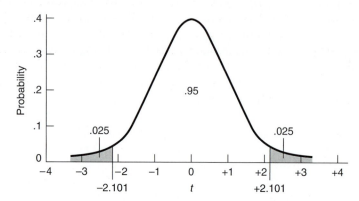

Critical value for two-tailed test with .05 significance level

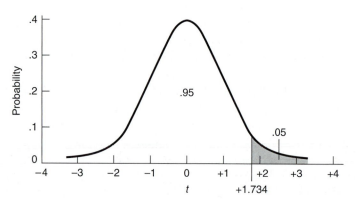

Critical value for one-tailed test with .05 significance level

**Figure 13.1**
Sampling distribution of *t* values with 18 degrees of freedom

The within-group variability is the amount of variability of scores about the mean. The denominator of the *t* formula is essentially an indicator of the amount of random error in your sample. Recall from Chapter 12 that *s*, the standard deviation, and $s^2$, the variance, are indicators of how much scores deviate from the group mean.

A concrete example of a calculation of a *t*-test should help clarify these concepts. The formula for the *t*-test for two groups with equal numbers of participants in each group is

$$t = \frac{\overline{X}_1 - \overline{X}_2}{\sqrt{\dfrac{s_1^2}{N_1} + \dfrac{s_2^2}{N_2}}}$$

The numerator of the formula is simply the difference between the means of the two groups. In the denominator, we first divide the variance ($s^2$) of each group by the number of subjects in the group and add these together. We then find the square root of the result; this converts the number from a squared score, the variance, to a standard deviation. Finally, we calculate our obtained t value by dividing the mean difference by this standard deviation. When the formula is applied to the data in Table 12.1, we find:

$$t = \frac{5.2 - 3.1}{\sqrt{\dfrac{1.289}{10} + \dfrac{1.433}{10}}}$$

$$= \frac{2.1}{\sqrt{.1289 + .1433}}$$

$$= 4.025$$

Thus, the *t* value calculated from the data is 4.025. Is this a significant result? A computer program analyzing the results would immediately tell you the probability of obtaining a *t* value of this size with a total sample size of 20. Without such a program, however, you can refer to a table of "critical values" of *t*, such as Table C.3 in Appendix C. We will discuss the use of the appendix tables in detail in Appendix B. Before going any further, you should know that the obtained result is significant. Using a significance level of .05, the critical value from the sampling distribution of *t* is 2.101. Any *t* value greater than or equal to 2.101 has a .05 or less probability of occurring under the assumptions of the null hypothesis. Because our obtained value is larger than the critical value, we can reject the null hypothesis and conclude that the difference in means obtained in the sample reflects a true difference in the population.

### Degrees of Freedom

You are probably wondering how the critical value was selected from the table. To use the table, you must first determine the **degrees of freedom** for the test (the term degrees of freedom is abbreviated as *df*). When comparing two means, the degrees of freedom are equal to $N_1 + N_2 - 2$, or the total number of participants in the groups minus the number of groups. In our experiment, the degrees of freedom would be $10 + 10 - 2 = 18$. The degrees of freedom are the number of scores free to vary once the means are known. For example, if the mean of a group is 6.0 and there are five scores in the group, there are 4 degrees of freedom; once you have any four scores, the fifth score is known because the mean must remain 6.0.

### One-Tailed Versus Two-Tailed Tests

In the table, you must choose a critical *t* for the situation in which your research hypothesis either (1) specified a direction of difference between the groups (e.g., group 1 will be greater than group 2) or (2) did not specify a predicted direction of difference (e.g., group 1 will differ from group 2). Somewhat different critical values of $t$ are used in the two situations: The first situation is called a one-tailed test, and the second situation is called a two-tailed test.

The issue can be visualized by looking at the sampling distribution of $t$ values for 18 degrees of freedom, as shown in Figure 13.1. As you can see, a value of 0.00 is expected most frequently. Values greater than or less than zero are less likely to occur. The first distribution shows the logic of a two-tailed test. We used the value of 2.101 for the critical value of $t$ with a .05 significance level because a direction of difference was not predicted. This critical value is the point beyond which 2.5% of the positive values and 2.5% of the negative values of $t$ lie (hence, a total probability of .05 combined from the two "tails" of the sampling distribution). The second distribution illustrates a one-tailed test. If a directional difference had been predicted, the critical value would have been 1.734. This is the value beyond which 5% of the values lie in only one "tail" of the distribution. Whether to specify a one-tailed or two-tailed test will depend on whether you originally designed your study to test a directional hypothesis.

## F *Test*

The **analysis of variance,** or **F test,** is an extension of the $t$-test. The analysis of variance is a more general statistical procedure than the $t$-test. When a study has only one independent variable with *two* groups, $F$ and $t$ are virtually identical— the value of $F$ equals $t^2$ in this situation. However, analysis of variance is also used when there are more than two levels of an independent variable and when a factorial design with two or more independent variables has been used. Thus, the $F$ test is appropriate for the simplest experimental design, as well as for the more complex designs discussed in Chapter 10. The $t$-test was presented because the formula allows us to demonstrate easily the relationship of the group difference and the within-group variability to the outcome of the statistical test. However, in practice, analysis of variance is the more common procedure. The calculations necessary to conduct an $F$ test are provided in Appendix B.

The $F$ statistic is a ratio of two types of variance: systematic variance and error variance (hence the term *analysis of variance*). **Systematic variance** is the deviation of the group means from the grand mean, or the mean score of all individuals in all groups. Systematic variance is small when the difference between group means is small and increases as the group mean differences increase. **Error variance** is the deviation of the individual scores in each group from their respective group means. Terms that you may see in research instead of systematic and error variance are *between-group variance* and *within-group variance*. Systematic variance is the variability of scores between groups, and error variance is the variability of scores within groups. The larger the $F$ ratio is, the more likely it is that the results are significant.

## *Calculating Effect Size*

The concept of effect size was discussed in Chapter 12. In addition to knowing whether there was a statistically significant effect of the independent variable, it is useful to know the magnitude of the effect. Therefore, we want to calculate an estimate of effect size. For a *t*-test, the calculation is

$$\text{effect size } r = \sqrt{\frac{t^2}{t^2 + df}}$$

where *df* is the degrees of freedom. Thus, using the obtained value of *t*, 4.025, and 18 degrees of freedom, we find

$$\text{effect size } r = \sqrt{\frac{(4.025)^2}{(4.025)^2 + 18}} = \sqrt{\frac{16.201}{34.201}} = .688$$

This value is a type of correlation coefficient that can range from 0.00 to 1.00. For additional information on effect size calculation, see Rosenthal (1991). The same distinction between *r* and $r^2$ that was made in Chapter 12 applies here as well.

Another effect size estimate used when comparing two means is called Cohen's *d*. Cohen's *d* expresses effect size in terms of standard deviation units. A *d* value of 1.0 tells you that the means are 1 standard deviation apart; a *d* of .5 indicates that the means are separated by .5 standard deviation. The value of *d* is larger than the corresponding value of *r*, but it is easy to convert *d* to a value of *r*. Both statistics provide information on the size of the relationship between the variables studied. You might note that both effect size estimates have a value of 0.00 when there is no relationship. The value of *r* has a maximum value of 1.00 but *d* has no maximum value.

### Confidence Intervals and Statistical Significance

Confidence intervals were described in Chapter 7. After obtaining a sample value, a confidence interval can be calculated. An interval of values defines the most likely range of actual population values. The interval has an associated confidence interval: a 95% confidence interval indicates that we are 95% sure that the population value lies within the range; a 99% interval would provide greater certainty but the range of values would be larger.

A confidence interval can be obtained for each of the means in the aggression experiment. The 95% confidence intervals for the two conditions are:

|  | Obtained sample value | Low population value | High population value |
|---|---|---|---|
| Model group | 5.20 | 4.39 | 6.01 |
| No-model group | 3.10 | 2.24 | 3.96 |

It is important to examine confidence intervals to obtain a greater understanding of the meaning of your obtained data. Although the obtained sample means provide the best estimate of the population values, you are able to see the likely range of possible values. The size of the interval is related to both the size of the sample and the confidence level. As the sample size increases, the confidence interval narrows. This is because sample means obtained with larger sample sizes are more likely to reflect the population mean. Second, higher confidence is associated with a larger interval. If you want to be almost certain that the interval contains the true population mean (e.g., a 99% confidence interval), you will need to include more possibilities. Note that the 95% confidence intervals for the two means do not overlap. This should be a clue to you that the difference is statistically significant. Indeed, examining confidence intervals is an alternative way of thinking about statistical significance. The null hypothesis is that the difference in population means is 0.00. However, if you were to subtract all the means in the 95% confidence interval for the no-model condition from all the means in the model condition, none of these differences would include the value of 0.00. We can be very confident that the null hypothesis should be rejected.

### Statistical Significance: An Overview

The logic underlying the use of statistical tests rests on statistical theory. There are some general concepts, however, that should help you understand what you are doing when you conduct a statistical test. First, the goal of the test is to allow you to make a decision about whether your obtained results are reliable; you want to be confident that you would obtain similar results if you conducted the study over and over again. Second, the significance level (alpha level) you choose indicates how confident you wish to be when making the decision. A .05 significance level says that you are 95% sure of the reliability of your findings; however, there is a 5% chance that you could be wrong. There are few certainties in life! Third, you are most likely to obtain significant results when you have a large sample size because larger sample sizes provide better estimates of true population values. Finally, you are most likely to obtain significant results when the effect size is large, i.e., when differences between groups are large and variability of scores within groups is small.

In the remainder of the chapter, we will expand on these issues. We will examine the implications of making a decision about whether results are significant, the way to determine a significance level, and the way to interpret nonsignificant results. We will then provide some guidelines for selecting the appropriate statistical test in various research designs.

## TYPE I AND TYPE II ERRORS

The decision to reject the null hypothesis is based on probabilities rather than on certainties. That is, the decision is made without direct knowledge of the true state of affairs in the population. Thus, the decision might not be correct; errors may result from the use of inferential statistics.

A decision matrix is shown in Figure 13.2. Notice that there are two possible decisions: (1) Reject the null hypothesis or (2) accept the null hypothesis. There are also two possible truths about the population: (1) The null hypothesis is true

Figure 13.2
Decision matrix Type I
and Type II errors

or (2) the null hypothesis is false. In sum, as the decision matrix shows, there are two kinds of correct decisions and two kinds of errors.

## Correct Decisions

One correct decision occurs when we reject the null hypothesis and the research hypothesis is true in the population. Here, our decision is that the population means are not equal, and in fact, this is true in the population. This is the decision you hope to make when you begin your study.

The other correct decision is to accept the null hypothesis, and the null hypothesis is true in the population: The population means are in fact equal.

## Type I Errors

A **Type I error** is made when we reject the null hypothesis but the null hypothesis is actually true. Our decision is that the population means are not equal when they actually are equal. Type I errors occur when, simply by chance, we obtain a large value of $t$ or $F$. For example, even though a $t$ value of 4.025 is highly improbable if the population means are indeed equal (less than 5 chances out of 100), this *can* happen. When we do obtain such a large $t$ value by chance, we *incorrectly* decide that the independent variable had an effect.

The probability of making a Type I error is determined by the choice of significance or alpha level (alpha may be shown as the Greek letter alpha—$\alpha$). When the significance level for deciding whether to reject the null hypothesis is .05, the probability of a Type I error (alpha) is .05. If the null hypothesis is rejected, there are 5 chances out of 100 that the decision is wrong. The probability of making a Type I error can be changed by either decreasing or increasing the significance level. If we use a lower alpha level of .01, for example, there is less chance of making a Type I error. With a .01 significance level, the null hypothesis is rejected only when the probability of obtaining the results is .01 or less if the null hypothesis is correct.

### Type II Errors

A **Type II error** occurs when the null hypothesis is accepted although in the population the research hypothesis is true. The population means are not equal, but the results of the experiment do not lead to a decision to reject the null hypothesis.

Research should be designed so that the probability of a Type II error (this probability is called beta or $\beta$) is relatively low. The probability of making a Type II error is related to three factors. The first is the significance (alpha) level. If we set a very low significance level to decrease the chances of a Type I error, we increase the chances of a Type II error. In other words, if we make it very difficult to reject the null hypothesis, the probability of incorrectly accepting the null hypothesis increases. The second factor is sample size. True differences are more likely to be detected if the sample size is large. The third factor is effect size. If the effect size is large, a Type II error is unlikely. However, a small effect size may not be significant with a small sample.

### The Everyday Context of Type I and Type II Errors

The decision matrix used in statistical analyses can be applied to the kinds of decisions people frequently must make in everyday life. For example, consider the decision made by a juror in a criminal trial. As is the case with statistics, a decision must be made on the basis of evidence: Is the defendant innocent or guilty? However, the decision rests with individual jurors and does not necessarily reflect the true state of affairs: that the person really is innocent or guilty.

The juror's decision matrix is illustrated in Figure 13.3. To continue the parallel to the statistical decision, assume as the null hypothesis that the defendant is innocent (i.e., the dictum that a person is innocent until proven guilty). Thus, rejection of the null hypothesis means deciding that the defendant is guilty, and acceptance of the null hypothesis means deciding that the defendant is innocent. The decision matrix also shows that the null hypothesis may actually be true or false. There are two kinds of correct decisions and two kinds of errors like those described in statistical decisions. A Type I error is finding the defendant guilty when the person really is innocent; a Type II error is finding the defendant innocent when the person actually is guilty. In our society, Type I errors by jurors generally are considered to be more serious than Type II errors. Thus, before finding someone guilty, the juror is asked to make sure that the person is guilty "beyond a reasonable doubt" or to consider that "it is better to have a hundred guilty persons go free than to find one innocent person guilty."

The decision that a doctor makes to operate or not operate on a patient provides another illustration of how a decision matrix works. The matrix is shown in Figure 13.4. Here, the null hypothesis is that no operation is necessary. The decision is whether to reject the null hypothesis and perform the operation or to accept the null hypothesis and not perform surgery. In reality, the surgeon is faced with two possibilities: Either the surgery is unnecessary (the null hypothesis is true) or the patient will die without the operation (a dramatic case of the

True state

|                          | Null is true (innocent) | Null is false (guilty) |
| ------------------------ | ----------------------- | ---------------------- |
| Reject null (find guilty) | Type I error            | Correct decision       |
| Accept null (find innocent) | Correct decision       | Type II error          |

Decision

Figure 13.3
Decision matrix for a juror

True state

|                          | Null is true (no operation needed) | Null is false (operation is needed) |
| ------------------------ | ---------------------------------- | ----------------------------------- |
| Reject null (operate on patient) | Type I error               | Correct decision                    |
| Accept null (don't operate) | Correct decision                | Type II error                       |

Decision

Figure 13.4
Decision matrix for a doctor

null hypothesis being false). Which error is more serious in this case? Most doctors would believe that not operating on a patient who really needs the operation—making a Type II error—is more serious than making the Type I error of performing surgery on someone who does not really need it.

One final illustration of the use of a decision matrix involves the important decision to marry someone. If the null hypothesis is that the person is "wrong" for you, and the true state is that the person is either "wrong" or "right," you must decide whether to go ahead and marry the person. You might try to construct a decision matrix for this particular problem. Which error is more costly: a Type I error or a Type II error?

## CHOOSING A SIGNIFICANCE LEVEL

Researchers traditionally have used either a .05 or a .01 significance level in the decision to reject the null hypothesis. If there is less than a .05 or a .01 probability that the results occurred because of random error, the results are said to be significant. However, there is nothing magical about a .05 or a .01 significance level. The significance level chosen merely specifies the probability of a Type I error if the null hypothesis is rejected. The significance level chosen by the researcher usually is dependent on the consequences of making a Type I versus a Type II error. As previously noted, for a juror, a Type I error is more serious than a Type II error; for a doctor, however, a Type II error may be more serious.

Researchers generally believe that the consequences of making a Type I error are more serious than those associated with a Type II error. If the null hypothesis is rejected, the researcher might publish the results in a journal, and the results might be reported by others in textbooks or in newspaper or magazine articles. Researchers don't want to mislead people or risk damaging their reputations by publishing results that aren't reliable and so cannot be replicated. Thus, they want to guard against the possibility of making a Type I error by using a very low significance level (.05 or .01). In contrast to the consequences of publishing false results, the consequences of a Type II error are not seen as being very serious.

Thus, researchers want to be very careful to avoid Type I errors when their results may be published. However, in certain circumstances, a Type I error is not serious. For example, if you were engaged in pilot or exploratory research, your results would be used primarily to decide whether your research ideas were worth pursuing. In this situation, it would be a mistake to overlook potentially important data by using a very conservative significance level. In exploratory research, a significance level of .25 may be more appropriate for deciding whether to do more research. Remember that the significance level chosen and the consequences of a Type I or a Type II error are determined by what the results will be used for.

## INTERPRETING NONSIGNIFICANT RESULTS

Although "accepting the null hypothesis" is convenient terminology, it is important to recognize that researchers are not generally interested in accepting the null hypothesis. Research is designed to show that a relationship between variables does exist, not to demonstrate that variables are unrelated.

More important, a decision to accept the null hypothesis when a single study does not show significant results is problematic, because negative or nonsignificant results are difficult to interpret. The results of a single study might be nonsignificant even when a relationship between the variables in the population does in fact exist. This is a Type II error. Sometimes, the reasons for a Type II error lie in the procedures used in the experiment. For example, a researcher might obtain nonsignificant results by providing incomprehensible instructions to the participants, by having a very weak manipulation of the independent variable, or by using a dependent measure that is unreliable and insensitive. Rather than concluding that the variables are not related, it may be that a more carefully conducted study would find that the variables are related.

We should also consider the statistical reasons for a Type II error. Recall that the probability of a Type II error is influenced by the significance (alpha) level, sample size, and effect size. Thus, nonsignificant results are more likely by being very cautious in choosing the alpha level. If the researcher uses a significance level of .001 in deciding whether to reject the null hypothesis, there is not much chance of a Type I error. However, a Type II error is possible, because the researcher has decreased the chances of wrongly rejecting the null hypothesis. In other words, a meaningful result is more likely to be overlooked when the significance level is very low.

A Type II error may also result from a sample size that is too small to detect a real relationship between variables. A general principle is that the larger the sample size is, the greater the likelihood of obtaining a significant result. This is because large sample sizes give more accurate estimates of the actual population than do small sample sizes. In any given study, the sample size may be too small to permit detection of a significant result.

A third reason for a nonsignificant finding is that the effect size is small. Very small effects are difficult to detect without a large sample size. In general, the sample size should be large enough to find a real effect, even if it is a small one.

The fact that it is possible for a very small effect to be statistically significant raises another issue. A very large sample size might enable the researcher to find a significant difference between means; however, this difference, even though statistically significant, might have very little *practical* significance. For example, if an expensive new psychiatric treatment technique significantly reduces the average hospital stay from 60 days to 59 days, it might not be practical to use the technique despite the evidence for its effectiveness. The additional day of hospitalization costs less than the treatment. There are other circumstances, however, in which a treatment with a very small effect size has considerable practical significance. Usually this occurs when a very large population is affected by a fairly inexpensive treatment. Suppose a simple flextime policy for employees reduces employee turnover by 1% per year. This doesn't sound like a large effect. However, if a company normally has a turnover of 2,000 employees each year and the cost of training a new employee is $10,000, the company saves $200,000 per year with the new procedure. This amount may have practical significance for the company.

The key point here is that you should not accept the null hypothesis just because the results are nonsignificant. Nonsignificant results do not necessarily indicate that the null hypothesis is correct. However, there must be circumstances in which we can accept the null hypothesis and conclude that two variables are, in fact, not related. Frick (1995) describes several criteria that can be used in a decision to accept the null hypothesis. For example, we should look for well-designed studies with sensitive dependent measures and evidence from a manipulation check that the independent variable manipulation had its intended effect. In addition, the research should have a reasonably large sample to rule out the possibility that the sample was too small. Further, evidence that the variables are not related should come from multiple studies. Under such circumstances, you are justified in concluding that there is in fact no relationship.

## CHOOSING A SAMPLE SIZE: POWER ANALYSIS

We noted in Chapter 9 that researchers often select a sample size based on what is typical in a particular area of research. An alternative approach is to select a sample size on the basis of a desired probability of correctly rejecting the null hypothesis. This probability is called the **power** of the statistical test. It is obviously related to the probability of a Type II error:

$$\text{Power} = 1 - p \text{ (Type II error)}$$

We previously indicated that the probability of a Type II error is related to significance level (alpha), sample size, and effect size. Statisticians such as Cohen (1988) have developed procedures for determining sample size based on these factors. Table 13.2 shows the total sample size needed for an experiment with two groups and a significance level of .05. In the table, effect sizes range from .10 to .50, and the desired power is shown at .80 and .90. Smaller effect sizes require larger samples to be significant at the .05 level. Higher desired power demands a greater sample size; this is because you want a more certain "guarantee" that your results will be statistically significant. Researchers usually use a power between .70 and .90 when using this method to determine sample size. Several computer programs have been developed to allow researchers to easily make the calculations necessary to determine sample size based on effect size estimates, significance level, and desired power.

You may never need to perform a power analysis. However, you should recognize the importance of this concept. If a researcher is studying a relationship with an effect size correlation of .20, a fairly large sample size is needed for statistical significance at the .05 level. An inappropriately low sample size in this situation is likely to produce a nonsignificant finding.

## THE IMPORTANCE OF REPLICATIONS

Throughout this discussion of statistical analysis, the focus has been on the results of a single research investigation. What were the means and standard devi-

**TABLE 13.2**    Total sample size needed to detect a significant difference for a *t* test

| Effect size *r* | Power = .80 | Power = .90 |
|---|---|---|
| .10 | 786 | 1052 |
| .20 | 200 | 266 |
| .30 | 88 | 116 |
| .40 | 52 | 68 |
| .50 | 28 | 36 |

*Note:* Effect sizes are correlations; based on two-tailed tests.

ations? Was the mean difference statistically significant? If the results are significant, you conclude that they would likely be obtained over and over again if the study were repeated. We now have a framework for understanding the results of the study. Be aware, however, that scientists do not attach too much importance to the results of a single study. A rich understanding of any phenomenon comes from the results of numerous studies investigating the same variables. Instead of inferring population values on the basis of a single investigation, we can look at the results of several studies that replicate previous investigations (see Cohen, 1994). The importance of replications is a central concept in Chapter 14.

## SIGNIFICANCE OF A PEARSON R CORRELATION COEFFICIENT

Recall from Chapter 12 that the Pearson $r$ correlation coefficient is used to describe the strength of the relationship between two variables when both variables have interval or ratio scale properties. However, there remains the issue of whether the correlation is statistically significant. The null hypothesis in this case is that the true population correlation is 0.00—the two variables are not related. What if you obtain a correlation of .27 (plus or minus)? A statistical significance test will allow you to decide whether to reject the null hypothesis and conclude that the true population correlation is, in fact, greater than 0.00. The technical way to do this is to perform a $t$-test that compares the obtained coefficient with the null hypothesis correlation of 0.00. The procedures for calculating a Pearson $r$ and determining significance are provided in Appendix B.

## COMPUTER ANALYSIS OF DATA

Although you can calculate statistics with a calculator using the formulas provided in this chapter, Chapter 12, and Appendix B, most data analysis is carried out via computer programs. Sophisticated statistical analysis software packages make it easy to calculate statistics for any data set. Descriptive and inferential statistics are obtained quickly, the calculations are accurate, and information on statistical significance is provided in the output. Computers also facilitate graphic displays of data.

Some of the major statistical software programs are SPSS, SAS, Minitab, Systat, and BMDP; other programs may be used on your campus as well. Many people do most of their statistical analyses using a spreadsheet program such as Microsoft Excel. You will need to learn the specific details of the computer system used at your college or university. No one program is better than another; they all differ in the appearance of the output and the specific procedures needed to input data and have the program perform the test. However, the general procedures for doing analyses are quite similar in all of the statistics programs.

The first step in doing the analysis is to input the data. Suppose you want to input the data in Table 12.1, the modeling and aggression experiment. Data are entered into columns. It is easiest to think of data for computer analysis as a matrix with rows and columns. Data for each research participant are the rows of the matrix. The columns contain each participant's scores on one or more measures, and an additional column may be needed to indicate a code to identify which condition the individual was in (e.g., Group 1 or Group 2). A data matrix in SPSS for Windows is shown in Figure 13.5. The numbers in the "group" column indicate whether the individual is in Group 1 (model) or Group 2 (no model), and the numbers in the "aggscore" column are the aggression scores from Table 12.1.

Other programs may require somewhat different methods of data input. For example, in Excel, it is usually easiest to set up a separate column for each group, as shown in Figure 13.5.

The next step is to provide instructions for the statistical analysis. Again, each program uses somewhat different steps to perform the analysis; most require you to choose from various menu options. When the analysis is completed, you are provided with the output that shows the results of the statistical procedure you performed. You will need to learn how to interpret the output. Figure 13.5 shows the output for a *t*-test using Excel.

When you are first learning to use a statistical analysis program, it is a good idea to practice with some data from a statistics text to make sure that you get the same results. This will ensure that you know how to properly input the data and request the statistical analysis.


## SELECTING THE APPROPRIATE SIGNIFICANCE TEST

Many statistical tests have been developed for different research designs. The appropriateness of a particular test of significance depends on the design used and the type of measurement scales employed for studying the variables. Recall from Chapter 12 that the values of variables have measurement scale properties. There are four such scales: (1) nominal, in which the values have no numerical properties; (2) ordinal, in which the values are only meaningful as a ranked order; (3) interval, in which the values are arranged along a continuum of equal intervals; and (4) ratio, in which there is a true zero point on the scale of values. This section will not provide guidelines for selecting a test in all situations; rather, only the appropriate tests for some of the more common designs will be presented.

### One Independent Variable—Two Groups Only

Nominal scale data    When individuals in two groups have been measured using a nominal scale, the appropriate test is a *chi-square test*. Chi-square tests are used with all nominal data. Check a statistics book for the formula for your application.

| | group | aggscore |
|---|---|---|
| 1 | 1 | 3 |
| 2 | 1 | 4 |
| 3 | 1 | 5 |
| 4 | 1 | 5 |
| 5 | 1 | 5 |
| 6 | 2 | 1 |
| 7 | 2 | 2 |
| 8 | 2 | 2 |
| 9 | 2 | 3 |
| 10 | 2 | 3 |
| 11 | 1 | 5 |
| 12 | 1 | 6 |
| 13 | 2 | 3 |
| 14 | 2 | 4 |
| 15 | 2 | 4 |

Data matrix in SPSS for Windows

| | A | B |
|---|---|---|
| 1 | Model | No Model |
| 2 | 3 | 1 |
| 3 | 4 | 2 |
| 4 | 5 | 2 |
| 5 | 5 | 3 |
| 6 | 5 | 3 |
| 7 | 5 | 3 |
| 8 | 6 | 4 |
| 9 | 6 | 4 |
| 10 | 6 | 4 |
| 11 | 7 | 5 |
| 12 | | |
| 13 | | |

Excel method of data input

*t*-Test: Two-Sample Assuming Equal Variances

| | *Model* | *No Model* |
|---|---|---|
| Mean | 5.200 | 3.100 |
| Variance | 1.289 | 1.433 |
| Observations | 10.000 | 10.000 |
| Pooled Variance | 1.361 | |
| Hypothesized Mean Difference | 0.000 | |
| df | 18.000 | |
| t Stat | 4.025 | |
| P(T<=t) one-tail | 0.000 | |
| t Critical one-tail | 1.734 | |
| P(T<=t) two-tail | 0.001 | |
| t Critical two-tail | 2.101 | |

Output for a *t*-test using Excel

Figure 13.5
Sample computer input and output using data from Figure 12.1
(modeling experiment).

**Ordinal scale data**     If an independent groups design was used, the Mann-Whitney $U$ test is the appropriate statistical significance test. For a repeated measures or matched participants design, Wilcoxon's $T$ or the sign test is used. The procedures for these tests may be found in many statistics texts (see Siegel & Castellan, 1988).

**Interval or ratio scale data**     For independent groups designs, the $t$-test described in this chapter or a one-way analysis of variance is used. The analysis of variance calculations are given in Appendix B. With repeated measures or matched groups designs, a $t$-test with a slightly different calculation procedure or a repeated measures analysis of variance should be employed. The calculations for a repeated measures analysis of variance are shown in Appendix B.

### One Independent Variable—Three or More Groups

**Nominal scale data**     A chi-square test is used in this situation.

**Ordinal scale data**     The Kruskal–Wallace $H$ test is appropriate for an independent groups design. For repeated measures designs, the Friedman $T$ test is appropriate. Consult a statistics text for details on calculating these tests.

**Interval or ratio scale data**     A one-way analysis of variance is used here. The procedures to calculate this test for both independent groups and repeated measures designs are provided in Appendix B.

### Two or More Independent Variables

**Nominal scale data**     Again, a chi-square test is appropriate for nominal scale data. The formula for a chi-square in which participants are classified on two variables, both with nominal scale properties, is provided in Appendix B.

**Ordinal scale data**     No appropriate statistical test is available.

**Interval or ratio scale data**     A two-way analysis of variance is used for factorial designs with two independent variables. Analysis of variance can be extended to designs with any number of independent variables. It is appropriate for independent groups, repeated measures, or mixed designs with both independent groups and repeated measures variables.

You have now considered how to generate research ideas, conduct research to test your ideas, and evaluate the statistical significance of your results. In the final chapter, we will examine issues of generalizing research findings beyond the specific circumstances in which the research was conducted.

## Study Terms

Alpha level                                Probability
Analysis of variance ($F$ test)            Research hypothesis
Chi-square test                            Sampling distribution
Degrees of freedom                         Statistical significance
Error variance                             Systematic variance
Inferential statistics                     $t$-test
Null hypothesis                            Type I error
Power                                      Type II error

## Review Questions

1. Distinguish between the null hypothesis and the research hypothesis. When does the researcher decide to reject the null hypothesis?

2. What is meant by statistical significance?

3. What factors are most important in determining whether obtained results will be significant?

4. Distinguish between a Type I and a Type II error. Why is your significance level the probability of making a Type I error?

5. What factors are involved in choosing a significance level?

6. What influences the probability of a Type II error?

7. What is the difference between statistical significance and practical significance?

8. Discuss the reasons that a researcher might obtain nonsignificant results.

## Activity Questions

1. In an experiment, one group of research participants is given 10 pages of material to proofread for errors. Another group proofreads the same material on a computer screen. The dependent variable is the number of errors detected in a 5-minute period. A .05 significance (alpha) level is used to evaluate the results.

   a. What statistical test would you use?

   b. What is the null hypothesis? The research hypothesis?

   c. What is the Type I error? The Type II error?

   d. What is the probability of making a Type I error?

2. In Professor Dre's study, the average number of errors detected in the print and computer conditions was 38.4 and 13.2, respectively; this difference was not statistically significant. When Professor Seuss conducted the same experiment, the means of the two groups were 21.1 and 14.7, but the difference was statistically significant. Explain how this could happen.

3. Suppose that you work for the child social services agency in your county. Your job is to investigate instances of possible child neglect or abuse. After collecting your evidence, which may come from a variety of sources, you must decide whether to leave the child in the home or place the child in protective custody. Specify the null and research hypotheses in this situation. What constitutes a Type I and a Type II error? Is a Type I or Type II error the more serious error in this situation? Why?

4. A researcher investigated attitudes toward individuals in wheelchairs. The question was: Would people react differently to a person they perceived as being temporarily confined to the wheelchair than to a person who had a permanent disability? Participants were randomly assigned to two groups. Individuals in one group each worked on various tasks with a confederate in a wheelchair; members of the other group worked with the same confederate in a wheelchair, but this time the confederate wore a leg cast. After the session was over, participants filled out a questionnaire regarding their reactions to the study. One question asked, "Would you be willing to work with your test partner in the future on a class assignment?" with "yes" and "no" as the only response alternatives. What would be the appropriate significance test for this experiment? Can you offer a critique of the dependent variable? If you changed the dependent variable, would it affect your choice of significance tests? If so, how?

# 14

# Generalizing Results

In this chapter, we will consider the issue of generalization of research findings. A single study is conducted with a particular sample and procedure. Can the results then be generalized to other populations of research participants, or to other ways of manipulating or measuring the variables? Recall that internal validity refers to the ability to infer that there is a causal relationship between variables. External validity is the extent to which the findings may be generalized.

## GENERALIZING TO OTHER POPULATIONS OF RESEARCH PARTICIPANTS

Even though a researcher randomly assigns participants to experimental conditions, rarely are they randomly selected from the general population. As we noted in Chapters 7 and 9, the individuals who participate in psychological research are usually selected because they are available, and the most available population consists of college students—or more specifically, freshmen and sophomores enrolled in the introductory psychology course to satisfy a general education requirement. They may also be from a particular college or university, may be volunteers, or may be mostly males or mostly females. Are our research findings limited to these types of subjects, or can we generalize our findings to a more general population? After considering these issues, we will examine the larger issue of culture.

### College Students

Smart (1966) found that college students were studied in over 70% of the articles published between 1962 and 1964 in the *Journal of Experimental Psychology* and the *Journal of Abnormal and Social Psychology.* Sears (1986) reported similar percentages in 1980 and 1985 in a variety of social psychology journals. The potential problem is that such studies use a highly restricted population. Sears points out that most of the students are freshmen and sophomores taking the introductory psychology class. They therefore tend to be very young and to possess the characteristics of late adolescence: a sense of self-identity that is still developing, social and political attitudes that are in a state of flux, a high need for peer approval, and unstable peer relationships. They also are intelligent, have high cognitive skills, and know how to win approval from authority (having done well enough in a school environment to get into college). Thus, what we know about "people in general" may actually be limited to a highly select and unusual group.

The problem of unrepresentative subjects is not confined to human research. A great deal of research with animals relies solely on the infamous white rat. Why? In part because, as Beach (1950) points out, "Rats are hardy, cheap, easy to rear, and well adapted to laboratory existence." Thus, like freshmen and sophomores, they are easy to obtain on a college campus.

## Volunteers

Researchers usually must ask people to volunteer to participate in the research. At many colleges, introductory psychology students are required either to volunteer for experiments or to complete an alternative project. If you are studying populations other than college students, you are even more dependent on volunteers—for example, asking people at a homeowners' association meeting to participate in a study of marital interaction or conducting research on the Internet in which people must go to your Web page and then agree to participate in the study. Research indicates that volunteers differ in various ways from nonvolunteers (Rosenthal & Rosnow, 1975). For instance, volunteers tend to be more highly educated, more in need of approval, and more social; they also tend to have a higher socioeconomic status.

Further, different kinds of people volunteer for different kinds of experiments. In colleges, there may be a sign-up board with the titles of many studies listed. Different types of people may be drawn to the study titled "problem solving" than to the one titled "interaction in small groups." Available evidence indicates that the title does influence who signs up (Hood & Back, 1971; Silverman & Margulis, 1973).

## Gender Considerations

Sometimes, researchers use either males or females (or a very disproportionate ratio of males to females) simply because this is convenient or the procedures seem better suited to either males or females. Given the possible differences between males and females, however, the results of such studies may not be generalizable (Denmark, Russo, Frieze, & Sechzer, 1988). Denmark et al. provide an example of studies on contraception practices that use only females because of stereotypical assumptions that only females are responsible for contraception. They also point out several other ways that gender bias may arise in psychological research, including confounding gender with age or job status and selecting response measures that are gender-stereotyped. The solution is to be aware of possible gender differences and include both males and females in our research investigations. Moreover, it is important to recognize the ways that males and females might differentially interpret independent variable manipulations or questions asked in a questionnaire.

## Locale

Participants in one locale may differ from participants in another locale. For example, students at UCLA may differ from students at a nearby state university, who, in turn, may differ from students at a community college. People in Iowa may differ from people in New York City. Thus, a finding obtained with the students in one type of educational setting or in one geographic region may not generalize to people in other settings or regions.

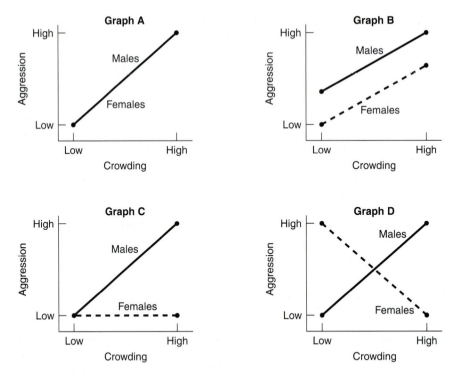

**FIGURE 14.1**

Outcomes of a hypothetical experiment on crowding and aggression.

Note: The presence of an interaction indicates that the results for males cannot be generalized to females.

### Generalization as a Statistical Interaction

The problem of generalization can be thought of as an interaction in a factorial design (see Chapter 10). An interaction occurs when a relationship between variables exists under one condition but not another or when the nature of the relationship is different in one condition than in another. Thus, if you question the generalizability of a study that used only males, you are suggesting that there is an interaction between gender and the independent variable. Suppose, for example, that a study examines the relationship between crowding and aggression among males and reports that crowding is associated with higher levels of aggression. You might then question whether the results are generalizable to females.

Figure 14.1 shows four potential outcomes of a hypothetical study on crowding and aggression that tested both males and females. In each graph, the relationship between crowding and aggression for males has been maintained. In Graph A, there is no interaction—the behavior of males and females is virtually identical. Thus, the results of the original all-male study could be generalized to females. In Graph B, there is also no interaction; the effect of crowding is identical for males and females. However, in this graph, males are more aggressive than females. Although such a difference is interesting, it is not a factor in generalization because the overall relationship between crowding and aggression is present for both males and females.

Graphs C and D do show interactions. In both, the original results with males cannot be generalized to females. In Graph C, there is no relationship between crowding and aggression for females. In Graph D, the interaction tells us that a positive relationship between crowding and aggression exists for males but that a negative relationship exists for females. As it turns out, Graph D describes the results of several studies (cf. Freedman, Levy, Buchanan, & Price, 1972).

Researchers can address generalization issues that stem from the use of different populations by including subject type as a variable in the study. By including variables such as gender, age, or ethnic group in the design of the study, the results may be analyzed to determine whether there are interaction effects like the ones illustrated in Figure 14.1.

### In Defense of College Students and Rats

It is easy to criticize research on the basis of subject characteristics, yet criticism by itself does not mean that the research necessarily is flawed. Although we need to be concerned about the potential problems of generalizing from unique populations such as college students (cf. Sears, 1986), we should also keep two things in mind when thinking about this issue. First, criticisms of the use of any particular type of subject, such as college students, in a study should be backed with good reasons that a relationship would not be found with other types of subjects. College students, after all, *are* human, and researchers should not be blamed for not worrying about generalization to a particular type of subject if there is no good reason to do so. Moreover, college students are increasingly diverse and representative of the society as a whole. Second, remember that replication of research studies provides a safeguard against limited generalizability. Studies are replicated at other colleges using different mixes of students, and many findings first established with college students are later applied to other populations, such as children, aging adults, and people in other countries. Also, although rats are, in fact, hardy and inexpensive, the value of studying rats has been demonstrated by research that applies findings to human problems. For example, research on reinforcement using rats and pigeons has been applied to modifying behavior, understanding personality, and studying choice behavior in humans.

## CULTURAL CONSIDERATIONS

Only a few years ago, the participants in most experiments conducted with college students in the United States were primarily White because this reflected the predominant population of college students. Today, however,

most samples of college students are ethnically diverse because the population of college students is increasingly diverse. The external validity of the research is enhanced, and it is much easier to compare ethnic groups to examine
group differences and similarities. Fewer than 10% of studies in social psychology in the late 1980s included comparisons of two or more cultures (Pepitone & Triandis, 1987). Today, there is much greater interest in studying
different cultures (Miller, 1999).

Much cultural research centers on identifying similarities and differences
that may exist in personality and other psychological characteristics as well as
ways that individuals from different cultures respond to the same environments (Matsumoto, 1994). For example, Cunningham, Roberts, Barbee,
Druen, and Wu (1995) conducted a series of studies to examine perceptions of
female physical attractiveness across cultures. In one study, White American
students and Asian and Hispanic students who had recently immigrated to the
United States rated the attractiveness of faces of Asian, Black, Hispanic, and
White females depicted in photographs. The ratings were highly similar across
groups—the average correlation was .93. There were certain cultural differences, however. For example, in a study in which Black and White American
males rated both faces and body types, the groups were similar in their ratings
of faces but differed in their ratings of different body types. Also, while most
people rated females who appear "sexually mature" as more attractive, Asians
were not influenced by sexual maturity.

This type of research informs us about the generality of findings across cultural groups. Miller (1999) encourages psychologists to take a broader view of
the importance of culture in which "culture is understood as shared meaning
systems that are embodied in artifacts and practices and that form a medium for
human development." Such cultural perspectives should be incorporated into
psychological theories.

Miller points to recent research on self-concept to illustrate the benefits of
incorporating culture into psychological theory. Traditional theories of self-
concept are grounded in the culture of the United States and Western Europe;
the "self" is an individualistic concept; people are independent from others and
self-enhancement comes from individual achievements. Kitayama and his colleagues take a cultural perspective: In contrast to the U.S. meaning of self, in
other cultures, the "self" is a collective concept in which self-esteem is derived
from relationships with others. Japanese engage in self-criticism, whereas Americans engage in self-enhancement—thus, very different activities contribute to
a positive self-concept in the two cultures (Kitayama, Markus, Matsumoto, &
Norasakkunkit, 1997).

It is also important to be aware of the ways that the operational definitions
of the constructs that we study are grounded in a particularly cultural meaning.
A measure of self-esteem that is appropriate for an individualistic culture is
probably not appropriate for use, and would yield misleading results, in a collective culture.

## GENERALIZING TO OTHER EXPERIMENTERS

The person who actually conducts the experiment is the source of another generalization problem. In most research, only one experimenter is used, and rarely is much attention paid to the personal characteristics of the experimenter (McGuigan, 1963). The main goal is to make sure that any influence the experimenter has on subjects is constant throughout the experiment. There is always the possibility, however, that the results are generalizable only to certain types of experimenters.

Some of the important characteristics of experimenters have been discussed by Kintz and his colleagues (Kintz, Delprato, Mettee, Persons, & Schappe, 1965). These include the experimenter's personality and gender and the amount of practice in the role of experimenter. A warm, friendly experimenter will almost certainly produce different results than will a cold, unfriendly experimenter. Participants also may behave differently with male and female experimenters. It has even been shown that rabbits learn faster when trained by experienced experimenters (Brogden, 1962)! The influence of the experimenter may depend as well on the characteristics of the participants. For example, participants seem to perform better when tested by an experimenter of the opposite sex (Stevenson & Allen, 1964).

One solution to the problem of generalizing to other experimenters is to use two or more experimenters, preferably both male and female, to conduct the research. A fine example of the use of multiple experimenters is a study by Rubin (1975), who sent several male and female experimenters to the Boston airport to investigate self-disclosure. The experimenters revealed different kinds of information about themselves to both male and female travelers and recorded the passengers' return disclosures.

## PRETESTS AND GENERALIZATION

Researchers are often faced with the decision of whether to give a pretest. Intuitively, pretesting seems to be a good idea. The researcher can be sure that the groups are equivalent on the pretest, and it is often more satisfying to see that individuals changed their scores than it is to look only at group means on a posttest. Pretesting, however, may limit the ability to generalize to populations that did not receive a pretest. In the real world, people are rarely given a pretest—attitudes are not measured prior to listening to a political speech or viewing an advertisement, for example (cf. Lana, 1969).

An important reason for using a pretest is that it enables the researcher to assess mortality effects when it is likely that some participants will withdraw from an experiment. If you give a pretest, you can determine whether the people who withdrew are different from those who completed the study. Recall from Chapter 8 that a Solomon four-group design (Solomon, 1949) can be used in situations in which a pretest is desirable but there is concern over the possible impact of taking the pretest. In the Solomon four-group design, half of the participants are given the pretest; the other half receive the posttest only. In other words, the same experiment is conducted with and without the pretest. Mortality effects can be assessed in the pretest conditions. Also, the researcher can examine whether there is an interaction between the independent variable and the pretest variable; that is, are posttest scores on the dependent variable different depending on whether the pretest was given? Sometimes, researchers find that it is not feasible to conduct the study with all four groups in a single experiment. In this case, the first study can include the pretest; the study can be replicated later without the pretest.

## GENERALIZING FROM LABORATORY SETTINGS

Research conducted in a laboratory setting has the advantage of allowing the experimenter to study the impact of independent variables under highly controlled conditions. The question arises, however, as to whether the artificiality of the laboratory setting limits the ability to generalize what is observed in the laboratory to real-life settings. Field experiments, discussed in Chapter 4, represent one method of counteracting laboratory artificiality. In a field experiment, the researcher manipulates the independent variable in a natural setting—a factory, a school, or a street corner, for example.

### Mundane and Experimental Realism

Aronson, Brewer, and Carlsmith (1985) point out that even field experiments can be contrived and artificial, with little real-world relevance. They propose a better distinction: mundane realism versus experimental realism. **Mundane realism** refers to whether the experiment bears similarity to events that occur in the real world. **Experimental realism** refers to whether the experiment has an impact on the participants, involves them, and makes them take the experiment seriously. Aronson et al. point out that experimental and mundane realism are separate, independent dimensions. An experiment may have considerable mundane realism (and thus be very similar to real life) but be totally boring and uninvolving and thus lacking in experimental realism. Consider two examples:

> *Example 1:* In a study on helping, an experimenter drops some pencils outside a building on campus and waits to see whether anyone stops to help pick them up. The dependent variable is the helping by observers of the "accident." This study would possess considerable mundane realism but little experimental realism.

> *Example 2:* In another experiment on helping, participants are seated in individual cubicles that are interconnected via an intercom system. During the course of the study, the individual hears another (supposed) participant having an epileptic seizure and must decide whether to help the person (Darley & Latané, 1968). This study has relatively little mundane realism but a great deal of experimental realism.

Other experimental procedures, in both laboratory and field settings, may rate either high or low on both mundane and experimental realism. Experiments that are low on both mundane realism (bearing little similarity to real-world events or tasks) and experimental realism (failing to engage the interest or involvement of participants) are not likely to yield valuable results. The key point here, however, is that laboratory experiments are not automatically artificial; even when an experiment lacks mundane realism, it may be very realistic in terms of experimental realism.

### Mutual Benefits of Lab and Field Research

Aronson et al. (1985) also point out that it is unwise to consider laboratory or field experiments in isolation. Conducting research in both laboratory and field settings provides the greatest opportunity for advancing our understanding of behavior. Recall the Langer and Rodin (1976) study on the effects of giving elderly nursing home residents greater control over decisions in their lives (see Chapter 4). This field experiment was part of a research tradition that includes laboratory studies of control over stressors using both animal and human subjects, the effects of stress in natural settings, and field experiments on the general effects of perceived control.

Anderson, Lindsay, and Bushman (1999) asked whether laboratory and field experiments that examine the same variables do in fact produce the same results. To answer this question, they found 38 pairs of studies for which a laboratory investigation had a field experiment counterpart. The studies were drawn from a variety of research areas including aggression, helping, memory, leadership style, and depression. Results of the laboratory and field experiments were in fact very similar—the magnitude of the effect of the independent variable on the dependent variable was very similar in the two types of studies. Thus, even though lab and field experiments are conducted in different settings, the results are complementary rather than contradictory.

## THE IMPORTANCE OF REPLICATIONS

**Replication** has been stressed as a way of overcoming any problems of generalization that occur in a single study. There are two types of replications to consider: exact replications and conceptual replications.

### Exact Replications

An **exact replication** is an attempt to replicate precisely the procedures of a study to see whether the same results are obtained. A researcher who obtains an unexpected finding will frequently attempt a replication to make sure that the finding is reliable. If you are starting your own work on a problem, you may try to replicate a crucial study to make sure that you understand the procedures and can obtain the same results. Often, exact replications occur when a researcher builds on the findings of a prior study. For example, suppose you are intrigued by Singh's (1993) research on waist-to-hip ratio that was mentioned in Chapter 5. Singh reports that males rate females with a ratio of .70 as most attractive. In your research, you might replicate the procedures used in the original study while expanding on the original research. For example, you might study this phenomenon with males similar to those in the original sample as well as males from different cultures or age groups. When you replicate the original research findings using very similar procedures, your confidence in the generality of the original findings is increased.

Sometimes, a researcher will be unable to replicate a previous finding. A single failure to replicate does not reveal much, though; it is unrealistic to assume, on the basis of a single failure to replicate, that the previous research is invalid. Failures to replicate share the same problems as nonsignificant results, discussed in Chapter 13. A failure to replicate could mean that the original results are invalid, but it could also mean that the replication attempt was flawed. For example, if the replication is based on the procedure as reported in a journal article, it is possible that the article omitted an important aspect of the procedure. For this reason, it is usually a good idea to write the researcher to obtain detailed information on all of the materials that were used in the study.

The "Mozart effect" provides us with an interesting example of the importance of replications. In the original study by Rauscher, Shaw, and Ky (1993), college students listened to 10 minutes of a particular Mozart sonata. These students then showed an increase in performance on a spatial-reasoning measure drawn from the Stanford-Binet Intelligence Scale. Subsequently, Rauscher, Shaw, and Ky (1995) replicated the effect using a different dependent spatial ability measure, the Stanford-Binet Paper Folding and Cutting task. Despite the fact that the effect was temporary, lasting about 10 minutes, these findings received a great deal of attention in the press as people quickly generalized it to the possibility of increasing children's intelligence with Mozart sonatas. In fact, one state governor began producing Mozart CDs to distribute in maternity wards, and entrepreneurs began selling Mozart kits to parents over the Internet. Over the next few years, however, there were many failures to replicate the Mozart effect (see Steele, Bass, and Crook, 1999). We noted above that failures to replicate may occur because the exact conditions for producing the effect were not used. In this case, Rauscher and Shaw (1998) responded to the many replication failures by precisely describing the conditions necessary to produce the Mozart effect. However, Steele et al. (1999) and McCutcheon (2000) were unable to obtain the effect even though they followed the recommendations of Rauscher and Shaw. Research on the Mozart effect continues. Some recent findings suggest that the effect is limited to music that also increases arousal; it is this arousal that can cause better performance following exposure to the music (Thompson, Schellenberg, & Husain, 2001).

A single failure to replicate is not adequate cause for discarding the original research finding. As we saw in the case of the Mozart effect, attempts to replicate do not occur in isolation, as many researchers attempt replications. Repeated failures to replicate may lead to a conclusion that the original results were a fluke—a Type I error was made. Another possibility is that the research will demonstrate that the results can be obtained only under certain limited circumstances. In a few cases, it may turn out that the original researcher misrepresented the results in some way (see Chapter 3 for a discussion of the role of replications in detecting instances of fraud).

## Conceptual Replications

The use of different procedures to replicate a research finding is called a **conceptual replication.** Conceptual replications are even more important than exact replications in furthering our understanding of behavior.

In most research, the goal is to discover whether a relationship between conceptual variables exists. The music manipulation in the original Mozart effect study was the first section of the Mozart Sonata for Two Pianos in D Major (K448). This is a specific operational definition for the purposes of studying the effect of music on a spatial performance. Likewise, the specific task chosen as the dependent measure is an operational definition of the more general performance variable.

In a conceptual replication, the same independent variable is manipulated in a different way (and possibly the dependent variable is measured in a different way, too). Conceptual replications are extremely important in the social sciences because the specific manipulations and measures are usually operational definitions of complex variables. A crucial generalization question is whether the relationship holds when other ways of manipulating or measuring the variables are studied. Sometimes the conceptual replication may involve an alternative stimulus (e.g., a different Mozart sonata, a selection by a different composer) or an alternative dependent measure (e.g., a different spatial-reasoning task). Or as we previously noted, the same variables are sometimes studied in both laboratory and field settings. When conceptual replications produce similar results, our confidence in the generalizability of relationships between variables is greatly increased.

This discussion should also alert you to an important way of thinking about research findings. The findings represent relationships between conceptual variables but are grounded in specific operations. You may read about the specific methods employed in a study conducted 20 years ago and question whether the study could be replicated today. You might also speculate that the methods used in a study are so unusual that they could never generalize to other situations. These concerns are not as serious when placed within the context of conceptual replications. Admittedly, a specific method from a study conducted at one time might not be effective today, given changes in today's political and cultural climate. A conceptual replication of the manipulation, however, would demonstrate that the relationship between the conceptual theoretical variables is still present. Similarly, the narrow focus of a particular study is less problematic if the general finding is replicated with different procedures.

## EVALUATING GENERALIZATIONS VIA LITERATURE REVIEWS AND META-ANALYSIS

Researchers have traditionally drawn conclusions about the generalizability of research findings by conducting literature reviews. In a literature review, a reviewer reads a number of studies that address a particular topic and then writes a paper that summarizes and evaluates the literature. The *Publication Manual of the American Psychological Association* provides the following description: "Review articles, including meta-analyses, are critical evaluations of material that has already been published. By organizing, integrating, and evaluating previously published material, the author of a review article considers the progress of current research toward clarifying a problem" (APA, 2001, p. 7). The literature review provides information that (1) summarizes what has been found, (2) tells the reader what findings are strongly supported and those that are only weakly supported in the literature, (3) points out inconsistent findings and areas in which research is lacking, and (4) discusses future directions for research.

Sometimes a review will be a narrative in which the author provides descriptions of research findings and draws conclusions about the literature. The conclusions in a narrative literature review are based on the subjective impressions of the reviewer. Another technique for comparing a large number of studies in an area has emerged in recent years. This technique is termed **meta-analysis** (Rosenthal, 1991). In a meta-analysis, the researcher combines the actual results of a number of studies. The analysis consists of a set of statistical procedures that employ effect sizes to compare a given finding across many different studies. Instead of relying on judgments obtained in a narrative literature review, statistical conclusions can be drawn. The statistical procedures need not concern you. They involve examining several features of the results of studies, including the effect sizes and significance levels obtained. The important point here is that meta-analysis is a method for determining the reliability of a finding by examining the results from many different studies.

An example of a meta-analysis is a study by Smith and Glass (1977) on the effectiveness of psychotherapy techniques as reported in 375 studies. The researchers examined the reported effects of different modes of therapy (e.g., behavioral, psychodynamic, and client-centered therapies) across many different studies that used several different outcome measures (e.g., anxiety reduction, self-esteem). They then applied appropriate statistical techniques to combine and compare the different results. Their research allowed them to conclude that therapy does have a beneficial effect. In fact, they concluded that the "typical therapy client is better off than 75% of untreated controls." They were also able to make general statements that applied to different types of therapies. For example, some therapies, such as systematic desensitization, produce very large changes in behavior compared to others; however, overall there was no difference between the "behavioral" types of therapies and the "traditional" ones.

The information obtained from a meta-analysis such as the one conducted by Smith and Glass is very informative. In a traditional literature review, it would be very difficult to provide the type of general conclusion that was reached with the meta-analysis. Anyone would find it difficult to easily integrate the results of so many studies with different experimental designs, subject types, and measures. In fact, if you read all the studies and someone asked you the simple question "Does psychotherapy work?" you might proceed to spend a day telling the person about all the specific studies and the complexities you noted in reading the literature. This would be the result of information overload and the fact that it is difficult to integrate information from diverse sources.

An interesting study by Cooper and Rosenthal (1980) actually demonstrated that researchers are more likely to draw strong conclusions about a set of findings when using meta-analysis than when using traditional judgments. In this study, the researchers read only seven articles on gender differences in task persistence; still, the researchers who used meta-analysis were more likely to conclude that females do show greater task persistence than do males.

Meta-analyses are increasingly used to examine relationships between variables. For example, Saks and Marti (1997) examined many studies that compared the outcomes of 6-person and 12-person juries. Some of the studies were experiments that manipulated the variable in mock juries; others used nonexperimental methods to compare the outcomes of actual juries in states that allow 6-person juries. Saks and Marti categorized the studies according to dependent variable outcomes such as deliberation time, minority representation, hung juries, and recall of testimony. They found that larger juries have greater minority representation and more hung juries. Based on a fairly small number of studies, it appears that larger juries also deliberate longer and recall testimony more accurately. One of the most important features of meta-analysis studies is the focus on effect size. This can lead to the conclusion that some findings are much weaker than previously thought. For example, many studies on the effects of physical attractiveness support a stereotype that "what is beautiful is good"; that is, physically attractive people are judged more favorably than less attractive persons. The fact that many studies support this conclusion can lead us to overestimate its importance: Meta-analyses of physical attractiveness studies conclude that the effect of physical attractiveness on many variables, including jury decisions, is very small (Eagly, Ashmore, Makhijani, & Longo, 1991; Mazzella & Feingold, 1994).

Both narrative reviews and meta-analyses provide valuable information and in fact are often complementary. A meta-analysis allows statistical, quantitative conclusions whereas the narrative review identifies trends in the literature and directions for future study—a more qualitative approach. A study by Bushman and Wells (2001) points to an interesting way in which knowledge of meta-analysis can improve the way that we interpret information for literature reviews. The reviewers in their study were undergraduates provided with both titles and information about the findings of 20 studies dealing with the effect of attitude similarity on attraction. Sometimes the titles were salient with respect to the findings ("Birds of a Feather Flock Together") and others were nonsalient ("Research Studies Who Likes

Whom"). Salient titles are obviously easier to remember. When asked to draw conclusions about the findings, naive reviewers with no knowledge of meta-analysis overestimated the size of the similarity–attraction relationship when provided with salient titles. Other reviewers were given brief training in meta-analysis; these reviewers drew accurate conclusions about the actual findings; they were not influenced by the article title. Thus, even without conducting a meta-analysis, a background in meta-analysis can be beneficial when reviewing research findings.

## USING RESEARCH TO IMPROVE LIVES

In a presidential address to the American Psychological Association, George Miller (1969) discussed "psychology as a means of promoting human welfare" and spoke of "giving psychology away." Miller was addressing the broadest issue of generalizability, taking what we know about human behavior and allowing it to be applied by many people in all areas of everyday life. Perhaps the strongest evidence for the generalizability of research findings is to view what has happened to psychology in the years since Miller urged us to give psychology away. The impact of psychological research can be seen in the fields of health care (programs to promote health-related behaviors related to stress, heart disease, and sexually transmitted diseases); the environment (designing work spaces that promote worker satisfaction and productivity, providing energy companies with ways of encouraging conservation); law (providing data on the effects of 6- versus 12-person juries, showing how law enforcement personnel can improve the accuracy of eyewitness identification); and education (providing methods for encouraging academic performance or reducing conflict among different ethnic groups). In addition, psychologists are using the Internet to provide information on parenting, education, mental health, and many other topics—for example, the Web sites of the American Psychological Association and the American Psychological Society (http://www.apa.org; http://www.psychologicalscience.org), Center for Mental Health Services (http://www.mentalhealth.org), and many individual psychologists who are sharing their expertise with the public. We have discussed only a few of the ways that basic research has been applied to improve lives. Despite all the potential problems of generalizing research findings that were highlighted in this chapter, the evidence suggests that we can generalize our findings to many aspects of our lives.

## *Study Terms* _____

| | |
|---|---|
| Conceptual replication | Meta-analysis |
| Exact replication | Mundane realism |
| Experimental realism | Replication |
| External validity | Solomon four-group design |
| Literature review | |

## Review Questions

1. Why should a researcher be concerned about generalizing to other subject populations? What are some of the subject population generalization problems that a researcher might confront?

2. What is the source of the problem of generalizing to other experimenters? How can this problem be solved?

3. Why is pretesting a problem for generalization important? Describe how pretesting can affect generalization.

4. Distinguish between mundane and experimental realism.

5. Distinguish between an exact replication and a conceptual replication. What is the value of a conceptual replication?

6. What is a meta-analysis?

## Activity Questions

1. It is easy to collect data for experiments and surveys on the Internet. Anyone in the world who is connected to the Internet can access a researcher's computer and take part in the study. Participate in a psychological research study on the Internet. What issues of generalization might arise when interpreting the results of such studies? Does the computer aspect of the research make this research less generalizable than traditional research, or does the fact that people throughout the world can participate make it more generalizable? Could you empirically answer this question?

2. Use *PsycINFO* to find abstracts of articles that included race, ethnicity, gender, or nationality as a variable in the studies discussed. What conclusions do the authors of these studies draw about generalization?

3. Find a meta-analysis published in a journal; two good sources are the *Review of Educational Research* and *Psychological Bulletin*. What conclusions were drawn from the meta-analysis? How were studies selected for the analysis? How was the concept of effect size discussed in the meta-analysis?

4. Obtain an article from a social psychology journal. After briefly summarizing the experimental procedure, discuss the experiment in terms of mundane realism and experimental realism.

# Appendix A
# Writing Research Reports

## INTRODUCTION

This appendix presents the information you will need to prepare a written report of your research for a course and for possible publication in a professional journal. In addition, an example article illustrates the stylistic features of a research report. We will consider the specific rules that should be followed in organizing and presenting research results. These rules are a great convenience for both the writer and the reader. They provide structure for the report and a uniform method of presentation, making it easier for the reader to understand and evaluate the report.

Specific rules vary from one discipline to another. A rule for presenting research results in psychology may not apply to the same situation in, for example, sociology research. Also, the rules may vary depending on whether you are preparing the report for a class, a thesis, or submission to a journal. Fortunately, the variation is usually minor, and the general rules of presentation are much the same across disciplines and situations.

The format presented here for writing research reports is drawn from the *Publication Manual of the American Psychological Association* (fifth edition, 2001). APA style is used in many journals in psychology, child development, family relations, and education. If you are concerned about specific rules for a particular journal, consult a recent issue of that journal. APA has also published a student workbook and training guide for the *Publication Manual* (Gelfand & Walker, 2001) and a computer program called *APA-Style Helper*. The computer program works with most word processors to ensure that your paper conforms to the rules of APA style. You may purchase the *Publication Manual, APA-Style Helper,* and other APA products through your college bookstore or directly from the American Psychological Association. (The APA Web sites at http://www. apa.org and http://www.apastyle.org provide the easiest method of ordering.) Other useful sources for preparing papers are brief books by Rosnow and Rosnow (2002) and Sternberg (1993). Kazdin (1995) and Bem (2002) also offer excellent guidelines for preparing research reports for publication.

The APA manual is guided by principles of "specificity and sensitivity." First, papers should be written at a level of specificity and detail that will allow others to replicate the research. Second, papers should be free of inappropriate language that might be interpreted as biased and insensitive. The manual also includes manuscript preparation guidelines that take advantage of the features of word processing software. Throughout this appendix, examples that are intended to appear as you would type them in your papers appear in a typewriter font to make spacing and other rules clear; this convention is also used in the APA manual. When typing your own paper with a word processor, you would not use this type of font. (Fonts are described below.)

## WRITING STYLE

In any format for preparing your report, writing style is important. A poorly written report that is difficult to understand is of no value (and almost certainly will bring you a poor grade!). Also, a good paper should be neatly typed and free of spelling and typographical errors.

### Clarity

Clarity in writing is essential. Be precise and clear in presenting ideas, and think about your intended audience. It is helpful to direct your paper to an audience that is unfamiliar with your general topic and the methods you used to study the topic. Eliminate jargon that most readers will not comprehend. Sometimes a researcher will develop an abbreviated notation for referring to a specific variable or procedure. Such abbreviations may be convenient when communicating with others who are directly involved in the research project, but they are confusing to the general reader. However, you should assume that the reader has a general familiarity with statistics and hypothesis testing. Statistical outcomes can usually be presented without defining terms such as the *mean, standard deviation,* or *significance.* These are only general guidelines, however. Rosnow and Rosnow (2002) point out that when your intended audience is your instructor you should pay close attention to what he or she has to say about expectations for the paper!

The entire report should have a coherent structure. Ideas should be presented in an orderly, logical progression to facilitate understanding. If you write your report for someone who is being introduced to your ideas and research findings for the first time, you will be more likely to communicate clearly with the reader.

One method of producing a more organized report is to use an outline. Many writers plan a paper by putting their thoughts and ideas into outline form. The outline then serves as a writing guide. This method forces writers to develop a logical structure before writing the paper. Other writers prefer to use a less structured approach for the first draft. They then try to outline what has been written. If the paper does not produce a coherent outline, the organization needs to be improved. Word processing programs usually have an outline feature to help you organize your paper; find this feature using the program's help menu.

Paragraphs should be well organized. It is a good idea for a paragraph to contain a topic sentence. Other sentences within a paragraph should be related to the topic sentence and develop the idea in this sentence by elaborating, expanding, explaining, or supporting the idea in the topic sentence. Also, avoid one-sentence paragraphs. If you find such paragraphs in your paper, expand the paragraph, include the idea in another paragraph, or delete the concept. After completing the first draft of your paper, it is a good idea to let it sit for a day or so before you reread it. Carefully proofread the paper, paying attention to grammar and spelling. Some grammatical considerations are described here; you can also use a computer word processor to check your spelling and grammar. After you make changes and corrections, you may want to get feedback from others. Find one or more people who will read your report critically and suggest improvements. Be prepared to write several drafts before you have a satisfactory finished product.

### Acknowledging the Work of Others

It is extremely important to clearly separate your own words and ideas from those obtained from other sources. If you use a passage drawn from an article or book, make sure the passage is presented as a direct quotation. There is nothing wrong with quoting another author as long as you acknowledge your source. Never present another person's idea as your own. This is plagiarism and is inexcusable.

Sometimes writers are tempted to fill a paper with quotes from other sources or to quote another paper at great length (e.g., several paragraphs or more). This practice is distracting and counterproductive. Be direct, and use your own descriptions and interpretations while acknowledging your sources. If you have any questions about how to properly include material from source articles in your own paper, consult your instructor.

### Active Versus Passive Voice

Many writers rely too much on the passive voice in their reports, perhaps because they believe that the passive voice makes their writing seem more "scientific." Consider the following sentences:

It was found by Yee and Johnson (1996) that adolescents prefer . . .

Participants were administered the test after a 10-minute rest period.

Participants were read the instructions by the experimenter.

Now try writing those sentences in a more active voice. For example:

Yee and Johnson (1996) found that adolescents prefer . . .

Participants took the test after a 10-minute rest period.

I read the instructions to the participants.

Prose that seems stilted using the passive voice is much more direct when phrased in the active voice.

Sometimes authors refer to themselves in the third person. Thus, they might say "The experimenter distributed the questionnaires" instead of "I distributed the questionnaires"—this is a more active voice but it introduces an ambiguity. It is unclear whether "the experimenter" is in fact the author or someone else. When authors refer to themselves in the paper, APA style calls for the use of "I" and "we" pronouns.

### Biased Language

APA style is guided by the principles of specificity and sensitivity. The principle of specificity leads to the recommendation of using the term *participants* to specifically distinguish between human and animal subjects. In addition, it is appropriate to describe participants as respondents in survey research, children, patients, clients, and so on if these terms more accurately describe the people who participated in the study.

Be sensitive to the possibility that your writing might convey a bias, however unintentional, regarding gender, sexual orientation, and ethnic or racial group. As a general principle, be as specific as possible when referring to groups of people. For example, referring to the participants in your study as "Korean Americans and Vietnamese Americans" is more specific and accurate than describing them as "Asians." Also, be sensitive to the use of labels that might be offensive to members of certain groups. In practice, this means that you refer to people using the terms that these people prefer. Also, avoid implicit labels by saying, "The lesbian sample, in contrast to the sample of normal women" or "We tested groups of autistics and normals." The latter phrase could be written as "We tested people with autism and without autism."

The APA manual has numerous examples of ways of being sensitive to gender, racial and ethnic identity, age, sexual orientation, and disabilities. The term *gender* refers to males and females as social groups. Thus, gender is the proper term to use in a phrase such as "gender difference in average salary." The term *sex* refers to biological aspects of men and women; for example, "sex fantasies" or "sex differences in the size of certain brain structures." The use of gender pronouns can be problematic. Do not use *he, his, man, man's,* and so on when both males and females are meant. Sentences can usually be rephrased or specific pronouns deleted to avoid linguistic biases. For example, "The worker is paid according to his productivity" can be changed to "The worker is paid according to productivity" or "Workers are paid according to their productivity." In the first case, *his* was simply deleted; in the second case, the subject of the sentence was changed to plural. Do *not* try to avoid sexist language by simply substituting *s/he* whenever that might appear convenient.

There are certain rules to follow when referring to racial and ethnic groups. The names of these groups are capitalized and never hyphenated; for example, Black, White, African American, Latino, Asian, Asian American. The manual also reminds us that the terms that members of racial and ethnic groups use to describe themselves may change over time, and there may be a lack of consensus about a preferred term. Currently, for example, both *Black* and *African American* are generally acceptable. Depending on a number of factors, participants may prefer to be called Hispanic, Latino, Chicana, or Mexican American. You are urged to use the term most preferred by your participants.

The APA manual includes a great deal of information and numerous examples to encourage sensitivity in writing reports. The best advice is to review your papers for possible problems at least once prior to writing your final draft. If you have any questions about appropriate language, consult the manual and colleagues whose opinions you respect.

## Typing and Word Processing

You will eventually have to prepare a typed copy of your paper. In APA style, the paper should be *entirely double-spaced*. The margins for text should be *at least 1 inch* on all four sides of the page. Page headers, the information that appears at the top of each page including the page number, are set approximately .5 inch from the top of the page. All pages are numbered except for figure pages at the end of the paper. Paragraphs are indented 5 to 7 spaces or .5 inch (use the tab function, not the space bar). Contractions are not used in APA-style writing. Words should never be hyphenated at the end of a line; lines should be a little short or a little long rather than breaking a word.

It has been common practice to insert two spaces after each sentence in a paper. However, you should place only one space between sentences, according to APA guidelines. Two spaces were appropriate for manual typewriters, but one space is more attractive and readable when using word processors with modern printer fonts. (Hint: If you have a hard time remembering this rule, use your word processor's "replace" feature to replace instances of two spaces with one space.)

Most students use word processing computer programs to prepare their papers. With a computer, you can improve your writing and submit a high-quality paper far more easily. Correcting, revising, moving, and deleting text and preparing several drafts is easy because you do not have to retype the paper each time you wish to make a change. Be sure to take advantage of the features of your word processing application. You can have a page header and a page number automatically placed at the top of each page, insert footnotes or endnotes, center text, check spelling and grammar, and so on.

Set the alignment of your text to the left margin. The font should be 12-point size throughout the paper. Use a serif font for all text and tables. The serif font should usually be Times Roman font style. Figures, however, should be prepared with a sans serif font, either Arial or Helvetica font style. Serif fonts have short lines at the ends of the strokes that form the letters; sans serif literally means "without serif" and so does not have serif lines. Here are examples:

This is serif text.
This is sans serif text.

When italics are called for, use the italics feature of your word processor. Italics are used for (a) titles and volume numbers of periodicals, (b) titles of books, (c) side margin and paragraph headings, (d) most statistical terms, (e) anchors of a scale, such as 1 (*strongly disagree*) to 5 (*strongly agree*), and (f) when you need to emphasize a particular word or phrase when first mentioned in the paper. Pay attention to the use of italics in the examples used throughout this appendix. Finally, there are few reasons to ever use boldface type.

### APA Style and Student Paper Formats

APA style is intended to provide a manuscript to a typesetter who then prepares the paper for publication in a journal; several APA style requirements are for the convenience of the typesetter. When you prepare a paper for a class report, an honors project, or a thesis, however, your paper may be the "final product" for your readers. In such cases, many aspects of APA style may be ignored so that your paper will closely resemble a printed report. For example, APA style calls for placement of tables and figures at the end of the paper; the typesetter inserts the tables and figures in the body of the paper for the published article. However, if your report is the final version for your readers, you may need to (a) place tables and figures on separate pages in the body of your report, or (b) actually insert the tables and figures in the text. Some of the ways that a student report may differ from APA style are described below. When you are getting ready to prepare your own report, be sure to check the particular requirements of your instructor or college.

## ORGANIZATION OF THE REPORT

A research report is organized into five major parts: Abstract, Introduction, Method, Results, and Discussion. References must be listed using a particular format. The report may also include tables and figures used in presenting the results. We will consider the parts of the paper in the order prescribed by APA style. Refer to the sample paper at the end of this appendix as you read the material that follows.

### Title Page

The first page of the paper is the title page. It is a separate page and is numbered page 1. Note that in the example paper the title page does in fact list the title; however, there are other important items of information as well.

At the top of the title page is a page header. The page header includes a short title, generally consisting of the first two or three words of the title of your paper, and a page number. These should be typed so the page number is flush to the right margin of the paper. If you are using a word processor, use the page header feature to create a header that prints approximately halfway between the text of the paper and the top of each page, usually .5 inch from the top. Do not try to manually type a page header and number at the top of every page of your paper; check your word processing program for how to create a page header. The page header appears on every page of your paper except the figure pages. The page header provides a heading for your readers; more important, if the pages get separated accidentally, it will be easy for the reader to put them together again in proper order.

The first line of the title page will be the *running head.* The running head has a very specific meaning and purpose: It is an abbreviated title and should be no more than 50 characters (letters, numbers, spaces) in length. If the paper is published in a journal, the running head is printed as a heading at the top of pages to help readers identify the article. On your title page, the running head is typed flush against the left margin; the running head line from the example article appears as follows when typed:

```
Running head: GENDERED PORTRAYALS OF ATHLETES BY THE MEDIA
```

Note that all letters in the running head are capitalized. The running head is used for publication purposes and appears only once in your paper—on the title page. The page header with the short title and page number, in contrast, is used by readers of your paper and appears on every page. Do not confuse the running head and the page header.

The remainder of the title page consists of the title, author byline, and institutional affiliation. All are centered on the page. The title should be fairly short (usually no more than 10 to 12 words) and should inform the reader of the nature of your research. A good way to do this is to include the names of your variables in the title. For example—the following titles are both short and informative:

Effect of Anxiety on Mathematical Problem Solving

Memory for Faces Among Elderly and Young Adults

Sometimes a colon in the title will help to convey the nature of your research or even add a bit of "flair" to your title, as in

Cognitive Responses in Persuasion: Affective and Evaluative Determinants

Comparing the Tortoise and the Hare: Gender Differences and Experience in Dynamic Spatial Reasoning Tasks

Another method of titling a paper is to pose the question that the research addresses. For example,

Do Rewards in the Classroom Undermine Intrinsic Motivation?

Does Occupational Stereotyping Still Exist?

One futher consideration in the choice of a title is that computer literature searches are most likely to find your article if the title includes words and phrases that people are most likely to use when conducting the search. This consideration also applies to the abstract.

## Abstract

The abstract is a brief summary of the research report and typically runs 100 to no more than 120 words in length. The purpose of the abstract is to introduce the article, allowing readers to decide whether the article appears relevant to their own interests. The abstract should provide enough information so that the reader can decide whether to read the entire report, and it should make the report easier to comprehend when it is read.

Although the abstract appears at the beginning of your report, it is easiest to write the abstract last. Read a few abstracts and you will get some good ideas for how to condense a full-length research report down to 8 or 10 information-packed sentences. A very informative exercise is to write an abstract for a published article, and then compare your abstract to the one written by the original authors.

Abstracts generally include a sentence or two about each of the four main sections in the body of the article. First, from the *Introduction* section, state the problem under study and the primary hypotheses. Second, from the *Method* section, include information on the characteristics of the participants (e.g., number, age, sex, and any special characteristics) and a brief summary of the procedure (e.g., self-report questionnaires, direct observation, repeated measurements on several occasions). Third, from the *Results* section, describe the pattern of findings for major variables. This is typically done by reporting the direction of differences without relying on numerical values. APA guidelines recommend including statistical significance levels, yet few authors comply (Ono, Phillips, & Leneman, 1996). Rely on guidelines provided by your instructor. Finally, the abstract will include implications of the study taken from the *Discussion* section. Informative comments about the findings are preferred to general statements such as "the implications of the study are addressed" (Kazdin, 1995).

The abstract is typed on a separate page and is numbered page 2. The word "Abstract" is centered at the top of the page. The abstract is always typed as a single paragraph with no paragraph indentation.

## Introduction

The Introduction section begins on a new page (page 3), with the title of your report typed at the top of the page. Note that the author's name does not appear on this page, which allows a reviewer to read the paper without knowing the name of the author. The Introduction section presents the specific problem under study, describes the research strategy, and presents the predicted outcomes of the research. After reading the introduction, the reader should know why you decided to do the research and how you decided to go about doing it. In general, the introduction progresses from broad theories and findings to specifics of the current research.

The introduction has three components, although no formal subsections are utilized. The components are (1) the problem under study, (2) the literature review, and (3) the rationale and hypotheses of the study.

The introduction should begin with an opening statement of the problem under study. In two or three sentences, give the reader an appreciation of the broad context and significance of the topic being studied (Bem, 1981, Kazdin, 1995). Specifically stating what problem is being investigated is worthwhile if it can be done; it helps readers, even those who are unfamiliar with the topic, understand and appreciate why the topic was studied in the first place.

Following the opening statement, the introduction provides a description of past research and theory. This is called the *literature review.* An exhaustive review of past theory and research is not necessary. (If there are major literature reviews of the topic, you would of course refer the reader to the reviews.) Rather, you want to describe only the research and theoretical issues that are clearly related to your study. State explicitly how this previous work is logically connected to your research problem. This tells the reader why your research was conducted and shows the connection to prior research.

The final part of the introduction tells the reader the *rationale* of the current study. Here you state what variables you are studying and what results you expect. The links between the research hypotheses, prior research, and the current research design are shown by explaining why the hypotheses are expected.

## Method

The Method section begins immediately after you have completed the introduction (on the same page if space permits). This section provides the reader with detailed information about how your study was conducted. Ideally, there should be enough information in the Method section to allow a reader to replicate your study.

The Method section is typically divided into a number of subsections. Both the order of the subsections and the number of subsections vary in published articles. Decisions about which subsections to include are guided by the complexity of the investigation. The sample paper in this appendix uses three subsections: *Participants, Design and Materials,* and *Procedure.* Some of the most commonly used subsections are discussed next.

**Overview**    If the experimental design and procedures used in the research are complex, a brief overview of the method should be presented to help the reader understand the information that follows.

**Participants**    A subsection on the participants or respondents is always necessary. The number and nature of the participants should be described. Age, sex, ethnicity, and any other relevant characteristics should be described. Special characteristics of participants are described, such as firstborn children, adolescent children of alcoholics, student teachers, or parents of hyperactive boys. State explicitly how participants were recruited and what incentives for participation might have been used. The number of individuals in each experimental condition also can be included here.

**Apparatus** An Apparatus subsection may be necessary if special equipment is used in the experiment. The brand name and model number of the equipment may be specified; some apparatus may be described in detail. Include this information if it is needed to replicate the experiment.

**Procedure** The Procedure subsection tells the reader exactly how the study was conducted. One way to report this information is to describe, step by step, what occurred in the experiment. Maintain the temporal sequence of events so the reader is able to visualize the sequence of events the participants experienced.

The Procedure subsection tells the reader what instructions were given to the participants, how the independent variables were manipulated, and how the dependent variables were measured. The methods used to control extraneous variables also should be described. These include randomization procedures, counterbalancing, and special means that were used to keep a variable constant across all conditions. Finally, the method of debriefing should be described. If your study used a nonexperimental method, you would still provide details on exactly how you conducted the study and the measurement techniques you used.

It is up to you to decide how much detail to include here. Use your own judgment to determine the importance of a specific aspect of the procedure and the amount of detail that is necessary for the reader to clearly understand what was done in the study. Include any detail that might be important in a replication of the study.

**Other subsections** Include other subsections if they are needed for clear presentation of the method. For example, a subsection on testing materials might be necessary instead of an Apparatus subsection. Other sections are customized by the authors to suit their study. If you glance through the recent issue of a journal, you will find that some studies have only two subsections and others have many more subsections. This reflects the varying complexity of the studies and the particular writing styles of the researchers.

### Results

In the Results section, present the results as clearly as possible. The Results section is a straightforward description of your analyses. Although it is tempting to explain your findings in the Results section, save that discussion for the next section of the paper.

Be sure to state the alpha (probability) level that you used in making decisions about statistical significance: This will usually be .05 or .01 and requires only a simple sentence such as "An alpha level of .05 was used for statistical analyses."

Present your results in the same order that your predictions are stated in the Introduction section of the paper. If a manipulation check was made, present it before you describe the major results.

The content of your Results section will vary according to the type of statistical test performed and the number of analyses you conducted. However, every Results section includes some basic elements. If applicable, describe any scoring or coding procedures performed on the data to prepare them for analysis. This is particularly important when coding qualitative data. (Sometimes data transformations are included in a subsection of the Method section.) State which statistical test was performed on the data ($t$-test, $F$ test, correlation, etc.). Justify the selection of a particular statistical comparison to address your hypothesis. Be sure to summarize each finding in words as well as to include the results of statistical tests in the form of statistical phrases. The fifth edition of the APA manual includes guidelines for reporting statistics that were recommended by an APA Task Force on Statistical Inference (Wilkinson, 1999). One major recommendation is to report exact probability values that are routinely provided by computer programs used to perform statistical analyses. In the past, most researchers reported probabilities as "less than" the standard probabilities shown in statistical tables, e.g., $p < .10$, $p < .05$, or $p < .01$. It is now possible to report exact probabilities of the null hypothesis being correct, e.g., $p = .085$, $p = .031$, or $p = .004$. This change allows readers to apply their own standards of statistical significance when evaluating the study.

A second recommendation is to report effect size. The manual recognizes that there are currently many indicators of effect size associated with different statistical procedures; the primary concern is to have an effect size in the published article.

The results should be stated in simple sentences. For example, the results of the modeling and aggression experiment described in Chapter 12 might be expressed as follows:

> As predicted, children who viewed the aggressive model were significantly more aggressive than children in the no-model condition, $t(18) = 4.025$, $p = .001$. The mean aggression score in the model group was 5.20 and the no-model mean was 3.10. The effect size $r$ associated with this finding was .688.

These brief sentences inform the reader of the general patterns of the results, the obtained means, statistical significance, and effect size. You should note the wording of the phrase that includes the symbol for the $t$-test, degrees of freedom, and significance level (probability).

If the results are relatively straightforward, they can be presented entirely in sentence form. If the study involved a complex design, tables and figures may be needed to clarify presentation of the results.

**Tables and figures**     Tables are generally used to present large arrays of data. For example, a table might be useful in a design with several dependent measures; the means of the different groups for all dependent measures would be presented in the table. Tables are also convenient when a factorial design has been used. For example, in a $2 \times 2 \times 3$ factorial design, a table could be used to present all 12 means.

Figures are used when a visual display of the results would help the reader understand the outcome of the study. Figures may be used to illustrate a significant interaction or show trends over time. When preparing a figure, you will need to decide whether to present the information as a pie chart, a bar graph, or a line graph. Pie charts are used when showing percentages or proportions. The entire pie represents 100% and is divided into slices. In this way, the whole is divided into separate groups or responses. Bar graphs are used when describing the responses of two or more groups—e.g., the mean aggression score of a model and a no-model group in an experiment. Line graphs are used when both the independent and dependent variables have quantitative properties, e.g., the average response time of two groups on days 1, 2, 3, 4, and 5 of an experiment. Nicol and Pexman (2003) provide detailed information on creating figures and other visual displays of data.

In APA style, tables and figures are not presented in the main body of the manuscript. Rather, they are placed at the end of the paper. Each table and figure appears on a separate page. A table or figure is noted in the text by referring to a table or figure number and describing the content of the table or figure. Never make a reference to the placement of the figure because the placement is determined by the typesetter. In the Results section, make a statement such as "As shown in Figure 2, the model group . . ." or "Table 1 presents the demographic characteristics of the survey respondents." Describe the important features of the table or figure rather than use a generic comment such as "See Figure 3."

Do not repeat the same data in more than one place. An informative table or figure supplements, not duplicates, the text. Using tables and figures does not diminish your responsibility to clearly state the nature of the results in the text of your report.

When you are writing a research report for a purpose other than publication—for example, to fulfill a course or degree requirement—it may be more convenient to place each figure and table on a separate page within the main body of the paper. Because rules about the placement of tables and figures may vary, check on the proper format before writing your report.

**Discussion of the results**     It is usually *not* appropriate to discuss the implications of the results in the Results section. However, the Results and Discussion sections may be combined if the discussion is brief and greater clarity is achieved by the combination.

### Discussion

The Discussion section is the proper place to discuss the implications of the results. One way to organize the discussion is to begin by summarizing the original purpose and expectations of the study, then to state whether the results were consistent with your expectations. If the results do support your original ideas, you should discuss how your findings contribute to knowledge of the problem you investigated. You will want to consider the relationship between your results and past research and theory. If you did not obtain the expected results, discuss possible explanations. The explanations would be quite different, of course, depending on whether you obtained results that were the opposite of what you expected or the results were not significant.

It is often a good idea to include your own criticisms of the study. Many published articles include limitations of the study. Try to anticipate what a reader might find wrong with your methodology. For example, if you used a nonexperimental research design, you might point out problems of cause and effect and possible extraneous variables that might be operating. Sometimes there may be major or minor flaws that could be corrected in a subsequent study (if you had the time, money, and so on). You can describe such flaws and suggest corrections. If there are potential problems in generalizing your results, state the problems and give reasons why you think the results would or would not generalize.

The results will probably have implications for future research. If so, you should discuss the direction that research might take. It is also possible that the results have practical implications—for example, for childrearing or improving learning in the classroom. Discussion of these larger issues is usually placed at the end of the discussion section. Finally, you will probably wish to have a brief concluding paragraph that provides "closure" to the entire paper.

### References

The list of references begins on a new page. The references must contain complete citations for all sources mentioned in your report. Do not omit any sources from the list of references; also, do not include any sources that are not mentioned in your report. The exact procedures for citing sources within the body of your report and in your list of references are described later in Appendix A. Follow the examples in recent publications.

### Appendix

An appendix is rarely provided in manuscripts submitted for publication. The APA *Publication Manual* notes that an appendix might be appropriate when necessary material would be distracting in the main body of the report. Examples of appendixes include a sample of a questionnaire or survey instrument, a complex mathematical proof, or a long list of words used as stimulus items. An appendix (or several appendixes) is much more appropriate for a student research project or a thesis. The appendix might include the entire questionnaire that was used, a new test that was developed, or other materials employed in the study. Check with your instructor concerning the appropriateness of an appendix for your paper. If an appendix is provided, it begins on a new page with the word "Appendix" centered at the top.

## Author Note

The author note begins with a paragraph that gives the department affiliations of the authors. Another paragraph may give details about the background of the study (e.g., that it is based on the first author's master's thesis) and acknowledgments (e.g., grant support, colleagues who assisted with the study, and so on). A final paragraph begins with "Correspondence concerning this article should be addressed to . . ." followed by the mailing address of the person designated for that purpose. E-mail addresses are routinely provided in the author note as well. An author note may be unnecessary for class research reports. The author note usually begins on a new page. However, sometimes your instructor (or a journal editor) will ask you to place the author note information at the bottom of the title page. This is done when the paper will have *masked review*. With a masked review, the person reviewing the paper has no information about the author of the paper. In this case, the title page will be separated from the rest of the paper prior to review to mask the identity of the author.

## Footnotes

Footnotes, if used, are not typed in the body of the text. Instead, all footnotes in the paper are typed on one page at the end of the paper. Avoid using footnotes unless they are absolutely necessary. They tend to be distracting to readers, and the information can and should be integrated into the body of the paper.

## Tables

Each table should be on a separate page. As noted previously, APA style requires placement of the table at the end of the paper, but for a class you may be asked to place your tables on separate pages within the body of the paper. In preparing your table, allow enough space so that the table does not appear cramped on a small portion of the page. Define areas of the table using typed horizontal lines (do not use vertical lines). Give some thought to the title so that it accurately and clearly describes the content of the table. You may wish to use an explanatory note in the table to show significance levels or the range of possible values on a variable. Before you make up your own tables, examine the tables in a recent issue of one of the journals published by the American Psychological Association.

## Figures

There are two special APA style rules for the placement and preparation of figures: (1) Figures are placed after the tables in the papers, and (2) a separate page containing the figure captions is provided before the figures. However, either or both of these rules may not be necessary for student reports or theses. You may be asked to place each figure on a separate page at the appropriate point in the body of the text, and you may not need a figure caption page (this is only for the convenience of typesetting and printing the paper). Also, if you are following true APA style, there is no page number or short title on the figure pages (the figure number is written on the back of the figure in pencil).

Sometimes it is necessary to prepare graphs by hand. However, you will find it much easier to use a computer program to create graphs. Most spreadsheet, word processing, and statistical analysis programs have graphing features. Independent and predictor variables are placed on the horizontal axis; dependent and criterion variables are placed on the vertical axis. Both the horizontal and vertical axes must be labeled. When you print the graph on a separate piece of paper, a rule of thumb is that the horizontal axis should be about 5 inches wide, and the vertical axis should be about 3.5 inches long. If you are inserting a graph into the text of your report (not using APA style), your graphs may be smaller than this.

Remember that the purpose of a figure is to increase comprehension of results by having a graphical display of data. If the graph is cluttered with information, it will confuse the reader and will not serve its purpose. Plan your graphs carefully to make sure that you are accurately and clearly informing the reader. If you become interested in the topic of how to display information in graphs and charts, two books by Tufte (1983, 1990) are recommended. Tufte explores a variety of ways of presenting data, factors that lead to data clarity, and ways that graphs can deceive the reader.

### Summary: Order of Pages

To summarize, the organization of your paper is as follows:

1. Title page (page 1)
2. Abstract (page 2)
3. Pages of text (start on new page 3)
   a. Title at top of first page begins the Introduction
   b. Method
   c. Results
   d. Discussion
4. References (start on new page)
5. Appendix (start on new page if included)
6. Author Note (start on new page)
7. Footnotes (start on new page if included)
8. Tables, with table captions (each table on a separate page)
9. Figure captions (all captions together on one separate page)
10. Figures (each figure on a separate page)

You should now have a general idea of how to structure and write your report. The remainder of Appendix A focuses on some of the technical rules that may be useful as you prepare your own research report.

# THE USE OF HEADINGS

Papers written in APA style use one to five levels of headings. Most commonly, you will use level 1 and level 3 headings, and you may need to use level 4 headings as well. These are as follows:

```
(Level 1)                        Centered heading
(Level 3)      Margin heading
                   The text begins indented on a new line.
(Level 4)          Paragraph heading.  The heading is indented
               and the text begins on the same line.
```

Level 2 and level 5 headings will not be described here because they are used in more complex papers in which multiple experiments are presented.

Level 1, or centered, headings are used to head major sections of the report: Abstract, Title (on page 3), Method, Results, Discussion, References, and so on. Level 1 headings are typed with uppercase and lowercase letters (i.e., the first letter of each word is capitalized).

Level 3, or margin, headings are used to divide major sections into subsections. Level 3 headings are typed flush to the left margin, with uppercase and lowercase letters (i.e., the first letter of each word is capitalized). For example, the Method section is divided into at least two subsections: Participants and Procedure. The correct format is

```
                         Method
  Participants
        The description of the participants begins on a new line.

  Procedure
        The procedure is now described in detail.
```

Level 4, or paragraph, headings are used to organize material within a subsection. For example, the Procedure subsection might be broken down into separate categories for describing instructions to participants, the independent variable manipulation, measurement of the dependent variable, and debriefing. Each of these would be introduced through the use of a paragraph heading.

Paragraph headings begin on a new line, indented 5 spaces or .5 inch. The first word begins with a capital letter; the remaining words are all typed in lowercase letters. The heading ends with a period. All information that appears between a paragraph heading and the next heading (of any level) must be related to the paragraph heading. Both level 3 and level 4 headings are italicized.

## CITING AND REFERENCING SOURCES

### Citation Style

Whenever you refer to information reported by other researchers, you *must* accurately identify the sources. APA journals use the author–date citation method: The author name(s) and year of publication are inserted at appropriate points. The citation style depends on whether the author names are part of the narrative or are in parentheses.

**One author**    When the author's name is part of the narrative, include the publication date in parentheses immediately after the name:

```
Markman (1991) found that marital discord can lead to
constructive resolution of conflict.
```

When the author's name is not part of the narrative, the name and date are cited in parentheses at the end of an introductory phrase or at the end of the sentence:

```
In one study (Markman, 1991), couples learned to discuss . . .

Couples have lower rates of divorce and marital violence
after problem-solving intervention (Markman, 1991).
```

**Two authors**    When the work has two authors, both names are included in each reference citation. The difference between narrative and parenthetical citations is in the use of the conjunction "and" and the ampersand "&" to connect authors' names. When the names are part of a sentence, use the word "and" to join the names of two authors. When the complete citation is in parentheses, use the "&" symbol:

```
Harris and Marmer (1996) reported that fathers in poor
families are less involved with their adolescent children
than fathers in non-poor families.

Fathers in poor families are less likely to spend time with
their adolescent children than fathers in non-poor families
(Harris & Marmer, 1996).
```

**Three to five authors**    When a report has three to five authors, all author names are cited the first time the reference occurs. Thereafter, cite the first author's surname followed by the abbreviation et al. ("and others") along with

the publication date. The abbreviation may be used in narrative and parenthetical citations:

*First citation*

Abernathy, Massad, and Romano-Dwyer (1995) reported that
female adolescents with low self-esteem are more likely to
smoke than their peers with high self-esteem.

Research suggests that low self-esteem is one reason teenage
girls are motivated to smoke (Abernathy, Massad, & Romano-
Dwyer, 1995).

*Subsequent citations*

Abernathy et al. (1995) also examined the relationship
between smoking and self-esteem in adolescent males.

For males, there is no relationship between smoking and
self-esteem, suggesting gender-specific motivations for
initiating smoking in adolescence (Abernathy et al.,
1995).

Another question about subsequent citations is whether to include the publication date each time an article is referenced. Within a paragraph, you do *not*
need to include the year in subsequent citations as long as the study cannot be
confused with other studies cited in your report.

*Citation within a paragraph*

In a recent study of reaction times, Yokoi and Jones
(1998) . . .

Yokoi and Jones also reported that . . .

When subsequent citations are in another paragraph or in another section of the
report, the publication date should be included.

**Six or more authors**     Occasionally you will reference a report with six or
more authors. In this case, use the abbreviation et al. after the first author's
last name in *every* citation. Although you would not list all author names in
the text, the citation in the references section of the report should include the
names of the first six authors followed by et al. for additional authors.

**References with no author**     When an article has no author (e.g., some newspaper or magazine articles), cite the first two or three words of the title in quotation marks, followed by the publication date:

*Citation in reference list*

```
Parental smoking kills 6,200 kids a year, study says. (1997,
     July 15). Orange County Register, p. 11.
```

*Citation in text*

```
     In an article on smoking ("Parental Smoking," 1997),
data obtained from . . .
```

**Multiple works within the same parentheses**     A convenient way to cite several studies on the same topic or several studies with similar findings is to reference them as a series within the same parentheses. When two or more works are by the same author(s), report them in order of year of publication, using commas to separate citations:

```
Schaie and Willis (1986, 1993) found . . .


Past research (Schaie & Willis, 1986, 1993) indicates . . .
```

When two or more works by different authors are cited within the same parentheses, arrange them in alphabetical order and separate citations by semicolons:

```
Investigations of families in economic distress consistently
report that girls react with internalization problems
whereas boys respond with externalization problems (Conger,
Ge, Elder, Lorenz, & Simons, 1994; Flanagan & Eccles, 1993;
Lempers, Clark-Lempers, & Simons, 1989).
```

## Reference List Style

The APA *Publication Manual* provides examples of 95 different reference formats for journal articles, books, book chapters, technical reports, convention presentations, dissertations, Web pages, and videos, among many others. Only a few of these are presented here. When in doubt about how to construct a reference, consult the APA manual. The general format for a reference list is as follows:

1. The references are listed in alphabetical order by the first author's last name. Do not categorize references by type (i.e., books, journal articles, and so on). Note the spacing in the typing of authors' names in the examples.

2. Elements of a reference (authors' names, article title, publication data) are separated by periods.

The first line of each reference is typed flush to the left margin; subsequent lines are indented. This is called a "hanging indent." When you type the reference, it will appear as follows:

```
Davis, J. L., & Rusbult, C. E. (2001). Attitude alignment in
     close relationships. Journal of Personality and Social
     Psychology, 81, 65-84.
```

Each reference begins on a new line (think of each reference as a separate paragraph). Most word processors will allow you to easily format the paragraph with a hanging indent so you do not have to manually insert spaces on the second and subsequent lines: Using Microsoft Word, begin the paragraph with Ctrl-t (control key and t pressed simultaneously); with WordPerfect, start the reference paragraph with Ctrl-F7.

**Format for journal articles**    Most journals are organized by volume and year of publication (e.g., Volume 57 of *American Psychologist* consists of journal issues published in 2002). A common confusion is whether to include the journal issue number in addition to the volume number. The rule is simple: If the issues in a volume are paginated consecutively throughout the volume, *do not* include the journal issue number. If each issue in a volume begins with page 1, the issue number should be included. Specific examples are shown next.

In the reference list, both the name of the journal and the volume number are italicized. Also, only the first letter of the first word in article titles is capitalized (except proper nouns and the first word after a colon or question mark). Here are some examples.

*One author—no issue number*

```
Newby, T. J. (1991). Classroom motivation strategies:
     Strategies of first-year teachers. Journal of
     Educational Psychology, 83, 195-200.
```

*Two authors—use of issue number*

```
Greenwald-Robbins, J., & Greenwald, R. (1994). Environmental
     attitudes conceptualized through developmental theory:
     A qualitative analysis. Journal of Social Issues,
     50(3), 29-47.
```

**Format for books**     When a book is cited, the title of the book is italicized. Only the first word of the title is capitalized; however, proper nouns and the first word after a colon or question mark are also capitalized. The city of publication and the publishing company follow the title. If the city is not well known, include the U.S. Postal Service two-letter abbreviation for the state (e.g., AZ, NY, MN, TX).

*One-author book*

Uba, L. (1994). *Asian Americans: Personality patterns,*
      *identity, and mental health.* New York: The Guilford Press.

*One-author book—second or later edition*

McAdoo, H. P. (1988). *Black families* (2nd ed.). Newbury
      Park, CA: Sage.

*Edited book*

Huston, A. H. (Ed.). (1991). *Children in poverty: Child*
      *development and public policy.* New York: Cambridge
      University Press.

**Format for articles in edited books**     For edited books, the reference begins with the names of the authors of the article, not the book. The title of the article follows. The name(s) of the book editor(s), the book title, the inclusive page numbers for the article, and the publication data for the book follow, in that order. Only the book title is italicized, and only the first letters of the article and book titles are capitalized. Here are some examples.

*One editor*

Brown, A. L., & Campione, J. C. (1994). Guided discovery in
      a community of learners. In K. McGilly (Ed.), *Classroom*
      *lessons: Integrating cognitive theory and classroom*
      *practice* (pp. 229–270). Cambridge, MA: MIT Press.

*Two editors*

Bates, J., Bayles, K., Bennett, D., Ridge, B., & Brown, M.
      (1991). Origins of externalizing behavior problems at
      eight years of age. In D. Pepler & K. Rubin (Eds.), *The*
      *development and treatment of childhood aggression*
      (pp. 93–120). Hillsdale, NJ: Erlbaum.

*Chapter from book in multivolume series*

Kagan, J. (1992). Temperamental contributions to emotion and social behavior. In M. S. Clark (Ed.), *Review of personality and social psychology: Vol. 14. Emotion and social behavior* (pp. 99–118). Newbury Park, CA: Sage.

**Format for "popular articles"**   The reference styles shown next should be used for articles from magazines and newspapers. As a general rule, popular press articles are used sparingly (e.g., when no scientific articles on a topic can be found or to provide an example of an event that is related to your topic).

*Magazine—continuous pages*

Begley, S. (1995, March 27). Gray matters. *Newsweek, 125,* 48–54.

*Newspaper—no author*

10-year-old is youngest to graduate from college. (1994, June 6). *Orange County Register,* p. 15.

*Newspaper—discontinuous pages*

Cole, K. C. (1995, May 1). Way the brain works may play role in bias, experts say. *Los Angeles Times,* pp. Al, A18.

**Format for papers and poster sessions presented at conferences**   Occasionally you may need to cite an unpublished paper or poster session that was presented at a professional meeting. Here are two examples:

*Paper*

Kee, D. W., McBride, D., Neale, P., & Segal, N. (1995, November). *Manual and cerebral laterality in hand-discordant monozygotic twins.* Paper presented at the annual meeting of the Psychonomic Society, Los Angeles, CA.

*Poster session*

Roach, M. A., Barratt, N. S., & Miller, J. F. (1997, April). *Maternal adaptation over time to children with Down Syndrome and typically developing children.* Poster session presented at the annual meeting of the Society for Research in Child Development, Washington, DC.

Secondary sources    Sometimes you need to cite an article, book, or book chapter that you read about through a textbook, an abstract, or a book review. Although it is always preferable to read primary sources, sometimes you may have to cite a secondary source instead.

Suppose you wish to cite an article that you read about in a book. When you refer to the article in your paper, you need to say that it was cited in the book. In the following example, a paper by Conway and Pleydell-Pearce is the secondary source:

```
Conway and Pleydell-Pearce (as cited in Woll, 2002)
suggested that autobiographical memory . . .
```

In the reference list at the end of the paper, simply provide the reference for the primary source you used (in this case, the Woll citation):

```
Woll, S. B. (2002). Everyday thinking: Memory, reasoning,
        and judgment in the real world. Mahwah, NJ: Erlbaum.
```

If you cite an abstract that was obtained from the *PsycINFO* database, simply cite the author(s) in your paper as you normally would. However, the reference will need to state that your citation is based on an abstract. Follow this example in which you provide the reference information but also state that you retrieved the abstract on the date specified:

```
Bieman-Copland, S., & Ryan, E. B. (2001). Social perceptions
        of failures in memory monitoring. Psychology and Aging,
        16, 357-361. Abstract retrieved September 20, 2001,
        from PsycINFO database.
```

## Reference Formats for Electronic Sources

The amount of information available on the Internet has exploded in the past few years. The American Psychological Association has developed guidelines for citing information obtained on the Internet. These guidelines are published in the APA manual as well as at http://www.apastyle.org. The most current formats are provided here, but these could easily change as technology continues to develop.

### Citing a Web site

Sometimes you want simply to cite a particular Web site in your paper without referring to a specific document. In this case, just provide the address of the Web site. No listing in the references is necessary. For example, the following might appear in the text of your paper:

```
The Methods in Behavioral Research text has a useful Web
site for students (http://methods.fullerton.edu).
```

*Citing specific Web documents/pages*

The methods for citing specific Web documents in your paper are the same as citing any document. Follow the rules that have already been described by providing an author and year of publication. For example, to cite the Web document that contains these guidelines, your text might read:

```
The American Psychological Association (2002) has prepared a
set of online guidelines for citing electronic resources.
```

In the reference list, the actual reference to the Web document would appear

```
American Psychological Association. (2001). Electronic
      references. Retrieved November 1, 2002, from
      http://www.apastyle.org/elecsource.html
```

Note that the citation treats the Web document as a publication with a publication date and publisher. Most important, information is provided on the date the document was retrieved and the exact location and file name (URL) of the document. The general rule is to give sufficient citation information to allow a reader to locate the information you are citing. Sometimes it will be difficult to provide all the information that you would have with a regular print publication. For example, there may be no date provided on the document. Here, you may use the abbreviation n.d. to indicate no date.

There is an important rule about typing the URL (location) of the document you are citing. It is acceptable to have the location carry over two lines if it will not fit on a single line. However, you should never allow your word processor to insert a hyphen; the hyphen is an additional character that is not part of the address and so it would be more difficult for the reader to obtain the information.

Electronic journals and newspapers are also becoming more common. Here is a citation from a psychology electronic journal called *Prevention & Treatment*.

```
Beutler, L. E. (2000, September 1). Empirically based
      decision making in clinical practice. Prevention
      & Treatment, 3, Article 27. Retrieved March 1,
      2001, from http://journals.apa.org/prevention/
      volume3/pre0030027a.html
```

Note that the journal provides volume number information, but there is no page number because the document is simply one file without separate pages. You also do not need a period at the end of the citation.

## ABBREVIATIONS

Abbreviations are not used extensively in APA-style papers. They can be distracting because the reader must constantly try to translate the abbreviation into its full meaning. However, APA style does allow for the use of abbreviations that are accepted as words in the dictionary (specifically, Webster's *Collegiate Dictionary*). These include IQ, REM, ESP, and AIDS.

Certain well-known terms may be abbreviated when it would make reading easier, but the full meaning should be given when first used in the paper. Examples of commonly used abbreviations are

| | |
|---|---|
| MMPI | Minnesota Multiphasic Personality Inventory |
| STM | short-term memory |
| CS | conditioned stimulus |
| RT | reaction time |
| CVC | consonant-vowel-consonant |
| ANOVA | analysis of variance |

Statistical terms are sometimes used in their abbreviated or symbol form. These are always italicized in a manuscript. For example,

| | |
|---|---|
| $M$ | mean |
| $SD$ | standard deviation |
| $Mdn$ | median |
| $df$ | degrees of freedom |
| $n$ | number of individuals in a group or experimental condition |
| $N$ | total number of participants or respondents |
| $p$ | probability (significance) level |
| $SS$ | sum of squares |
| $MS$ | mean square |
| $F$ | value of $F$ in analysis of variance |
| $r$ | Pearson correlation coefficient |
| $R$ | multiple correlation coefficient |

Some scientific abbreviations for various measurement units that are frequently used include:

| | |
|---|---|
| cm | centimeter |
| g | gram |
| hr | hour |

| | |
|---|---|
| in | inch |
| kg | kilogram |
| km | kilometer |
| m | meter |
| mg | milligram |
| min | minute |
| ml | milliliter |
| mm | millimeter |
| ms | millisecond |
| s | second |

Finally, certain abbreviations of Latin and Middle English terms are regularly used in papers. Some of these abbreviations and their meanings are:

| | | |
|---|---|---|
| cf. | compare | (from Latin *confer*) |
| e.g., | for example | (from Latin *exempli gratia*) |
| etc. | and so forth | (from Latin *et cetera*) |
| i.e., | that is | (from Latin *id est*) |
| viz. | namely | |
| vs. | versus | |

## SOME GRAMMATICAL CONSIDERATIONS

### Transition Words and Phrases

One way to produce a clearly written research report is to pay attention to how you connect sentences within a paragraph and connect paragraphs within a section. The transitions between sentences and paragraphs should be smooth and consistent with the line of reasoning. Some commonly used transition words and phrases and their functions are described in this section.

**Adverbs**    Adverbs can be used as introductory words in sentences. However, you must use them to convey their implied meanings.

| Adverb | Implied meaning |
|---|---|
| (Un)fortunately | It is (un)fortunate that . . . |
| Similarly | In a similar manner . . . |
| Certainly | It is certain that . . . |
| Clearly | It is clear that . . . |

One adverb that is frequently misused as an introductory or transition word is *hopefully*. *Hopefully* means "in a hopeful manner," *not* "it is hoped that . . . ."

> *Incorrect:* Hopefully, this is not the case.
>
> *Correct:* I hope this is not the case.

**Words suggesting contrast**    Some words and phrases suggest a contrast or contradiction between what was written immediately before and what is now being written:

| *Between sentences* | *Within sentences* |
| --- | --- |
| By contrast, | whereas |
| On the other hand, | although |
| However, | but |

The words in the left list refer to the previous sentence. The words in the right list connect phrases within a sentence; that is, they refer to another point in the same sentence.

**Words suggesting a series of ideas**    Words and phrases that suggest that information after the transition word is related or similar to information in the sentence are:

| | | | |
| --- | --- | --- | --- |
| First | In addition | Last | Further |
| Second | Additionally | Finally | Moreover |
| Third | Then | Also | Another |

**Words suggesting implication**    These words and phrases indicate that the information following the transition word is implied by or follows from the previous information:

| | |
| --- | --- |
| Therefore | If . . . then |
| It follows that | Thus |
| In conclusion | Then |

When you use transition words, be sure that they convey the meaning you intend. Sprinkling them around to begin sentences leads to confusion on the reader's part and defeats your purpose.

## Troublesome Words and Phrases

**"That" versus "which"**    *That* and *which* are relative pronouns that introduce subordinate clauses and reflect the relationship of the subordinate clause to the main clause. *That* clauses are called restrictive clauses and are essential to the meaning of the sentence; *which* clauses are nonrestrictive and simply add more information. Note the different meanings of the same sentence using *that* and *which:*

> The mice that performed well in the first trial were used in the second trial.
>
> The mice, which performed well in the first trial, were used in the second trial.

The first sentence states that only mice that performed well in the first trial were used in the second. The second sentence states that all the mice were used in the second trial and they also happened to perform well in the first trial.

**"While" versus "since"**    *While* and *since* are subordinate conjunctions that also introduce subordinate clauses. To increase clarity in scientific writing, the APA manual suggests that *while* and *since* should be used only to refer to time. *While* is used to describe simultaneous events, and *since* is used to refer to a subsequent event:

> The participants waited together while their personality tests were scored.
>
> Since the study by Elder (1974), many studies have been published on this topic.

The APA manual suggests other conjunctions to use to link phrases that do not describe temporal events. *Although, whereas,* and *but* can be used in place of *while,* and *because* should be substituted for *since.*

> *Incorrect:* While the study was well designed, the report was poorly written.
>
> *Correct:* Although the study was well designed, the report was poorly written.

**"Effect" versus "affect"**    A common error in student reports is incorrect use of *effect* and *affect. Effect* is a noun that is used in scientific reports to mean "what is produced by a cause," as in the sentence: "The movie had a strong effect on me." *Affect* can be a noun or a verb. As a noun it means emotion, as in "The patient seemed depressed but she displayed very little affect." As a verb it means "to have an influence on," as in "The listeners' responses were affected by the music they heard."

> *Incorrect:* The independent variable effected their responses.
>
> *Correct:* The independent variable affected their responses.
>
> *Incorrect:* The independent variable had only a weak affect on the participants' behavior.
>
> *Correct:* The independent variable had only a weak effect on the participants' behavior.

**Singular and plural**    The following words are often misused. The left list shows singular nouns requiring singular verb forms. The right list contains plural nouns that must be used with plural verbs.

| *Singular* | *Plural* |
| --- | --- |
| datum | data |
| stimulus | stimuli |
| analysis | analyses |
| phenomenon | phenomena |
| medium | media |
| hypothesis | hypotheses |
| schema | schemas |

Probably the most frequently misused word is *data*.

> *Incorrect:* The data *was* coded for computer analysis.
> *Correct:* The data *were* coded for computer analysis.

**Some spelling considerations**    Here are words that are frequently mis-spelled or used with incorrect capitalization:

questionnaire
database
e-journal
e-mail
Web
Internet
URL

## REPORTING NUMBERS AND STATISTICS

Virtually all research papers report numbers: number of participants, number of groups, the values of statistics such as $t$, $F$, or $r$. Should you use numbers (e.g., "*43*"), or should you use words (e.g., "*forty-three*")? The general rule is to use words when expressing the numbers zero through nine but to use numbers for 10 and above. There are some important qualifications, however.

If you start a sentence with a number, you should use words even if the number is 10 or larger (e.g., "*Eighty-five student teachers participated in the study.*"). Starting a sentence with a number is often awkward, especially with large numbers. Therefore, you should try to revise the sentence to avoid the problem (e.g., "*The participants were 85 students enrolled in teaching credential classes.*").

When numbers both above and below 10 are being compared in the same sentence, use numerals for both (e.g., "*Participants read either 8 or 16 paragraphs.*"). However, this sentence contains an appropriate mix of numbers and words: "*Participants read eight paragraphs and then answered 20 multiple-choice questions.*" The sentence is correct because the paragraphs and the questions are different entities and so are not being compared.

When reporting a percentage, always use numerals followed by a percent sign except when beginning a sentence. This is true regardless of whether the number is less than 10 (e.g., "*Only 6% of the computer games appealed to females.*") or greater than 10 (e.g., "*When using this technique, 85% of the participants improved their performance.*").

Always use numbers when describing ages (e.g., "*5-year-olds*"), points on a scale (e.g., "*a 3 on a 5-point scale*"), units of measurement (e.g., "*the children stood 2 m from the target*"), sample size (e.g., "*6 girls and 6 boys were assigned to each study condition*"), and statistics (e.g., "*the mean score in the no-model group was 3.10*"). An odd but sensible exception to the word–number rule occurs when two different types of numbers must appear together. An example is "*Teachers identified fifteen 7-year-olds as the most aggressive.*" This sentence avoids an awkward juxtaposition of two numbers.

For a multiplication sign, use either a lowercase x or the multiplication symbol used by your word processor. This is true whether you are describing a mathematical operation or a factorial design (e.g., a $2 \times 2$ design). For a minus sign, use a hyphen with a space both before and after the hyphen.

Finally, you need to know about presenting statistical results within your paper. As noted previously, statistical terms are abbreviated and typed with italics (e.g., *M, r, t, F*). In addition, when reporting the results of a statistical significance test, provide the name of the test, the degrees of freedom, the value of the test statistic, and the probability level. Here are two examples of sentences that describe statistical results:

> As predicted, participants in the high-anxiety condition took longer to recognize the words ($M$ = 2.63) than did the individuals in the low-anxiety condition ($M$ = 1.42), $t(20)$ = 2.54, $p$ = .019.

> Job satisfaction scores were significantly correlated with marital satisfaction, $r(50)$ = .48, $p$ < .001.

Recall that exact probabilities are reported as they appear in the computer printout of your statistical analysis. However, sometimes the computer does not report very low probabilities that are below .001; in these cases, it is acceptable to use the < (less than) symbol.

If your printer cannot produce a particular symbol, you may draw it in with black ink. Pay attention to the way statistics are described in the articles you read. You will find that you can vary your descriptions of results to best fit your data and presentation, as well as vary your sentence constructions.

## CONCLUSION

When you have completed your research report, you should feel proud of your effort. You have considered past research on a problem, conducted a research project, analyzed the results, and reported the findings. Such a research effort may result in a publication or presentation at a convention. This is not the most important part of your research, however. What is most important is that you have acquired new knowledge and that your curiosity has been aroused so you will want to learn even more.

## SAMPLE PAPER

The remainder of this appendix consists of a typed manuscript of a paper that was published in a professional journal. This is intended to be a useful guide when you write your own reports in APA style. The margin notes point out important elements of APA style. Read through the manuscript, paying particular attention to the general format, and make sure you understand the rules concerning page numbering, section headings, reference citation, and the format of figures. Writing your first research report is always a challenging task. It will become easier as you read the research of others and practice by writing reports of your own.

Jennifer L. Knight and Traci A. Giuliano graciously gave their permission to reprint their paper to illustrate elements of APA style. The comments at the side alert you to features of APA style that you will need to know about when writing your own papers. Be aware, though, that every paper will include slightly different types of information depending on the particular topic, method, and results. Your paper will follow the general guidelines of APA style but many of the details will be determined by the needs of your study.

You may note that the title of this paper is longer than the 10 to 12 words recommended by APA style. A briefer (but less intriguing) title might be *Consequences of Gender-Stereotypical Portrayals of Male and Female Athletes in Print Media.*

He's a Laker   1

Running head: GENDERED PORTRAYALS OF ATHLETES BY THE MEDIA

He's a Laker; She's a "Looker": The Consequences of
Gender-Stereotypical Portrayals of Male
and Female Athletes by the Print Media

Jennifer L. Knight and Traci A. Giuliano
Southwestern University

*Each page has a header with a paper identification and page number. The paper identification is the first few words of the title.*

*The running head is an abbreviated title that will appear at the top of each page when the article is published. It is 50 spaces maximum and capitalized.*

*Title, author(s), and affiliation are centered and appear in the upper half of the page.*

*The title is usually 10 to 12 words in length.*

*Double-space the entire paper.*

*Set margins to at least 1 inch (default word processor settings are usually appropriate).*

He's a Laker    2

*Abstract begins on a new page.*

*The word "Abstract" is centered and in regular type.*

*There is no paragraph indentation in the abstract.*

*The abstract is generally no more than 120 words in length.*

*Use one space only after periods, commas, colons, and semicolons.*

Abstract

Although qualitative research shows that coverage of women's sport often focuses on female athletes' attractiveness (to the exclusion of their athleticism), there is a dearth of quantitative research examining the effect of this coverage on people's perceptions of athletes. As part of a 2 × 2 between-subjects design, 92 undergraduates (40 men, 52 women) read a fictitious newspaper profile about an Olympic athlete that focused on either the athlete's attractiveness or athleticism. Interestingly, participants neither had favorable impressions of nor liked articles about female and male athletes when attractiveness was the main focus of an article. These findings suggest that the media should be cognizant of the impressions that can result from portraying athletes in terms of their personal attributes rather than their athletic accomplishments.

He's a Laker   3

He's a Laker; She's a "Looker": The Consequences
of Gender-Stereotypical Portrayals of Male
and Female Athletes by the Print Media

In an era in which men's professional sport is
becoming characterized by multimillion-dollar contracts,
players' union lockouts, illegal steroid use, and an
individualistic mentality, disgruntled sports fans are
increasingly turning to women's professional sport for
entertainment. Indeed, leagues such as the Women's
National Basketball Association (WNBA), the Ladies'
Professional Golf Association (LPGA), the Women's Pro
Softball League (WPSL), the Women's Pro Tennis Tour
(WTA), and the Women's United Soccer Association (WUSA)
are a welcome sign for fans searching for team-oriented
play, affordable seats, and accessible sports stars
(Wulf, 1997). In addition to the burgeoning field of
women's professional sport, the Olympic Games have also
been a showcase for successful female athletes. In the
1996 Atlanta Games, U.S. women's teams earned gold
medals in gymnastics, soccer, softball, and basketball
(with the softball and basketball teams reclaiming their
titles at the 2000 Sydney Games). Their Winter
counterparts in the 1998 Nagano Games also fared well,
with the first-place women's hockey team and with
individual stars Picabo Street, Tara Lipinski, and
Christine Witty securing victories.

Female athletes competing at the interscholastic and
intercollegiate levels have also made great strides. The
Title IX court decision of 1972 requires all federally
funded programs, including athletics, to provide equal
treatment and opportunity for participation for men and

*The main body of the paper begins on page 3. The body of the paper includes the introduction, method, results, and discussion sections.*

*Center the title and then begin typing the introduction. Do not include the names of the authors.*

*Use the author's last name and date for reference citations.*

He's a Laker   4

*Use the "&"
symbol when
multiple authors'
names are within
parentheses. Use
"and" when
authors' names are
part of the text.*

women. The implication for sports programs was that high schools and public universities subsequently were required to spend equivalent amounts of time and money for male and female athletes' scholarships, recruitment, facilities, supplies, travel, and services (Curtis & Grant, 2001). In part because of these improved opportunities, girls' and women's involvement in sport has reached an all-time high. Whereas in 1971, only 1 in 27 girls participated in high school athletics, over 1 in 3 participated in 1997 (Women's Sports Foundation, 1998).

*Provide all
authors' names in
the first citation.
When there are
three to five
authors, use "et
al." for subsequent
citations. See text
for the exception
with more than
five authors.*

Although women's participation in professional, Olympic, intercollegiate, and interscholastic sport has reached unprecedented highs, research shows that media coverage of female athletes still lags behind that of men's (e.g., Duncan, Messner, & Williams, 1991; Fink, 1998; Tuggle & Owen, 1999). For example, women were featured on the cover of *Sports Illustrated* a scant 4 times out of 53 issues in 1996 (Women's Sports Foundation, 1998). A longitudinal study of *Sports Illustrated* feature articles from the mid-1950s to the late 1980s also revealed that the popular sport magazine allots far fewer column inches and photographs per article for women's sport as compared to men's (Lumpkin & Williams, 1991; Salwen & Wood, 1994). A similar pattern was exhibited in television coverage of the Olympics, both in 1992 (Higgs & Weiller, 1994) and in 1996–purportedly "the year of women's sports" (Eastman & Billings, 1999). Even coverage of collegiate and high school sport is gender biased–boys receive more and longer articles

*When several
references are cited
together, separate
with a semicolon.*

*Use italics for titles
of books, journals,
and magazines.*

*Note that there is
no apostrophe in a
decade, such as the
1950s.*

*Note rules for
reporting
numbers: 4 and 53
used in the same
sentence so 4 is not
spelled out.*

He's a Laker    5

than do girls (e.g., Sagas, Cunningham, Wigley, & Ashley, 2000; Woodcock, 1995). In effect, this "symbolic annihilation" (Gerbner, 1972) of women's sport by the media conveys the inaccurate idea that women's sport is inferior to and not as noteworthy as men's sport.

*e.g. means "for example" and i.e. means "that is"*

Coverage of women's sport is inferior to that of men's not only in quantity but in quality as well (e.g., Birrell & Theberge, 1994; Daddario, 1998; Duncan, 1990, Duncan & Messner, 2000; Kane & Parks, 1992). Sport commentators and writers often allude or explicitly refer to a female athlete's attractiveness, emotionality, femininity, and heterosexuality (all of which effectively convey to the audience that her stereotypical gender role is more salient than her athletic role), yet male athletes are depicted as powerful, independent, dominating, and valued (Hilliard, 1984; Messner, 1988; Sabo & Jansen, 1992). Because competitively participating in sports is inconsistent with society's prescribed female role, the media coverage of female athletes seems to be trying to protect female athletes from rejection (or, more cynically, giving the public what they think it "wants") by emphasizing other aspects of their "femaleness," such as their attractiveness (Kane, 1996). For instance, although Gabrielle Reese, Anna Kournikova, Katarina Witt, and Jan Stephenson are all exceptional athletes, the media often focus on their attractiveness, a problem that is much less common for male athletes. In effect, the media tend to represent female athletes as women first (i.e., through focusing on their hair, nails, clothing, and attractiveness) and as athletes second;

however, male athletes for the most part are portrayed solely in terms of their athleticism (Boutilier & SanGiovanni, 1983).

This trivialization of women athletes is consistent with schema theory, which proposes that people have implicit cognitive structures that provide them with expectancies when processing information (Fiske & Taylor, 1991). One of the most socially constructed and dichotomous stereotypes is that of gender (Burn, O'Neal, & Nederend, 1996). Gender schema theory argues that people are socialized (e.g., through parents, teachers, peers, toys, and the popular media) to believe that gender differences are significant and worth maintaining (Bem, 1981). Although there is actually more variability within than between the sexes, the concept of distinct and exclusive gender differences persists nonetheless (Martin, 1987).

When people do violate our well-ingrained schemas (as would a female truck driver or a male secretary), they are consequently perceived more negatively than are people who are schema-consistent (e.g., Knight, Giuliano, & Sanchez-Ross, 2001; Rosenthal & Jacobson, 1968). It may be, then, that men are readily portrayed by the media as athletes first because being an athlete is consistent with the traditional male role (Coakley & White, 1992). However, for women, being an athlete contradicts the conventional female role, and thus media coverage emphasizes other aspects of their "femaleness" (such as their attractiveness). Consequently, the narratives of male athletes are free to focus on their athletic accomplishments, whereas the portrayals of female athletes focus on aspects of their femininity, possibly to make these female athletes appear more gender-role consistent.

The trivialization of women's sport by the media is well established, but researchers have yet to empirically investigate how differential portrayals of male and female athletes affect the public's view of the athletes. Although researchers have speculated as to how people's beliefs might be influenced by biased coverage (e.g., Fasting, 1999), there is a dearth of research on the actual consequences of these differential portrayals as well as on the extent to which the media can truly influence people's perceptions of athletes. In addition, members of the media argue that they simply provide coverage that "the public wants," yet this also remains to be substantiated by empirical research. In other words, to what end the media merely reflect or actively refract public opinion is still unknown. As such, the purpose of the present investigation was to address these previously unanswered questions in the sport literature. To explore how gender-consistent and gender-inconsistent portrayals of athletes affect people's perceptions, a hypothetical Olympic profile was designed in which the focal point of the article was either a male or female athlete's physical attractiveness (a typically female portrayal) or athleticism (a typically male portrayal).

In general, it was predicted that female athletes described as attractive would be perceived more positively (e.g., as more likable, more dedicated to sports, and more heroic) than female athletes who were not described in such a manner, because being attractive "softens" the

He's a Laker   8

perceived gender-role inconsistency of a female athlete. Conversely, male athletes described as attractive were expected to be perceived more negatively than would males not described as such, because the gender schema for male athletes leads people to expect that a man's athleticism, rather than his physical attractiveness, should be the focus of a magazine article.

Furthermore, we expected that the results would be qualified by the gender of the participant. Because women typically are more accepting of schema-inconsistency (e.g., Fiala, Giuliano, Remlinger, & Braithwaite, 1999; Greendorfer, 1993) and of female athletes in general (Nixon, Maresca, & Silverman, 1979), three-way interactions were expected such that male participants would perceive gender-typical behavior (i.e., articles about attractive female athletes and athletic male athletes) positively, whereas female participants would be more likely to value atypical, out-of-role behavior (i.e., articles about athletic female athletes or attractive male athletes).

Method

*Participants*

The participants were 92 predominantly White undergraduate students (40 men, 52 women) at a small liberal arts university in the Southwest. Participants were recruited primarily from introductory psychology and economics classes and were given extra credit in their courses for completing the study. Additional participants were recruited from the men's and women's Division III soccer teams at the university, and they were given small prizes as incentives.

*The Method section begins immediately after the introduction (no new page). The word "Method" is centered in regular type.z*

*Subsection headings such as "Participants" are italicized, typed flush to the left margin, and stand alone on the line.*

He's a Laker     9

*Design and Materials*

*INDENT* →   A 2 (Gender of the Athlete: Female or Male) × 2 (Gender
of the Participant: Female or Male) × 2 (Focus of the
Article: Physical Attractiveness or Athleticism)
between-subjects design was used to explore perceptions
of athletes as a function of their gender and the focus
of an article. Because newspaper and magazine articles
rarely just *describe* physical attributes, a picture of
the hypothetical athlete was included in the article.
To minimize potential confounds, a pilot test was
conducted to match male and female targets on
attractiveness and age. From a pool of 12 "head shot"
color photographs, one male target (*M* attractiveness
= 6.47 on a 7-point scale; *M* age = 19.43) and one
female target (*M* attractiveness = 6.93; *M* age = 21.20)
were selected because they received similar scores on
these attributes.

In the article emphasizing the athlete's physical
attractiveness, the athlete was described as "becoming
known as much for his [her] incredible body as for his
[her] powerful strokes," as being one of *People
Magazine*'s "Fifty Most Beautiful People in the World,"
and as having recently signed a modeling contract to
make a "Wet and Wild" calendar for Speedo swimwear
after the Olympics. By contrast, in the article that
focused on the athlete's athleticism, he or she was
described as "becoming known both for his [her]
incredible speed and his [her] powerful strokes," as
being one of *Sports Illustrated*'s "Fifty Up-and-Coming
Athletes," and as having recently signed a contract to
model for a Speedo promotional calendar.

*The authors determined that a "Design and Materials" subsection would help organize the paper. A paper you write might not have such a subsection, or it might have one section for Design and another for Materials. The main goal is to make it easy for a reader to understand your methodology.*

*Statistical symbols such as M for the mean are italicized.*

He's a Laker    10

Each article was followed by a response sheet designed to assess participants' reactions to the profile. Specifically, participants were asked to rate on 10-point scales ranging from 1 (*not at all*) to 10 (*very much*) several different characteristics of the athlete, including how feminine (i.e., tender, cheerful, affectionate, sympathetic, gentle, compassionate, and warm; Cronbach's alpha = .93), respectable (i.e., acting as a leader, respectable, ambitious, a good representative of the USA, and a good role model; Cronbach's alpha = .90), athletic (i.e., athletic, competitive, talented, serious about sports, and dedicated to sports; Cronbach's alpha = .84), and aggressive (i.e., aggressive, dominant, and forceful; Cronbach's alpha = .85) they perceived him or her to be. Using the same scale, participants also made other judgments about the athlete, such as how likable, heroic, similar to the "ideal" man/woman, and physically attractive they perceived the athlete to be. Participants were then given the opportunity to record open-ended responses about their overall impression of the athlete.

In addition, because the media have argued that gender-consistent coverage is "what the public wants" (Kane, 1996), we used a secondary category of dependent variables to assess participants' liking of the hypothetical article. Thus, participants also rated (on the same 10-point scale) how much they liked the article (i.e., how flattering the coverage was to the athlete, how interested they would be in reading more about the athlete, and how accurately the coverage

*The anchors of scales (not at all) or (very much) are italicized.*

*This paper does not use paragraph headings. You may see other articles in which the subsections such as Procedure are further divided by paragraph headings.*

He's a Laker    11

depicted the athlete; Cronbach's alpha = .87).
Participants then provided open-ended responses about
their overall impression of the article.

A number of control procedures were used to control
for extraneous variables. First, because the gender-
appropriateness of an athlete's sport is so salient, it
was necessary to choose a sport that was not perceived
as especially masculine or feminine. To determine
whether or not a sport was considered gender-neutral,
15 participants rated the gender-appropriateness of 16
sports on a 7-point scale ranging from 1 (*appropriate
for men*) to 7 (*appropriate for women*). The sport of
swimming (*M* = 4.07) was chosen as the athlete's sport
in this study because it was perceived as gender-
neutral, consistent with previous research (Metheny,
1965). Next, to ensure a balanced gender representation
in the sample, a randomized block design was used to
assign equal numbers of male and female participants to
each of the four conditions. Finally, to minimize
additional error variance, the athlete's reported age
(i.e., 21 years old) and name (depending on the
condition, either *Nick Gleason* or *Nicole Gleason*) were
consistent across conditions.

*Procedure*

Potential participants were approached and told that
the current study was "an investigation of people's
perceptions of Olympic athletes." After agreeing to
complete the questionnaire, participants read a
hypothetical newspaper account about an athlete (who
ostensibly had competed in the 1996 Summer Olympic
Games) and then made judgments in response to the

*Quotation marks are placed outside of the period.*

*Note the spelling of "questionnaire."*

He's a Laker    12

coverage and the athlete involved. All participants saw identical profiles, except that the first names (i.e., the gender) and type of coverage (i.e., attractive- or athletic-focused) varied according to each of the four specific experimental conditions.

After reading four profiles (three additional hypothetical profiles were included as part of a separate investigation) and completing the corresponding response sheets, participants recorded their answers to demographic questions (e.g., age, gender, athletic status, and the amount of time they spend following sports through the media) and other personality measures, including the Bem Sex-Role Inventory (Bem, 1974) and the Sex-Role Egalitarianism Scale (Beere, King, Beere, & King, 1984).[1] Upon completion of the questionnaire, participants were told that the article was hypothetical, thanked for their participation, and dismissed.

Results

The data were analyzed using a 2 (Gender of the Athlete: Female or Male) × 2 (Gender of the Participant: Female or Male) × 2 (Focus of the Article: Physical Attractiveness or Athleticism) between-subjects analysis of variance (ANOVA). Because there was no effect of participant gender, the reported results collapse across gender. An Athlete Gender × Focus of the Article interaction was obtained for participants' ratings of the athlete's attractiveness, $F(1,83) = 5.56$, $p = .021$. As expected, female athletes depicted in terms of their attractiveness ($M = 8.90$) were seen as more attractive than those depicted in terms of their athleticism only

*In general, avoid using footnotes. A footnote, if used, is indicated by a superscript number; the text of the footnote is typed on a separate page at the end of the paper.*

*The Results section begins immediately following the Method section. The word "Results" is centered in regular type.*

*Note that the word "data" is a plural noun; thus, it is correct to indicate that "the data are ..."*

*Exact probabilities are shown although sometimes it is appropriate to use "ns" to indicate that a result is nonsignificant.*

*When presenting the outcome of a statistical test, the name of the test is italicized and followed by the degrees of freedom in parentheses. The p refers to the probability of obtaining the result if the null hypothesis is correct.*

He's a Laker    13

($M = 6.54$; $t(43) = 5.14$, $p = .0001$); by contrast, there was no difference in the perceived attractiveness of male athletes described as attractive ($M = 8.18$) or as athletic ($M = 7.46$; $t < 1$, $ns$), as Figure 1 shows. The effect size $r$ associated with the comparison of perceived attractiveness of the female described as attractive or athletic was .617.

Additionally, there were several main effects of the focus of the article. Athletes whose coverage focused on their attractiveness were viewed as less talented ($M = 8.08$) than were athletes who were described in an athletic manner ($M = 8.96$), $F(1,83) = 11.68$, $p = .001$. Athletes described as attractive were also seen as less aggressive ($M = 6.22$) than were athletes described as athletic ($M = 6.97$), $F(1,83) = 4.05$, $p = .047$. Furthermore, athletes portrayed as attractive were viewed as less heroic ($M = 5.43$) than were athletes portrayed as athletic ($M = 6.52$), $F(1,83) = 5.74$, $p = .019$. Finally, when attractiveness was the focus of the article, people liked the article less ($M = 5.18$) than when the coverage focused on the athlete's athletic ability ($M = 6.14$), $F(1,83) = 5.09$, $p = .027$.

*Figures and tables, when used, must be mentioned in the text.*

Discussion

The results of the present study confirm that perceptions of athletes are influenced by the gender of the athlete and by the type of media coverage provided in the article. Interestingly, although the same picture was used in each condition, a female athlete whose attractiveness was the main focus of an article was perceived to be more physically attractive than was a female athlete whose athletic accomplishments were

*The Discussion section immediately follows the Results section. The word "Discussion" is centered in regular type.*

the focus of the article. However, the same pattern was not found with male athletes. Previous research has demonstrated that people have weaker schemas for ideal athletes than for ideal persons because the general public has fewer experiences (and thus, fewer cognitive associations) with the very specific category of "an ideal athlete" as opposed to the broader category of "an ideal person" (Martin & Martin, 1995). It follows that perhaps the schema for a female athlete is not as strong as that for a male athlete (because of less "mere exposure" through their "symbolic annihilation" by the media; Gerbner, 1972), and thus people's perceptions (especially of attractiveness, it seems) of a female athlete are more malleable and open to alteration. As such, this study implies that people are more apt to rely on peripheral information (such as the angle provided by the type of coverage) to form impressions of a female athlete.

Regardless of athlete gender, however, focusing on attractiveness to the exclusion of athletic ability had striking consequences on how athletes were perceived. Interestingly, our results indicate that male athletes are also affected by trivializing coverage; however, since men are rarely portrayed by the media in terms of their attractiveness (as female athletes often are), this marginalizing coverage seems to predominantly affect female athletes. Because of this negative effect on impressions of female and male athletes, the media need to be cognizant of (a) the damage that focusing on athletes' attractiveness can have on people's perceptions, (b) the fact that people might prefer articles that focus on an athlete's athleticism more than ones that focus on attractiveness, and (c) the reality that they do not merely reflect public opinion; they, in fact, can actively shape it.

Interestingly, participant gender was not a significant factor in ratings of the athlete or the article—a finding contrary to some previous research (e.g., Fisher, Genovese, Morris, & Morris, 1977), but consistent with other research (e.g., Michael, Gilroy, & Sherman, 1984). Perhaps this heralds a change in men's attitudes toward female athletes. Although women have traditionally been more accepting than men of female athletes (Nixon, Maresca, & Silverman, 1979), with the accomplishments of female athletes at the professional, Olympic, college, and high school levels, men might now be more aware and, hence, more accepting of women's sport.

An examination of the open-ended responses further confirmed what the quantitative data revealed. For example, one female participant shrewdly noted about the female athlete whose coverage centered on her attractiveness, "If I were her, I would be offended that this article talked more about my physical appearance than my talent—a typical attitude toward women. They can't resist talking about your appearance." A male participant similarly remarked, "If this was done in an edition of *Cosmopolitan* I might have liked it, but it told me nothing about her as an *athlete*." Yet another male participant said, "I wonder what her priorities are . . . is she using the 'swimming thing' to parlay a sweet modeling career?"

Open-ended responses about male athletes portrayed as
attractive revealed that they, too, were perceived in a
negative light. A female participant wrote that this
athlete was "a snobby rich kid who is a good swimmer
and is used to everyone telling him how great he is."
Another female participant remarked, "The article gave
no mention of sports or athletic profile, only
appearance. When speaking of an athlete in an Olympic
sport, that is disconcerting."

There were several limitations of the present study.
Most notably, the kind of methodology used (i.e.,
"effects" research) cannot truly simulate the long-term
consequences of the media as a tool of socialization
(Lewis, 1991). Although this kind of research does have
certain limitations, other researchers have recognized
its potential theoretical and practical value. For
instance, in their research involving *face-ism*, Archer
and his colleagues took a qualitative finding (i.e.,
that pictures of women in the media often feature their
entire body, whereas photographs of men usually feature
only their heads) and experimentally determined through
a quantitative methodology that this pattern results in
men appearing smarter and in women appearing
objectified (Archer, Iritani, Kimes, & Barrios, 1983).
In a similar vein, the current research has shown the
negative impressions and effects that can occur from
articles that focus exclusively on an athlete's
attractiveness. It is through this process of
triangulation and examining the same phenomenon from
different paradigms and disciplinary perspectives that

we will begin to be able to truly understand social patterns and their potential effect on society.

Another potential limitation was that some of the conditions within the study lacked external validity (i.e., male athletes are seldom depicted in terms of their attractiveness). Although articles such as these are rarely found in the print media, it was important to include them in the present study so that it could be empirically determined how gender-atypical portrayals of male and female athletes affect people's perceptions. That is, a conscious decision was made to trade internal for external validity in the present case. Finally, participants were not asked to report their race, and thus, the race of the participant was not taken into account in analyses. Although the majority of participants were White, previous research shows that White and Black participants weigh certain characteristics differently when evaluating the attractiveness of White and Black individuals (e.g., Hebl & Heatherton, 1998). Diverse audiences (in terms of age, socioeconomic status, education level, sexual orientation, and political orientation) might also differ with regards both to how much they like articles that focus on male and female athletes' attractiveness and athleticism and to their subsequent impressions of the athletes.

Opportunities are rife for future quantitative research in the area of gendered portrayals in the sport media. For example, the photographs selected for inclusion in the present study were both of White targets. Because people have different expectations and

*Racial and ethnic categories are capitalized in APA style.*

schemas for Black female athletes, the results from the
present study might not generalize to athletes of other
races. For instance, it traditionally is more
acceptable for minority and working-class female
athletes to participate in gender-inappropriate sports
(e.g., basketball, soccer, hockey) than for White and
middle-class female athletes because of the former
group's more dynamic perceptions of femininity (Cahn,
1994; Metheny, 1965). As such, further research is
necessary to investigate the potential interactions
among participant race, participant gender, athlete
race, and athlete gender (Gissendaner, 1994).

In a broader scope, more experimental quantitative
research should be conducted to empirically verify what
descriptive qualitative studies have been reporting all
along–that female athletes receive trivializing
coverage from the media. For instance, *gender marking*
(i.e., qualifying athletic contests and teams for women
as though men's contests are the norm or standard) is
very prevalent in television coverage of female
athletes (Kane, 1996). Sports writers and commentators
often use gendered labels to describe games in which
female athletes participate (e.g., the *"Women's* Final
Four"), yet male athletic contests are not referred to
in these gendered terms (e.g., the "Final Four" rather
than the *"Men's* Final Four"). Although researchers have
speculated that this type of coverage marginalizes
female athletes by making them appear to be "the other"
rather than the norm, research has yet to empirically
demonstrate the consequences of gender marking.
Exploring how these and other types of gender–

stereotypical portrayals affect both male and female athletes is an important next step in the sport literature.

In the meantime, the present study provides an empirical perspective to the burgeoning psychological and sociological fields that study the media, sport, and gender. At no other time in history have women had as much personal encouragement (Weiss & Barber, 1995) or as many opportunities to participate in sport (Women's Sports Foundation, 1998) as they do now, yet coverage of women's sport still lags behind men's coverage in both quantity and quality. The media need to be cognizant of the effects of their trivializing and marginalizing coverage and of the fact that this type of coverage may not be "what the public wants" after all. Hopefully, with a sustained and diligent commitment from the media, sport will be viewed as an

*References begins on a new page. The word "References" is centered at the top of the page.*

*Each reference begins on a new line and is considered a paragraph. The format of the paragraph is a "hanging indent" in which the first line is flush to the left margin and subsequent lines are indented. Use the hanging indent feature of your word processor to do this.*

*Titles of books and journals are italicized, as are volume numbers of journals.*

*Note that the "&" symbol is used throughout.*

*These references illustrate books, edited books, journal articles, articles in the popular press, and material from the Internet. The APA* Publication Manual *describes virtually every type of reference you might use.*

← other page

unconditionally acceptable and beneficial activity for

women.

He's a Laker     20

New page →

References

Archer, D., Iritani, B., Kimes, D. D., & Barrios, M. (1983). Five studies of sex differences in facial prominence. *Journal of Personality and Social Psychology, 45,* 725–735.

Beere, C. A., King, D. W., Beere, D. B., & King, L. A. (1984). The Sex-Role Egalitarianism Scale: A measure of attitudes toward equality between the sexes. *Sex Roles, 10,* 563–576.

Bem, S. L. (1981). Gender schema theory: A cognitive account of sex typing. *Psychological Review, 88,* 354–364.

Bem, S. L. (1974). The measurement of psychological androgyny. *Journal of Consulting and Clinical Psychology, 42,* 155 162.

Birrell, S., & Theberge, N. (1994). Ideological control of women in sport. In D. M. Costa & S. R. Guthrie (Eds.), *Women and sport: Interdisciplinary perspectives.* Champaign, IL: Human Kinetics.

Book

Boutilier, M. A., & SanGiovanni, L. (1983). *The sporting woman.* Champaign, IL: Human Kinetics.

Burn, S. M., O'Neal, K. A., & Nederend, S. (1996). Childhood tomboyism and adult androgyny. *Sex Roles, 34,* 419–428.

Cahn, S. K. (1994). *Coming on strong: Gender and sexuality in twentieth-century women's sport.* New York: Free Press.

He's a Laker   21

Coakley, J. J., & White, A. (1992). Making decisions: Gender and sport participation among British adolescents. *Sociology of Sport Journal, 9,* 20-35.

Curtis, M. C., & Grant, C. H. B. (2001). *Gender equity in sports.* Retrieved July 15, 2001, from http://bailiwick.lib.uiowa.edu/ge/

Daddario, G. (1998). *Women's sport and spectacle: Gendered television coverage and the Olympic Games.* Westport, CT: Praeger.

Duncan, M. C. (1990). Sport photographs and sexual difference: Images of women and men in the 1984 and 1988 Olympic Games. *Sociology of Sport Journal, 7,* 22-43.

Duncan, M. C., & Messner, M. A. (2000). *Gender stereotyping in televised sports: 1989, 1993, and 1999.* Los Angeles: Amateur Athletic Foundation of Los Angeles.

Eastman, S. T., & Billings, A. C. (1999). Gender parity in the Olympics: Hyping women athletes, favoring men athletes. *Journal of Sport and Social Issues, 23,* 140-170.

Fasting, K. (1999). Women and sport. *Olympic Review, 26,* 43-45.

Fiala, S. E., Giuliano, T. A., Remlinger, N. M., & Braithwaite, L. C. (1999). Lending a helping hand: The effects of gender stereotypes and gender on likelihood of helping. *Journal of Applied Social Psychology, 29,* 2164-2176.

Fink, J. S. (1998). Female athletes and the media: Strides and stalemates. *Journal of Physical Education, Recreation, & Dance, 69,* 37–45.

Fisher, A., Genovese, P., Morris, K., & Morris, H. (1977). Perceptions of females in sport. In D. Landers & R. Christina (Eds.), *Psychology of motor behavior and sport* (pp. 96–118). Champaign, IL: Human Kinetics.

Fiske, S. T., & Taylor, S. E. (1991). *Social cognition* (2nd ed.). New York: McGraw-Hill.

Gerbner, G. (1972). Violence in television drama: Trends and symbolic functions. In G. A. Comstock and I. A. Rubinstein (Eds.), *Media content and control: Television and social behavior, Vol. 1,* (pp. 28–187). Washington, DC: U.S. Government Printing Office.

Gissendaner, C. H. (1994). African-American women and competitive sport, 1920-1960. In S. Birrell and C. L. Cole (Eds.), *Women, sport, and culture* (pp. 81–92). Champaign, IL: Human Kinetics.

Greendorfer, S. L. (1993). Gender role stereotypes and early childhood socialization. *Psychology of Women Quarterly, 18,* 85–104.

Hebl, M. R., & Heatherton, T. F. (1998). The stigma of obesity in women: The difference is Black and White. *Personality and Social Psychology Bulletin, 24* (4), 417–426.

Higgs, C. T., & Weiller, K. H. (1994). Gender bias and the 1992 Summer Olympic Games: An analysis

He's a Laker 23

of television coverage. *Journal of Sport and Social Issues, 3,* 234–246.

Hilliard, D. C. (1984). Media images of male and female professional athletes: An interpretive analysis of magazine articles. *Sociology of Sport Journal, 1,* 251–262.

Kane, M. J. (1996). Media coverage of the post Title IX female athlete. *Duke Journal of Gender Law & Policy, 3,* 95–127.

Kane, M. J., & Parks, J. B. (1992). The social construction of gender difference and hierarchy in sport journalism—Few new twists on very old themes. *Women in Sport and Physical Activity Journal, 1,* 49–83.

Knight, J. L., Giuliano, T. A., & Sanchez-Ross, M. G. (2001). Famous or infamous? The influence of celebrity status and race on perceptions of responsibility for rape. *Basic and Applied Social Psychology, 23,* 183–190.

Lewis, J. (1991). *The ideological octopus.* New York: Routledge.

Lumpkin, A., & Williams, L. D. (1991). An analysis of *Sports Illustrated* feature articles, 1954–1987. *Sociology of Sport Journal, 8,* 1–15.

Martin, B. A., & Martin, J. H. (1995). Compared perceived sex role orientations of the ideal male and female athlete to the ideal male and female person. *Journal of Sport Behavior, 18,* 286–301.

Martin, E. (1987). *The woman in the body.* Boston: Beacon Press.

He's a Laker   24

Messner, M. (1988). Sports and male domination: The female athlete as contested ideological terrain. *Sociology of Sport Journal, 5,* 197–211.

Metheny, E. (1965). Symbolic forms of movement: The feminine image in sports. In E. Metheny (Ed.), *Connotations of movement in sport and dance* (pp. 43–56). Dubuque, IA: Wm. C. Brown.

Michael, M. E., Gilroy, F. D., & Sherman, M. F. (1984). Athletic similarity and attitudes toward women as factors in the perceived physical attractiveness and liking of a female varsity athlete. *Perceptual and Motor Skills, 59,* 511–518.

Nixon, H. L., Maresca, P. J., & Silverman, M. A. (1979). Sex differences in college students' acceptance of females into sport. *Adolescence, 14,* 755–764.

Rosenthal, R., & Jacobson, L. F. (1968). *Pygmalion in the classroom: Teacher expectations and pupils' intellectual development.* New York: Holt, Rinehart & Winston.

Sabo, D., & Jansen, S. C. (1992). Images of men in sport media: The social reproduction of gender order. *Masculinity and the media.* Newbury Park, CA: Sage.

Sagas, M., Cunningham, G. B., Wigley, B. J., & Ashley, F. B. (2000). Internet coverage of university softball and baseball websites: The inequity continues. *Sociology of Sport Journal, 17* (2), 198–212.

He's a Laker  25

Salwen, M. B., & Wood, N. (1994). Depictions of
    female athletes on *Sports Illustrated* covers,
    1957–89. *Journal of Sport Behavior, 17*, 98–107.

Tuggle, C. A., & Owen, A. (1999). A descriptive
    analysis of NBC's coverage of the Centennial
    Olympics. *Journal of Sport and Social Issues,
    23* (2), 171–182.

Weiss, M. R., & Barber, H. (1995). Socialization
    influences of collegiate female athletes: A
    tale of two decades. *Sex Roles, 33*, 129–140.

*The Women's Sports Foundation Report: Sport and Teen
    Pregnancy.* (1998, May). East Meadow, NY: The
    Women's Sports Foundation.

Woodcock, A. T. (1995). Media coverage of boys' and
    girls' high school ice hockey in Minnesota.
    *Melpomene Journal, 14*, 27–29.

Wulf, S. (1997, August 4). The NBA's sister act: Pro
    hoops gets a new season and a new gender with
    the successful start-up of the WNBA. *Time*,
    41–43.

He's a Laker   26

*The Author Note is typed on a separate page.*

*The first paragraph provides the institutional affiliation of the author(s). The second paragraph indicates any changes in author affiliation. The final paragraph lists contact information. The Author Note is limited to four paragraphs.*

*Some journals and instructors may ask for the Author Note to be on the title page.*

Author Note

Jennifer L. Knight and Traci A. Giuliano, Department of Psychology, Southwestern University.

Jennifer L. Knight is now at the Department of Psychology, Rice University.

We are grateful to Dan Hilliard and Jacqueline Muir-Broaddus for their input in the design phase of the project and to Marie Helweg-Larsen for her helpful comments on an earlier draft of this manuscript. We also wish to thank three anonymous reviewers for their helpful insights and suggestions. A version of this article was presented at the 12th annual meeting of the American Psychological Society, Miami, 2000.

Correspondence concerning this paper should be addressed to Jennifer Knight, Department of Psychology, MS-25, Rice University, P.O. Box 1892, Houston, TX 77251-1892. E-mail: jknight@rice.edu or giuliant@southwestern.edu

He's a Laker    27

Footnote

*Footnotes, if used, are typed on a separate page.*

[1]These demographic and personality variables (e.g., athletic status, age, BSRI [Bem, 1974], and SRES [Beere et al., 1984]) were included to explore the potential moderating effects that they might have on the interactions and main effects. However, preliminary analyses revealed no significant pattern of results, and thus these variables are not discussed further.

He's a Laker    28

Figure Caption

*Figure 1.* Perceived attractiveness of the athlete as a function of athlete gender and focus of the article (attractiveness or athleticism).

*Begin the figure captions on a new page. All figure captions will go on this page.*

*The figure number is italicized. Only the first word of the figure caption is capitalized.*

*The figure caption page may not be necessary for student reports. Instead, the figure caption would appear on the figure page (as it would in the published paper).*

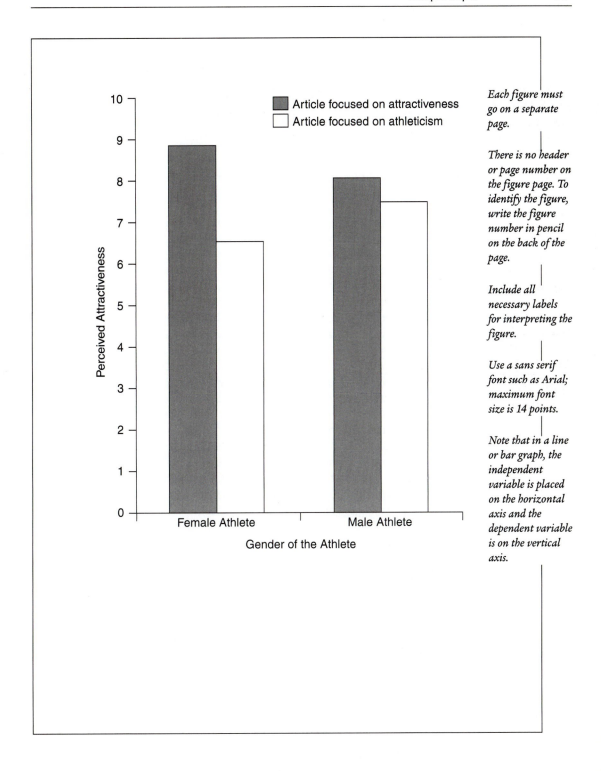

*Each figure must go on a separate page.*

*There is no header or page number on the figure page. To identify the figure, write the figure number in pencil on the back of the page.*

*Include all necessary labels for interpreting the figure.*

*Use a sans serif font such as Arial; maximum font size is 14 points.*

*Note that in a line or bar graph, the independent variable is placed on the horizontal axis and the dependent variable is on the vertical axis.*

# Appendix B
# Statistical Tests

The purpose of this appendix is to provide the formulas and calculational procedures for analysis of data. All possible statistical tests are not included, but a variety of tests are given that should be appropriate for many of the research designs you might use.

We will examine both descriptive and inferential statistics. Before you study the statistics, however, you should review the properties of measurement scales described in Chapter 5. Remember that there are four types of measurement scales: nominal, ordinal, interval, and ratio. Nominal scales have no numerical properties, ordinal scales provide rank-order information only, and interval and ratio scales have equal intervals between the points on the scale. In addition, ratio scales have a true zero point. You will also recall from Chapter 13 that the appropriate statistical analysis is determined by the type of design and by the measurement scale that was used in the study. As we proceed, the discussion of the various statistical tests will draw to your attention the relevant measurement scale restrictions that apply.

The examples here use small and simple data sets so the calculations can be easily done by hand using a calculator. However, you will find that the calculations become tedious and that you are more likely to make errors when working with large data sets and when you have to perform many statistical analyses in your study. Computer programs to perform statistical analyses have been developed to make the process easier and reduce calculation errors.

## DESCRIPTIVE STATISTICS

With a knowledge of the types of measurement scales, we can turn to a consideration of statistical techniques. We can start with two ways of describing a set of scores: central tendency and variability.

### Measures of Central Tendency

A measure of central tendency gives a single number that describes how an entire group scores as a whole, or on the average. Three different central tendency measures are available: the mode, the median, and the mean.

**The mode** The mode is the most frequently occurring score. Table B.1 shows a set of scores and the descriptive statistics that are discussed in this section. The most frequently occurring score in these data is 5: No calculations are necessary to find the mode. The mode can be used with any of the four types of measurement scales. However, it is the only measure of central tendency that can be used with nominal scale data. If you are measuring gender and find there are 100 females and 50 males, the mode is "female" because this is the most frequently occurring category on the nominal scale.

**The median** The median is the score that divides the group in half: 50% of the scores are below the median and 50% are above the median. When the scores have been ordered from lowest to highest (as in Table B.1), the median is easily found. If there are an odd number of scores, you simply find the middle score. (For example, if there are 11 scores, the sixth score is the median, because there are 5 lower and 5 higher scores.) If there are an even number of scores, the median is the midpoint between the two middle scores. In the data in Table B.1, there are 10 scores, so the fifth and sixth scores are the two middle scores. To find the median, we add the two middle scores and divide by 2. Thus, in Table B.1, the median is

$$\frac{5 + 5}{2} = 5$$

The median can be used with ordinal, interval, or ratio scale data. It is most likely to be used with ordinal data, however. This is because calculation of the median considers only the rank ordering of scores and not the actual size of the scores.

**TABLE B.1** Descriptive statistics for a set of scores

| Score | Descriptive statistic |
|---|---|
| 1 | Mode = 5 |
| 2 | |
| 4 | Median = 5 |
| 4 | |
| 5 | $\bar{X} = \dfrac{\Sigma X}{N} = 4.5$ |
| 5 | |
| 5 | |
| 6 | Range = 6 |
| 6 | |
| 7 | $s^2 = \dfrac{\Sigma(X - \bar{X})^2}{N - 1} = \dfrac{\Sigma X^2 - N\bar{X}^2}{N - 1} = \dfrac{233 - 202.5}{9} = 3.388$ |
| $\Sigma X = 45$ | |
| $\Sigma X^2 = 233$ | $s = \sqrt{s^2} = 1.84$ |
| $N = 10$ | |

**The mean**    The mean does take into account the actual size of the scores. Thus, the mean is based on more information about the scores than either the mode or the median. However, it is appropriate only for interval or ratio scale data.

     The mean is the sum of the scores in a group divided by the number of scores. The calculational formula for the mean can be expressed as

$$\overline{X} = \frac{\Sigma X}{N}$$

where $\overline{X}$ is the symbol for the mean. In this formula, $X$ represents a score obtained by an individual, and the $\Sigma$ symbol indicates that scores are to be summed or added. The symbol $\Sigma X$ can be read as "sum of the $X$s" and simply is an indication that the scores are to be added. Thus, $\Sigma X$ in the data from Table B.1 is

$$1 + 2 + 4 + 4 + 5 + 5 + 5 + 6 + 6 + 7 = 45$$

The $N$ in the formula symbolizes the number of scores in the group. In our example, $N = 10$. Thus, we can now calculate the mean:

$$\overline{X} = \frac{\Sigma X}{N} = \frac{45}{10} = 4.5$$

### Measures of Variability

In addition to describing the central tendency of the set of scores, we want to describe how much the scores vary among themselves. How much spread is there in the set of scores?

**The range**    The range is the highest score minus the lowest score. In our example, the range is 6. The range is not a very useful statistic, however, because it is based on only two scores in the distribution. It does not take into account all of the information that is available in the entire set of scores.

**The variance and standard deviation**    The variance, and a related statistic called the standard deviation, uses all the scores to yield a measure of variability. The variance indicates the degree to which scores vary about the group mean. The formula for the variance (symbolized as $s^2$) is

$$s^2 = \frac{\Sigma(X - \overline{X})^2}{N - 1}$$

where $(X - \overline{X})^2$ is an individual score, $X$, minus the mean, $\overline{X}$, and then squared. Thus $(X - \overline{X})^2$ is the squared deviation of each score from the mean. The $\Sigma$ sign indicates that these squared deviation scores are to be summed. Finally, dividing by $N - 1$ gives the mean of the squared deviations. The variance, then, is the mean of the squared deviations from the group mean. (Squared deviations are used because simple deviations would add up to zero. $N - 1$ is used in most cases for statistical purposes because the scores represent a sample and not an entire population. As the sample size becomes larger, it makes little difference whether $N$ or $N - 1$ is used.)

The data in Table B.1 can be used to illustrate calculation of the variance. $\Sigma(X - \overline{X})^2$ is equal to

$$(1 - 4.5)^2 + (2 - 4.5)^2 + (4 - 4.5)^2 + (4 - 4.5)^2 + (5 - 4.5)^2 + (5 - 4.5)^2 + (5 - 4.5)^2 + (6 - 4.5)^2 + (6 - 4.5)^2 + (7 - 4.5)^2 = 30.50$$

The next step is to divide $\Sigma(X - \overline{X})^2$ by $N - 1$. The calculation for the variance, then, is

$$s^2 = \frac{\Sigma(X - \overline{X})^2}{N - 1} = \frac{30.50}{9} = 3.388$$

A simpler calculational formula for the variance is

$$s^2 = \frac{\Sigma X^2 - N\overline{X}^2}{N - 1}$$

where $\Sigma X^2$ is the sum of the squared individual scores, and $\overline{X}^2$ is the mean squared. You can confirm that the two formulas are identical by computing the variance using this simpler formula. (Remember that $\Sigma X^2$ tells you to square each score and then sum the squared scores.) This simpler formula is much easier to work with when there are many scores, because each deviation does not have to be calculated.

The standard deviation is the square root of the variance. Because the variance uses squared scores, the variance does not describe the amount of variability in the same units of measurement as the original scale. The standard deviation ($s$) corrects this problem. Thus, the standard deviation is the average deviation of scores from the mean.

## STATISTICAL SIGNIFICANCE TESTS

This section describes several statistical significance tests. These tests are used to determine the probability that the outcome of the research was due to the operation of random error. All use the logic of the null hypothesis discussed in Chapter 13. We will consider two significance tests in this section: the chi-square test and the analysis of variance or $F$ test.

### Chi-Square ($\chi^2$)

The chi-square (Greek letter chi, squared) test is used when dealing with nominal scale data. It is used when the data consist of frequencies—the number of subjects who fall into each of several categories.

Chi-square can be used with either the experimental or the correlational method. It is used in conjunction with the experimental method when the dependent variable is measured on a nominal scale. It is used with the correlational method when both variables are measured on nominal scales.

**Example**    Suppose you want to know whether there is a relationship between gender and hand dominance. To do this, you sample 50 males and 50 females and ask whether they are right-handed, left-handed, or ambidextrous (use both hands with equal skill). Your data collection involves classifying each person as male or female and as right-handed, left-handed, or ambidextrous.

Fictitious data for such a study are presented in Table B.2. The frequencies labeled as "O" in each of the six cells in the table refer to the number of male and female subjects who fall into each of the three hand-dominance categories. The frequencies labeled "E" refer to frequencies that are expected if the null hypothesis is correct. It is important that each subject falls into only one of the cells when using chi-square (that is, no subject can be counted as both male and female or both right- and left-handed).

The chi-square test examines the extent to which the frequencies that are actually observed in the study differ from the frequencies that are expected if the null hypothesis is correct. The null hypothesis states that there is no relationship between sex and hand dominance: Males and females do not differ on this characteristic.

The formula for computing chi-square is

$$\chi^2 = \Sigma \frac{(O - E)^2}{E}$$

where O is the *observed* frequency in each cell, E is the *expected* frequency in each cell, and the symbol $\Sigma$ refers to summing over all cells. The steps in calculating the value of $\chi^2$ are:

*Step 1:* Arrange the observed frequencies in a table such as Table B.2. Note that in addition to the observed frequencies in each cell, the table presents row totals, column totals, and the total number of observations (*N*).

*Step 2:* Calculate the expected frequencies for each of the cells in the table. The expected frequency formula is

$$E = \frac{\text{row total} \times \text{column total}}{N}$$

where the row total refers to the row total for the cell, and the column total refers to the column total for the cell. Thus, the expected frequency for cell 1 (male right-handedness) is

$$E_1 = \frac{50 \times 50}{100} = 25$$

The expected frequencies for each of the cells are shown in Table B.2 below the observed frequencies.

TABLE B.2    Data for hypothetical study on hand dominance: Chi-square test

| Sex of subject | Hand dominance | | | Row totals |
| | Right | Left | Ambidextrous | |
|---|---|---|---|---|
| Male | $O_1 = 15$ | $O_2 = 30$ | $O_3 = 5$ | 50 |
| | $E_1 = 25$ | $E_2 = 20$ | $E_3 = 5$ | |
| Female | $O_4 = 35$ | $O_5 = 10$ | $O_6 = 5$ | 50 |
| | $E_4 = 25$ | $E_5 = 20$ | $E_6 = 5$ | |
| Column totals | 50 | 40 | 10 | $N = 100$ |

| Computations: | Cell number | $\dfrac{(O - E)^2}{E}$ | |
|---|---|---|---|
| | 1 | 4.00 | |
| | 2 | 5.00 | |
| | 3 | 0.00 | |
| | | | $\chi^2 = \Sigma \dfrac{(O - E)^2}{E}$ |
| | 4 | 4.00 | |
| | 5 | 5.00 | $= 18.00$ |
| | 6 | 0.00 | |
| | | $\Sigma = 18.00$ | |

*Step 3:* Calculate the quantity $(O - E)^2/E$ for each cell. For cell 1, this quantity is

$$\frac{(15 - 25)^2}{25} = \frac{100}{25} = 4.00$$

*Step 4:* Find the value of $\chi^2$ by summing the $(O - E)^2/E$ values found in step 3. The calculations for obtaining $\chi^2$ for the example data are shown in Table B.2.

**Significance of chi-square**    The significance of the obtained $\chi^2$ value can be evaluated by consulting a table of critical values of $\chi^2$. A table of critical $\chi^2$ values is presented as Table C.2 in Appendix C. The critical $\chi^2$ values indicate the value that the *obtained* $\chi^2$ must equal or exceed to be significant at the .10 level, the .05 level, and the .01 level.

To be able to use the table of critical values of $\chi^2$ as well as most other statistical tables, you must understand the concept of *degrees of freedom (df )*. The critical value of $\chi^2$ for any given study depends on the degrees of freedom. Degrees of freedom refers to the number of scores that are free to vary. In the table of categories for a chi-square test, the number of degrees of freedom is the number of cells in which the frequencies are free to vary once we know the row totals and column totals. The degrees of freedom for chi-square is easily calculated:

$$df = (R - 1)(C - 1)$$

where R is the number of rows in the table and C is the number of columns. In our example in Table B.1, there are two rows and three columns, so there are 2 degrees of freedom. In a study with three rows and three columns, there are 4 degrees of freedom, and so on.

To use Table C.2, find the correct degrees of freedom and then determine the critical value of $\chi^2$ necessary to reject the null hypothesis at the chosen significance level. With 2 degrees of freedom, the obtained $\chi^2$ value must be *equal to* or *greater than* the critical value of 5.991 to be significant at the .05 level. There is only a .05 probability that a $\chi^2$ of 5.991 would occur if only random error is operating. Because the obtained $\chi^2$ from our example is 18.00, we can reject the null hypothesis that there is no relationship between sex and hand dominance. (The chi-square was based on fictitious data, but it would be relatively easy for you to determine for yourself whether there is in fact a relationship.)

**Concluding remarks**   The chi-square test is extremely useful and is used frequently in all of the behavioral sciences. The calculational formula described is generalizable to expanded studies in which there are more categories on either of the variables. One note of caution, however: When both variables have only two categories, so that there are only two rows and two columns, the formula for calculating chi-square changes slightly. In such cases, the formula is

$$\chi^2 = \Sigma \frac{(|O - E|) - .5)^2}{E}$$

where $|O - E|$ is the absolute value of $O - E$, and .5 is a constant that is subtracted for each cell.

## Analysis of Variance (F *Test*)

The analysis of variance, or *F* test, is used to determine whether there is a significant difference between groups that have been measured on either interval or ratio scales. The groups may have been formed using either the experimental or the correlational method; the important thing is that at least an interval scale measure was used. The analysis of variance may be used with either independent groups or repeated measures designs. Procedures for calculating *F* for both types of designs are presented.

## Analysis of Variance: One Independent Variable

To illustrate the use of the analysis of variance, let's consider a hypothetical experiment on physical distance and self-disclosure. You think that people will reveal more about themselves to an interviewer when they are sitting close to the interviewer than they will when sitting farther away. To test this idea, you conduct an experiment on interviewing. Participants are told that interviewing techniques are being studied. Each participant is seated in a room; the interviewer comes into the room and sits at one of three distances from the participant: close (2 feet, or .61 meter), medium (4 feet, or 1.22 meters), or far (6 feet, or 1.83 meters). The distance chosen by the interviewer is the independent variable manipulation. Participants are randomly assigned to the three distance conditions, and the interviewer's behavior is constant in all conditions. The interview consists of a number of questions, and the dependent variable is the number of personal, revealing statements made by the participant during the interview.

Fictitious data for such an experiment are shown in Table B.3. Note that this is an independent groups design with five subjects in each group. The calculations of the systematic variance and error variance involve computing the *sum of squares* for the different types of variance.

**Sum of squares**   Sum of squares stands for the *sum of squared deviations from the mean*. Computing an analysis of variance for the data in Table B.3 involves three sums of squares: (1) $SS_{TOTAL}$, the sum of squared deviations of each individual score from the grand mean; (2) $SS_A$, the sum of squared deviations of each of the group means from the grand mean; and (3) $SS_{ERROR}$, the sum of squared deviations of the individual scores from their respective group means. The "$A$" in $SS_A$ is used to indicate that we are dealing with the systematic variance associated with independent variable $A$.

The three sums of squares are deviations from a mean. (Recall that we calculated such deviations earlier when discussing the variance in a set of scores.) We could calculate the deviations directly with the data in Table B.3, but such calculations are hard to work with, so we will use simplified formulas for computational purposes. The computational formulas are

$$SS_{TOTAL} = \Sigma X^2 - \frac{G^2}{N}$$

$$SS_A = \Sigma \frac{T_a^2}{n_a} - \frac{G^2}{N}$$

$$SS_{ERROR} = \Sigma X^2 - \Sigma \frac{T_a^2}{n_a}$$

You might note here that $SS_{TOTAL} = SS_A + SS_{ERROR}$. The actual computations are shown in Table B.3.

$SS_{TOTAL}$   The formula for $SS_{TOTAL}$ is

$$\Sigma X^2 - \frac{G^2}{N}$$

**TABLE B.3**   Data for hypothetical experiment on distance and self-disclosure: Analysis of variance

| | Distance (A) | |
|---|---|---|
| Close (A1) | Medium (A2) | Far (A3) |
| 33 | 21 | 20 |
| 24 | 25 | 13 |
| 31 | 19 | 15 |
| 29 | 27 | 10 |
| 34 | 26 | 14 |
| $T_{A1} = 151$ | $T_{A2} = 118$ | $T_{A3} = 72$ |
| $n_{A1} = 5$ | $n_{A2} = 5$ | $n_{A3} = 5$ |
| $X_{A1} = 30.20$ | $X_{A2} = 23.60$ | $X_{A3} = 14.40$ |
| $\Sigma X_{A1}^2 = 4623$ | $\Sigma X_{A2}^2 = 2832$ | $\Sigma X_{A3}^2 = 1090$ |
| $T_{A1}^2 = 22801$ | $T_{A2}^2 = 13924$ | $T_{A3}^2 = 5184$ |

$$SS_{TOTAL} = \Sigma X^2 - \frac{G^2}{N} = (4623 + 2832 + 1090) - \frac{(151 + 118 + 72)^2}{15}$$
$$= 8545 - 7752.07$$
$$= 792.93$$
$$SS_A = \Sigma \frac{T_a^2}{n_a} - \frac{G^2}{N} = \left[ \frac{(151)^2}{5} + \frac{(118)^2}{5} + \frac{(72)^2}{5} \right] - 7752.07$$
$$= 8381.80 - 7752.07$$
$$= 629.73$$
$$SS_{ERROR} = \Sigma X^2 = \Sigma \frac{T_a^2}{n_a} = 8545 - 8381.80$$
$$= 163.20$$

$\Sigma X^2$ is the sum of the squared scores of all subjects in the experiment. Each of the scores is squared first and then added. Thus, for the data in Table B.3, $\Sigma X^2$ is $33^2 + 24^2 + 31^2$ and so on until all of the scores have been squared and added. If you are doing the calculations by hand or with a pocket calculator, it may be convenient to find the $\Sigma X^2$ for the scores in each group and then add these up for your final computation. This is what I did for the data in the table. The G in the formula stands for the grand total of all of the scores. This involves adding up the scores for all subjects. The grand total is then squared and divided by N, the total number of subjects in the experiment. When computing the sum of squares, you should always keep the calculations clearly labeled, because you can simplify later calculations by referring to these earlier ones. Once you have computed $SS_{TOTAL}$, $SS_A$ can be calculated.

$SS_A$   The formula for $SS_A$ is

$$\Sigma \frac{T_a^2}{n_a} - \frac{G^2}{N}$$

The $T_a$ in this formula refers to the total of the scores in Group $a$ of independent variable $A$. ($T_a$ is a shorthand notation for $\Sigma X$ in each group. [Recall the computation of $\Sigma X$ from our discussion of the mean.] The $T_a$ symbol is used to avoid having to deal with too many $\Sigma$ signs in our calculation procedures.) The $a$ is used to symbolize the particular group number; thus, $T_a$ is a general symbol for $T_1$, $T_2$, and $T_3$. Looking at our data in Table B.3, $T_1 = 151$, $T_2 = 118$, and $T_3 = 72$. These are the sums of the scores in each of the groups. After $T_a$ has been calculated, $T_a^2$ is found by squaring $T_a$. Now, $T_a^2$ is divided by $n_a$, the number of subjects in Group $a$. Once the quantity $T_a^2/n_a$ has been computed for each group, the quantities are summed as indicated by the $\Sigma$ symbol.

Note that the second part of the formula, $G^2/N$, was calculated when $SS_{TOTAL}$ was obtained. Because we already have this quantity, it need not be calculated again when computing $SS_A$. After obtaining $SS_A$, we can now compute $SS_{ERROR}$.

$SS_{ERROR}$   The formula for $SS_{ERROR}$ is

$$\Sigma X^2 - \Sigma \frac{T_a^2}{n_a}$$

Both of these quantities were calculated above in obtaining $SS_{TOTAL}$ and $SS_A$. To obtain $SS_{ERROR}$, we merely have to find these quantities and perform the proper subtraction.

As a check on the calculations, we can make sure that $SS_{TOTAL} = SS_A + SS_{ERROR}$.

The next step in the computation of the analysis of variance is to find the *mean square* for each of the sums of squares. We can then find the value of $F$. The necessary computations are shown in an analysis of variance summary table in Table B.4. Constructing a summary table is the easiest way to complete the computations.

**Mean squares**   After obtaining the sum of squares, it is necessary to compute the mean squares. Mean square stands for the *mean of the sum of the squared deviations from the mean* or, more simply, the mean of the sum of squares. The mean square ($MS$) is the sum of squares divided by the degrees of freedom. The degrees of freedom are determined by the number of scores in the sum of squares that are free to vary. The mean squares are the variances that are used in computing the value of $F$.

From Table B.4, you can see that the mean squares that concern us are the mean square for $A$ (systematic variance) and the mean square for error (error variance). The formulas are

$$MS_A = SS_A / df_A$$

$$MS_{ERROR} = SS_{ERROR} / df_{ERROR}$$

where $df_A = a - 1$ (the number of groups minus one) and $df_{ERROR} = N - a$ (the total number of subjects minus the number of groups).

**Obtaining the F value**   The obtained $F$ is found by dividing $MS_A$ by $MS_{ERROR}$. If only random error is operating, the expected value of $F$ is 1.0. The greater the $F$ value, the lower the probability that the results of the experiment were due to chance error.

**Significance of F**   To determine the significance of the obtained $F$ value, it is necessary to compare the obtained $F$ to a critical value of $F$. Table C.4 in Appendix C shows critical values of $F$ for significance levels of .10, .05, and .01. To find the critical value of $F$, locate on the table the degrees of freedom for the numerator of the ratio (the systematic variance) and the degrees of freedom for the denominator of the $F$ ratio (the error variance). The intersection of these two degrees of freedom on the table is the critical $F$ value.

The appropriate degrees of freedom for our sample data are 2 and 12 (see Table B.4). The critical $F$ value from Table C.4 is 3.89 for a .05 level of significance. For the results to be significant, the obtained $F$ value must be equal to or greater than the critical value. Because the obtained value of $F$ in Table B.4 (23.15) is greater than the critical value, we conclude that the results are significant and reject the null hypothesis that the means of the groups are equal in the population.

**Concluding remarks**   The analysis of variance for one independent variable with an independent groups design can be used when there are two or more groups in the experiment. The general formulas described are appropriate for all such designs. Also, the calculations are the same whether the experimental or the correlational method is used to form the groups. The formulas are also applicable to cases in which the number of subjects in each group is not equal (although you should have approximately equal numbers of subjects in the groups).

When the design of the experiment includes more than two levels of the independent variable (as in our example experiment, which had three groups), the

**TABLE B.4**   Analysis of variance summary table

| Source of variance | Sum of squares | df | Mean square | F |
|---|---|---|---|---|
| A | $SS_A$ | $a - 1$ | $SS_A/df_A$ | $MS_A/MS_{ERROR}$ |
| Error | $SS_{ERROR}$ | $N - a$ | $SS_{ERROR}/df_{ERROR}$ | |
| Total | $SS_{TOTAL}$ | $N - 1$ | | |
| A | 629.73 | 2 | 314.87 | 23.15 |
| Error | 163.20 | 12 | 13.60 | |
| Total | 792.93 | 14 | | |

obtained $F$ value does not tell us whether any two specific groups are significantly different from one another. One way to examine the difference between two groups in such a study is to use the formula for $SS_A$ to compute the sum of squares and the mean square for the two groups (the $df$ in this case is 2 – 1). When doing this, the previously calculated $MS_{ERROR}$ should be used as the error variance term for computing $F$. More complicated procedures for evaluating the difference between two groups in such designs are available, but these are beyond the scope of this book.

## Analysis of Variance: Two Independent Variables

In this section, we will describe the computations for analysis of variance with a factorial design containing two independent variables. The formulas apply to an $A \times B$ factorial design with any number of levels of the independent variables. The formulas apply only to a completely independent groups design with different subjects in each group, and the number of subjects in each group must be equal. Once you understand this analysis, however, you should have little trouble understanding the analysis for more complicated designs with repeated measures or unequal numbers of subjects. With these limitations in mind, let's consider example data from a hypothetical experiment.

The experiment uses a $2 \times 2$ IV $\times$ PV factorial design. Variable $A$ is the type of instruction used in a course, and variable $B$ is the intelligence level of the students. The students are classified as of either "low" or "high" intelligence on the basis of intelligence test scores and are randomly assigned to one of two types of classes. One class uses the traditional lecture method; the other class uses an individualized learning approach with frequent testing over small amounts of material, proctors to help individual students, and a stipulation that students master each section of material before going on to the next section. The information presented to students in the two classes is identical. At the end of the course, all students take the same test, which covers all of the material presented in the course. The score on this examination is the dependent variable.

Table B.5 shows fictitious data for such an experiment, with five subjects in each condition. This design allows us to evaluate three effects—the main effect of $A$, the main effect of $B$, and the $A \times B$ interaction. The main effect of $A$ is whether one type of instruction is superior to the other; the main effect of $B$ is whether high-intelligence students score differently on the test than do low-intelligence students; the $A \times B$ interaction examines whether the effect of one independent variable is different depending on the particular level of the other variable.

The computation of the analysis of variance starts with calculation of the sum of squares for the following sources of variance in the data: $SS_{TOTAL}$, $SS_A$, $SS_B$, $SS_{A \times B}$, and $SS_{ERROR}$. The procedures for calculation are similar to the calculations performed for the analysis of variance with one independent variable. The numerical calculations for the example data are shown in Table B.6. We can now consider each of these calculations.

$SS_{TOTAL}$    The $SS_{TOTAL}$ is computed in the same way as the previous analysis formula. The formula is

$$SS_{TOTAL} = \Sigma X^2 - \frac{G^2}{N}$$

where $\Sigma X^2$ is the sum of the squared scores of all subjects in the experiment, $G$ is the grand total of all of the scores, and $N$ is the total number of subjects. It is usually easiest to calculate $\Sigma X^2$ and $G$ in smaller steps by calculating subtotals separately for each group in the design. The subtotals are then added. This is the procedure followed in Tables B.5 and B.6.

**TABLE B.5**    Data for hypothetical experiment on the effect of type of instruction and intelligence level on exam score: Analysis of variance

| | Intelligence ($B$) | | |
| --- | --- | --- | --- |
| | Low ($B1$) | High ($B2$) | |
| Traditional lecture ($A1$) | 75 | 90 | |
| | 70 | 95 | |
| | 69 | 89 | |
| | 72 | 85 | |
| | 68 | 91 | |
| | $T_{A1B1} = 354$ | $T_{A1B2} = 450$ | $T_{A1} = 804$ |
| | $\Sigma X^2_{A1B1} = 25094$ | $\Sigma X^2_{A1B2} = 40552$ | $n_{A1} = 10$ |
| | $n_{A1B1} = 5$ | $n_{A1B2} = 5$ | $\overline{X}_{A1} = 80.40$ |
| | $\overline{X}_{A1B1} = 70.80$ | $\overline{X}_{A1B2} = 90.00$ | |
| Individualized method ($A2$) | 85 | 87 | |
| | 87 | 94 | |
| | 83 | 93 | |
| | 90 | 89 | |
| | 89 | 92 | |
| | $T_{A2B1} = 434$ | $T_{A2B2} = 455$ | $T_{A2} = 889$ |
| | $\Sigma X^2_{A2B1} = 37704$ | $\Sigma X^2_{A2B2} = 41439$ | $n_{A2} = 10$ |
| | $n_{A2B1} = 5$ | $n_{A2B2} = 5$ | $\overline{X}_{A2} = 88.90$ |
| | $\overline{X}_{A2B1} = 86.80$ | $\overline{X}_{A2B2} = 91.00$ | |
| | $T_{B1} = 788$ | $T_{B2} = 905$ | |
| | $n_{B1} = 10$ | $n_{B2} = 10$ | |
| | $\overline{X}_{B1} = 78.80$ | $\overline{X}_{B2} = 90.50$ | |

$SS_A$     The formula for $SS_A$ is

$$SS_A = \frac{\Sigma T_a^2}{n_a} - \frac{G^2}{N}$$

where $\Sigma T_a^2$ is the sum of the squared totals of the scores in each of the groups of independent variable $A$, and $n_a$ is the number of subjects in each level of independent variable $A$. When calculating $SS_A$, we consider only the groups of independent variable $A$ without considering the particular level of $B$. In other words, the totals for each group of the $A$ variable are obtained by considering all subjects in that level of $A$, irrespective of which condition of $B$ the subject may be in. The quantity of $G^2/N$ was previously calculated for $SS_{TOTAL}$.

$SS_B$     The formula for $SS_B$ is

$$SS_B = \frac{\Sigma T_b^2}{n_b} - \frac{G^2}{N}$$

$SS_B$ is calculated in the same way as $SS_A$. The only difference is that we are calculating totals of the groups of independent variable $B$.

$SS_{A \times B}$     The formula for $SS_{A \times B}$ is

$$SS_{A \times B} = \frac{\Sigma T_{ab}^2}{n_{ab}} - \frac{G^2}{N} - SS_A - SS_B$$

The sum of squares for the A × B interaction is computed by first calculating the quantity $\Sigma T_{ab}^2$. This involves squaring the total of the scores in each of the ab conditions in the experiment. In our example experiment in Table B.5, there are four conditions; the interaction calculation considers *all* of the groups. Each of the group totals is squared, and then the sum of the squared totals is obtained. This sum is divided by $n_{ab}$, the number of subjects in each group. The other quantities in the formula for $SS_{A \times B}$ have already been calculated, so the computation of $SS_{A \times B}$ is relatively straightforward.

$SS_{ERROR}$     The quantities involved in the $SS_{ERROR}$ formula have already been calculated. The formula is

$$SS_{ERROR} = \Sigma X^2 - \frac{\Sigma T_{ab}^2}{n_{ab}}$$

These quantities were calculated previously, so we merely have to perform the proper subtraction to complete the computation of $SS_{ERROR}$.

At this point, you may want to practice calculating the sums of squares using the data in Table B.5. As a check on the calculations, make sure that $SS_{TOTAL} = SS_A + SS_B + SS_{A \times B} + SS_{ERROR}$.

**TABLE B.6** Computations for analysis of variance with two independent variables

$$SS_{TOTAL} = \Sigma X^2 - \frac{G^2}{N}$$

$$= (25094 + 40552 + 37704 + 41439)$$

$$- \frac{(354 + 450 + 434 + 455)^2}{20}$$

$$= 144789 - 143312.45$$

$$= 1476.55$$

$$SS_A = \frac{\Sigma T_a^2}{n_a} - \frac{G^2}{N}$$

$$= \frac{(804)^2 + (889)^2}{10} - 143312.45$$

$$= 143673.70 - 143312.45$$

$$= 361.25$$

$$SS_B = \frac{\Sigma T_b^2}{n_b} - \frac{G^2}{N}$$

$$= \frac{(788)^2 + (905)^2}{10} - 143312.45$$

$$= 143996.90 - 143312.45$$

$$= 684.45$$

$$SS_{A \times B} = \frac{\Sigma T_{ab}^2}{n_{ab}} - \frac{G^2}{N} - SS_A - SS_B$$

$$= \frac{(354)^2 + (450)^2 + (434)^2 + (455)^2}{5}$$

$$- 143312.45 - 361.25 - 684.45$$

$$= 144639.40 - 143312.45 - 361.25 - 684.45$$

$$= 281.25$$

$$SS_{ERROR} = \Sigma X^2 - \frac{\Sigma T_{ab}^2}{n_{ab}}$$

$$= 144789 - 144639.40$$

$$= 149.60$$

After obtaining the sums of squares, the next step is to find the mean square for each of the sources of variance. The easiest way to do this is to use an analysis of variance summary table like Table B.7.

**Mean square**    The mean square for each of the sources of variance is the sum of squares divided by the degrees of freedom. The formulas for the degrees of freedom and the mean square are shown in the top portion of Table B.7, and the computed values are shown in the bottom portion of the table.

**Obtaining the F value**    The F value for each of the three sources of systematic variance (main effects for A and B, and the interaction) is obtained by dividing the appropriate mean square by the $MS_{ERROR}$. We now have three obtained F values and can evaluate the significance of the main effects and the interaction.

**Significance of F**    To determine whether an obtained F is significant, we need to find the critical value of F from Table C.4 in Appendix C. For all of the Fs in

TABLE B.7    Analysis of variance summary table: Two independent variables

| Source of variance | Sum of squares | df | Mean square | F |
|---|---|---|---|---|
| A | $SS_A$ | $a - 1$ | $SS_A/df_A$ | $MS_A/MS_{ERROR}$ |
| B | $SS_B$ | $B - 1$ | $SS_B/df_B$ | $MS_B/MS_{ERROR}$ |
| $A \times B$ | $SS_{A \times B}$ | $(a - 1)(b - 1)$ | $SS_{A \times B}/df_{A \times B}$ | $MS_{A \times B}/MS_{ERROR}$ |
| Error | $SS_{ERROR}$ | $N - ab$ | $SS_{ERROR}/df_{ERROR}$ | |
| Total | $SS_{TOTAL}$ | | | |
| A | 361.25 | 1 | 361.25 | 38.64 |
| B | 684.45 | 1 | 684.45 | 73.20 |
| $A \times B$ | 281.25 | 1 | 281.25 | 30.08 |
| Error | 149.60 | 16 | 9.35 | |
| Total | 1476.55 | 19 | | |

the analysis of variance summary table, the degrees of freedom are 1 and 16. Let's assume that a .01 significance level for rejecting the null hypothesis was chosen. The critical F at .01 for 1 and 16 degrees of freedom is 8.53. If the obtained F is larger than 8.53, we can say that the results are significant at the .01 level. By referring to the obtained Fs in Table B.7, you can see that the main effects and the interaction are all significant. I will leave it to you to interpret the main effect means and to graph the interaction. If you do not recall how to do this, you should review the material in Chapter 10.

## Analysis of Variance: Repeated Measures and Matched Subjects

The analysis of variance computations considered thus far have been limited to independent groups designs. This section considers the computations for analysis of variance of a repeated measures or a matched random assignment design with one independent variable.

Fictitious data for a hypothetical experiment using a repeated measures design are presented in Table B.8. The experiment examines the effect of a job candidate's physical attractiveness on judgments of the candidate's competence. The independent variable is the candidate's physical attractiveness; the dependent variable is judged competence on a 10-point scale. Participants in the experiment view two videotapes of different females performing a mechanical aptitude task that involved piecing together a number of parts. Both females do equally well, but one is physically attractive and the other is unattractive. The order of presentation of the two tapes is counterbalanced to control for order effects.

The main difference between the repeated measures analysis of variance and the independent groups analysis described earlier is that the effect of subject differences becomes a source of variance. There are four sources of variance in

**TABLE B.8**   Data for hypothetical experiment on attractiveness and judged competence: Repeated measures analysis of variance

| Subjects (or subject pairs) | Condition (A) | | $T_s$ | $T_s^2$ |
|---|---|---|---|---|
| | Unattractive candidate (A1) | Attractive candidate (A2) | | |
| #1 | 6 | 8 | 14 | 196 |
| #2 | 5 | 6 | 11 | 121 |
| #3 | 5 | 9 | 14 | 196 |
| #4 | 7 | 6 | 13 | 169 |
| #5 | 4 | 6 | 10 | 100 |
| #6 | 3 | 5 | 8 | 64 |
| #7 | 5 | 5 | 10 | 100 |
| #8 | 4 | 7 | 11 | 121 |
| | $T_{A1} = 39$ | $T_{A2} = 52$ | $\Sigma T_s^2 = 1067$ | |
| | $\Sigma X_{A1}^2 = 201$ | $\Sigma X_{A2}^2 = 352$ | | |
| | $n_{A1} = 8$ | $n_{A2} = 8$ | | |
| | $\overline{X}_{A1} = 4.88$ | $\overline{X}_{A2} = 6.50$ | | |

$$SS_{TOTAL} = \Sigma X^2 - \frac{G^2}{N} = (201 + 352) - \frac{(39 + 52)^2}{16}$$

$$= 553 - 517.56$$

$$= 35.44$$

$$SS_A = \frac{\Sigma T_a^2}{n_a} - \frac{G^2}{N} = \frac{(39)^2 + (52)^2}{8} - 517.56$$

$$= 528.13 - 517.56$$

$$= 10.57$$

$$SS_{SUBJECTS} = \frac{\Sigma T_s^2}{n_s} - \frac{G^2}{N} = \frac{1067}{2} - 517.56$$

$$= 533.50 - 517.56$$

$$= 15.94$$

$$SS_{ERROR} = SS_{TOTAL} - SS_A - SS_{SUBJECTS} = 35.44 - 10.57 - 15.94$$

$$= 8.93$$

the repeated measures analysis of variance, and so four sums of squares are calculated:

$$SS_{TOTAL} = \Sigma X^2 - \frac{G^2}{N}$$

$$SS_A = \frac{\Sigma T_a^2}{n_a} - \frac{G^2}{N}$$

$$SS_{SUBJECTS} = \frac{\Sigma T_s^2}{n_s} - \frac{G^2}{N}$$

$$SS_{ERROR} = SS_{TOTAL} - SS_A - SS_{SUBJECTS}$$

The calculations for these sums of squares are shown in the lower portion of Table B.8. The quantities in the formula should be familiar to you by now. The only new quantity involves the calculation of $SS_{SUBJECTS}$. The term $T_s^2$ refers to the squared total score of each subject—that is, the squared total of the scores that each subject gives when measured in the different groups in the experiment. The quantity $\Sigma T_s^2$ refers to the sum of these squared totals for all subjects. The calculation of $SS_{SUBJECTS}$ is completed by dividing $\Sigma T_s^2$ by $n_s$ and then subtracting by $G^2/N$. The term $n_s$ refers to the number of scores that each subject gives. Because our hypothetical experiment has two groups, $n_s = 2$, the total for each subject is based on two scores.

An analysis of variance summary table is shown in Table B.9. The procedures for computing the mean squares and obtaining $F$ are similar to our previous calculations. Note that the mean square and $F$ for the subjects' source of variance are not computed. There is usually no reason to know or care whether subjects differ significantly from one another. The ability to calculate this source of variance does have the advantage of reducing the amount of error variance—in an independent groups design, subject differences are part of the error variance. Because there is only one score per subject in the independent groups design, it is impossible to estimate the influence of subject differences.

You can use the summary table and the table of critical $F$ values to determine whether the difference between the two groups is significant. The procedures are identical to those discussed previously.

### Analysis of Variance: Conclusion

The analysis of variance is a very useful test that can be extended to any type of factorial design, including those that use both independent groups and repeated measures in the same design. The method of computing analysis of variance is much the same regardless of the complexity of the design. A section on analysis of variance as brief as this cannot hope to cover all of the many aspects of such a general statistical technique. However, you should now have the background to compute an analysis of variance and to understand the more detailed discussions of analysis of variance in advanced statistics texts.

**TABLE B.9**    Analysis of variance summary table: Repeated measures design

| Source of variance | Sum of squares | df | Mean square | F |
|---|---|---|---|---|
| A | $SS_A$ | $a - 1$ | $SS_A/df_A$ | $MS_A/MS_{ERROR}$ |
| Subjects | $SS_{SUBJECTS}$ | $s - 1$ | — | |
| Error | $SS_{ERROR}$ | $(a - 1)(s - 1)$ | $SS_{ERROR}/df_{ERROR}$ | |
| Total | $SS_{TOTAL}$ | $N - 1$ | | |
| A | 10.57 | 1 | 10.57 | 8.26 |
| Subjects | 15.94 | 7 | — | |
| Error | 8.93 | 7 | 1.28 | |
| Total | 35.44 | 15 | | |

## CORRELATION AND EFFECT SIZE

Finally, we will examine calculations for measures of correlation and effect size; these are indicators of the strength of association between variables. These are very important measures because they provide a common metric number that can be used in all types of studies. These numbers range from 0.00, indicating no relationship, to 1.00; correlations above .50 are considered to be indicative of very strong relationships. In much research, expect correlations between about .25 and .50. Correlations between about .10 and .25 are weaker, but correlations of this size can be statistically significant with large sample sizes; they can also be important for theoretical and even practical reasons.

### Effect Size for the Chi-Square Statistic

The chi-square ($\chi^2$) test was described previously. In addition to determining whether there is a significant relationship, you want an indicator of effect size to tell you the strength of association between the variables. This is obtained by calculating a phi coefficient, symbolized as $\phi$. Phi is computed after obtaining the value of chi-square. The formula is

$$\phi = \sqrt{\frac{x^2}{N}}$$

Thus, the value of $\phi$ for the sex and hand-dominance study analyzed previously (see Table B.2) is

$$\phi = \sqrt{\frac{18.00}{100}} = \sqrt{.18} = .42$$

Because the significance of the chi-square value has already been determined, no further significance testing is necessary. Note: A related statistic called Cramer's V is used with larger tables.

## Effect Size for the F Statistic

After computing an analysis of variance and evaluating the significance of the $F$ statistic, you need to examine effect size. *Eta* is a type of correlation coefficient that can be easily calculated. The formula is

$$\text{eta} = \sqrt{\frac{\text{between group (systematic) variance}}{\text{total variance}}}$$

In the experiment on interpersonal distance and disclosure previously described, the $SS_A$ was 629.73, and the $SS_{TOTAL}$ was 792.93. The value of eta then would be

$$\text{eta} = \sqrt{\frac{629.73}{792.93}}$$

$$= .89$$

This is a very high correlation, reflecting the fact that the data were all manufactured for ease of computation.

## Pearson Product-Moment Correlation Coefficient

The Pearson product–moment correlation coefficient ($r$) is used to find the strength of the relationship between two variables that have been measured on interval or ratio scales.

**Example**   Suppose you want to know whether travel experiences are related to knowledge of geography. In your study, you give a 15-item quiz on North American geography, and you also ask how many states and Canadian provinces participants have visited. After obtaining the pairs of observations from each participant, a Pearson $r$ can be computed to measure the strength of the relationship between travel experience and knowledge of geography.

Table B.10 presents fictitious data from such a study along with the calculations for $r$. The calculational formula for $r$ is

$$r = \frac{N\Sigma XY - \Sigma X/\Sigma Y}{\sqrt{N\Sigma X^2 - (\Sigma X)^2}\ \sqrt{N\Sigma Y^2 - (\Sigma Y)^2}}$$

where $X$ refers to a subject's score on variable $X$, and $Y$ is a subject's score on variable $Y$. In Table B.10, the travel experience score is variable $X$, and the geography knowledge score is variable $Y$. In the formula, $N$ is the number of paired observations (that is, the number of participants measured on both variables).

**TABLE B.10**    Data for hypothetical study on travel and knowledge of geography: Pearson $r$

| Subject identification number | Travel score ($X$) | Knowledge score ($Y$) | $XY$ |
|:---:|:---:|:---:|:---:|
| 01 | 4 | 10 | 40 |
| 02 | 6 | 15 | 90 |
| 03 | 7 | 8 | 56 |
| 04 | 8 | 9 | 72 |
| 05 | 8 | 7 | 56 |
| 06 | 12 | 10 | 120 |
| 07 | 14 | 15 | 210 |
| 08 | 15 | 13 | 195 |
| 09 | 15 | 15 | 225 |
| 10 | 17 | 14 | 238 |

$$\Sigma X = 106 \qquad \Sigma Y = 116 \qquad \Sigma XY = 1302$$
$$\Sigma X^2 = 1308 \qquad \Sigma Y^2 = 1434$$
$$(\Sigma X)^2 = 11236 \qquad (\Sigma Y)^2 = 13456$$

Computation:

$$r = \frac{N\Sigma XY - \Sigma X \Sigma Y}{\sqrt{N\Sigma X^2 - (\Sigma X)^2}\ \sqrt{N\Sigma Y^2 - (\Sigma Y)^2}}$$

$$= \frac{10(1302) - (106)(116)}{\sqrt{10(1308) - 11236}\ \sqrt{10(1434) - 13456}}$$

$$= \frac{13020 - 12296}{\sqrt{13080 - 11236}\ \sqrt{14340 - 13456}}$$

$$= \frac{724}{\sqrt{1844}\ \sqrt{884}}$$

$$= \frac{724}{1276.61}$$

$$= .567$$

The calculation of $r$ requires a number of arithmetic operations on the $X$ and $Y$ scores. $\Sigma X$ is simply the sum of the scores on variable $X$. $\Sigma X^2$ is the sum of the squared scores on $X$ (each score is first squared and then the sum of the squared scores is obtained). The quantity $(\Sigma X)^2$ is the square of the sum of the scores: The total of the $X$ scores ($\Sigma X$) is first calculated and then this total is squared. It is important not to confuse the two quantities, $\Sigma X^2$ and $(\Sigma X)^2$. The same calculations are made, using the $Y$ scores, to obtain $\Sigma Y$, $\Sigma Y^2$, and $(\Sigma Y)^2$. To find $\Sigma XY$, each participant's $X$ score is multiplied by the score on $Y$; these values are then summed for all subjects. When these calculations have been made, $r$ is computed using the formula for $r$ given above.

At this point, you may wish to examine carefully the calculations shown in Table B.10 to familiarize yourself with the procedures for computing $r$. You might then try calculating $r$ from another set of data, such as the seating pattern and exam score study shown in Table 12.2.

**Significance of $r$**  To test the null hypothesis that the population correlation coefficient is in fact 0.00, we consult a table of critical values of $r$. Table C.5 in Appendix C shows critical values of $r$ for .10, .05, and .01 levels of significance. To find the critical value, you first need to determine the degrees of freedom. The $df$ for the significance test for $r$ is $N - 2$. In our example study on travel and knowledge, the number of paired observations is 10, so the $df = 8$. For 8 degrees of freedom, the critical value of $r$ at the .05 level of significance is .632 (plus or minus). The obtained $r$ must be greater than the critical $r$ to be significant. Because our obtained $r$ (from Table B.10) of .567 is less than the critical value, we do not reject the null hypothesis.

Notice that we do not reject the null hypothesis in this case, even though the magnitude of $r$ is fairly large. Recall the discussion of nonsignificant results from Chapter 13. It is possible that you would obtain a significant correlation if you used a larger sample size or more sensitive and reliable measures of the variables.

# Appendix C
# Statistical Tables

## RANDOM NUMBER TABLE

The random numbers between 0 and 99 in Table C.1 can be used to randomly assign participants to conditions in an experiment or randomly select individuals from a population. To obtain a series of random numbers, enter the table at any arbitrary point and read in sequence either across or down.

For random assignment, first order the participants in some way. For example, suppose that 15 individuals will be participating in your experiment. You could simply arrange them in order from the first to the last individual, as shown in the following table. You can now use the random number table to assign them to conditions in the experiment. Suppose that you need to assign these 15 individuals to three groups. Enter the random number table and assign a number to each of the 15 participants. (If there is a duplicate number, ignore it and use the next number in the sequence.) In the example here, the table was entered in the upper left-hand corner and was read downward. Now assign the participants to the three groups: The five with the lowest random numbers are assigned to Group 1, the next five are assigned to Group 2, and the five with the highest numbers are assigned to Group 3. These general procedures can be followed with any number of groups in an experiment.

To use the random number table for random sampling, first make a list of all members of your population. Enter the random number table and assign a number to each member of the population. Determine your desired sample size ($N$). Your sample then will be composed of the first $N$ individuals. For example, if you want to take a random sample of 25 faculty members at your school, use the random number table to give each faculty member a number. The 15 faculty members with the lowest numbers would be selected for the sample.

You now have computer-based alternatives to random number tables such as Table C.1. Spreadsheet programs such as Excel have a function for producing random numbers, and there is a useful Web site for random assignment and selection at http://www.randomizer.org.

| Participant order | Random number | Group assignment |
|---|---|---|
| 1 | 56 | 2 |
| 2 | 57 | 2 |
| 3 | 51 | 2 |
| 4 | 10 | 1 |
| 5 | 69 | 2 |
| 6 | 9 | 1 |
| 7 | 75 | 3 |
| 8 | 5 | 1 |
| 9 | 78 | 3 |
| 10 | 90 | 3 |
| 11 | 79 | 3 |
| 12 | 4 | 1 |
| 13 | 79 | 3 |
| 14 | 48 | 1 |
| 15 | 57 | 2 |

## TABLE C.1    Random number table

| | | | | | | | | | | | | | | | | | | | | | | |
|---|---|---|---|---|---|---|---|---|---|---|---|---|---|---|---|---|---|---|---|---|---|---|
| 56 | 54 | 77 | 81 | 67 | 11 | 27 | 56 | 76 | 67 | 16 | 71 | 93 | 68 | 33 | 31 | 90 | 67 | 52 | 32 | 81 | 64 | 3 |
| 57 | 63 | 49 | 93 | 11 | 26 | 57 | 88 | 94 | 65 | 80 | 23 | 82 | 16 | 58 | 86 | 90 | 70 | 54 | 71 | 13 | 50 | 60 |
| 51 | 1 | 35 | 56 | 36 | 28 | 18 | 97 | 49 | 47 | 80 | 43 | 56 | 73 | 22 | 69 | 58 | 37 | 55 | 52 | 56 | 69 | 34 |
| 10 | 34 | 73 | 74 | 9 | 24 | 14 | 31 | 97 | 62 | 15 | 80 | 51 | 49 | 64 | 48 | 61 | 9 | 14 | 29 | 81 | 65 | 16 |
| 69 | 59 | 39 | 53 | 82 | 97 | 70 | 98 | 90 | 22 | 12 | 22 | 13 | 87 | 10 | 69 | 61 | 11 | 27 | 60 | 50 | 42 | 96 |
| 9 | 94 | 34 | 81 | 9 | 79 | 41 | 30 | 35 | 27 | 54 | 82 | 49 | 95 | 79 | 3 | 26 | 2 | 10 | 12 | 93 | 15 | 12 |
| 75 | 9 | 76 | 33 | 71 | 87 | 5 | 39 | 13 | 98 | 68 | 43 | 32 | 46 | 52 | 75 | 27 | 71 | 66 | 62 | 37 | 70 | 14 |
| 5 | 54 | 84 | 29 | 60 | 75 | 35 | 6 | 31 | 82 | 39 | 31 | 98 | 45 | 97 | 73 | 56 | 3 | 39 | 48 | 36 | 49 | 4 |
| 78 | 23 | 95 | 76 | 61 | 61 | 12 | 52 | 68 | 57 | 72 | 64 | 65 | 12 | 88 | 42 | 8 | 29 | 58 | 56 | 10 | 32 | 32 |
| 90 | 18 | 61 | 31 | 11 | 45 | 44 | 6 | 15 | 90 | 74 | 69 | 72 | 38 | 94 | 35 | 75 | 27 | 75 | 76 | 25 | 91 | 33 |
| | | | | | | | | | | | | | | | | | | | | | | |
| 79 | 70 | 44 | 70 | 2 | 61 | 6 | 4 | 49 | 96 | 17 | 37 | 3 | 78 | 63 | 82 | 57 | 50 | 24 | 55 | 43 | 53 | 84 |
| 4 | 53 | 53 | 85 | 61 | 99 | 99 | 0 | 34 | 17 | 24 | 65 | 59 | 66 | 75 | 80 | 16 | 95 | 96 | 25 | 61 | 36 | 2 |
| 79 | 50 | 9 | 86 | 37 | 60 | 76 | 80 | 13 | 80 | 78 | 16 | 46 | 87 | 56 | 6 | 71 | 17 | 96 | 58 | 63 | 80 | 43 |
| 48 | 13 | 20 | 30 | 35 | 34 | 99 | 51 | 32 | 90 | 6 | 8 | 56 | 61 | 12 | 94 | 86 | 6 | 51 | 89 | 53 | 26 | 13 |
| 57 | 66 | 6 | 29 | 10 | 3 | 33 | 73 | 0 | 69 | 19 | 95 | 35 | 2 | 52 | 88 | 31 | 49 | 40 | 53 | 90 | 46 | 10 |
| 82 | 47 | 37 | 12 | 59 | 51 | 55 | 24 | 35 | 83 | 27 | 34 | 53 | 50 | 87 | 15 | 2 | 20 | 31 | 65 | 15 | 91 | 7 |
| 64 | 38 | 48 | 70 | 7 | 46 | 86 | 42 | 24 | 34 | 68 | 58 | 84 | 54 | 41 | 13 | 23 | 38 | 69 | 29 | 22 | 5 | 27 |
| 98 | 19 | 18 | 8 | 57 | 56 | 76 | 69 | 92 | 64 | 69 | 11 | 79 | 93 | 98 | 3 | 70 | 76 | 6 | 72 | 70 | 83 | 28 |
| 4 | 53 | 16 | 78 | 53 | 54 | 31 | 33 | 2 | 64 | 29 | 24 | 25 | 48 | 30 | 82 | 24 | 25 | 81 | 25 | 22 | 43 | 3 |
| 51 | 12 | 24 | 74 | 1 | 35 | 67 | 55 | 45 | 43 | 88 | 54 | 52 | 90 | 18 | 73 | 92 | 8 | 25 | 0 | 59 | 34 | 75 |
| | | | | | | | | | | | | | | | | | | | | | | |
| 31 | 33 | 22 | 54 | 64 | 88 | 52 | 70 | 43 | 44 | 84 | 43 | 42 | 6 | 57 | 34 | 25 | 34 | 90 | 95 | 54 | 25 | 18 |
| 13 | 73 | 99 | 45 | 24 | 5 | 54 | 90 | 55 | 99 | 24 | 67 | 50 | 58 | 52 | 33 | 36 | 84 | 9 | 92 | 79 | 77 | 5 |
| 73 | 12 | 17 | 38 | 11 | 41 | 25 | 86 | 12 | 85 | 24 | 18 | 3 | 27 | 80 | 54 | 59 | 92 | 51 | 71 | 34 | 58 | 65 |
| 10 | 80 | 53 | 35 | 0 | 10 | 52 | 55 | 19 | 94 | 20 | 43 | 63 | 48 | 44 | 2 | 70 | 26 | 94 | 28 | 92 | 38 | 86 |
| 12 | 5 | 47 | 41 | 45 | 77 | 99 | 91 | 87 | 9 | 34 | 67 | 63 | 61 | 22 | 63 | 37 | 17 | 87 | 89 | 80 | 27 | 24 |
| 34 | 64 | 18 | 70 | 39 | 71 | 85 | 67 | 11 | 70 | 55 | 33 | 21 | 72 | 84 | 92 | 43 | 99 | 6 | 14 | 77 | 36 | 54 |
| 40 | 7 | 10 | 35 | 99 | 37 | 94 | 70 | 17 | 75 | 34 | 82 | 27 | 47 | 62 | 2 | 61 | 69 | 99 | 57 | 50 | 34 | 36 |
| 24 | 46 | 26 | 12 | 98 | 54 | 6 | 83 | 73 | 11 | 69 | 11 | 30 | 90 | 69 | 15 | 5 | 90 | 2 | 40 | 90 | 78 | 64 |
| 85 | 73 | 53 | 28 | 25 | 32 | 79 | 24 | 29 | 54 | 77 | 69 | 38 | 45 | 9 | 3 | 14 | 5 | 42 | 26 | 57 | 51 | 89 |
| 10 | 34 | 23 | 44 | 5 | 98 | 79 | 55 | 92 | 99 | 49 | 53 | 12 | 24 | 42 | 27 | 83 | 69 | 77 | 92 | 90 | 13 | 28 |
| | | | | | | | | | | | | | | | | | | | | | | |
| 69 | 17 | 91 | 38 | 2 | 46 | 98 | 5 | 97 | 22 | 62 | 19 | 48 | 96 | 38 | 11 | 5 | 15 | 30 | 79 | 33 | 64 | 7 |
| 18 | 71 | 29 | 18 | 3 | 17 | 56 | 39 | 69 | 19 | 40 | 69 | 68 | 64 | 98 | 7 | 32 | 33 | 52 | 33 | 95 | 7 | 57 |
| 32 | 28 | 12 | 9 | 99 | 92 | 52 | 98 | 56 | 5 | 12 | 71 | 42 | 23 | 3 | 64 | 4 | 5 | 33 | 62 | 5 | 34 | 46 |
| 61 | 57 | 16 | 77 | 65 | 62 | 39 | 89 | 68 | 82 | 51 | 42 | 91 | 73 | 53 | 25 | 59 | 1 | 93 | 57 | 28 | 4 | 17 |
| 10 | 66 | 15 | 18 | 62 | 62 | 79 | 88 | 79 | 84 | 47 | 21 | 86 | 0 | 6 | 21 | 57 | 66 | 12 | 55 | 72 | 31 | 6 |
| 83 | 32 | 65 | 27 | 30 | 50 | 32 | 60 | 81 | 99 | 86 | 83 | 90 | 2 | 70 | 82 | 55 | 24 | 1 | 79 | 12 | 64 | 32 |
| 82 | 69 | 70 | 0 | 64 | 77 | 55 | 41 | 71 | 42 | 5 | 40 | 76 | 10 | 74 | 62 | 24 | 36 | 8 | 85 | 0 | 24 | 25 |
| 94 | 15 | 11 | 46 | 59 | 85 | 81 | 54 | 89 | 93 | 70 | 20 | 4 | 79 | 9 | 18 | 5 | 48 | 77 | 52 | 84 | 32 | 68 |
| 57 | 83 | 28 | 41 | 10 | 6 | 11 | 22 | 48 | 33 | 34 | 35 | 51 | 77 | 38 | 7 | 26 | 34 | 72 | 49 | 52 | 59 | 47 |
| 76 | 58 | 72 | 63 | 41 | 58 | 67 | 40 | 79 | 28 | 36 | 63 | 27 | 79 | 47 | 97 | 61 | 12 | 84 | 97 | 7 | 97 | 41 |

| 4 | 52 | 15 | 69 | 32 | 65 | 40 | 39 | 11 | 63 | 30 | 53 | 29 | 21 | 70 | 67 | 57 | 85 | 92 | 95 | 64 | 72 | 61 |
|---|----|----|----|----|----|----|----|----|----|----|----|----|----|----|----|----|----|----|----|----|----|----|
| 86 | 4 | 49 | 39 | 55 | 71 | 47 | 73 | 78 | 42 | 48 | 32 | 68 | 13 | 65 | 43 | 54 | 44 | 61 | 32 | 16 | 21 | 10 |
| 15 | 98 | 53 | 34 | 70 | 37 | 65 | 88 | 0 | 58 | 3 | 65 | 57 | 45 | 5 | 43 | 93 | 18 | 19 | 31 | 4 | 86 | 69 |
| 10 | 21 | 90 | 40 | 38 | 58 | 1 | 28 | 18 | 98 | 40 | 37 | 1 | 19 | 76 | 62 | 54 | 29 | 6 | 27 | 96 | 61 | 34 |
| 20 | 0 | 53 | 71 | 35 | 49 | 81 | 60 | 51 | 87 | 25 | 13 | 16 | 77 | 31 | 43 | 60 | 49 | 27 | 66 | 1 | 56 | 9 |
| 28 | 48 | 61 | 31 | 66 | 66 | 26 | 62 | 90 | 11 | 86 | 34 | 55 | 95 | 26 | 12 | 39 | 20 | 51 | 85 | 77 | 18 | 81 |
| 63 | 34 | 49 | 96 | 18 | 31 | 59 | 61 | 26 | 18 | 34 | 86 | 31 | 97 | 23 | 77 | 44 | 25 | 24 | 31 | 79 | 94 | 8 |
| 63 | 77 | 79 | 43 | 44 | 26 | 3 | 13 | 21 | 56 | 31 | 71 | 71 | 57 | 23 | 0 | 15 | 57 | 57 | 46 | 53 | 38 | 59 |
| 46 | 74 | 49 | 18 | 77 | 16 | 74 | 10 | 55 | 23 | 2 | 50 | 82 | 63 | 17 | 76 | 63 | 99 | 40 | 26 | 35 | 89 | 42 |
| 58 | 28 | 44 | 4 | 39 | 69 | 71 | 59 | 68 | 28 | 18 | 18 | 6 | 4 | 99 | 75 | 64 | 64 | 87 | 59 | 11 | 37 | 42 |
| 46 | 76 | 17 | 53 | 46 | 94 | 82 | 43 | 71 | 41 | 30 | 13 | 51 | 48 | 28 | 52 | 97 | 13 | 19 | 70 | 58 | 37 | 55 |
| 45 | 98 | 45 | 44 | 70 | 83 | 73 | 99 | 86 | 85 | 4 | 86 | 45 | 29 | 80 | 94 | 78 | 79 | 32 | 25 | 76 | 5 | 70 |
| 27 | 70 | 86 | 16 | 32 | 59 | 99 | 71 | 31 | 22 | 62 | 44 | 39 | 80 | 52 | 27 | 30 | 82 | 73 | 23 | 51 | 36 | 79 |
| 38 | 32 | 43 | 34 | 10 | 3 | 36 | 24 | 91 | 24 | 26 | 62 | 19 | 70 | 31 | 53 | 69 | 1 | 73 | 52 | 6 | 8 | 21 |
| 37 | 79 | 13 | 76 | 64 | 55 | 48 | 79 | 84 | 81 | 19 | 48 | 71 | 72 | 47 | 85 | 75 | 7 | 6 | 41 | 74 | 51 | 59 |
| 46 | 98 | 85 | 52 | 65 | 48 | 9 | 36 | 54 | 50 | 55 | 1 | 92 | 7 | 2 | 50 | 4 | 35 | 35 | 39 | 66 | 71 | 31 |
| 66 | 12 | 25 | 53 | 23 | 83 | 97 | 13 | 61 | 93 | 44 | 12 | 15 | 46 | 50 | 56 | 15 | 12 | 20 | 84 | 23 | 89 | 64 |
| 60 | 6 | 52 | 97 | 15 | 78 | 31 | 36 | 41 | 89 | 52 | 71 | 63 | 1 | 23 | 16 | 60 | 78 | 86 | 47 | 15 | 3 | 82 |
| 99 | 73 | 76 | 80 | 73 | 84 | 6 | 51 | 96 | 76 | 50 | 25 | 14 | 61 | 17 | 46 | 1 | 74 | 43 | 71 | 72 | 99 | 73 |
| 88 | 58 | 26 | 18 | 5 | 60 | 0 | 41 | 6 | 59 | 65 | 43 | 0 | 57 | 91 | 2 | 9 | 30 | 44 | 78 | 94 | 95 | 72 |
| 92 | 94 | 3 | 46 | 42 | 12 | 52 | 26 | 95 | 48 | 71 | 74 | 98 | 50 | 12 | 69 | 62 | 42 | 20 | 50 | 1 | 1 | 70 |
| 95 | 64 | 66 | 18 | 69 | 33 | 82 | 71 | 32 | 56 | 42 | 63 | 35 | 56 | 96 | 18 | 3 | 14 | 80 | 25 | 80 | 41 | 84 |
| 68 | 19 | 20 | 17 | 34 | 27 | 27 | 51 | 97 | 71 | 35 | 99 | 2 | 37 | 25 | 81 | 52 | 39 | 91 | 4 | 36 | 28 | 31 |
| 57 | 96 | 79 | 5 | 89 | 24 | 90 | 32 | 69 | 37 | 2 | 16 | 38 | 89 | 22 | 25 | 9 | 87 | 21 | 82 | 87 | 24 | 90 |
| 60 | 45 | 57 | 82 | 98 | 25 | 41 | 41 | 35 | 8 | 84 | 62 | 55 | 90 | 59 | 15 | 35 | 63 | 14 | 87 | 69 | 86 | 3 |
| 40 | 8 | 48 | 28 | 46 | 86 | 71 | 71 | 56 | 79 | 61 | 52 | 33 | 38 | 74 | 90 | 87 | 82 | 17 | 11 | 72 | 31 | 79 |
| 90 | 32 | 23 | 16 | 91 | 48 | 32 | 76 | 77 | 68 | 97 | 84 | 72 | 31 | 23 | 44 | 37 | 90 | 97 | 17 | 11 | 76 | 88 |
| 96 | 61 | 45 | 64 | 81 | 15 | 33 | 99 | 55 | 92 | 69 | 3 | 46 | 80 | 64 | 48 | 32 | 76 | 47 | 39 | 27 | 2 | 31 |
| 38 | 66 | 94 | 89 | 57 | 57 | 31 | 84 | 64 | 11 | 51 | 55 | 55 | 4 | 11 | 24 | 80 | 94 | 76 | 81 | 42 | 65 | 90 |
| 72 | 69 | 51 | 48 | 31 | 9 | 46 | 32 | 13 | 23 | 95 | 93 | 34 | 82 | 78 | 0 | 97 | 75 | 65 | 30 | 21 | 97 | 24 |
| 76 | 15 | 55 | 72 | 55 | 21 | 5 | 90 | 12 | 20 | 85 | 80 | 57 | 80 | 17 | 93 | 86 | 78 | 30 | 18 | 30 | 48 | 77 |
| 16 | 17 | 89 | 69 | 42 | 75 | 33 | 11 | 22 | 7 | 12 | 43 | 38 | 58 | 89 | 41 | 58 | 4 | 34 | 73 | 83 | 20 | 10 |
| 30 | 67 | 23 | 66 | 19 | 43 | 84 | 14 | 6 | 26 | 19 | 22 | 0 | 68 | 47 | 82 | 77 | 5 | 7 | 22 | 76 | 37 | 6 |
| 7 | 84 | 19 | 23 | 54 | 13 | 36 | 62 | 49 | 14 | 91 | 61 | 46 | 20 | 2 | 15 | 44 | 22 | 55 | 48 | 87 | 18 | 5 |
| 69 | 74 | 59 | 7 | 66 | 96 | 42 | 21 | 16 | 87 | 44 | 47 | 87 | 99 | 60 | 63 | 83 | 51 | 14 | 93 | 33 | 41 | 76 |
| 92 | 80 | 5 | 3 | 81 | 7 | 10 | 56 | 50 | 2 | 22 | 90 | 93 | 82 | 39 | 42 | 52 | 74 | 52 | 79 | 33 | 14 | 20 |
| 43 | 46 | 11 | 66 | 75 | 70 | 26 | 19 | 39 | 24 | 68 | 16 | 77 | 81 | 30 | 90 | 38 | 88 | 34 | 90 | 93 | 96 | 98 |
| 21 | 36 | 36 | 12 | 35 | 27 | 95 | 98 | 2 | 32 | 1 | 43 | 20 | 77 | 24 | 26 | 96 | 0 | 57 | 39 | 70 | 85 | 92 |
| 26 | 41 | 22 | 42 | 17 | 8 | 97 | 67 | 74 | 13 | 87 | 63 | 5 | 81 | 8 | 18 | 23 | 39 | 94 | 28 | 25 | 34 | 14 |
| 98 | 3 | 56 | 19 | 5 | 83 | 82 | 23 | 98 | 7 | 0 | 59 | 73 | 84 | 82 | 70 | 12 | 8 | 51 | 73 | 20 | 5 | 86 |

(continued)

```
28  33  51  32   6  50   6  86  67   4  68   0  15  80  16  15  82  91  61  22  47   2  23
30  12   3  27  98  73  17  67  91  82  56  24   9  34  63  44  89  43  41  73  80   2  91
10  34  45  83  27  17  21  70  66  73  14   3  84  92  53  56   0  11  74  19  31  38  47
55  72  22  83  89  32  48  41  48  88  90  84   1  11  35   8  93  43  45  13  78  47  31
39  61  21  65  72  49  63   5  65  64  12  25  69   8  32  61  86  15  16  87  35  89  72
49  74  40  83  29  55  79  69   1  79  73   0  73  88  16  10   3  34  25  54   8  27  22
11  65  53  34  53  78  51  55   0  85  91  68  17  46   4  72  90   8  56  88  24  85  96
10  63  78  95  46  99   9  37  42  15  53  59  80  26  15  74  82  60  30  10  74  74  70
49  86  40  80  73  20  64  72  55  12  17  80  45  95   8  40  70  87  80   1   9  30  19
60   4  79  64  53  28   9  10  91  24  44  27   5  55  15  96  17  77   1  26  87  20  38

76  99  24  90   2  63  59  39  21   4  76  26  80  12  12  83  28   7  10  93  65  85  54
65  14   4  40  99  87  73  41  65  21  81  94  22  23  52   0  25  73  10  74  92  87  24
27  15  19  37   3  52  87  27  30  76  22  82  20  46  76  40  27  90  89  59  93   6  28
56  82  81  89  30  12  51  48  37  76  94  31  97  36  23  93  82  16  89  29  96  80  99
 1  60  99  69  77  20   9   5  84  82  10  20  87  67  87  48  95   5  83  28  24   6  87
60  77  63  82  24  30  29  95  38  30  70  66  78  13  38  41  16  60  63  39  44  70   8
78   5  70  38   3  49  85  15  42  47  12  20   1   6   7  87  61  73  91  19  37  77  73
25  16   0  86  71  60  76  27  80  27  26  89  94  46  22  51  62  29  83  21  90  37  71
66  33  96  63  95  69  53  61  40  37  73  42  16  62  13   0  20  85   4  71  25   7  43
57  20  42  96  94  96  70  53  71  48  26  84  94  37  62  31  19  84  28  88  61  40  58

73  33  16  26  56  63  91   2  13  81  60  13  88  31  86  63  14  76  24  35  87  35  37
21  91  74  11  28  24  62  67  44  65  90  27  14  92  10  28  22  50  22  68  73  79   3
 9  61  60  69  97  11  85  59   0   6  59  16  12   7  85   2  16  20  39  59  33  81  14
16  62  92  65  82  67  26   8  36  86   9  73  68  79  60  10  32  48  59  70  83  95   5
25  45  23  46  19  70  36   7  75  26  41  14  36  32  25  87  34  30  74  57  39  61  76
85  83  20  36   4  20  69  12  59  32  53  33  33  68  38  37  18   4  38  63  16  73  85
31  63  91  65  30  40  27  30  15  65  31  43  58  99  30  53  97  91  95   2  89  53   0
54  94  59  67  69  98  22  50  74  63   3  39  46  22  35  40   4  77  61  14  21  57   2
82  86  93  17   2  30  12  23  28  24  34  41  74  53  35  88   0  19  71   6  59  38   0
32  93  35  64   4  86  60  12  80  30  45  75  18  41  11  47  99  30  55  72  53  99  92

82  79  45  35  16  95  16  44  36  95  36  88  13  55  26  81   3  55  42  65  65  12  93
85  13  56  62  53  14  35  18  87  26  27  17  72  79  83  81  89  64  89  33  86  52  16
 3  21  83  18  41  64  54  36  89  49  46  11   6  87  97  77  12  36  59  75  81  59  20
15  98  56  37  29  75  56  72  44  28   8  77  45  74  44  51  75  90  63  55  20  97  47
15   0  33   3  96  88  88  88  97  62  36  95  92  94   4  63  61  77  21  42  62  20  21
39  51  58  87  73  15  47  34  81  60  99  40  18  50  86  80  88  99  77  79  93  19  27
22  42  18  32  49  40  72   4  46  56   2  60  59  91  47  22  27  77  35  66  72  88  11
87  73   0  50  32  20   7  46  65  85  43  73  97  46  73  65   0   8  38  34  11   0  81
85  99  68  83  67   9  29  40  78  71  93  93  67  56  36  50  76  65   2  83   1  41  27
34  10  45  58  47  11   9  20  37  33  48  82   9  73   6   2  79  51  99  44  83  49  82
```

| | | | | | | | | | | | | | | | | | | | | | | |
|---|---|---|---|---|---|---|---|---|---|---|---|---|---|---|---|---|---|---|---|---|---|---|
| 24 | 30 | 59 | 32 | 34 | 58 | 6 | 54 | 13 | 2 | 86 | 18 | 65 | 26 | 61 | 61 | 38 | 38 | 72 | 60 | 55 | 92 | 88 |
| 76 | 92 | 62 | 70 | 77 | 89 | 0 | 75 | 5 | 2 | 44 | 84 | 28 | 51 | 64 | 40 | 82 | 60 | 39 | 4 | 88 | 49 | 45 |
| 41 | 27 | 22 | 49 | 79 | 21 | 20 | 58 | 10 | 25 | 74 | 73 | 62 | 81 | 99 | 99 | 61 | 21 | 18 | 66 | 96 | 81 | 43 |
| 83 | 71 | 66 | 90 | 13 | 22 | 39 | 47 | 79 | 32 | 23 | 53 | 42 | 17 | 45 | 82 | 3 | 74 | 22 | 47 | 5 | 46 | 76 |
| 68 | 49 | 85 | 27 | 2 | 8 | 25 | 5 | 99 | 93 | 61 | 68 | 2 | 64 | 50 | 82 | 8 | 43 | 48 | 1 | 21 | 52 | 13 |
| 86 | 26 | 41 | 11 | 48 | 77 | 93 | 15 | 54 | 99 | 95 | 71 | 81 | 91 | 8 | 26 | 67 | 73 | 52 | 5 | 2 | 66 | 24 |
| 25 | 58 | 61 | 79 | 7 | 48 | 8 | 14 | 8 | 78 | 93 | 56 | 70 | 45 | 92 | 58 | 31 | 10 | 92 | 0 | 12 | 47 | 70 |
| 73 | 35 | 64 | 61 | 48 | 69 | 14 | 40 | 24 | 91 | 84 | 56 | 83 | 36 | 50 | 59 | 0 | 72 | 58 | 44 | 57 | 96 | 34 |
| 41 | 12 | 91 | 81 | 45 | 33 | 73 | 79 | 21 | 26 | 58 | 0 | 20 | 2 | 37 | 61 | 17 | 19 | 87 | 28 | 16 | 70 | 88 |
| 81 | 80 | 97 | 64 | 80 | 19 | 31 | 11 | 85 | 23 | 76 | 28 | 72 | 71 | 3 | 43 | 50 | 39 | 64 | 89 | 41 | 65 | 54 |
| | | | | | | | | | | | | | | | | | | | | | | |
| 41 | 40 | 11 | 55 | 45 | 99 | 71 | 7 | 55 | 75 | 31 | 73 | 41 | 0 | 18 | 36 | 31 | 45 | 88 | 67 | 40 | 51 | 83 |
| 50 | 15 | 71 | 99 | 43 | 88 | 59 | 6 | 94 | 75 | 95 | 58 | 7 | 30 | 80 | 99 | 12 | 91 | 57 | 53 | 90 | 26 | 12 |
| 77 | 54 | 33 | 43 | 1 | 15 | 86 | 91 | 58 | 84 | 97 | 65 | 75 | 46 | 25 | 39 | 80 | 59 | 95 | 75 | 60 | 27 | 51 |
| 79 | 66 | 68 | 73 | 40 | 96 | 6 | 15 | 21 | 97 | 83 | 25 | 30 | 69 | 36 | 19 | 91 | 40 | 86 | 62 | 28 | 92 | 56 |
| 21 | 3 | 62 | 2 | 69 | 74 | 50 | 6 | 83 | 92 | 93 | 86 | 65 | 80 | 74 | 25 | 51 | 93 | 46 | 74 | 94 | 25 | 14 |
| 82 | 62 | 93 | 95 | 44 | 83 | 31 | 29 | 78 | 41 | 24 | 74 | 41 | 10 | 29 | 14 | 49 | 43 | 83 | 46 | 83 | 76 | 46 |
| 58 | 72 | 90 | 3 | 89 | 15 | 64 | 72 | 45 | 15 | 73 | 14 | 14 | 47 | 3 | 29 | 1 | 19 | 75 | 70 | 3 | 16 | 73 |
| 81 | 57 | 48 | 9 | 34 | 27 | 23 | 81 | 44 | 48 | 26 | 7 | 19 | 74 | 43 | 71 | 46 | 11 | 98 | 5 | 14 | 64 | 78 |
| 65 | 65 | 86 | 84 | 54 | 33 | 80 | 15 | 77 | 34 | 85 | 97 | 42 | 98 | 72 | 31 | 88 | 42 | 23 | 47 | 78 | 54 | 45 |
| 90 | 75 | 83 | 5 | 91 | 6 | 95 | 23 | 89 | 44 | 5 | 96 | 61 | 7 | 35 | 88 | 71 | 97 | 59 | 72 | 64 | 73 | 85 |

TABLE C.2    Critical values of chi-square

| Degrees of freedom | Probability level | | |
|---|---|---|---|
| | .10 | .05 | .01 |
| 1 | 2.706 | 3.841 | 6.635 |
| 2 | 4.605 | 5.991 | 9.210 |
| 3 | 6.251 | 7.815 | 11.345 |
| 4 | 7.779 | 9.488 | 13.277 |
| 5 | 9.236 | 11.070 | 15.086 |
| 6 | 10.645 | 12.592 | 16.812 |
| 7 | 12.017 | 14.067 | 18.475 |
| 8 | 13.362 | 15.507 | 20.090 |
| 9 | 14.684 | 16.919 | 21.666 |
| 10 | 15.987 | 18.307 | 23.209 |
| 11 | 17.275 | 19.675 | 24.725 |
| 12 | 18.549 | 21.026 | 26.217 |
| 13 | 19.812 | 22.362 | 27.688 |
| 14 | 21.064 | 23.685 | 29.141 |
| 15 | 22.307 | 24.996 | 30.578 |
| 16 | 23.542 | 26.296 | 32.000 |
| 17 | 24.769 | 27.587 | 33.409 |
| 18 | 25.989 | 28.869 | 34.805 |
| 19 | 27.204 | 30.144 | 36.191 |
| 20 | 28.412 | 31.410 | 37.566 |

*Source:* Table adapted from Fisher and Yates, *Statistical Tables for Biological, Agricultural, and Medical Research* (1974, 6th ed.), London: Longman. Reprinted by permission.

TABLE C.3    Critical values of $t$

| | Significance level* | | | |
|---|---|---|---|---|
| | .05 | .025 | .01 | .005 |
| $df$ | .10 | .05 | .02 | .01 |
| 1 | 6.314 | 12.706 | 31.821 | 63.657 |
| 2 | 2.920 | 4.303 | 6.965 | 9.925 |
| 3 | 2.353 | 3.182 | 4.541 | 5.841 |
| 4 | 2.132 | 2.776 | 3.747 | 4.604 |
| 5 | 2.015 | 2.571 | 3.365 | 4.032 |
| 6 | 1.943 | 2.447 | 3.143 | 3.707 |
| 7 | 1.895 | 2.365 | 2.998 | 3.499 |
| 8 | 1.860 | 2.306 | 2.896 | 3.355 |
| 9 | 1.833 | 2.262 | 2.821 | 3.250 |
| 10 | 1.812 | 2.228 | 2.764 | 3.169 |
| 11 | 1.796 | 2.201 | 2.718 | 3.106 |
| 12 | 1.782 | 2.179 | 2.681 | 3.055 |
| 13 | 1.771 | 2.160 | 2.650 | 3.012 |
| 14 | 1.761 | 2.145 | 2.624 | 2.977 |
| 15 | 1.753 | 2.131 | 2.602 | 2.947 |
| 16 | 1.746 | 2.120 | 2.583 | 2.921 |
| 17 | 1.740 | 2.110 | 2.567 | 2.898 |
| 18 | 1.734 | 2.101 | 2.552 | 2.878 |
| 19 | 1.729 | 2.093 | 2.539 | 2.861 |
| 20 | 1.725 | 2.086 | 2.528 | 2.845 |
| 21 | 1.721 | 2.080 | 2.518 | 2.831 |
| 22 | 1.717 | 2.074 | 2.508 | 2.819 |
| 23 | 1.714 | 2.069 | 2.500 | 2.807 |
| 24 | 1.711 | 2.064 | 2.492 | 2.797 |
| 25 | 1.708 | 2.060 | 2.485 | 2.787 |
| 26 | 1.706 | 2.056 | 2.479 | 2.779 |
| 27 | 1.703 | 2.052 | 2.473 | 2.771 |
| 28 | 1.701 | 2.048 | 2.467 | 2.763 |
| 29 | 1.699 | 2.045 | 2.462 | 2.756 |
| 30 | 1.697 | 2.042 | 2.457 | 2.750 |
| 40 | 1.684 | 2.021 | 2.423 | 2.704 |
| 60 | 1.671 | 2.000 | 2.390 | 2.660 |
| 120 | 1.658 | 1.980 | 2.358 | 2.617 |
| ∞ | 1.645 | 1.960 | 2.326 | 2.576 |

*Use the top significance level when you have predicted a specific directional difference (a one-tailed test; e.g., Group 1 will be greater than Group 2). Use the bottom significance level when you have predicted only that Group 1 will differ from Group 2 without specifying the direction of the difference (a two-tailed test).

## TABLE C.4    Critical values of *F*

| df for deno-minator (error) | α | \multicolumn{12}{c}{df for numerator (systematic)} |
|---|---|---|---|---|---|---|---|---|---|---|---|---|---|
| | | 1 | 2 | 3 | 4 | 5 | 6 | 7 | 8 | 9 | 10 | 11 | 12 |
| 1 | .10 | 39.9 | 49.5 | 53.6 | 55.8 | 57.2 | 58.2 | 58.9 | 59.4 | 59.9 | 60.2 | 60.5 | 60.7 |
| | .05 | 161 | 200 | 216 | 225 | 230 | 234 | 237 | 239 | 241 | 242 | 243 | 244 |
| 2 | .10 | 8.53 | 9.00 | 9.16 | 9.24 | 9.29 | 9.33 | 9.35 | 9.37 | 9.38 | 9.39 | 9.40 | 9.41 |
| | .05 | 18.5 | 19.0 | 19.2 | 19.2 | 19.3 | 19.3 | 19.4 | 19.4 | 19.4 | 19.4 | 19.4 | 19.4 |
| | .01 | 98.5 | 99.0 | 99.2 | 99.2 | 99.3 | 99.3 | 99.4 | 99.4 | 99.4 | 99.4 | 99.4 | 99.4 |
| 3 | .10 | 5.54 | 5.46 | 5.39 | 5.34 | 5.31 | 5.28 | 5.27 | 5.25 | 5.24 | 5.23 | 5.22 | 5.22 |
| | .05 | 10.1 | 9.55 | 9.28 | 9.12 | 9.01 | 8.94 | 8.89 | 8.85 | 8.81 | 8.79 | 8.76 | 8.74 |
| | .01 | 34.1 | 30.8 | 29.5 | 28.7 | 28.2 | 27.9 | 27.7 | 27.5 | 27.3 | 27.2 | 27.1 | 27.1 |
| 4 | .10 | 4.54 | 4.32 | 4.19 | 4.11 | 4.05 | 4.01 | 3.98 | 3.95 | 3.94 | 3.92 | 3.91 | 3.90 |
| | .05 | 7.71 | 6.94 | 6.59 | 6.39 | 6.26 | 6.16 | 6.09 | 6.04 | 6.00 | 5.96 | 5.94 | 5.91 |
| | .01 | 21.2 | 18.0 | 16.7 | 16.0 | 15.5 | 15.2 | 15.0 | 14.8 | 14.7 | 14.5 | 14.4 | 14.4 |
| 5 | .10 | 4.06 | 3.78 | 3.62 | 3.52 | 3.45 | 3.40 | 3.37 | 3.34 | 3.32 | 3.30 | 3.28 | 3.27 |
| | .05 | 6.61 | 5.79 | 5.41 | 5.19 | 5.05 | 4.95 | 4.88 | 4.82 | 4.77 | 4.74 | 4.71 | 4.68 |
| | .01 | 16.3 | 13.3 | 12.1 | 11.4 | 11.0 | 10.7 | 10.5 | 10.3 | 10.2 | 10.1 | 9.96 | 9.89 |
| 6 | .10 | 3.78 | 3.46 | 3.29 | 3.18 | 3.11 | 3.05 | 3.01 | 2.98 | 2.96 | 2.94 | 2.92 | 2.90 |
| | .05 | 5.99 | 5.14 | 4.76 | 4.53 | 4.39 | 4.28 | 4.21 | 4.15 | 4.10 | 4.06 | 4.03 | 4.00 |
| | .01 | 13.7 | 10.9 | 9.78 | 9.15 | 8.75 | 8.47 | 8.26 | 8.10 | 7.98 | 7.87 | 7.79 | 7.72 |
| 7 | .10 | 3.59 | 3.26 | 3.07 | 2.96 | 2.88 | 2.83 | 2.78 | 2.75 | 2.72 | 2.70 | 2.68 | 2.67 |
| | .05 | 5.59 | 4.74 | 4.35 | 4.12 | 3.97 | 3.87 | 3.79 | 3.73 | 3.68 | 3.64 | 3.60 | 3.57 |
| | .01 | 12.2 | 9.55 | 8.45 | 7.85 | 7.46 | 7.19 | 6.99 | 6.84 | 6.72 | 6.62 | 6.54 | 6.47 |
| 8 | .10 | 3.46 | 3.11 | 2.92 | 2.81 | 2.73 | 2.67 | 2.62 | 2.59 | 2.56 | 2.54 | 2.52 | 2.50 |
| | .05 | 5.32 | 4.46 | 4.07 | 3.84 | 3.69 | 3.58 | 3.50 | 3.44 | 3.39 | 3.35 | 3.31 | 3.28 |
| | .01 | 11.3 | 8.65 | 7.59 | 7.01 | 6.63 | 6.37 | 6.18 | 6.03 | 5.91 | 5.81 | 5.73 | 5.67 |
| 9 | .10 | 3.36 | 3.01 | 2.81 | 2.69 | 2.61 | 2.55 | 2.51 | 2.47 | 2.44 | 2.42 | 2.40 | 2.38 |
| | .05 | 5.12 | 4.26 | 3.86 | 3.63 | 3.48 | 3.37 | 3.29 | 3.23 | 3.18 | 3.14 | 3.10 | 3.07 |
| | .01 | 10.6 | 8.02 | 6.99 | 6.42 | 6.06 | 5.80 | 5.61 | 5.47 | 5.35 | 5.26 | 5.18 | 5.11 |
| 10 | .10 | 3.29 | 2.92 | 2.73 | 2.61 | 2.52 | 2.46 | 2.41 | 2.38 | 2.35 | 2.32 | 2.30 | 2.28 |
| | .05 | 4.96 | 4.10 | 3.71 | 3.48 | 3.33 | 3.22 | 3.14 | 3.07 | 3.02 | 2.98 | 2.94 | 2.91 |
| | .01 | 10.0 | 7.56 | 6.55 | 5.99 | 5.64 | 5.39 | 5.20 | 5.06 | 4.94 | 4.85 | 4.77 | 4.71 |

TABLE C.4    Critical values of *F* (*continued*)

| *df* for de-nom-inator (error) | α | \| | 1 | 2 | 3 | 4 | 5 | 6 | 7 | 8 | 9 | 10 | 11 | 12 |
|---|---|---|---|---|---|---|---|---|---|---|---|---|---|---|
| | | | | | | | *df* for numerator (systematic) | | | | | | | |
| 11 | .10 | | 3.23 | 2.86 | 2.66 | 2.54 | 2.45 | 2.39 | 2.34 | 2.30 | 2.27 | 2.25 | 2.23 | 2.21 |
| | .05 | | 4.84 | 3.98 | 3.59 | 3.36 | 3.20 | 3.09 | 3.01 | 2.95 | 2.90 | 2.85 | 2.82 | 2.79 |
| | .01 | | 9.65 | 7.21 | 6.22 | 5.67 | 5.32 | 5.07 | 4.89 | 4.74 | 4.63 | 4.54 | 4.46 | 4.40 |
| 12 | .10 | | 3.18 | 2.81 | 2.61 | 2.48 | 2.39 | 2.33 | 2.28 | 2.24 | 2.21 | 2.19 | 2.17 | 2.15 |
| | .05 | | 4.75 | 3.89 | 3.49 | 3.26 | 3.11 | 3.00 | 2.91 | 2.85 | 2.80 | 2.75 | 2.72 | 2.69 |
| | .01 | | 9.33 | 6.93 | 5.95 | 5.41 | 5.06 | 4.82 | 4.64 | 4.50 | 4.39 | 4.30 | 4.22 | 4.16 |
| 13 | .10 | | 3.14 | 2.76 | 2.56 | 2.43 | 2.35 | 2.28 | 2.23 | 2.20 | 2.16 | 2.14 | 2.12 | 2.10 |
| | .05 | | 4.67 | 3.81 | 3.41 | 3.18 | 3.03 | 2.92 | 2.83 | 2.77 | 2.71 | 2.67 | 2.63 | 2.60 |
| | .01 | | 9.07 | 6.70 | 5.74 | 5.21 | 4.86 | 4.62 | 4.44 | 4.30 | 4.19 | 4.10 | 4.02 | 3.96 |
| 14 | .10 | | 3.10 | 2.73 | 2.52 | 2.39 | 2.31 | 2.24 | 2.19 | 2.15 | 2.12 | 2.10 | 2.08 | 2.05 |
| | .05 | | 4.60 | 3.74 | 3.34 | 3.11 | 2.96 | 2.85 | 2.76 | 2.70 | 2.65 | 2.60 | 2.57 | 2.53 |
| | .01 | | 8.86 | 6.51 | 5.56 | 5.04 | 4.69 | 4.46 | 4.28 | 4.14 | 4.03 | 3.94 | 3.86 | 3.80 |
| 15 | .10 | | 3.07 | 2.70 | 2.49 | 2.36 | 2.27 | 2.21 | 2.16 | 2.12 | 2.09 | 2.06 | 2.04 | 2.02 |
| | .05 | | 4.54 | 3.68 | 3.29 | 3.06 | 2.90 | 2.79 | 2.71 | 2.64 | 2.59 | 2.54 | 2.51 | 2.48 |
| | .01 | | 8.68 | 6.36 | 5.42 | 4.89 | 4.56 | 4.32 | 4.14 | 4.00 | 3.89 | 3.80 | 3.73 | 3.67 |
| 16 | .10 | | 3.05 | 2.67 | 2.46 | 2.33 | 2.24 | 2.18 | 2.13 | 2.09 | 2.06 | 2.03 | 2.01 | 1.99 |
| | .05 | | 4.49 | 3.63 | 3.24 | 3.01 | 2.85 | 2.74 | 2.66 | 2.59 | 2.54 | 2.49 | 2.46 | 2.42 |
| | .01 | | 8.53 | 6.23 | 5.29 | 4.77 | 4.44 | 4.20 | 4.03 | 3.89 | 3.78 | 3.69 | 3.62 | 3.55 |
| 17 | .10 | | 3.03 | 2.64 | 2.44 | 2.31 | 2.22 | 2.15 | 2.10 | 2.06 | 2.03 | 2.00 | 1.98 | 1.96 |
| | .05 | | 4.45 | 3.59 | 3.20 | 2.96 | 2.81 | 2.70 | 2.61 | 2.55 | 2.49 | 2.45 | 2.41 | 2.38 |
| | .01 | | 8.40 | 6.11 | 5.18 | 4.67 | 4.34 | 4.10 | 3.93 | 3.79 | 3.68 | 3.59 | 3.52 | 3.46 |
| 18 | .10 | | 3.01 | 2.62 | 2.42 | 2.29 | 2.20 | 2.13 | 2.08 | 2.04 | 2.00 | 1.98 | 1.96 | 1.93 |
| | .05 | | 4.41 | 3.55 | 3.16 | 2.93 | 2.77 | 2.66 | 2.58 | 2.51 | 2.46 | 2.41 | 2.37 | 2.34 |
| | .01 | | 8.29 | 6.01 | 5.09 | 4.58 | 4.25 | 4.01 | 3.84 | 3.71 | 3.60 | 3.51 | 3.43 | 3.37 |
| 19 | .10 | | 2.99 | 2.61 | 2.40 | 2.27 | 2.18 | 2.11 | 2.06 | 2.02 | 1.98 | 1.96 | 1.94 | 1.91 |
| | .05 | | 4.38 | 3.52 | 3.13 | 2.90 | 2.74 | 2.63 | 2.54 | 2.48 | 2.42 | 2.38 | 2.34 | 2.31 |
| | .01 | | 8.18 | 5.93 | 5.01 | 4.50 | 4.17 | 3.94 | 3.77 | 3.63 | 3.52 | 3.43 | 3.36 | 3.30 |
| 20 | .10 | | 2.97 | 2.59 | 2.38 | 2.25 | 2.16 | 2.09 | 2.04 | 2.00 | 1.96 | 1.94 | 1.92 | 1.89 |
| | .05 | | 4.35 | 3.49 | 3.10 | 2.87 | 2.71 | 2.60 | 2.51 | 2.45 | 2.39 | 2.35 | 2.31 | 2.28 |
| | .01 | | 8.10 | 5.85 | 4.94 | 4.43 | 4.10 | 3.87 | 3.70 | 3.56 | 3.46 | 3.37 | 3.29 | 3.23 |

(*continued*)

**TABLE C.4    Critical values of *F* (*continued*)**

| *df* for denominator (error) | α | \multicolumn{12}{c}{df for numerator (systematic)} |||||||||||| |
|---|---|---|---|---|---|---|---|---|---|---|---|---|---|
| | | 1 | 2 | 3 | 4 | 5 | 6 | 7 | 8 | 9 | 10 | 11 | 12 |
| 22 | .10 | 2.95 | 2.56 | 2.35 | 2.22 | 2.13 | 2.06 | 2.01 | 1.97 | 1.93 | 1.90 | 1.88 | 1.86 |
| | .05 | 4.30 | 3.44 | 3.05 | 2.82 | 2.66 | 2.55 | 2.46 | 2.40 | 2.34 | 2.30 | 2.26 | 2.23 |
| | .01 | 7.95 | 5.72 | 4.82 | 4.31 | 3.99 | 3.76 | 3.59 | 3.45 | 3.35 | 3.26 | 3.18 | 3.12 |
| 24 | .10 | 2.93 | 2.54 | 2.33 | 2.19 | 2.10 | 2.04 | 1.98 | 1.94 | 1.91 | 1.88 | 1.85 | 1.83 |
| | .05 | 4.26 | 3.40 | 3.01 | 2.78 | 2.62 | 2.51 | 2.42 | 2.36 | 2.30 | 2.25 | 2.21 | 2.18 |
| | .01 | 7.82 | 5.61 | 4.72 | 4.22 | 3.90 | 3.67 | 3.50 | 3.36 | 3.26 | 3.17 | 3.09 | 3.03 |
| 26 | .10 | 2.91 | 2.52 | 2.31 | 2.17 | 2.08 | 2.01 | 1.96 | 1.92 | 1.88 | 1.86 | 1.84 | 1.81 |
| | .05 | 4.23 | 3.37 | 2.98 | 2.74 | 2.59 | 2.47 | 2.39 | 2.32 | 2.27 | 2.22 | 2.18 | 2.15 |
| | .01 | 7.72 | 5.53 | 4.64 | 4.14 | 3.82 | 3.59 | 3.42 | 3.29 | 3.18 | 3.09 | 3.02 | 2.96 |
| 28 | .10 | 2.89 | 2.50 | 2.29 | 2.16 | 2.06 | 2.00 | 1.94 | 1.90 | 1.87 | 1.84 | 1.81 | 1.79 |
| | .05 | 4.20 | 3.34 | 2.95 | 2.71 | 2.56 | 2.45 | 2.36 | 2.29 | 2.24 | 2.19 | 2.15 | 2.12 |
| | .01 | 7.64 | 5.45 | 4.57 | 4.07 | 3.75 | 3.53 | 3.36 | 3.23 | 3.12 | 3.03 | 2.96 | 2.90 |
| 30 | .10 | 2.88 | 2.49 | 2.28 | 2.14 | 2.05 | 1.98 | 1.93 | 1.88 | 1.85 | 1.82 | 1.79 | 1.77 |
| | .05 | 4.17 | 3.32 | 2.92 | 2.69 | 2.53 | 2.42 | 2.33 | 2.27 | 2.21 | 2.16 | 2.13 | 2.09 |
| | .01 | 7.56 | 5.39 | 4.51 | 4.02 | 3.70 | 3.47 | 3.30 | 3.17 | 3.07 | 2.98 | 2.91 | 2.84 |
| 40 | .10 | 2.84 | 2.44 | 2.23 | 2.09 | 2.00 | 1.93 | 1.87 | 1.83 | 1.79 | 1.76 | 1.73 | 1.71 |
| | .05 | 4.08 | 3.23 | 2.84 | 2.61 | 2.45 | 2.34 | 2.25 | 2.18 | 2.12 | 2.08 | 2.04 | 2.00 |
| | .01 | 7.31 | 5.18 | 4.31 | 3.83 | 3.51 | 3.29 | 3.12 | 2.99 | 2.89 | 2.80 | 2.73 | 2.66 |
| 60 | .10 | 2.79 | 2.39 | 2.18 | 2.04 | 1.95 | 1.87 | 1.82 | 1.77 | 1.74 | 1.71 | 1.68 | 1.66 |
| | .05 | 4.00 | 3.15 | 2.76 | 2.53 | 2.37 | 2.25 | 2.17 | 2.10 | 2.04 | 1.99 | 1.95 | 1.92 |
| | .01 | 7.08 | 4.98 | 4.13 | 3.65 | 3.34 | 3.12 | 2.95 | 2.82 | 2.72 | 2.63 | 2.56 | 2.50 |
| 120 | .10 | 2.75 | 2.35 | 2.13 | 1.99 | 1.90 | 1.82 | 1.77 | 1.72 | 1.68 | 1.65 | 1.62 | 1.60 |
| | .05 | 3.92 | 3.07 | 2.68 | 2.45 | 2.29 | 2.17 | 2.09 | 2.02 | 1.96 | 1.91 | 1.87 | 1.83 |
| | .01 | 6.85 | 4.79 | 3.95 | 3.48 | 3.17 | 2.96 | 2.79 | 2.66 | 2.56 | 2.47 | 2.40 | 2.34 |
| 200 | .10 | 2.73 | 2.33 | 2.11 | 1.97 | 1.88 | 1.80 | 1.75 | 1.70 | 1.66 | 1.63 | 1.60 | 1.57 |
| | .05 | 3.89 | 3.04 | 2.65 | 2.42 | 2.26 | 2.14 | 2.06 | 1.98 | 1.93 | 1.88 | 1.84 | 1.80 |
| | .01 | 6.76 | 4.71 | 3.88 | 3.41 | 3.11 | 2.89 | 2.73 | 2.60 | 2.50 | 2.41 | 2.34 | 2.27 |
| ∞ | .10 | 2.71 | 2.30 | 2.08 | 1.94 | 1.85 | 1.77 | 1.72 | 1.67 | 1.63 | 1.60 | 1.57 | 1.55 |
| | .05 | 3.84 | 3.00 | 2.60 | 2.37 | 2.21 | 2.10 | 2.01 | 1.94 | 1.88 | 1.83 | 1.79 | 1.75 |
| | .01 | 6.63 | 4.61 | 3.78 | 3.32 | 3.02 | 2.80 | 2.64 | 2.51 | 2.41 | 2.32 | 2.25 | 2.18 |

**TABLE C.5**     Critical values of *r* (Pearson product–moment correlation coefficient)

| df | Level of significance for two-tailed test* | | |
|---|---|---|---|
| | .10 | .05 | .01 |
| 1 | .988 | .997 | .9999 |
| 2 | .900 | .950 | .990 |
| 3 | .805 | .878 | .959 |
| 4 | .729 | .811 | .917 |
| 5 | .669 | .754 | .874 |
| 6 | .622 | .707 | .834 |
| 7 | .582 | .666 | .798 |
| 8 | .549 | .632 | .765 |
| 9 | .521 | .602 | .735 |
| 10 | .497 | .576 | .708 |
| 11 | .476 | .553 | .684 |
| 12 | .458 | .532 | .661 |
| 13 | .441 | .514 | .641 |
| 14 | .426 | .497 | .623 |
| 15 | .412 | .482 | .606 |
| 16 | .400 | .468 | .590 |
| 17 | .389 | .456 | .575 |
| 18 | .378 | .444 | .561 |
| 19 | .369 | .433 | .549 |
| 20 | .360 | .423 | .537 |
| 25 | .323 | .381 | .487 |
| 30 | .296 | .349 | .449 |
| 35 | .275 | .325 | .418 |
| 40 | .257 | .304 | .393 |
| 45 | .243 | .288 | .372 |
| 50 | .231 | .273 | .354 |
| 60 | .211 | .250 | .325 |
| 70 | .195 | .232 | .303 |
| 80 | .183 | .217 | .283 |
| 90 | .173 | .205 | .267 |
| 100 | .164 | .195 | .254 |

*The significance level is halved for a one-tailed test.

# Appendix D
# Constructing a Latin Square

A Latin square to determine the orders of any *N* number of conditions will have *N* arrangements of orders. Thus, if there are four conditions, there will be four orders in a 4 × 4 Latin square; eight conditions will produce an 8 × 8 Latin square. The method for constructing a Latin square shown below will produce orders in which (1) each condition or group appears once at each order and (2) each condition precedes and follows each other condition one time.

Use the following procedures for generating a Latin square when there are an even number of conditions:

1. Determine the number of conditions. Use letters of the alphabet to represent your *N* conditions: ABCD for four conditions, ABCDEF for six conditions, and so on.

2. Determine the order for the first row, using the following ordering:

$$A, B, L, C, L-1, D, L-2, E$$

and so on. *L* stands for the last or final treatment. Thus, if you have four conditions (ABCD), your order will be

$$A, B, D, C$$

With six conditions (ABCDEF), the order will be

$$A, B, F, C, E, D$$

because F is the final treatment (*L*), and E is the next to final treatment (*L* – 1).

3. Determine the order for the second row, by increasing one letter at each position of the first row. The last letter cannot be increased, of course, so it reverts to the first letter. With six conditions, the order of the second row becomes

$$B, C, A, D, F, E$$

4. Continue this procedure for the third and subsequent rows. For the third row, increase one letter at each position of the second row:

$$C, D, B, E, A, F$$

The final 6 × 6 Latin square will be

```
A  B  F  C  E  D
B  C  A  D  F  E
C  D  B  E  A  F
D  E  C  F  B  A
E  F  D  A  C  B
F  A  E  B  D  C
```

5. Randomly assign each of your conditions to one of the letters to determine which condition will be in the A position, the B position, and so on.

If you have an odd number of conditions, you must make two Latin squares. For the first square, simply follow the procedures we have shown. Now create a second square that reverses the first one; that is, in each row, the first condition becomes the last, the second condition is next to last, and so on. Join the two squares together to create the final Latin square (actually a rectangle!). Thus, if there are five conditions, you will have 10 possible orders to run in your study.

# Glossary

**alternative explanation** Part of causal inference; a potential alternative cause of an observed relationship between variables.

**analysis of covariance** A statistical technique to control for the correlation between a subject variable and a dependent variable in an experiment. This procedure removes the error variance that results from the fact that variability in scores on the dependent variable is due in part to the effect of the subject variable.

**analysis of variance** *See F* test.

**archival research** The use of existing sources of information for research. Sources include statistical records, survey archives, and written records.

**autonomy (Belmont Report)** Principle that individuals in research investigations are capable of making a decision of whether to participate.

**bar graph** Using bars to depict frequencies of responses, percentages, or means in two or more groups.

**baseline** In a single case design, the subject's behavior during a control period before introduction of the experimental manipulation.

**beneficence (Belmont Report)** Principle that research should have beneficial effects while minimizing any harmful effects.

**carry-over effect** A problem that may occur in repeated measures designs if the effects of one treatment are still present when the next treatment is given.

**case study** A descriptive account of the behavior, past history, and other relevant factors concerning a specific individual.

**ceiling effect** Failure of a measure to detect a difference because it was too easy (*also see* floor effect).

**central tendency** A single number or value that describes the typical or central score among a set of scores.

**cluster sampling** A method of sampling in which clusters of individuals are identified. Clusters are sampled, and then all individuals in each cluster are included in the sample.

**coding system** A set of rules used to categorize observations.

**cohort** A group of people born at about the same time and exposed to the same societal events; cohort effects are confounded with age in a cross-sectional study.

**conceptual replication** Replication of research using different procedures for manipulating or measuring the variables.

**concurrent validity** The construct validity of a measure is assessed by examining whether groups of people differ on the measure in expected ways.

**confederate** A person posing as a participant in an experiment who is actually part of the experiment.

**confidence interval** An interval of values within which there is a given level of confidence (e.g., 95%) where the population value lies.

**confounding** An uncontrolled variable varies systematically with an independent variable; it is impossible to separate the effect of the independent variable from the confounding variable.

**confounding variable** A variable that is not controlled in a research investigation. In an experiment, the experimental groups differ on both the independent variable and the confounding variable.

**construct validity** The degree to which a measurement device accurately measures the theoretical construct it is designed to measure.

**content analysis** Systematic analysis of the content of written records.

**control series design** An extension of the interrupted time series quasi-experimental design in which there is a comparison or control group.

**convergent validity** The construct validity of a measure is assessed by examining the extent to which scores on the measure are related to scores on other measures of the same construct or similar constructs.

**correlation coefficient** An index of how strongly two variables are related to each other.

**correlational method** *See* nonexperimental method.

**counterbalancing** A method of controlling for order effects in a repeated measures design by either including all orders of treatment presentation or randomly determining the order for each subject.

**covariation of cause and effect** Part of causal inference; observing that a change in one variable is accompanied by a change in a second variable.

**criterion-oriented validity** Techniques for determining construct validity that rely on assessing the relationship between scores on the measure and a criterion or outcome.

**Cronbach's** *alpha* An indicator of internal consistency reliability assessed by examining the average correlation of each item (question) in a measure with every other question.

**cross-sectional method** A developmental research method in which persons of different ages are studied at only one point in time; con-ceptually similar to an independent groups design.

**curvilinear relationship** A relationship in which increases in the values of the first variable are accompanied by both increases and decreases in the values of the second variable.

**debriefing** Explanation of the purposes of the research that is given to participants following their participation in the research.

**degrees of freedom (*df*)** A concept used in tests of statistical significance; the number of observations that are free to vary to produce a known outcome.

**demand characteristics** Cues that inform the subject how he or she is expected to behave.

**dependent variable** The variable that is the subject's response to, and dependent on, the level of the manipulated independent variable.

**descriptive statistics** Statistical measures that describe the results of a study; descriptive statistics include measures of central tendency (e.g., mean), variability (e.g., standard deviation), and correlation (e.g., Pearson *r*).

**discriminant validity** The construct validity of a measure is assessed by examining the extent to which scores on the measure are not related to scores on conceptually unrelated measures.

**effect size** The extent to which two variables are associated. In experimental research, the magnitude of the impact of the independent variable on the dependent variable.

**electroencephalogram (EEG)** A measure of the electrical activity of the brain.

**electromyogram (EMG)** A measure of the electrical activity of muscles, including muscle tension.

**empiricism** Use of objective observations to answer a question about the nature of behavior.

**error variance** Random variability in a set of scores that is not the result of the independent variable. Statistically, the variability of each score from its group mean.

**exact replication**    Replication of research using the same procedures for manipulating and measuring the variables that were used in the original research.

**experimental method**    A method of determining whether variables are related in which the researcher manipulates the independent variable and controls all other variables either by randomization or by direct experimental control.

**experimental realism**    The extent to which the independent variable manipulation has an impact on and involves subjects in an experiment.

**experimenter bias (expectancy effects)**    Any intentional or unintentional influence that the experimenter exerts on subjects to confirm the hypothesis under investigation.

**external validity**    The degree to which the results of an experiment may be generalized.

***F* test (analysis of variance)**    A statistical significance test for determining whether two or more means are significantly different. *F* is the ratio of systematic variance to error variance.

**face validity**    The degree to which a measurement device appears to accurately measure a variable.

**factorial design**    A design in which all levels of each independent variable are combined with all levels of the other independent variables. A factorial design allows investigation of the separate main effects and interactions of two or more independent variables.

**field experiment**    An experiment that is conducted in a natural setting rather than in a laboratory setting.

**filler items**    Items included in a questionnaire measure to help disguise the true purpose of the measure.

**floor effect**    Failure of a measure to detect a difference because it was too difficult (*also see* ceiling effect).

**frequency distribution**    An arrangement of a set of scores from lowest to highest that indicates the number of times each score was obtained.

**frequency polygon**    A graphic display of a frequency distribution in which the frequency of each score is plotted on the vertical axis, with the plotted points connected by straight lines.

**functional MRI**    Magnetic resonance imaging uses a magnet to obtain scans of structures of the brain. Functional magnetic resonance imaging (fMRI) provides information on the amount of activity in different brain structures.

**galvanic skin response (GSR)**    The electrical conductance of the skin, which changes when sweating occurs.

**haphazard (convenience) sampling**    Selecting subjects in a haphazard manner, usually on the basis of availability, and not with regard to having a representative sample of the population; a type of nonprobability sampling.

**history effect**    As a threat to the internal validity of an experiment, refers to any outside event that is not part of the manipulation that could be responsible for the results.

**hypothesis**    A statement that makes an assertion about what is true in a particular situation; often, a statement asserting that two or more variables are related to one another.

**independent groups design**    An experiment in which different subjects are assigned to each group. Also called between-subjects design.

**independent variable**    The variable that is manipulated to observe its effect on the dependent variable.

**inferential statistics**    Statistics designed to determine whether results based on sample data are generalizable to a population.

**informed consent**    In research ethics, the principle that participants in an experiment be informed in advance of all aspects of the research that might influence their decision to participate.

**Institutional Review Board (IRB)**    An ethics review committee established to review research proposals. The IRB is composed of scientists, nonscientists, and legal experts.

**instrument decay**   As a threat to internal validity, the possibility that a change in the characteristics of the measurement instrument is responsible for the results.

**interaction**   The differing effect of one independent variable on the dependent variable, depending on the particular level of another independent variable.

**internal consistency reliability**   Reliability assessed with data collected at one point in time with multiple measures of a psychological construct. A measure is reliable when the multiple measures provide similar results.

**internal validity**   The certainty with which results of an experiment can be attributed to the manipulation of the independent variable rather than to some other, confounding variable.

**interrater reliability**   An indicator of reliability that examines the agreement of observations made by two or more raters (judges).

**interrupted time series design**   A design in which the effectiveness of a treatment is determined by examining a series of measurements made over an extended time period both before and after the treatment is introduced. The treatment is not introduced at a random point in time.

**interval scale**   A scale of measurement in which the intervals between numbers on the scale are all equal in size.

**interviewer bias**   Intentional or unintentional influence exerted by an interviewer in such a way that the actual or interpreted behavior of respondents is consistent with the interviewer's expectations.

**IV × PV design**   A factorial design that includes both an experimental independent variable (IV) and a nonexperimental participant variable (PV).

**justice (Belmont Report)**   Principle that all individuals and groups should have fair and equal access to the benefits of research participation as well as potential risks of research participation.

**Latin square**   A technique to control for order effects without having all possible orders.

**longitudinal method**   A developmental research method in which the same persons are observed repeatedly as they grow older; conceptually similar to a repeated measures design.

**main effect**   The direct effect of an independent variable on a dependent variable.

**manipulation check**   A measure used to determine whether the manipulation of the independent variable has had its intended effect on a subject.

**matched pairs design**   A method of assigning subjects to groups in which pairs of subjects are first matched on some characteristic and then individually assigned randomly to groups.

**maturation effect**   As a threat to internal validity, the possibility that any naturally occurring change within the individual is responsible for the results.

**mean**   A measure of central tendency, obtained by summing scores and then dividing the sum by the number of scores.

**measurement error**   The degree to which a measurement deviates from the true score value.

**median**   A measure of central tendency; the middle score in a distribution of scores that divides the distribution in half.

**meta-analysis**   A set of statistical procedures for combining the results of a number of studies in order to provide a general assessment of the relationship between variables.

**mixed factorial design**   A design that includes both independent groups (between-subjects) and repeated measures (within-subjects) variables.

**mode**   A measure of central tendency; the most frequent score in a distribution of scores.

**moderator variable**   A variable that influences the nature of the relationship between two other variables (an independent variable and a dependent variable). In a factorial design, the effect of the moderator variable is revealed as an interaction.

**mortality**   The loss of subjects who decide to leave an experiment. Mortality is a threat to internal validity when the mortality rate is related to the nature of the experimental manipulation.

**multiple baseline design**   Observing behavior before and after a manipulation under multiple circumstances (across different individuals, different behaviors, or different settings).

**multiple correlation**   A correlation between one variable and a combined set of predictor variables.

**mundane realism**   The extent to which the independent variable manipulation is similar to events that occur in the real world.

**naturalistic observation**   Descriptive method in which observations are made in a natural social setting. Also called field observation.

**negative case analysis**   In field observation, an examination of observations that do not fit with the explanatory structure devised by the researcher.

**negative linear relationship**   A relationship in which increases in the values of the first variable are accompanied by decreases in the values of the second variable.

**nominal scale**   A scale of measurement with two or more categories that have no numerical (less than, greater than) properties.

**nonequivalent control group design**   A quasi-experimental design in which nonequivalent groups of subjects participate in the different experimental groups, and there is no pretest.

**nonequivalent control group pretest-posttest design**   A quasi-experimental design in which nonequivalent groups are used, but a pretest allows assessment of equivalency and pretest-posttest changes.

**nonexperimental method**   Use of measurement of variables to determine whether variables are related to one another. Also called correlational method.

**nonprobability sampling**   Type of sampling procedure in which one cannot specify the probability that any member of the population will be included in the sample.

**null hypothesis**   The hypothesis, used for statistical purposes, that the variables under investigation are not related in the population, that any observed effect based on sample results is due to random error.

**one-group posttest-only design**   A quasi-experimental design that has no control group and no pretest comparison; a very poor design in terms of internal validity.

**one-group pretest-posttest design**   A quasi-experimental design in which the effect of an independent variable is inferred from the pretest-posttest difference in a single group.

**operational definition**   Definition of a concept that specifies the operation used to measure or manipulate the concept.

**order effect**   In a repeated measures design, the effect that the order of introducing treatment has on the dependent variable.

**ordinal scale**   A scale of measurement in which the measurement categories form a rank order along a continuum.

**panel study**   In survey research, questioning the same people at two or more points in time.

**partial correlation**   The correlation between two variables with the influence of a third variable statistically controlled for.

**path analysis**   A method used to develop models of possible relationships among a set of variables that were studied with the nonexperimental method.

**Pearson product–moment correlation coefficient**    A type of correlation coefficient used with interval and ratio scale data. In addition to providing information on the strength of relationship between two variables, the Pearson product-moment correlation coefficient indicates the direction (positive or negative) of the relationship.

**pie chart**    Graphic display of data in which frequencies or percentages are represented as "slices" of a pie.

**pilot study**    A small-scale study conducted prior to conducting an actual experiment; designed to test and refine procedures.

**placebo group**    In drug research, a group given an inert substance to assess the psychological effect of receiving a treatment.

**population**    The defined group of individuals from which a sample is drawn.

**positive linear relationship**    A relationship in which increases in the values of the first variable are accompanied by increases in the values of the second variable.

**posttest-only design**    A true experimental design in which the dependent variable (posttest) is measured only once, after manipulation of the independent variable.

**power**    The probability of correctly rejecting the null hypothesis.

**prediction**    A statement that makes an assertion concerning what will occur in a particular research investigation.

**predictive validity**    The construct validity of a measure is assessed by examining the ability of the measure to predict a future behavior.

**pretest-posttest design**    A true experimental design in which the dependent variable is measured both before (pretest) and after (posttest) manipulation of the independent variable.

**probability**    The likelihood that a given event (among a specific set of events) will occur.

**probability sampling**    Type of sampling procedure in which one is able to specify the probability that any member of the population will be included in the sample.

**program evaluation**    Research designed to evaluate programs (e.g., social reforms, innovations) that are designed to produce certain changes or outcomes in a target population.

**psychobiography**    A type of case study in which the life of an individual is analyzed using psychological theory.

**quasi-experimental design**    A type of design that approximates the control features of true experiments to infer that a given treatment did have its intended effect.

**quota sampling**    A sampling procedure in which the sample is chosen to reflect the numerical composition of various subgroups in the population. A haphazard sampling technique is used to obtain the sample.

**randomization**    Controlling for the effects of extraneous variables by ensuring that the variables operate in a manner determined entirely by chance.

**ratio scale**    A scale of measurement in which there is an absolute zero point, indicating an absence of the variable being measured. An implication is that ratios of numbers on the scale can be formed (generally, these are physical measures such as weight or timed measures such as duration or reaction time).

**reactivity**    A problem of measurement in which the measure changes the behavior being observed.

**regression equation**    A mathematical equation that allows prediction of one behavior when the score on another variable is known.

**regression toward the mean**    Also called statistical regression; principle that extreme scores on a variable tend to be closer to the mean when a second measurement is made.

**reliability**    The degree to which a measure is consistent.

**repeated measures design**  An experiment in which the same subjects are assigned to each group. Also called within-subjects design.

**replication**  Repeating a research study to determine whether the results can be duplicated.

**research hypothesis**  The hypothesis that the variables under investigation are related in the population, that the observed effect based on sample data is true in the population.

**response rate**  The percentage of people selected for a sample who actually completed a survey.

**response set**  A pattern of individual response to questions on a self-report measure that is not related to the content of the questions.

**reversal design**  A single case design in which the treatment is introduced after a baseline period and then withdrawn during a second baseline period. It may be extended by adding a second introduction of the treatment. Sometimes called a "withdrawal" design.

**role-playing**  A procedure for studying behavior in which individuals are asked to indicate how they would respond to a given situation rather than being observed in action in the situation.

**sampling**  The process of choosing members of a population to be included in a sample.

**sampling frame**  The individuals or clusters of individuals in a population who might actually be selected for inclusion in the sample.

**selection differences**  Differences in the type of subjects who make up each group in an experimental design; this situation occurs when participants elect which group they are to be assigned to.

**sensitivity**  The ability of a measure to detect differences between groups.

**sequential method**  A combination of the cross-sectional and longitudinal design to study developmental research questions.

**simple main effect**  In a factorial design, the effect of one independent variable at a particular level of another independent variable.

**simple random sampling**  A sampling procedure in which each member of the population has an equal probability of being included in the sample.

**single case experiment**  An experiment in which the effect of the independent variable is assessed using data from a single participant.

**split-half reliability**  A reliability coefficient determined by the correlation between scores on half of the items on a measure with scores on the other half of a measure.

**standard deviation**  The average deviation of scores from the mean (the square root of the variance).

**statistical significance**  Rejection of the null hypothesis when an outcome has a low probability of occurrence (usually .05 or less) if, in fact, the null hypothesis is correct.

**stratified random sampling**  A sampling procedure in which the population is divided into strata followed by random sampling from each stratum.

**structural model**  A model of an expected pattern of relationships among a set of variables. The proposed pattern is based on a theory of how the variables are causally related to one another.

**systematic observation**  Observations of one or more specific variables, usually made in a precisely defined setting.

**systematic variance**  Variability in a set of scores that is the result of the independent variable; statistically, the variability of each group mean from the grand mean of all subjects.

**temporal precedence**  Part of causal inference; the cause precedes the effect in a time sequence.

**testing effect**  A threat to internal validity in which taking a pretest changes behavior without any effect on the independent variable.

**test-retest reliability**  A reliability coefficient determined by the correlation between scores on a measure given at one time with scores on the same measure given at a later time.

**true score**   An individual's actual score on a variable being measured, as opposed to the score the individual obtained on the measure itself.

**_t_-test**   A statistical significance test used to compare differences between means.

**Type I error**   An incorrect decision to reject the null hypothesis when it is true.

**Type II error**   An incorrect decision to accept the null hypothesis when it is false.

**validity**   *See* construct validity, external validity, internal validity.

**variability**   The amount of dispersion of scores about some central value.

**variable**   Any event, situation, behavior, or individual characteristic that varies—that is, has at least two values.

**variance**   A measure of the variability of scores about a mean; the mean of the sum of squared deviations of scores from the group mean.

# References

Aiello, J. R., Baum, A., & Gormley, F. P. (1981). Social determinants of residential crowding stress. *Personality and Social Psychology Bulletin, 4,* 643–649.

Ajzen, I., & Fishbein, M. (1980). *Understanding attitudes and predicting social behavior.* Englewood Cliffs, NJ: Prentice-Hall.

American Psychological Association. (2002a). *Ethical principles of psychologists and code of conduct.* Retrieved October 20, 2002, from http://www.apa.org/ethics/code2002.html

American Psychological Association. (2002b). *Guidelines for ethical conduct in the care and use of animals.* Retrieved March 2, 2003, from http://www.apa.org/science/anguide.html

American Psychological Association. (2001). *Publication manual of the American Psychological Association* (5th ed.). Washington, DC: Author.

Anderson, C. A., & Anderson, D. C. (1984). Ambient temperature and violent crime: Test of the linear and curvilinear hypotheses. *Journal of Personality and Social Psychology, 46,* 91–97.

Anderson, C. A., Lindsay, J. J., & Bushman, B. J. (1999). Research in the psychological laboratory: Truth or triviality? *Current Directions in Psychological Science, 8,* 3–9.

Anderson, D. R., Lorch, E. P., Field, D. E., Collins, P. A., & Nathan, J. G. (1986). TV viewing at home. *Child Development, 57,* 1024–1033.

Aristotle. (1954). Rhetoric. In *Aristotle, rhetoric, and poetics* (W. Rhys Roberts, Trans.). New York: Modern Library.

Aronson, E., Brewer, M., & Carlsmith, J. M. (1985). Experimentation in social psychology. In G. Lindzey & E. Aronson (Eds.), *Handbook of social psychology* (3rd ed.). New York: Random House.

Asch, S. (1956). Studies of independence and conformity: A minority of one against a unanimous majority. *Psychological Monographs, 709* (Whole No. 416).

Astin, A. (1987). *The American freshman: Twenty year trends, 1966–1985.* Los Angeles: Higher Education Research Institute, Graduate School of Education, University of California.

Bakeman, R., & Brownlee, J. R. (1980). The strategic use of parallel play: A sequential analysis. *Child Development, 51,* 873–878.

Bakeman, R., & Gottman, J. M. (1986). *Observing interaction.* Cambridge: Cambridge University Press.

Bales, R. F., & Cohen, S. P. (1979). *SYMLOG: A system for the multiple level observation of groups.* New York: Free Press.

Barlow, D. H., & Hersen, M. (1984). *Single case experimental designs.* New York: Pergamon Press.

Baron, R. A. (1997). The sweet smell of . . . helping: Effects of pleasant ambient fragrance on prosocial behavior in shopping malls. *Personality and Social Psychology Bulletin, 23,* 498–503.

Baron, R. M., & Kenney, D. A. (1986). The moderator-mediator variable distinction in social psychological research: Conceptual, strategic, and statistical considerations. *Journal of Personality and Social Psychology, 51,* 1173–1182.

Barton, E. M., Baltes, M. M., & Orzech, M. J. (1980). Etiology of dependence in older nursing home residents during morning care; the role of staff behavior. *Journal of Personality and Social Psychology, 38,* 423–431.

Baum, A., Gachtel, R. J., & Schaeffer, M. A. (1983). Emotional, behavioral, and psychological effects of chronic stress at Three Mile Island. *Journal of Consulting and Clinical Psychology, 51,* 565–572.

Baumeister, R. F., & Newman, L. S. (1994). How stories make sense of personal experiences: Motives that shape autobiographical narratives. *Personality and Social Psychology Bulletin, 20,* 676–690.

Beach, F. A. (1950). The snark was a boojum. *American Psychologist, 5,* 115–124.

Becker, H. S. (1963). *Outsiders: Studies in the sociology of deviance.* New York: Free Press.

Bem, D. J. (1981). Writing the research report. In L. H. Kidder (Ed.), *Research methods in social relations.* New York: Holt, Rinehart & Winston.

Bem, D. J. (2002). *Writing the empirical journal article.* Retrieved August 15, 2002, from http://comp9. psych.cornell.edu/dbem/writing_article.html

Berry, T. D., & Geller, E. S. (1991). A single-subject approach to evaluative vehicle safety belt reminders: Back to basics. *Journal of Applied Behavior Analysis, 24,* 13–22.

Berscheid, E., Baron, R. S., Dermer, M., & Libman, M. (1973). Anticipating informed consent: An empirical approach. *American Psychologist, 28,* 913–925.

Bornstein, B. H. (1998). From compassion to compensation: The effect of injury severity on mock jurors' liability judgments. *Journal of Applied Social Psychology, 28,* 1477–1502.

Bortnik, K., Henderson, L., & Zimbardo, P. (2002). *The Shy Q, a measure of chronic shyness: Associations with interpersonal motives and interpersonal values.* Retrieved November 10, 2002, from http:// www.shyness.com/documents/2002/SITAR2002 poster_handout.pdf

Bouchard, T. J., Jr., & McGue, M. (1981). Familial studies of intelligence: A review. *Science, 212,* 1055–1059.

Broberg, A. G., Wessels, H., Lamb, M. E., & Hwang, C. P. (1997). Effects of day care on the development of cognitive abilities in 8-year-olds: A longitudinal study. *Developmental Psychology, 33,* 62–69.

Bröder, A. (1998). Deception can be acceptable. *American Psychologist, 53,* 805–806.

Brogden, W. J. (1962). The experimenter as a factor in animal conditioning. *Psychological Reports, 11,* 239–242.

Brooks, C. I., & Rebata, J. L. (1991). College classroom ecology: The relation of sex of student to classroom performance and seating preference. *Environment and Behavior, 23,* 305–313.

Brown, A. S., & Rahhal, T. A. (1994). Hiding valuables: A questionnaire study of mnemonically risky behavior. *Applied Cognitive Psychology, 8,* 141–154.

Bruning, N. S., & Frew, D. R. (1987). Effects of exercise, relaxation, and management skills training on physiological stress indicators: A field experiment. *Journal of Applied Psychology, 72,* 515–521.

Bushman, B. J., & Wells, G. L. (2001). Narrative impressions of the literature: The availability bias and the corrective properties of meta-analytic approaches. *Personality and Social Psychology Bulletin, 27,* 1123–1130.

Buss, D. M. (1989). Sex differences in human mate preferences: Evolutionary hypotheses tested in 37 cultures. *Behavioral and Brain Sciences, 12,* 1–49.

Buss, D. M. (1998). *Evolutionary psychology: The new science of the mind.* Boston: Allyn & Bacon.

Byrne, D., Ervin, C. R., & Lamberth, J. (1970). Continuity between the experimental study of attraction and real-life computer dating. *Journal of Personality and Social Psychology, 16,* 157–165.

Byrne, G. (1988, October 7). Breuning pleads guilty. *Science, 242,* 27–28.

Cacioppo, J. T., & Tassinary, L. G. (1990). Inferring psychological significance from physiological signals. *American Psychologist, 45,* 16–28.

Campbell, D. T. (1968). Quasi-experimental design. In D. L. Gillis (Ed.), *International encyclopedia of the social sciences* (Vol. 5). New York: Macmillan and Free Press.

Campbell, D. T. (1969). Reforms as experiments. *American Psychologist, 24,* 409–429.

Campbell, D. T., & Stanley, J. C. (1966). *Experimental and quasi-experimental designs for research.* Chicago: Rand McNally.

Carroll, M. E., & Overmier, J. B. (Eds.). (2001). *Animal research and human health: Advancing human welfare through behavioral science.* Washington, DC: American Psychological Association.

Caspi, A., & Silva, P. T. (1995). Temperamental qualities at age three predict personality traits in young adulthood: Longitudinal evidence from a birth cohort. *Child Development, 66,* 486–498.

Cavan, S. (1966). *Liquor license: An ethnography of bar behavior.* Chicago: Aldine.

Chaiken, S., & Pliner, P. (1987). Women, but not men, are what they eat: The effect of meal size and gender on perceived femininity and masculinity. *Personality and Social Psychology Bulletin, 13,* 166–176.

Chastain, G. D., & Landrum, R. E. (Eds.). (1999). *Protecting human subjects: Department subject pools and institutional review boards.* Washington, DC: American Psychological Association.

Christensen, L. (1988). Deception in psychological research: When is its use justified? *Personality and Social Psychology Bulletin, 14,* 664–675.

Cialdini, R. B. (1988). *Influence: Science and practice* (2nd ed.). Glenview, IL: Scott, Foresman.

Clark, K. B., & Clark, M. P. (1947). Racial identification and preference in Negro children. In T. M. Newcomb & E. L. Hartley (Eds.), *Readings in social psychology.* New York: Holt, Rinehart & Winston.

Cohen, D., Nisbett, R. E., Bowdle, B. F., & Schwarz, N. (1996). Insult, aggression, and the southern culture of honor: An "experimental ethnography." *Journal of Personality and Social Psychology, 70,* 945–960.

Cohen, J. (1988). *Statistical power analysis for the behavioral sciences.* Hillsdale, NJ: Erlbaum.

Cohen, J. (1994). The earth is round ($p < .05$). *American Psychologist, 49,* 997–1003.

Coile, D. C., & Miller, N. E. (1984). How radical animal activists try to mislead humane people. *American Psychologist, 39,* 700–701.

Coltheart, V., & Langdon, R. (1998). Recall of short word lists presented visually at fast rates: Effects of phonological similarity and word length. *Memory & Cognition, 26,* 330–342.

Conoley, J. C., & Kramer, J. J. (1989). *Tenth mental measurements yearbook.* Lincoln: Buros Institute of Mental Measurements, University of Nebraska–Lincoln.

Converse, J. M., & Presser, S. (1986). *Survey questions: Handcrafting the standardized questionnaire.* Newbury Park, CA: Sage.

Cooper, H. M., & Rosenthal, R. (1980). Statistical versus traditional procedures for summarizing research findings. *Psychological Bulletin, 87,* 442–449.

Costa, P. T., Jr., & McCrae, R. R. (1985). *The NEO Personality Inventory manual.* Odessa, FL: Psychological Assessment Resources.

Cunningham, M. R., Druen, P. B., & Barbee, A. P. (1997). Angels, mentors, and friends: Trade-offs among evolutionary, social, and individual variables in physical appearance. In J. A. Simpson & D. T. Kenrick (Eds.), *Evolutionary social psychology* (pp. 109–140). Mahwah, NJ: Erlbaum.

Cunningham, M. R., Roberts, R., Barbee, A. P., Druen, P. B., & Wu, C. (1995). "Their ideas of beauty are, on the whole, the same as ours": Consistency and variability in the cross-cultural perception of female physical attractiveness. *Journal of Personality and Social Psychology, 68,* 261–279.

Curtiss, S. R. (1977). *Genie: A psycholinguistic study of a modern-day "wild child."* New York: Academic Press.

Darley, J. M., & Latané, B. (1968). Bystander intervention in emergencies: Diffusion of responsibility. *Journal of Personality and Social Psychology, 8,* 377–383.

Denmark, F., Russo, N. P., Frieze, I. H., & Sechzer, J. A. (1988). Guidelines for avoiding sexism in psychological research: A report of the Ad Hoc Committee on Nonsexist Research. *American Psychologist, 43,* 582–585.

Department of Health and Human Services. (2001). Protection of human subjects. Retrieved March 19, 2003, from http:/ohrp. osophs.dhhs.gov/humansubjects/guidance/ 45cfr46.htm

Dermer, M. L., & Hoch, T. A. (1999). Improving descriptions of single-subject experiments in research texts written for undergraduates. *Psychological Record, 49,* 49–66.

Dill, C. A., Gilden, E. R., Hill, P. C., & Hanslka, L. L. (1982). Federal human subjects regulations: A methodological artifact? *Personality and Social Psychology Bulletin, 8,* 417–425.

Dillman, D. A. (2000). *Mail and Internet surveys: The tailored design method* (2nd ed.). New York: Wiley.

Duncan, S., Rosenberg, M. J., & Finklestein, J. (1969). The paralanguage of experimenter bias. *Sociometry, 32,* 207–219.

Eagly, A. H., Ashmore, R. D., Makhijani, M. G., & Longo, L. C. (1991). What is beautiful is good, but . . . : A meta-analytic review of research on the physical attractiveness stereotype. *Psychological Bulletin, 110,* 109–128.

Eagly, A. M., & Wood, W. (1999). The origins of sex differences in human behavior: Evolved dispositions versus social roles. *American Psychologist, 54,* 408–423.

Ellsworth, P. C., Carlsmith, J. M., & Henson, A. (1972). The stare as a stimulus to flight in human beings: A series of field experiments. *Journal of Personality and Social Psychology, 21,* 302–311.

Elms, A. C. (1994). *Uncovering lives: The uneasy alliance of biography and psychology.* New York: Oxford University Press.

Ennett, S. T., Tobler, N. S., Ringwalt, C. L., & Flewelling, R. L. (1994). How effective is drug abuse resistance education? A meta-analysis of Project D.A.R.E. outcome evaluations. *American Journal of Public Health, 84,* 1394–1401.

Epstein, Y. M., Suedfeld, P., & Silverstein, S. J. (1973). The experimental contract: Subjects' expectations of and reactions to some behaviors of experimenters. *American Psychologist, 28,* 212–221.

Everett, P. B., Hayward, S. C., & Meyers, A. W. (1974). The effects of a token reinforcement procedure on bus ridership. *Journal of Applied Behavior Analysis, 7,* 1–10.

Fazio, R. H., Cooper, M., Dayson, K., & Johnson, M. (1981). Control and the coronary-prone behavior pattern: Responses to multiple situational demands. *Personality and Social Psychology Bulletin, 7,* 97–102.

Feldman Barrett, L., & Barrett, D. J. (2001). Computerized experience-sampling: How technology facilitates the study of conscious experience. *Social Science Computer Review, 19,* 175–185.

Fischer, K., Schoeneman, T. J., & Rubanowitz, D. E. (1987). Attributions in the advice columns: II. The dimensionality of actors' and observers' explanations of interpersonal problems. *Personality and Social Psychology Bulletin, 13,* 458–466.

Fiske, S. T., Bersoff, D. N., Borgida, E., Deaux, K., & Heilman, M. E. (1991). Social science research on trial: Use of sex stereotyping in Price Waterhouse v. Hopkins. *American Psychologist, 46,* 1049–1060.

Fiske, S. T., & Taylor, S. E. (1984). *Social cognition.* New York: Random House.

Flavell, J. H. (1996). Piaget's legacy. *Psychological Science, 7,* 200–203.

Fowler, F. J., Jr. (1984). *Survey research methods.* Newbury Park, CA: Sage.

Frank, M. G., & Gilovich, T. (1988). The dark side of self- and social perception: Black uniforms and aggression in professional sports. *Journal of Personality and Social Psychology, 54,* 74–85.

Freedman, J. L. (1969). Role-playing: Psychology by consensus. *Journal of Personality and Social Psychology, 13,* 107–114.

Freedman, J. L., Klevansky, S., & Ehrlich, P. R. (1971). The effect of crowding on human task performance. *Journal of Applied Social Psychology, 1,* 7–25.

Freedman, J. L., Levy, A. S., Buchanan, R. W., & Price, J. (1972). Crowding and human aggressiveness. *Journal of Experimental Social Psychology, 8,* 528–548.

Frick, R. W. (1995). Accepting the null hypothesis. *Memory and Cognition, 25,* 132–138.

Fried, C. B. (1999). Who's afraid of rap: Differential reactions to music lyrics. *Journal of Applied Social Psychology, 29,* 705–721.

Friedman, H. S., Tucker, J. S., Schwartz, J. E., Tomlinson-Keasy, C., Martin, L. R., Wingard, D. L., & Criqui, M. H. (1995). Psychosocial and behavioral predictors of longevity: The aging and death of the "Termites." *American Psychologist, 50,* 69–78.

Furnham, A., Gunter, B., & Peterson, E. (1994). Television distraction and the performance of introverts and extroverts. *Applied Cognitive Psychology, 8,* 705–711.

Gallup, G. G., & Suarez, S. D. (1985). Alternatives to the use of animals in psychological research. *American Psychologist, 40,* 1104–1111.

Gardner, G. T. (1978). Effects of federal human subjects regulations on data obtained in environmental stressor research. *Journal of Personality and Social Psychology, 34,* 774–781.

Gardner, L. E. (1988). A relatively painless method of introduction to the psychological literature search. In M. E. Ware & C. L. Brewer (Eds.), *Handbook for teaching statistics and research methods.* Hillsdale, NJ: Erlbaum.

Gaulin, S. J. C., & McBurney, D. (2000). *Psychology: An evolutionary approach.* Upper Saddle River, NJ: Prentice-Hall.

Gelfand, H., & Walker, C. J. (2001). *Mastering APA style.* Washington, DC: American Psychological Association.

Geller, E. S., Russ, N. W., & Altomari, M. G. (1986). Naturalistic observations of beer drinking among college students. *Journal of Applied Behavior Analysis, 19,* 391–396.

Gilovich, T. (1991). *How we know what isn't so: The fallibility of human reason in everyday life.* New York: Free Press.

Goodstein, D. (2000). *How science works.* Retrieved February 10, 2002, from http://www.its.caltech.edu/~dg/HowScien.pdf

Graesser, A. C., Kennedy, T., Wiemer-Hastings, P., & Ottati, V. (1999). The use of computational cognitive methods to improve questions on surveys and questionnaires. In M. G. Sirkin, D. J. Hermann, S. Schechter, N. Schwarz, J. M. Tanur, & R. Tourangeau (Eds.), *Cognition and survey methods research* (pp. 199–216). New York: Wiley.

Green, J., & Wallaf, C. (1981). *Ethnography and language in educational settings.* New York: Ablex.

Greenfield, D. N. (1999). *Nature of Internet addiction: Psychological factors in compulsive Internet use.* Paper presented at the meeting of the American Psychological Association, Boston, MA.

Greenwald, A. G. (1976). Within-subjects designs: To use or not to use? *Psychological Bulletin, 83,* 314–320.

Gross, A. E., & Fleming, I. (1982). Twenty years of deception in social psychology. *Personality and Social Psychology Bulletin, 8,* 402–408.

Gwaltney-Gibbs, P. A. (1986). The institutionalization of premarital cohabitation: Estimates from marriage license applications, 1970 and 1980. *Journal of Marriage and the Family, 48,* 423–434.

Haney, C., & Zimbardo, P. G. (1998). The past and future of U.S. prison policy: Twenty-five years after the Stanford Prison Experiment. *American Psychologist, 53,* 709–727.

Harris, R. (2002). *Anti-plagiarism strategies for research papers.* Retrieved September 10, 2002, from http://www.virtualsalt.com/antiplag.htm

Hawking, S. W. (1988). *A brief history of time: From the big bang to black holes.* New York: Bantam Books.

Hearnshaw, L. S. (1979). *Cyril Burt, psychologist.* Ithaca, NY: Cornell University Press.

Henle, M., & Hubbell, M. B. (1938). "Egocentricity" in adult conversation. *Journal of Social Psychology, 9,* 227–234.

Herman, D. B., Struening, E. L., & Barrow, S. M. (1994). Self-reported needs for help among homeless men and women. *Evaluation and Program Planning, 17,* 249–256.

Hill, C. T., Rubin, Z., & Peplau, L. A. (1976). Breakups before marriage: The end of 103 affairs. *Journal of Social Issues, 32,* 147–168.

Hill, L. (1990). Effort and reward in college: A replication of some puzzling findings. In J. W. Neuliep (Ed.), *Handbook of replication in the behavioral and social sciences* [Special issue]. *Journal of Social Behavior and Personality, 5*(4), 151–161.

Holden, C. (1987). Animal regulations: So far, so good. *Science, 238,* 880–882.

Hood, T. C., & Back, K. W. (1971). Self-disclosure and the volunteer: A source of bias in laboratory experiments. *Journal of Personality and Social Psychology, 17,* 130–136.

Hostetler, A. J. (1987, May). Fraud inquiry revives doubt: Can science police itself? *APA Monitor,* 1, 12.

Humphreys, L. (1970). *Tearoom trade.* Chicago: Aldine.

Jones, R., & Cooper, J. (1971). Mediation of experimenter effects. *Journal of Personality and Social Psychology, 20,* 70–74.

Josselson, R., & Lieblich, A. (1993). *The narrative study of lives.* Newbury Park, CA: Sage.

Jourard, S. M. (1969). The effects of experimenters' self-disclosure on subjects' behavior. In C. Spielberger (Ed.), *Current topics in community and clinical psychology.* New York: Academic Press.

Joy, L. A., Kimball, M. M., & Zabrack, M. L. (1986). Television and children's aggressive behavior. In T. M. Williams (Ed.), *The impact of television: A natural experiment in three communities.* Orlando, FL: Academic Press.

Judd, C. M., Smith, E. R., & Kidder, L. H. (1991). *Research methods in social relations* (6th ed.). Ft. Worth, TX: Holt, Rinehart & Winston.

Kamin, L. G. (1974). *The science and politics of IQ.* New York: Wiley.

Kazdin, A. E. (1995). Preparing and evaluating research reports. *Psychological Assessment, 7,* 228–237.

Kazdin, A. E. (2001). *Behavior modification in applied settings* (6th ed.). Belmont, CA: Wadsworth.

Kelman, H. C. (1967). Human use of human subjects: The problem of deception in social psychological experiments. *Psychological Bulletin, 67,* 1–11.

Kenny, D. A. (1979). *Correlation and causality.* New York: Wiley.

Keyser, D. J., & Sweetland, R. C. (Eds.). (1991). *Test critiques.* Kansas City, MO: Test Corporation of America.

Kimmel, A. (1998). In defense of deception. *American Psychologist, 53,* 803–805.

Kintz, N. L., Delprato, D. J., Mettee, D. R., Persons, C. E., & Schappe, R. H. (1965). The experimenter effect. *Psychological Bulletin, 63,* 223–232.

Kirsch, I., Moore, T. J., Scoboria, A., & Nicholls, S. S. (2002). The emperor's new drugs: An analysis of antidepressant medication data submitted to the U.S. Food and Drug Administration. *Prevention & Treatment, 5,* Article 23. Retrieved November 1, 2002, from http://www.journals.apa.org/prevention/volume5/pre0050023a.html

Kitayama, S., Markus, H. R., Matsumoto, H., & Norasakkunkit, V. (1997). Individual and collective processes in the construction of the self: Self-enhancement in the United States and self-criticism in Japan. *Journal of Personality and Social Psychology, 72,* 1245–1267.

Koocher, G. P. (1977). Bathroom behavior and human dignity. *Journal of Personality and Social Psychology, 35,* 120–121.

Koop, C. E. (1987). Report of the Surgeon General's workshop on pornography and public health. *American Psychologist, 42,* 944–945.

Korn, J. H. (1997). *Illusions of reality: A history of deception in social psychology.* Albany: State University of New York Press.

Korn, J. H. (1998). The reality of deception. *American Psychologist, 53,* 805.

Koss, M. P. (1992). The underdetection of rape: Methodololgical choices influence incident estimates. *Journal of Social Issues, 48*(1), 61–75.

Krantz, J. H., Ballard, J., & Scher, J. (1997). Comparing the results of laboratory and World Wide Web samples on the determinants of female attractiveness. *Behavior Research Methods, Instrumentation, and Computers, 29,* 264–269.

Labranche, E. R., Helweg-Larsen, M., Byrd, C. E., & Choquette, R. A., Jr. (1997). To picture or not to picture: Levels of erotophobia and breast self-examination brochure techniques. *Journal of Applied Social Psychology, 27,* 2200–2212.

Lana, R. E. (1969). Pretest sensitization. In R. Rosenthal & R. L. Rosnow (Eds.), *Artifacts in behavioral research.* New York: Academic Press.

Langer, E. J., & Abelson, R. P. (1974). A patient by any other name . . . : Clinical group difference in labeling bias. *Journal of Consulting and Clinical Psychology, 42,* 4–9.

Langer, E. J., & Rodin, J. (1976). The effects of choice and enhanced personal responsibility for the aged: A field experiment in an institutional setting. *Journal of Personality and Social Psychology, 34,* 191–198.

Latané, B., Williams, K., & Harkins, S. (1979). Many hands make light the work: The causes and consequences of social loafing. *Journal of Personality and Social Psychology, 37,* 822–832.

Leventhal, H. (1970). Findings and theory in the study of fear communications. In L. Berkowitz (Ed.), *Advances in experimental social psychology* (Vol. 5). New York: Academic Press.

Levin, J. R. (1983). Pictorial strategies for school learning: Practical illustrations. In M. Pressley & J. R. Levin (Eds.), *Cognitive strategy research: Educational applications* (pp. 213–238). New York: Springer-Verlag.

Levine, R. V. (1990). The pace of life. *American Scientist, 78,* 450–459.

Linz, D., Donnerstein, E., & Penrod, S. (1987). The findings and recommendations of the Attorney General's Commission on Pornography: Do the psychological "facts" fit the political fury? *American Psychologist, 42,* 946–953.

Loehlin, J. C. (1998). *Latent variable models: An introduction to factor, path, and structural analysis.* Mahwah, NJ: Erlbaum.

Lofland, J., & Lofland, L. H. (1995). *Analyzing social settings: A guide to qualitative observation and analysis* (3rd ed.). Belmont, CA: Wadsworth.

Loftus, E. (1979). *Eyewitness testimony.* Cambridge, MA: Harvard University Press.

Luria, A. R. (1968). *The mind of a mnemonist.* New York: Basic Books.

Macintosh, N. J. (Ed.). (1995). *Cyril Burt: Fraud or framed?* New York: Oxford University Press.

Marlatt, G. A., & Rohsenow, D. R. (1980). Cognitive processes in alcohol use: Expectancy and the balanced placebo design. In N. K. Mello (Ed.), *Advances in substance abuse* (Vol. 1). Greenwich, CT: JAI Press.

Maruyama, G. M. (1998). *Basics of structural equation modeling.* Thousand Oaks, CA: Sage.

Matsumoto, D. (1994). *Cultural influences on research methods and statistics.* Belmont, CA: Brooks/Cole.

Matteson, M. T., & Ivancevich, J. M. (1983). Note on tension discharge rate as an employee health status predictor. *Academy of Management Journal, 26,* 540–545.

Mazzella, R., & Feingold, A. (1994). The effects of physical attractiveness, race, socioeconomic status, and gender of defendants and victims on judgments of mock jurors: A meta-analysis. *Journal of Applied Social Psychology, 24,* 1315–1344.

McCutcheon, L. E. (2000). Another failure to generalize the Mozart effect. *Psychological Reports, 87,* 325–330.

McGuigan, F. J. (1963). The experimenter: A neglected stimulus. *Psychological Bulletin, 60,* 421–428.

Middlemist, R. D., Knowles, E. S., & Matter, C. F. (1976). Personal space invasion in the lavatory: Suggestive evidence for arousal. *Journal of Personality and Social Psychology, 33,* 541–546.

Middlemist, R. D., Knowles, E. S., & Matter, C. F. (1977). What to do and what to report: A reply to Koocher. *Journal of Personality and Social Psychology, 35,* 122–124.

Milgram, S. (1963). Behavioral study of obedience. *Journal of Abnormal and Social Psychology, 67,* 371–378.

Milgram, S. (1964). Group pressure and action against a person. *Journal of Abnormal and Social Psychology, 69,* 137–143.

Milgram, S. (1965). Some conditions of obedience and disobedience to authority. *Human Relations, 18,* 57–76.

Miller, A. G. (1972). Role-playing: An alternative to deception? *American Psychologist, 27,* 623–636.

Miller, A. G. (1986). *The obedience experiments: A case study of controversy in social science.* New York: Praeger.

Miller, G. A. (1969). Psychology as a means of promoting human welfare. *American Psychologist, 24,* 1063–1075.

Miller, J. G. (1999). Cultural psychology: Implications for basic psychological theory. *Psychological Science, 10,* 85–91.

Miller, N. E. (1985). The value of behavioral research on animals. *American Psychologist, 40,* 423–440.

Montee, B. B., Miltenberger, R. G., & Wittrock, D. (1995). An experimental analysis of facilitated communication. *Journal of Applied Behavior Analysis, 28,* 189–200.

Morgan, D. L., & Morgan, R. K. (2001). Single-participant research design: Bringing science to managed care. *American Psychologist, 56,* 119–127.

Murray, B. (2002). Research fraud needn't happen at all. *APA Monitor, 33*(2). Retrieved July 31, 2002, from http://www.apa.org/monitor/feb02/fraud.html

National Commission for the Protection of Human Subjects of Biomedical and Behavioral Research. (April 18, 1979). *The Belmont Report: Ethical principles and guidelines for the protection of human subjects of research.* Retrieved March 19, 2003, from http://ohsr.od.nih.gov/mpa/belmont.php3

Nicol, A. A. M., & Pexman, P. M. (2003). *Displaying your findings: A practical guide for creating figures, posters, and presentations.* Washington, DC: American Psychological Association.

Nisbett, R. E., & Ross, L. (1980). *Human inference: Strategies and shortcomings of social judgment.* Englewood Cliffs, NJ: Prentice-Hall.

Nisbett, R. E., & Wilson, T. D. (1977). Telling more than we can know: Verbal reports on mental processes. *Psychological Review, 84,* 231–259.

Ono, H., Phillips, K. A., & Leneman, M. (1996). Content of an abstract: De jure and de facto. *American Psychologist, 51,* 1338–1340.

Orne, M. T. (1962). On the social psychology of the psychological experiment: With particular reference to demand characteristics and their implications. *American Psychologist, 17,* 776–783.

Ortmann, A., & Hertwig, R. (1997). Is deception acceptable? *American Psychologist, 52,* 746–747.

Osgood, C. E., Suci, G. J., & Tannenbaum, P. H. (1957). *The measurement of meaning.* Urbana: University of Illinois Press.

Patterson, G. R., & Moore, D. (1979). Interactive patterns as units of behavior. In M. E. Lamb,

S. J. Sumoi, & G. L. Stephenson (Eds.), *Social interaction analysis: Methodological issues* (pp. 77–96). Madison: University of Wisconsin Press.

Paulus, P. B., Annis, A. B., Seta, J. J., Schkade, J. K., & Matthews, R. W. (1976). Crowding does affect task performance. *Journal of Personality and Social Psychology, 34,* 248–253.

Pepitone, A., & Triandis, H. (1987). On the universality of social psychological theories. *Journal of Cross-Cultural Psychology, 18,* 471–499.

Petty, R. E., & Cacioppo, J. T. (1986). *Communication and persuasion: Central and peripheral routes to attitude change.* New York: Springer-Verlag.

Petty, R. E., Cacioppo, J. T., & Goldman, R. (1981). Personal involvement as a determinant of argument-based persuasion. *Journal of Personality and Social Psychology, 41,* 847–855.

Pfungst, O. (1911). *Clever Hans (the horse of Mr. von Osten): A contribution to experimental, animal, and human psychology* (C. L. Rahn, Trans.). New York: Holt, Rinehart & Winston. (Republished 1965.)

Piaget, J. (1952). *The origins of intelligence in children.* New York: International Universities Press.

Plous, S. (1996a). Attitudes toward the use of animals in psychological research and education: Results from a national survey of psychologists. *American Psychologist, 51,* 1167–1180.

Plous, S. (1996b). Attitudes toward the use of animals in psychological research and education: Results from a national survey of psychology majors. *Psychological Science, 7,* 352–363.

Punnett, B. J. (1986). Goal setting: An extension of the research. *Journal of Applied Psychology, 71,* 171–172.

Rauscher, F. H., & Shaw, G. L. (1998). Key components of the Mozart effect. *Perceptual and Motor Skills, 86,* 835–841.

Rauscher, F. H., Shaw, G. L., & Ky, K. N. (1993). Music and spatial task performance. *Nature, 365,* 611.

Rauscher, F. H., Shaw, G. L., & Ky, K. N. (1995). Listening to Mozart enhances spatial-temporal reasoning: Towards a neurophysiological basis. *Neuroscience Letters, 185,* 44–47.

Reed, J. G., & Baxter, P. M. (2003). *Library use: A handbook for psychology* (3rd ed.). Washington, DC: American Psychological Association.

Reeve, D. K., & Aggleton, J. P. (1998). On the specificity of expert knowledge about a soap opera: An everyday story of farming folk. *Applied Cognitive Psychology, 12,* 35–42.

Reifman, A. S., Larrick, R. P., & Fein, S. (1991). Temper and temperature on the diamond: The heat-aggression relationship in major league baseball. *Personality and Social Psychology Bulletin, 17,* 580–585.

Reverby, S. M. (Ed.). (2000). *Tuskegee's truths: Rethinking the Tuskegee syphilis study.* Chapel Hill, NC: University of North Carolina Press.

Ring, K. (1967). Experimental social psychology: Some sober questions about frivolous values. *Journal of Experimental Social Psychology, 3,* 113–123.

Ring, K., Wallston, K., & Corey, M. (1970). Mode of debriefing as a factor affecting subjective reaction to a Milgram-type obedience experiment: An ethical inquiry. *Representative Research in Social Psychology, 1,* 67–68.

Riordan, C. A., & Marlin, N. A. (1987). Some good news about some bad practices. *American Psychologist, 42,* 104–106.

Roberson, M. T., & Sundstrom, E. (1990). Questionnaire design, return rates, and response favorableness in an employee attitude questionnaire. *Journal of Applied Psychology, 75,* 354–357.

Robinson, J. P., Athanasiou, R., & Head, K. B. (1969). *Measures of occupational attitudes and occupational characteristics.* Ann Arbor, MI: Institute for Social Research.

Robinson, J. P., Rusk, J. G., & Head, K. B. (1968). *Measures of political attitudes.* Ann Arbor, MI: Institute for Social Research.

Robinson, J. P., Shaver, P. R., & Wrightsman, L. S. (1991). *Measures of personality and social psychological attitudes* (Vol. 1). San Diego, CA: Academic Press.

Rodin, J., & Langer, E. J. (1977). Long-term effects of a control-relevant intervention with the institutionalized aged. *Journal of Personality and Social Psychology, 35,* 897–902.

Rosenbaum, D. P., & Hanson, G. S. (1998). Assessing the effects of school-based drug education: A six-year multilevel analysis of Project D.A.R.E. *Journal of Research in Crime and Delinquency, 35,* 381–412.

Rosenblatt, P. C., & Cozby, P. C. (1972). Courtship patterns associated with freedom of choice of spouse. *Journal of Marriage and the Family, 34,* 689–695.

Rosenhan, D. (1973). On being sane in insane places. *Science, 179,* 250–258.

Rosenthal, R. (1966). *Experimenter effects in behavior research.* New York: Appleton-Century-Crofts.

Rosenthal, R. (1967). Covert communication in the psychological experiment. *Psychological Bulletin, 67,* 356–367.

Rosenthal, R. (1969). Interpersonal expectations: Effects of the experimenter's hypothesis. In R. Rosenthal & R. L. Rosnow (Eds.), *Artifacts in behavioral research.* New York: Academic Press.

Rosenthal, R. (1991). *Meta-analytic procedures for social research* (Rev. ed.). Newbury Park, CA: Sage.

Rosenthal, R., & Jacobson, L. (1968). *Pygmalion in the classroom: Teacher expectation and pupils' intellectual development.* New York: Holt, Rinehart & Winston.

Rosenthal, R., & Rosnow, R. L. (1975). *The volunteer subject.* New York: Wiley.

Rosnow, R. L., & Rosnow, M. (2002). *Writing papers in psychology* (6th ed.). Belmont, CA: Wadsworth.

Rossi, P. H., Freeman, H. E., & Lipsey, M. W. (1999). *Evaluation: A systematic approach.* Thousand Oaks, CA: Sage.

Ruback, R. B., & Juieng, D. (1997). Territorial defense in parking lots: Retaliation against waiting drivers. *Journal of Applied Social Psychology, 27,* 821–834.

Rubin, Z. (1970, December). Jokers wild in the lab. *Psychology Today, 18,* 20, 22–24.

Rubin, Z. (1973). Designing honest experiments. *American Psychologist, 28,* 445–448.

Rubin, Z. (1975). Disclosing oneself to a stranger: Reciprocity and its limits. *Journal of Experimental Social Psychology, 11,* 233–260.

Rubin, Z. (1985). Deceiving ourselves about deception: Comment on Smith and Richardson's "Amelioration of deception and harm in psychological research." *Journal of Personality and Social Psychology, 48,* 252–253.

Russell, C. H., & Megaard, I. (1988). *The general social survey, 1972–1986: The state of the American people.* New York: Springer-Verlag.

Russell, D., Peplau, L. A., & Cutrona, C. E. (1980). The revised UCLA Loneliness Scale: Concurrent and discriminant validity. *Journal of Personality and Social Psychology, 39,* 472–480.

Saks, M. J., & Marti, M. W. (1997). A meta-analysis of the effects of jury size. *Law and Human Behavior, 21,* 451–467.

Schachter, S. (1959). *The psychology of affiliation.* Stanford, CA: Stanford University Press.

Schaie, K. W. (1986). Beyond calendar definitions of age, time, and cohort: The general developmental model revisited. *Developmental Review, 6,* 252–277.

Schlenger, W. E., Caddell, J. M., Ebert, L., Jordan, B. K., Rourke, K. M., Wilson, D., Thajii, L., Dennis, J. M., Fairbank, J. A., & Kulka, R. A. (2002). Psychological reactions to terrorist attacks: Findings from the National Study of Americans' Reactions to September 11. *Journal of the American Medical Association, 288,* 581–588.

Schoeneman, T. J., & Rubanowitz, D. E. (1985). Attributions in the advice columns: Actors and observers, causes and reasons. *Personality and Social Psychology Bulletin, 11,* 315–325.

Schwarz, N. (1999). Self-reports: How the questions shape the answers. *American Psychologist, 54,* 93–105.

Scribner, S. (1997). Studying literacy at work: Bringing the laboratory to the field. In E. Torbach, R. J. Falmagne, M. B. Parlee, L. M. W. Martin, & A. S. Kapelman (Eds.), *Mind and social practice: Selected writings of Sylvia Scribner.* Cambridge: Cambridge University Press.

Sears, D. O. (1986). College sophomores in the laboratory: Influences of a narrow data base on social psychology's view of human nature. *Journal of Personality and Social Psychology, 51,* 515–530.

Sebald, H. (1986). Adolescents' shifting orientation toward parents and peers: A curvilinear trend over recent decades. *Journal of Marriage and the Family, 48,* 5–13.

Shadish, W. R., Cook, T. D., & Campbell, D. T. (2002). *Experimental and quasi-experimental designs for generalized causal inference.* Boston: Houghton Mifflin.

Shepard, R. N., & Metzler, J. (1971). Mental rotation of three-dimensional objects. *Science, 171,* 701–703.

Sidman, M. (1960). *Tactics of scientific research.* New York: Basic Books.

Sieber, J. E. (1992). *Planning ethically responsible research: A guide for students and internal review boards.* Newbury Park, CA: Sage.

Sieber, J. E., Iannuzzo, R., & Rodriguez, B. (1995). Deception methods in psychology: Have they changed in 23 years? *Ethics and Behavior, 5,* 67–85.

Siegel, S., & Castellan, N. J. (1988). *Nonparametric statistics for the behavioral sciences.* New York: McGraw-Hill.

Sigall, H., & Mills, J. (1998). Measures of independent variables and mediators are useful in social psychology experiments. But are they necessary? *Personality and Social Psychology Review, 2,* 218–226.

Silverman, I. (1975). Nonreactive methods and the law. *American Psychologist, 30,* 764–769.

Silverman, I., & Margulis, S. (1973). Experiment title as a source of sampling bias in commonly used "subject-pool" procedures. *Canadian Psychologist, 14,* 197–201.

Singh, D. (1993). Adaptive significance of female physical attractiveness: Role of waist-to-hip ratio. *Journal of Personality and Social Psychology, 65,* 293–307.

Skinner, B. F. (1953). *Science and human behavior.* New York: Macmillan.

Smart, R. (1966). Subject selection bias in psychological research. *Canadian Psychologist, 7,* 115–121.

Smith, C. P. (1983). Ethical issues: Research on deception, informed consent, and debriefing. In L. Wheeler & P. Shaver (Eds.), *Review of personality and social psychology* (Vol. 4). Newbury Park, CA: Sage.

Smith, M. L., & Glass, G. V. (1977). Meta-analysis of psychotherapy outcome studies. *American Psychologist, 32,* 752–760.

Smith, R. J., Lingle, J. H., & Brock, T. C. (1978). Reactions to death as a function of perceived similarity to the deceased. *Omega, 9,* 125–138.

Smith, S. M., & Shaffer, D. R. (1991). Celerity and cajolery: Rapid speech may promote or inhibit persuasion through its impact on message elaboration. *Personality and Social Psychology Bulletin, 17,* 663–669.

Smith, S. S., & Richardson, D. (1983). Amelioration of harm in psychological research: The important role of debriefing. *Journal of Personality and Social Psychology, 44,* 1075–1082.

Smith, S. S., & Richardson, D. (1985). On deceiving ourselves about deception: A reply to Rubin. *Journal of Personality and Social Psychology, 48,* 254–255.

Smith, V. L., & Ellsworth, P. C. (1987). The social psychology of eyewitness accuracy: Misleading questions and communicator expertise. *Journal of Applied Psychology, 72,* 294–300.

Solomon, R. L. (1949). An extension of control group design. *Psychological Bulletin, 46,* 137–150.

Stanton, J. M. (1998). An empirical assessment of data collection using the Internet. *Personnel Psychology, 51,* 709–725.

Steele, K. M., Bass, K. E., & Crook, M. D. (1999). The mystery of the Mozart effect: Failure to replicate. *Psychological Science, 10,* 366–369.

Steinberg, L., & Dornbusch, S. M. (1991). Negative correlates of part-time employment during adolescence: Replication and elaboration. *Developmental Psychology, 27,* 304–313.

Stephan, W. G. (1983). Intergroup relations. In D. Perlman & P. C. Cozby (Eds.), *Social psychology.* New York: Holt, Rinehart & Winston.

Sternberg, R. J. (1993). *The psychologist's companion: A guide to scientific writing for students and researchers.* Cambridge: Cambridge University Press.

Stevenson, H. W., & Allen, S. (1964). Adult performance as a function of sex of experimenter and sex of subject. *Journal of Abnormal and Social Psychology, 68,* 214–216.

Stone, V. E., Cosmides, L., Tooby, J., Kroll, N., & Knight, R. T. (2002). Selective impairment of reasoning about social exchange in a patient with bilateral limbic system damage. *Proceedings of the National Academy of Sciences, 99*(17), 11531–11536. Retrieved November 1, 2002, from http://www.pnas.org/cgi/content/full/99/17/11531

Sullivan, D. S., & Deiker, T. E. (1973). Subject-experimenter perceptions of ethical issues in human research. *American Psychologist, 28,* 587–591.

Terman, L. M. (1925). *Genetic studies of genius: Vol. 1. Mental and physical traits of a thousand gifted children.* Stanford, CA: Stanford University Press.

Terman, L. M., & Oden, M. H. (1947). *Genetic studies of genius: Vol. 4. The gifted child grows up: Twenty-five years' follow-up of a superior group.* Stanford, CA: Stanford University Press.

Terman, L. M., & Oden, M. H. (1959). *Genetic studies of genius: Vol. 5. The gifted group in mid-life: Thirty-five years' follow-up of the superior child.* Stanford, CA: Stanford University Press.

Thomas, G. V., & Blackman, D. (1992). The future of animal studies in psychology. *American Psychologist, 47,* 1678.

Thombs, D. L. (2000). A retrospective study of DARE: Substantive effects not detected in undergraduates. *Journal of Alcohol and Drug Education, 46,* 27–40.

Thompson, W. F., Schellenberg, E. G., & Husain, G. (2001). Arousal, mood, and the Mozart effect. *Psychological Science, 12,* 248–251.

Trochim, W. M. (2000). *The Research Methods Knowledge Base* (2nd ed.). Retrieved March 6, 2003, http://trochim.human.cornell.edu/kb/index.htm

Tucker, W. H. (1997). Re-considering Burt: Beyond a reasonable doubt. *Journal of the History of the Behavioral Sciences, 33,* 145–162.

Tufte, E. R. (1983). *The visual display of quantitative information.* Cheshire, CT: Graphics Press.

Tufte, E. R. (1990). *Envisioning information.* Cheshire, CT: Graphics Press.

U.S. Department of Justice. (1999). *Eyewitness evidence: A guide for law enforcement.* Retrieved July 10, 2002, from http://www.ncjrs.org/pdffiles1/nij/178240.pdf

Vincent, P. C., Peplau, L. A., & Hill, C. T. (1998). A longitudinal application of the theory of reasoned action to women's career behavior. *Journal of Applied Social Psychology, 28,* 761–778.

Vitz, P. C. (1966). Preference for different amounts of visual complexity. *Behavioral Science, 11,* 105–114.

Webb, E. J., Campbell, D. T., Schwartz, R. D., Sechrest, R., & Grove, J. B. (1981). *Nonreactive measures in the social sciences* (2nd ed.). Boston: Houghton Mifflin.

Weber, R. P. (1990). *Basic content analysis* (2nd ed.). Newbury Park, CA: Sage.

Wells, G. L. (2001). Eyewitness lineups: Data, theory, and policy. *Psychology, Public Policy, and Law, 7,* 791–801.

Wells, G. L., Small, M., Penrod, S. J., Malpass, R. S., Fulero, S. M., & Brimacombe, C. A. E. (1998). Eyewitness identification procedures: Recommendations for lineups and photospreads. *Law and Human Behavior, 22,* 603–647.

Wilkinson, L., & the Task Force on Statistical Inference. (1999). Statistical methods in psychology journals: Guidelines and explanations. *American Psychologist, 54,* 594–604.

Wilson, D. W., & Donnerstein, E. (1976). Legal and ethical aspects of nonreactive social psychological research. *American Psychologist, 31,* 765–773.

Wilson, W. H., Ellinwood, E. H., Mathew, R. J., & Johnson, K. (1994). Effects of marijuana on performance of a computerized cognitive-neuromotor test battery. *Psychiatry Research, 51,* 115–125.

Winograd, E., & Soloway, R. M. (1986). On forgetting the location of things stored in special places. *Journal of Experimental Psychology: General, 115,* 366–372.

Yin, R. K. (1994). *Case study research: Design and methods.* Newbury Park, CA: Sage.

Zimbardo, P. G. (1973). The psychological power and pathology of imprisonment. In E. Aronson & R. Helmreich (Eds.), *Social psychology.* New York: Van Nostrand.

Zuckerman, M. (1979). *Sensation seeking: Beyond the optimal level of arousal.* Hillsdale, NJ: Erlbaum.

# Credits

**Chapter 2** p. 25, Netscape browser window © 2002 Netscape Communications Corporation. Used with permission. Netscape Communications has not authorized, sponsored, or endorsed, or approved this publication and is not responsible for its content; reprinted with permission of the American Psychological Association, publisher of the PsychINFO Database, all rights reserved. May not be reproduced without prior permission. **Chapter 7** p. 116, Fig. 7.1, "Negative Correlates of Part-Time Employment During Adolescence," by L. Steinberg and S. M. Dornbusch, 1991, *Developmental Psychology, 27,* pp. 304–313. Copyright © 1991 by the American Psychological Association. Reprinted by permission. **Chapter 8** p. 148, Fig. 8.2, reprinted with permission from "Mental Rotation of Three-Dimensional Objects," by R. N. Shepard and J. Metzler, 1971, *Science, 171,* pp. 701–703. Copyright © 1971 American Association for the Advancement of Science. **Chapter 11** p. 203, Fig. 11.2 and p. 204, Fig. 11.3, "Reforms as Experiments," by D. T. Campbell, 1969, *American Psychologist, 24,* pp. 409–429. Copyright © 1969 by the American Psychological Association. Reprinted with permission. **Appendix C** p. 360, Table C.2, table adapted from Fisher and Yates, *Statistical Tables for Biological, Agricultural, and Medical Research* (1974, 6th ed.), London: Longman. Copyright © 1963 by R. A. Fisher and F. Yates. Reprinted by permission of Pearson Education Limited.

# Index